SURVEY OF UNITED STATES INTERNATIONAL FINANCE 1951

BY

GARDNER PATTERSON

AND

JACK N. BEHRMAN

INTERNATIONAL FINANCE SECTION

DEPARTMENT OF ECONOMICS AND SOCIAL INSTITUTIONS

PRINCETON UNIVERSITY

PRINCETON UNIVERSITY PRESS

London: Geoffrey Cumberlege, Oxford University Press

Printed in the United States of America
by the Vail-Ballou Press, Inc., Binghamton, N.Y.

PREFACE

THIS IS the third volume of an experimental series entitled *Survey of United States International Finance.* The present document covers the calendar year 1951, and, except for the inclusion of enough background material to make the record as here presented intelligible, we have resorted to frequent references to the previous two volumes for information on 1949 and 1950.

This document has been prepared in the hope that a reasonable number of persons, both in the United States and abroad and including not only students in the usual sense but also those more directly affected by the international economic activities of the United States, may find it a source of reasonably current information and a useful reference on the myriad international financial policies and transactions of the United States. In a document such as this a source could be cited for nearly every statement, but such extensive documentation was considered unnecessary. However, since this is a survey and no subject has been treated exhaustively, citations have been made to what are regarded as the most useful and important sources—usually original documents. These cited sources will provide additional details for those interested in pursuing a subject further than has seemed desirable here.

As in the previous two volumes, our objective is only that of accurate and orderly reporting. We have therefore refrained from any independent analysis or conclusions on the many topics covered but have attempted to order the facts so as to bring out trends, progress toward stated goals, shifts in policies, and important conflicts and inconsistencies. For national security reasons, an increasing portion of the facts on the international financial affairs of the United States during the year under review were not made public. Such gaps in the record are probably not great, however, and it is hoped that the present document gives a fairly complete summary of the developments covered.

Most of the statistical information on foreign aid and financial transactions of the United States is compiled by several different

Government agencies and for various purposes, with the result that public data on the same transaction often differ. Considerable pains have been taken in the present document to reconcile such differences and, where possible, notes explaining the discrepancies have been added to the statistical tables. Further, in some cases, statistics are published only on a cumulative basis and the not infrequent revisions of the cumulative figures make for errors in the data for any given quarter or year. Where we have so calculated yearly or quarterly data we believe the errors are not serious. In any case, most of the financial statistics on international transactions are estimates, and the Government, especially the Department of Commerce—whose *Foreign Transactions of the U.S. Government* and *Survey of Current Business* are the two most important sources of statistical data on international transactions of the United States—frequently revises previously published data. Relevant revisions for previous years have been incorporated in the present volume of this *Survey*, with the result that the data given here for the years 1949 and 1950 sometime differ from those given in the previous volumes.

As in previous years, we received the generous cooperation of the other members of the Department of Economics and Social Institutions of Princeton University. Great assistance was received from Mrs. Mary B. Fernholz, of the International Finance Section; Miss Dorothea Collins, Librarian of the Pliny Fisk Library of Economics and Finance; and Mrs. Evelyn R. Barr, Librarian of the International Relations Collection, of the Princeton University Library. Several persons outside the University have been most generous in checking the various parts of the document for accuracy. Our debt to them is great. Most of these persons hold official positions in the U.S. Government or international organizations, but their help was asked for, and given, on an unofficial and informal basis. In view of their official responsibilities and the fact that none of them was given an opportunity to see the document in its final form, it would not be fair to cite them here by name. Full responsibility for the accuracy and the form of presentation is borne by Mr. Jack N. Behrman and the undersigned.

GARDNER PATTERSON, *Director*
INTERNATIONAL FINANCE SECTION

Princeton University
April 1952

CONTENTS

LIST OF TABLES

LIST OF TABLES

ABBREVIATIONS FREQUENTLY USED

CCC—Commodity Credit Corporation

ECA—Economic Cooperation Administration

ECOSOC—United Nations Economic and Social Council

EIB—Export-Import Bank of Washington

EPU—European Payments Union

ERP—European Recovery Program

Fund—International Monetary Fund

GATT—General Agreement on Tariffs and Trade

IBRD—International Bank for Reconstruction and Development

MDAP—Mutual Defense Assistance Program

MSA—Mutual Security Agency

MSP—Mutual Security Program

NAC—National Advisory Council on International Monetary and Financial Problems

NATO—North Atlantic Treaty Organization

OEEC—Organization for European Economic Cooperation

RFC—Reconstruction Finance Corporation

TCA—Technical Cooperation Administration

UN—United Nations Organization

Survey—1949—*Survey of United States International Finance—1949*, International Finance Section, Princeton University

Survey—1950—*Survey of United States International Finance—1950*, International Finance Section, Princeton University

INTRODUCTION

The "containment" of Communism became a major goal of United States foreign policy in 1947. The U.S. Government believed that as far as its international economic and financial policies were concerned the most effective way of accomplishing this was by helping the non-Communist countries to raise their standards of living, both by supplying them with large quantities of consumer goods and raw materials, and, more important, by helping them—with financial aid, easier access to the American market, and advice—to restore their own production facilities and to reorient their economic activities toward the many changes that had taken place in the previous two decades in the structure of world demand and production. The U.S. Government also hoped by these and related activities to foster policies abroad which would encourage and permit throughout the non-Communist world the adoption of currency convertibility and nondiscriminatory multilateral trade, the elimination of quantitative restrictions on trade and payments, and the progressive reduction of trade barriers and of direct government controls over internal and external transactions.

From the very beginning, the United States recognized that in certain cases—notably Greece and Turkey—this policy of "containment" of Communism required it to furnish some military equipment; and, in 1949, as the differences between the West and the Soviet bloc became greater, a Mutual Defense Assistance Program was inaugurated. This program—based on certain earlier political decisions, especially the Rio Pact of 1947, the 1948 Vandenburg resolution, and the 1949 North Atlantic Pact—called for the provision of increased amounts of military supplies, equipment and advice to many foreign nations, but the emphasis was to be on Western Europe. One of the major justifications by the Administration of the program was that by serving to reduce the insecurity and fear of aggression in Europe it would further the economic recovery of the area. The Administration presented the first year's military aid program, involving some $1.3 billion of appropriations and contract authorizations, as the largest to be requested but stated that additional assistance probably would be needed for several years.

During the first half of 1950, the Administration planned that aggregate foreign aid from the U.S. Government would and should be sharply reduced. Thus, while Congress was requested to provide slightly larger funds for the second year of the Mutual Defense Assistance Program than had been provided for the first year, nearly all of the other grant programs—European Recovery, Occupied Areas, China Aid, Philippine Rehabilitation, etc., etc.—were scheduled to taper off sharply. One important exception was the so-called "Point Four Program" for the "improvement and growth of underdeveloped areas," which the Administration intended to expand in geographic coverage but which it anticipated would involve only small official financial contributions, with most of the capital assistance required coming from private sources. At the same time, the U.S. Government opposed proposals of various countries that the resources of the International Bank and the International Monetary Fund be made more readily and amply available to member nations.

Because of the prospect of large reductions in American exports as official foreign aid declined, and in keeping with the established long-term commercial policy goals, much attention was given during the first half of 1950, especially by the Administration, to methods of expanding imports. Thus, preparations went forward for participating in the third round of tariff negotiations under the GATT; foreign nations were aided in many ways to expand their exports to the dollar area (including pressure on them by the United States to "integrate their economies," which, it was argued, would increase their total production and productivity and so would enhance their ability to compete in third markets); Congress was told that the United States must pursue an import policy in keeping with its creditor position; and, in particular, the Administration prepared to ask Congress to approve the ITO Charter and to simplify customs administration. Both for security considerations and as a means of increasing dollar earnings of foreign countries, many urged that the official stockpile program of the U.S. Government be accelerated; at the same time export controls were simplified and, except for strategic items, relaxed.

Following the outbreak of fighting in Korea in June 1950, which brought with it the conviction that the Communist countries were prepared, when they thought conditions were favorable, to resort to direct military aggression on a large scale, the overriding objective of United States international economic and financial policy became that of quickly strengthening the military defenses of the free world and then maintaining them at a high level for an indefinitely long period of time. This change in objectives called for a wholesale reassessment of the nation's international economic policies. As a result, some of the policies that were being previously pursued were abandoned, others were intensified, and several new ones were inaugurated. Few indeed were the policies or activities which were unaffected as the United States took the initiative in the rearmament drive of the non-Communist countries.

The most spectacular shift in policy during 1950 was, of course, the increase by several-fold in the size of the program for military assistance. But by the beginning of 1951 only small amounts of military matériel had actually been shipped; few of the economic problems of building "balanced collective forces" in the North Atlantic area had been solved, and many had not yet arisen. The Administration quickly dropped the earlier policy that economic recovery abroad should have a clear priority over rearmament, but the United States still faced the problem of the extent to which aid provided to Europe should be in the form of civilian-type as against military-type goods and the related question of continuing, in reduced amounts, financial support for the European Recovery Program. Following the events in Korea, United States officials stated that the necessity of rearming made it even more desirable than before that the Western European nations "integrate" their economies, but as the year ended the uneven impact of the rearmament efforts of the various European nations' internal and external financial and economic affairs was undercutting some of the assumptions on which the particular devices to accomplish integration had been based, and, as a result, many new problems were in prospect for 1951.

With the growing conviction that the threat of Communism anywhere in the world was a threat to American security, the U.S. Government gave more attention to aiding the non-European areas of the free world. As 1950 ended, plans were under way in the United States to provide larger amounts of both military supplies and so-called economic assistance to these areas. With respect to the latter, United States emphasis was shifting away from the previously stressed "broad economic development" projects to encouraging the production of strategic and critical raw materials in these areas. It was apparent, however, that the officials of the underdeveloped countries opposed this change in the emphasis of the program and that, in addition, questions of amounts of aid, its form (technical versus capital assistance), its source (public versus private), and its terms (grants versus loans) would have to be reexamined.

With the Korean crisis many changes were also inaugurated in United States commercial policies. In the face of increasing domestic demand for exportable goods, supplemented by growing foreign demands, concern over the problem of maintaining exports (which had been so acute in the first part of the year) was replaced, for many commodities, with concern over the inflation and physical shortages which might result from unrestricted exports. This, together with the problems of distributing the available supplies of many goods so as to "maximize their benefit to the security of the free world," resulted in the subjection of additional goods to United States export controls. In addition, expanded efforts were made by the United States to get the other nations allied with her to restrict still further their trade with the Soviet bloc countries. As the year ended, many difficult problems of implementing these general policies were being faced; for example, the establishing of priorities among needs of the United States and foreign countries, and among military and civilian demands, and the settling of questions of, and determining policies with respect to, the relative importance to the West and to the East of trade between the two areas. An acceleration after Korea in the rate of procurement for both the official and private stockpiles was providing certain areas with additional dollars which had been so urgently sought earlier in the year, but many nations complained that the United States was largely responsible for the skyrocketing prices of these goods and was "hogging" scarce materials to such an extent that the ability of the Western European countries to rearm was being impaired. The United States shared the concern over rising prices and the failure of the free market to achieve an "equitable and effective international distribution" of many such materials, and as the year ended it was taking the initiative in encouraging (where it had previously discouraged) the establishment of new intergovernmental machinery designed to allocate such goods, as well as to expand their output and restrict what were considered as non-essential uses. The methods being planned were largely voluntary, however, and thus created problems quite different from those which had been met during the period of World War II when many materials had been allocated by international agencies. While many believed that the physical shortages and inflationary pressures in the United States called for an energetic pursuit of the goals of the Reciprocal Trade Agreements Program of lowering barriers to imports in the United States, there were also many, in addition to the confirmed protectionists, who believed that the times were so uncertain and the threat of war so great that it would be unwise to take any action which might injure domestic producers. These and related questions were due to be canvassed early in 1951 since the Reciprocal Trade Agreements Act was up before Congress for a three-year extension.

The following chapters compose a record of the actions and decisions taken by the U.S. Government during 1951, and the reasons given therefor, to meet the unsettled problems carried over from 1950 and the new ones which developed.

I · GRANT PROGRAMS

THE broad objectives of most of the United States official grant programs during the three years immediately prior to the outbreak of the war in Korea in mid-1950 were (a) the "containment" of Communism by raising consumption standards in non-Communist countries and by helping such countries to rebuild their economies and reorient them to post World War II conditions of production and trade, and (b) the promotion of practices and policies abroad which the United States hoped would lead to a return to a world-wide system of nondiscriminatory multilateral trade and payments, with a progressive reduction of trade barriers and of direct governmental control of economic activities. Beginning in 1947, military supplies and equipment were provided in increasing amounts to various countries—notably Greece and Turkey, the North Atlantic Treaty countries, and, for a time, China. Such military aid was small, however, as compared with grants in the form of civilian-type goods and services, and amounted to only about 20 percent of the total value of official United States foreign grants in 1950.

Because of the evidence in the last half of 1950 that the Communist countries were willing to resort to direct military aggression, the second objective of the grant programs cited above was overshadowed by the growing conviction that American security depended in the near future on the immediate strengthening of the non-Communist world militarily against external aggression, as well as economically and politically against internal subversion.

A. *MUTUAL SECURITY PROGRAM*

Legislative Issues[1]

INTRODUCTION

In his January 1951 budget message to Congress, the President stated that he would shortly request Congress to appropriate $9.7

[1] For official documents on the program, which are the source of most of the information contained in this section, see "The Mutual Security Program," Presi-

billion for military and economic assistance to foreign countries for the approaching fiscal year. The difficulties within the Administration in determining the details as to amounts it should request from Congress—the countries to be aided were slow in providing estimates as to what they could do themselves—and the purposes[2] and direction of the new grant program, together with Congressional preoccupation with the "Great Debate" over sending additional American troops to Europe, combined to delay the submission of proposals for a "Mutual Security Program" until late May. The Administration's program—the request was reduced to $8.5 billion, of which nearly three-fourths was "military assistance"—was an omnibus one in that it included almost all of the anticipated foreign grant activities in one measure.[3] The Executive Branch stated that such a presentation was desirable since it tied together all facets of the "single-purposed drive for peace and security" and since political, economic, military, and spiritual strength depended on each other; but it did not attempt to "unify" the various aid programs into an "integrated whole." The proposal was in the form

---

dent's Message to Congress, Department of State, General Foreign Policy Series 52, May 24, 1951; Department of State, "Mutual Security for the Free World," General Foreign Policy Series 49, April 1951; "The Mutual Security Program for Fiscal Year 1952," *Committee Print* (Basic Data Supplied by the Executive Branch), House Committee on Foreign Affairs and Senate Committee on Foreign Relations, 82d Cong., 1st Sess., 1951; "The Mutual Security Program," *Hearings (on H.R. 5020 and H.R. 5113)*, House of Rep., Committee on Foreign Affairs, 82d Cong., 1st Sess., June-July 1951; "Mutual Security Act of 1951," *Hearings on S. 1762*, U.S. Senate, Committee on Foreign Relations and Committee on Armed Services, 82d Cong., 1st Sess., July-August 1951; "Mutual Security Program Appropriations for 1952," *Hearings, Parts 1-3*, House of Rep., Committee on Appropriations, 82d Cong., 1st Sess., September-October 1951; "Mutual Security Appropriations for 1952," *Hearings on H.R. 5684*, U.S. Senate, Committee on Appropriations, 82d Cong., 1st Sess., October 1951; and the *Congressional Record*, 82d Cong., 1st Sess. (The specific numbers and pages of the *Congressional Record* may be found conveniently in its index under the above-listed bills.)

[2] The National Advisory Council determined that "Economic assistance on a grant basis should not be extended for the purpose of increasing gold and dollar reserves, nor should countries participating in the defense effort be required to reduce their present level of reserves as a prerequisite for receiving United States aid." But "where a country is making a satisfactory contribution to mutual defense, an unanticipated accumulation of reserves resulting from the vigorous application of appropriate economic and financial policies should not automatically result in a reduction of aid." (*Semiannual Report to the President and to the Congress* [for the period October 1, 1950-March 31, 1951], September 18, 1951, pp. 9-10, and [for the period April 1-September 30, 1951] February 14, 1952, p. 14.)

[3] Aid to the occupied areas in the Far East was treated separately. Aid through the International Children's Emergency Fund was excluded since no new contributions were then being considered.

of a request for certain amendments to existing aid legislation and authority to continue these programs. That is, it included a continuation of, and amendments to, the legislation authorizing the previous programs of mutual defense assistance, European recovery, Korean aid, China aid, Southeast Asia aid, Palestine refugee relief, and technical assistance (Point Four).[4]

In his message, the President asked for funds for only one year. But during the hearings on his proposal Administration spokesmen stated (under direct questioning and apparently without much previous study) that if the then agreed-upon plans for the military build-up of the West were to be fulfilled, aid of similar dimensions would probably be required for two more years—that is, a three-year $25 billion program would have to be anticipated. Some members of Congress were reluctant to make any commitments beyond one year, even though many believed that an estimate of three years was optimistic in view of past experiences and the outlook as they saw it. The Mutual Security Act of 1951 specified that the authority to extend aid was to expire on June 30, 1954, save for some winding-up operations.[5]

In considering this omnibus grant program, Congress repeatedly expressed concern as to the ability of the United States economy to "bear the cost." The Administration apparently had not carried out a study of national capabilities comparable to that made when it was planning the European Recovery Program in 1947 and 1948, but spokesmen for the Executive Branch stated that they had carefully studied the effects of the program on thirty or forty key commodities, that the United States economy was not beyond the limit (unspecified) of its ability to extend aid, and that the proposed expenditures had been "carefully worked out to give this country maximum security per dollar cost."[6] Detailed and concrete justifications for these assertions were not provided in the public hearings but may have been in the executive sessions. During this discussion, the Administration admitted that domestic inflation

[4] The laws involved were: Mutual Defense Assistance Act of 1949, as amended; Economic Cooperation Act of 1948, as amended; Act for International Development; and Information and Educational Exchange Act of 1948.

[5] Administration spokesmen testified that this specific termination date was acceptable to them if it were recognized by Congress that it might have to be extended.

[6] *Hearings on H.R. 5020, op.cit.*, p. 7; also pp. 86-129 and 289. See also *Hearings on S. 1762, op.cit.*, pp. 28 and 53-54.

had "startlingly" reduced the amount of real aid voted in 1950; but, in reply to Congressmen expressing worry over the inflationary aspects of the program, witnesses asserted that to a large extent the expenditures anticipated under this program would induce greater United States production and not just drain off current production.

There was little sentiment in Congress for stopping all foreign grants, but those supporting continued aid emphasized strongly the Administration's statement that the broad purposes of all the programs were to maintain the security of the United States through strengthening her allies. Both branches of the Government saw the threat of Communism as immediate and of indefinite duration and agreed that American security could be most quickly and efficiently obtained by the cooperative efforts of all non-Communist nations to increase their military strength. The majority of Congress agreed with the Administration that some aid from the United States would "yield a faster and larger return in terms of our national security than we could obtain by increasing the budget for our own Armed Forces by the same amount."[7] Most of the increased strength abroad was scheduled to come from the domestic efforts of the European countries, with United States aid seen as the marginal contribution which would allow a multiple expansion of the military potential in the recipient nations. That is, for all practical purposes the international transfer of goods and services was to be from the United States, but the supporters of the program stressed that it was a "mutual" one in that American security would be strengthened by the enlarged defense forces of the aided areas.

The program was designed to "deter, defend, and develop." The *deter* aspect was that of gaining a "parity of power" so as to strengthen the hand of the West in negotiations with the Soviet bloc; the *defend* aspect was that of being prepared to win a war if it should come; the *develop* aspect referred to the belief that economic development was a means of combatting subversion, of making people in backward areas sympathetic to the United States aims, and of increasing the supply of strategic materials needed in the rearmament programs of the NATO countries. Neither the

[7] *Hearings on H.R. 5020, op.cit.,* p. 7.

Administration nor Congress stressed the humanitarian aspects of aiding foreign nations or of using grants to help create American-style "democracy" abroad; in fact, both groups eschewed the latter on the ground that the aim was to insure independence of governments abroad so that they could decide their own forms of government.

The major policy debates and discussions,[8] in Congress on the program revolved around the questions of (a) the amounts of aid to be extended to each area, (b) the amount which should be sent as military end-items, and (c) the amount and character of aid for economic recovery, production of military end-items, and economic development abroad. The President's request for new appropriations was divided as between "economic" and "military" aid and between areas, as follows:

	Military	*Economic* (millions of dollars)	*Total*
Europe	5,293	1,675	6,968
Near East and Africa	415	125	540
Asia and the Pacific	555	375*	930
Latin America	40	22	62
Total	6,303	2,197	8,500

(* *Including $112.5 million for the United States contribution to the* Korean Rehabilitation Agency.)

Before surveying the details of the major debates on the MSP it should be noted that it is particularly difficult for the public to assay the issues in Congress because a large portion of the hearings

[8] Though a detailed summary is outside the scope of this document, it should be recorded that Congress spent much time discussing the question of whether the administration of the program should be centralized. The Executive Branch favored a continuation of the existing organizational arrangements under which, in broad terms, ECA would continue to have primary authority for administering all economic aid, except for Point Four, which would remain in the State Department; the Defense Department would administer aid extended in the form of military end-items; and the State Department would coordinate all the programs and activities. Sentiment in the House, however, was strongly in favor of establishing a single agency to administer all aid, and that body passed a bill placing all such authority in one agency. The Senate was unwilling to go this far. The Act as finally approved continued the authority of the Department of Defense to administer military end-item assistance and the authority of the Technical Cooperation Administration of the State Department to administer the technical assistance extended under the Point Four Program, but ECA was terminated as an agency with its powers transferred to a new Mutual Security Agency. A new post, Director for Mutual Security, was created, and in it was placed the responsibility previously held by the State

was in executive (closed) session. The public record of the hearings does not provide evidence, however, that the Executive Branch was adequately prepared to justify its requests—especially those for non-military items.[9]

a. GEOGRAPHIC SCOPE OF THE PROGRAM

The Administration requested that the program be authorized, and funds provided by Congress, on a regional rather than individual country basis. The four regions specified were Europe, Near East and Africa, Asia and the Pacific, and Latin America. This approach was justified primarily on the grounds that (a) the individual countries in each of these areas have roughly similar problems and so the aid could be administered on a fairly uniform basis within each area and (b) aid on a regional rather than a country basis would permit greater flexibility in the geographic allocation of the aid in order to meet unforeseen developments and to take advantage of different degrees of effective use made of the assistance by individual countries.[1] The Administration requested even more flexibility by asking that authority be given to transfer up to 10 percent of the funds for any one area to another area, and also,

---

Department for coordinating all the foreign-aid programs. The Director for Mutual Security was also charged with administering the Government policy of restricting East-West trade (see Chapter VI). The President appointed Mr. Averell Harriman as Director for Mutual Security, and during late 1951 the latter spent most of his time in Europe as United States representative on the Temporary Council Committee of NATO. (See Department of State *Bulletin*, January 28, 1952, p. 124 ff., for certain official statements on the new organizational structure. See also the *First Report to Congress on the Mutual Security Program*, Washington, D.C., December 31, 1951, pp. 14-18. For an unofficial analysis of administrative problems in connection with foreign economic activities in general, see Parks, W. J., *United States Administration of its International Economic Affairs*, Johns Hopkins University Press, 1951. See also Brookings Institution, *The Administration of Foreign Affairs and Overseas Operation*, Washington, D.C., 1951.)

[9] For example, the Committee on Foreign Affairs, which conducted the House hearings, reported that "the whole basis for economic aid was on guess-estimates based on projected balances of payments. . . . Time and again it was obvious that the witnesses either did not know or would not tell about their program. . . . we often could not get answers to simple fundamental questions from anyone present." (*Congressional Record*, August 16, 1951, pp. 10364-10365.) This feeling on the part of Congress that the Administration had not adequately justified the program for economic aid was seen by some as an important factor in the final Congressional reductions from amounts requested.

[1] Congress itself justified the area approach on the grounds that it was especially appropriate for meeting the threat of Soviet expansion, since Russia thought in terms of areas rather than of nations. (See especially *H. Rpt. No. 872*, August 14, 1951, p. 8.)

within areas, to transfer up to 5 percent from either of the categories ("military" and "economic") to the other.

Except for Europe, the Administration did not anticipate that these areas would organize themselves on any regional basis, either for purposes of building up military forces or for "coordinating" their economic activities. As in previous years,[2] some Congressmen thought that such regional cooperation should be "encouraged" by the United States, but Administration spokesmen, while not questioning its desirability, argued that conditions in two of the other areas were not conducive to the establishment of regional cooperation along the lines being followed in Europe: in the Middle East and Africa area, among other reasons, because of the disputes between Israel and the Arab States,[3] and in the Far East because of the character of the economies and the general reluctance of the governments to form any bloc against the Soviet Union. With respect to Latin America, the Administration believed that existing inter-American organizations were adequate. Even those in the Administration and Congress who favored regional organizations abroad accepted without question that, as in the past, United States aid would not be extended through such organizations but to individual countries under bilateral agreements.

Of the four regions, Europe was to continue to receive most of the assistance on the grounds that its security was the most vital to the United States and that it was capable of utilizing larger amounts more effectively, that is, that military strength could be increased fastest there. Administration spokesmen insisted, however, that the smaller volume of aid to the other areas did not mean that they were to receive only "crumbs from the European table" but that there were several factors which limited the need for, or appropriateness of, aid to these countries: their reluctance, in some cases, to accept aid for fear of compromising their independence, the absence of institutions and personnel to make use of larger economic grants and an inability to maintain large armed forces even if the United States supplied the equipment, their relatively large current dollar earnings, and the availability of foreign aid from

[2] See *Survey—1950*, pp. 61-62.

[3] The Administration testified, however, that until a settlement of these disputes was arranged and regional cooperation attained, the adoption of large-scale agrarian and irrigation projects, necessary to economic development, would be delayed.

the Export-Import Bank, the International Bank, and under the Colombo Plan.[4]

The major issues with respect to the geographic scope of the European program centered around the inclusion of Western Germany, Yugoslavia, and Spain as active participants in Western defense and therefore as eligible for military aid.[5] The Administration witnesses agreed with most of their Congressional questioners that Western European defense would be strengthened if the resources, manpower, and geographic positions of these three nations could be utilized, and stated that they were in various stages of developing appropriate arrangements toward this end with these countries.[6] The Administration urged, however, that these countries not be specifically mentioned in the law since to do so might hamper the American negotiators. Further, such specification, they argued, was unnecessary since the proposed law authorized the President to extend aid "to any other area," if deemed in the security interests of the United States, and thus permitted the granting of military assistance to these three countries. The Executive Branch also asserted that it was not prepared to justify specific amounts of aid since detailed plans for these three nations had either not been developed or were confidential.[7]

Congress was satisfied that the Administration was anxious to work out mutual defense arrangements with Germany and Yugoslavia (several in Congress were unenthusiastic about aiding the latter), but many in both Houses were skeptical as to the Administration's intentions toward Spain and sentiment was strong for the specific inclusion of that country as being eligible for aid. Spokesmen for the Executive Branch opposed this action for the above reasons and also because of the offense it might cause to other

[4] See Rusk, D., "The Underlying Principles of Far Eastern Policy," Department of State *Bulletin*, November 19, 1951, pp. 823-824, for a more detailed statement of limitations on aid to these areas.

[5] Germany had been receiving economic aid since the end of the war, first under the Occupied Areas Program (GARIOA) and subsequently under the ERP. Yugoslavia was receiving American grant assistance under an Emergency Food Program begun in 1950, and in the same year Congress specified that $62.5 million of the ECA appropriations for the year ending in June 1951 were to be available in the form of a loan to Spain. (See *Survey—1950*, pp. 16, 17, 44, 46, and 54-56, for brief statements of aid to these countries during 1950.)

[6] See the Section on "Implementation, military assistance," below, for a summary of the activities vis-à-vis Germany.

[7] See *Hearings on H.R. 5020, op.cit.*, pp. 1196-1197 and 1201, and *Hearings on S. 1762, op.cit.*, pp. 115-118.

European nations which had made it known that they did not want Spain in the NATO.[8] Congress respected the Administration's wishes in the authorization act, but the law appropriating funds for the MSP specifically set aside $100 million for Spain, without specification as to type of aid or whether it was to be on a grant or loan basis.[9]

Except for its general interest in reducing the amount of foreign aid, Congress raised few objections to the amounts proposed for the Near East and Africa,[1] Asia and the Pacific, and Latin America, but it did insist on pruning the requests for economic aid to Europe.

b. MILITARY VERSUS ECONOMIC AID

The major problem confronting the Government in formulating the Mutual Security Program was the decision as to what constituted "security" and how best to achieve it. The Administration had decided that while most of the grants should be for military end-items, the security objectives of the United States demanded that economic aid—that is, aid which took the form of goods other than military end-items—should also be provided. Such economic aid, it argued, would serve the purposes of (a) forestalling political and economic crises abroad by helping to maintain living standards and (b) providing an effective and cheap means of expanding the production of military matériel in Europe and strategic raw materials in other areas.[2]

[8] Some members of the Foreign Affairs Committee urged the United States to seek Spain's inclusion in NATO on the grounds that it had a stable government, was willing to fight, hated Communism, and needed military equipment badly. (*Hearings on H.R. 5020, op.cit.*, pp. 581-582.) For a statement of economic and political problems in Spain, its possible contribution to the Western defense system, and a conclusion that Spain was both unwilling and unable to do much for NATO, see Schwarz, U., "Report on Spain," *Swiss Review of World Affairs*, July 1951, pp. 1-5.

[9] For some statements on the question of aiding Spain, see *Congressional Record*, February 14, 1951, pp. 1301-1302; July 23, p. 8858; and July 24, p. A4834; May, A. W., "Spain High-lights Difficulties in U.S. Foreign Aid Policies," *Commercial and Financial Chronicle*, New York, July 12, 1951, p. 1 ff.

[1] Specific and vociferous objections were raised, however, to the character of the aid and to the Administrations proposal that it be extended in the form of grants rather than loans (see Section c (3) below).

[2] The Administration did not present, and Congress did not discuss, the views of the potential recipients as to the distribution of the aid between military and non-military goods.

(1) *Military end-item assistance*

Under the Mutual Defense Assistance Program, the Government was already committed to providing large amounts of military matériel and, save for a small amount of "economizing," Congress was not disposed to prune seriously the Administration's 1951 requests for funds for these purposes. As noted above, the bulk of this military aid was destined for Europe—Greece, Turkey, and Iran were included in the area "Near East and Africa" and accounted for practically all the military aid scheduled for that general region, but aid to them was justified as being essential to the defense of Western Europe. The thesis of the Administration, which was accepted by the majority of Congress, was that if a general war were to break out in the near future it was likely to be centered in Europe, that loss of Europe to Russia would be most disastrous for United States security, and that the Western European nations, along with Greece and Turkey, were in a position to make the most effective use of additional military matériel since they had already formulated specific rearmament programs.

Congress also shared the Administration's view that only relatively small amounts of military end-items could be put to use by the other countries of the world and that, as compared with Europe, the emphasis of the American aid programs in these other areas should be proportionately more "upon building security through helping the people and governments of these areas to solve pressing economic problems."[3] Nonetheless, for all the non-European areas combined (excluding Greece, Turkey, and Iran) the value of the proposed shipments of military end-items was some two-thirds of the total aid program. In the area of Asia and the Pacific, military supplies were scheduled only for Formosa, the Philippines, Indochina, and Thailand. Except for these nations and South Korea, (the latter was receiving military supplies directly from United States forces there and financed from the regular appropriations for the Department of Defense) the other countries in this area either had not requested military equipment or were said to have no "need" for it. The Administration hoped that these relatively small amounts of military supplies would permit these countries to resist Communist aggression, but stated that rearmament pro-

[3] Budget Message of the President, January 15, 1951.

grams on the dimensions of those being pursued in Europe were not regarded as feasible from the point of view of United States capabilities, nor were they desired by these countries. Congress did not seriously question these conclusions. The Administration also proposed to give small amounts of military matériel to Latin America with the aim of securing the sources of, and access to, strategic materials and of reducing the probability of having to station large numbers of American troops in that area, as had been done during World War II. Although Congress appropriated practically all the funds requested for Latin America, many members were not satisfied that these nations were "doing all that was necessary" for their own security or genuinely accepting rearmament as their own responsibility.

Most of the discussions on military aid related to Europe.[4] In general terms, the program was "designed to supply only those items which represent net deficiencies in European requirements after determining what each country has on hand, what it can produce for itself, and what it can obtain through mutual assistance arrangements with its neighbors."[5] In these discussions the Administration admitted, however, that "very little progress" had been made in getting "each European country to specialize in the manufacture of those particular things which they can do best and discouraging them from trying to make every single article of military equipment for themselves."[6]

Spokesmen for the Executive Branch admitted also that the level of European rearmament was not up to the targets which had been promulgated by Supreme Headquarters, Allied Powers, Europe (SHAPE) but asserted that the programs were being accelerated and that such delays as had taken place were the result of economic, political, and social "realities" and not of any general

[4] For a country-by-country justification of the Administration's program of aid to Europe, see *Hearings, Pt. 1, op.cit.*, pp. 101-376. The programs as then planned by the individual European nations, as well as their individual economic, political, and social conditions, were examined by a Senate subcommittee during mid-1951; their findings are reported in "United States Foreign-Aid Programs in Europe," *Hearings on United States Economic and Military Assistance to Free Europe*, U.S. Senate, Subcommittee of the Committee on Foreign Relations, 82d Cong., 1st Sess., July 1951, and in *S. Doc. No. 56*, August 13, 1951.

[5] "The Mutual Security Program for Fiscal Year 1952," *Committee Print, op.cit.*, p. 16. The Administration later stated that in estimating the domestic contribution of each nation, it had taken into account not only the current rearmament budget but also possible increases via heavier taxation and lower domestic consumption.

[6] *Hearings on S. 1762, op.cit.*, p. 180.

unwillingness to put forth maximum efforts to improve their own defense. At the same time, the Administration stated that military end-items would be provided only if they could be used and that economic aid would be used as a lever to encourage greater rearmament efforts. Some Congressmen saw the higher percentage of United States defense expenditures to gross national product and the higher per capita expenditures devoted to defense as indications that other countries were failing to contribute a "fair share." The Administration replied that this conclusion was unwarranted since per capita incomes in the United States were much larger than those in Europe.[7]

To those members of Congress who urged that the total amount of military aid to Europe be reduced, the Administration replied with a series of statements and arguments: the amounts proposed were necessary if the Europeans were to get their defenses up to the desired levels;[8] a reduction would mean that some of the military units being formed in Europe would not be equipped; it would seriously reduce the flexibility of the program by making it impossible to take advantage of higher rates of progress in certain European countries toward rearmament goals; and it would have a seriously adverse morale and psychological impact in Europe since several of the countries were "just looking for excuses" for not doing more[9] and would interpret a Congressional cut in aid as meaning that the United States thought their efforts were not important.[1] These arguments were accepted by Congress, and the appropriation for military end-items was only some 5 percent below the Administration's request, as shown in Table 1 on page 29.

The Administration requested two rather minor amendments in the previously existing authority (the Mutual Defense Assistance Act) to extend military aid to foreign nations.[2] It asked that the

[7] For some detailed statistical estimates on incomes, taxes, and budgets, see *Hearings on H.R. 5020, op.cit.*, pp. 231-232. See also the *First Report to Congress on the Mutual Security Program, op.cit.*, pp. 12-13.

[8] *Hearings on S. 1762, op.cit.*, pp. 494-495.

[9] This statement is in contradiction to the prior one that slow progress was not due to unwillingness to put forth maximum efforts.

[1] *Hearings on H.R. 5020, op.cit.*, p. 1379.

[2] For the major provisions of this Act, see *Survey—1950*, pp. 40-43. In March 1951, Congress prohibited the transfer of large naval vessels under MDAP without the specific authorization of Congress (P.L. 3, 82d Cong., 1st Sess.). In September, it approved the transfer of twenty-four destroyer escorts (P.L. 146, 82d Cong., 1st Sess.).

ceiling on the amount of "excess" United States military equipment which could be sent abroad under the program be raised by $450 million (procurement cost). Nearly all of the existing authority, $700 million, had been obligated, and Defense Department spokesmen testified that additional amounts of equipment purchased in the past by the United States Military Establishment from its own appropriated funds were and would be available as "excess" because of the development of new models and the changing requirements of American forces. Since the goods were already in existence and only the costs of rehabilitating, packing, and shipping would be charged against the foreign-aid funds, witnesses argued that the requested authority served to reduce the amount of new appropriations which would otherwise be necessary. Congress saw no objection to this use of equipment if it were really in "excess" but expressed some doubts that this much would, or should, be available; it authorized the sending of only an additional $300 million after June 30, 1951. With but little discussion, Congress approved another Administration request, raising from $100 million to $500 million the amount of reimbursable contracts that could be outstanding at one time. The major effect of this amendment was to facilitate Canadian purchases of United States military equipment.

(2) *Economic assistance*

While there was no serious Congressional questioning of the desirability of giving military end-items to friendly foreign nations, sharp differences arose between the Executive and Legislative Branches on providing other than military end-items—the so-called economic assistance. The Administration asked for a total of $2,197 million for economic assistance, distributed among areas as shown above.[3] The Administration spokesmen argued that this aid was for various types of economic support of the military effort in the recipient countries, that it would directly and indirectly strengthen United States security, and so was an integral and "indivisible" part of the Mutual Security Program.[4]

[3] For detailed statements of the methods and assumptions used in arriving at this figure, see *Hearings on H.R. 5020, op.cit.*, pp. 434-438, and *Hearings on H.R. 5684, op.cit.*, pp. 132-150.

[4] For an official statement of the development of this Administration position, see *Fourth Semiannual Report to Congress on the Mutual Defense Assistance Program, H. Doc. No.* 352, February 14, 1952, pp. 74-77.

Nonetheless, the economic part of the program was statistically separated from the request for the military end-item assistance and was presented and justified by a different group of officials. This procedure, together with the fact that most of the persons presenting the case for economic aid simply were not well informed of the case being presented by the officials justifying military aid (and vice versa), facilitated Congressional attacks on the economic aid as a dispensable part of the program. The Administration justified its requests for economic aid on three broad fronts—(1) to forestall political and economic crises as the European nations diverted more of their own resources to rearmament, (2) to facilitate the expansion of military production in Europe, and (3) to increase the supply from the less developed areas of raw materials needed for rearmament and to strengthen their political affiliations with the Atlantic Community.

i. abandonment of European recovery

With respect to economic aid for Europe, many Congressmen were determined to divide the Administration's request into that portion designed to facilitate "recovery" along the lines of the previous ECA program and that part used to hasten rearmament. Administration officials replied that such a division could not be made since increased rearmament in Europe was dependent on expanded industrial and agricultural production. Nonetheless, under Congressional insistence and with great reluctance, ECA officials estimated that perhaps some $670 million would have been requested for continuing the recovery program had not rearmament intervened, but they stated that the character of such a program would have been different from that financed out of the present request. Despite its different character, ECA officials admitted that some aid would be of the ERP type since recovery was not completed, but they argued that the total amount of economic aid requested was necessary if some of the past economic recovery was not to be lost and Europe pushed back at a later date into its 1947 position,[5] that it was a necessary cushion for the inevitable rearmament-induced reductions in consumption and in-

[5] Administration spokesmen testified that with respect to a few countries—especially Greece, Italy, and Austria—economic help of the ECA variety would probably be requested in future years as well.

vestment if internal inflation and politically unacceptable standards of living were to be avoided and full moral support for the rearmament program obtained, and that provision of this sort of help would permit the Europeans to devote a larger amount of their own resources to producing military goods.

The Administration, which had for years been impressing Congress with the great strides toward economic recovery made by Europe, with the help of ECA aid, found the majority of that body unsympathetic to the pleas for continued "recovery" aid, and Congress concluded that the need for the European Recovery Program was ended well ahead of schedule. In the search for ways to reduce the cost of the new program, they concentrated on those parts of the Administration's proposal which they believed to be for general recovery purposes. Thus, the Administration's request for economic aid to Europe was trimmed by nearly $700 million and the funds finally appropriated for the so-called economic programs for Europe (excluding Spain) totalled slightly more than $1 billion.[6] Congress had, however, some second thoughts on this question and in the conference between the two houses agreed to increase to 10 percent (the Administration had originally requested only 5 percent) the amount which the Administration was authorized to transfer from the "military" to the "economic" category and vice versa. Nonetheless, in the debates, though not in the letter of the final law, Congress emphasized that these "economic" funds should be used for expanding the production of military matériel in Europe.[7] And the final law did stipulate that the authority to extend "recovery" aid was to expire on June 30, 1952.

ii. aid for military production

The Mutual Defense Assistance Act of 1949, as amended in 1950, empowered the Administration to send tools, equipment, and materials to Europe for use in producing military matériel there.[8]

[6] Of which $10 million were earmarked to aid migration out of Europe (see below).

[7] The Administration apparently failed to impress upon Congress that most of the "recovery" aid was for materials and tools which would facilitate in a fairly direct way the production of such matériel. (For comment, see *The Economist*, September 1, 1951, p. 508.) The Administration attempted to correct the impression held by Congress in its *First Report to Congress on the Mutual Security Program*, Washington, D.C., December 31, 1951, pp. 1-7.

[8] See *Survey—1949*, p. 38n, and *Survey—1950*, pp. 42-43 and 46-47.

In its 1951 aid proposals, the Administration requested that this authority be extended and stated that it was planned to help finance the construction of new, and expansion of existing, production facilities and also to contribute to the cost of military "infrastructure."[9] The Administration asserted that the program of aiding the expansion of facilities to produce military goods in Europe was warranted on several counts: it would cost the United States less than providing end-items; it brought the source of supply closer to the location of use; many military goods could be produced more cheaply in Europe than in the United States; and it would advance Europe toward self-sufficiency in military production[1] and so would ultimately relieve the United States of providing aid.[2] One of the major problems in this program was recognizedly that of determining which facilities should be aided in each country. The Administration set forth no general rules or principles, but it reported that in making these decisions it would take into account such factors as the speed with which the needed end-items could be produced, the existing and proposed facilities in the United States for producing certain goods, the cost of production and possibilities of increasing productivity abroad, the ability of a given country to direct more of its own resources to military goods output once the plant existed, the possibility of intra-European specialization, and strategic considerations as to plant location.[3] Congress raised no serious objections to this aspect of the program, and it was authorized in the final law.

Administration spokesmen testified that they also planned to facilitate the production of military end-items in Europe both by the direct procurement in Europe of some of the military matériel

[9] "Infrastructure" was the term applied to facilities such as airfields, harbors, communications, etc., which were to be used by several countries in the joint defense.

[1] A Defense Department representative stated that military self-sufficiency as here used did not necessarily mean production of all types of matériel within a given nation but in some cases included ability to buy items elsewhere. (*Hearings, Part 1, op.cit.*, p. 99.)

[2] Again, however, the Administration did not hold out the promise of any early relief to the United States from the necessity of supplying large amounts of military end-items to Europe.

[3] Importantly, American military officials gave no indication that they contemplated any serious reliance on Europe to produce matériel needed for United States forces.

to be given to Europe under the end-item part of the program and by the use of local currency counterpart funds generated by the economic aid grants from the United States. The direct purchase with dollars of military matériel, which in turn would be given to Europe, was seen primarily as a means of utilizing existing excess capacity and of reducing the total dollar cost of American support of Europe's rearmament effort, while providing Europe with some "free" dollars, rather than as a method of encouraging new investment in war goods producing facilities.[4] Nonetheless, the Administration testified that it had been and was reluctant to make such purchases on a large scale, lest it induce a drop in the amount of European domestic military purchases. Further, the officials reported, the amounts to be so spent would not be great because of the unavailability of items and because of their high cost as compared with the United States. Congress raised no serious objections to the Administration's making such purchases out of the funds appropriated for military end-item assistance.

In 1950, ECA had taken an adamant position that counterpart funds[5] should be used only for "economic" purposes, but in 1951 the Administration proposed that the existing law be amended so as to insure that a large part of these funds be directed to rearmament purposes. Although it was not firmly established Administration policy, a senior ECA official told Congress that these counterpart funds should be made available "preferably for use by the North Atlantic Treaty Organization itself for the procurement of certain military end items"[6] anywhere in Europe. The law as passed removed the restriction that the 5 percent counterpart funds could be used only within the depositing country and required the Administrator of the MSA to make agreements with countries receiving grant aid such that not less than the equivalent

[4] See *Hearings on H.R. 5020, op.cit.*, pp. 1275, 1357, 1366, and *Hearings, Part 1, op.cit.*, pp. 90-98 and *Part 2*, pp. 759-760.

[5] In most of the recent "economic" aid programs, each country receiving grant assistance is required to deposit in special accounts amounts of its own currency—called counterpart funds—equal to the dollar cost of United States financed goods and services received by it on a grant basis. Under the various ERP agreements, 95 percent of these deposits were to be used by the recipient country for purposes agreed upon by ECA and that country, and 5 percent were reserved for the use of the United States in that country.

[6] *Hearings on H.R. 5020, op.cit.*, p. 1276.

of $500 million of the 95 percent counterpart funds (existing and to be deposited for fiscal year 1952 aid) should be used for military production, construction, and equipment.[7]

iii. other economic aid

In addition to the economic aid for Europe, the Administration proposed that relatively small amounts of assistance other than military end-items be extended to various nations in the Near East and Africa, the Far East and the Pacific, and Latin America. These less industrially developed areas were not expected to contribute large contingents of armed forces or to produce military matériel, but Administration witnesses argued that the security of the West would be strengthened if those peoples and governments were aided in meeting their more pressing internal economic problems. They also testified that such assistance would not only be in support of American security objectives by giving these areas faith in the future with the free world but would also "generate in . . . [them] a sense of full partnership in the free world and a full awareness of the insidious character of the Communist threat and the means to eliminate it."[8] Additional strength would accrue to the West, they stated, if a portion of the American aid were devoted, as was planned, to expanding the production of strategic and critical materials, shortages of which were hindering the mobilization efforts of the United States and Western Europe. They emphasized the desirability of extending aid to increase the production of strategic materials but made it clear that a considerable part of the requested funds would be used to provide both consumer and capital goods to facilitate the more general economic development of these areas and for technical assistance.[9]

[7] The law did not specify which currencies were to be so used, or whether a given currency could be used outside the issuing country, nor did it make any restrictions on the use of such funds for purchasing end-items as against investment and production facilities.

MSA reported that, as of December 31, 1951, this minimum would probably be substantially exceeded and that in some cases the funds would be used directly for procurement of military equipment and construction, and in others would finance such production in private plants.

[8] *Hearings on H.R. 5020, op.cit.*, pp. 154-155.

[9] In line with the latter, the Administration requested (and Congress granted) authority to contribute $13 million to the UN technical assistance program; these funds were to be taken from any MSP area but not necessarily spent by the UN in that area.

For the Near East and Africa—an area seen as of great importance to American security by virtue of its strategic location and as a source of oil—the Administration requested $125 million, including $50 million for the UN Palestine Refugee Program.[1] The State Department testified that the general aim of United States foreign policy in this part of the world was that of overcoming the 'anti-Westernism" and "neutralism" which existed there.[2] Congress spent much time discussing the proposed aid to Iran in view of its existing dispute with Britain over Iranian oil properties. Some in Congress found it difficult to justify extending dollar aid to a country which they thought was denying itself foreign exchange as a result of nationalization schemes. The Administration asserted that, regardless of any mismanagement of her affairs from the West's standpoint, aid to Iran was justified as a means of frustrating Soviet intervention there,[3] and Congress finally agreed to the proposed expenditures.

More complicated was the problem of aid to Israel and the Arab States, including contributions to the UN Palestine Refugee Program. The major justification offered for aid to these areas was that it would prepare the way for a resolution of the differences between the Arabs and Israeli and so would strengthen the solidarity of the whole area with the West. Congress did not seriously question the desirability of contributing to the Palestine Refugee Program—which the Administration warned would continue for at least three years—but many members of Congress saw it as aid essentially to the Arab States. Earlier in the year, Israel had asked the United States for $150 million to assist it in meeting problems arising from immigration, claiming that it was assuming expenses for refugees who otherwise would have been under the care of the UN or of the occupying forces in Europe. Without the official blessing of the Administration, separate bills were introduced in

[1] Economic aid for Greece and Turkey was included in the funds provided for Europe. The funds requested for the Near East and Africa were scheduled to be distributed among Iran, Israel, the Arab States, Libya, Liberia, and Ethiopia.

[2] For a subsequent official statement of the economic, social, and political problems and "The Development of United States Policy in the Near East, 1945-1951," see Department of State *Bulletin,* November 19 and 26, 1951, pp. 809-816 and 839-843.

[3] See *Hearings on H.R. 5020, op.cit.,* pp. 49-50, and 368-375. In the debates, though not in the law, Congress made it clear that it disapproved using the aid in such a way (e.g., by providing heavy farm machinery) as to encourage the perpetuation of the existing land tenure system in Iran.

both Houses to provide United States assistance to Israel, and in discussing the Administration's MSP proposals various members of Congress stated their belief that the amount tentatively earmarked for Israel was insufficient. These legislators maintained that more aid could be justified on the grounds that Israel was a new state, had a large immigration problem, would use the aid to "productive advantage," and that diplomatic considerations required the equalization of aid between Israel and the Arab States.[4] After several different proposals had been considered, Congress, subjected to competing pro-Arab and pro-Israel lobbies, finally raised the total of economic aid for the Near East and Africa area to $160 million—taking the funds for the $35 million increase over the Administration's request from the military aid requested—and provided that Israel on the one hand and the Arab States on the other should receive the same amount, counting the $50 million for the UN Palestine Refugee Program as aid to the Arab States.

For economic aid to the Asia and Pacific area, the Administration requested a new authorization of $262.5 million,[5] plus $112.5 million for the United States contribution to the UN Korean Rehabilitation Agency. With respect to the UN Korean program, the Administration stated that it would not begin operations until hostilities ceased but that funds should be provided now in order that policies and specific programs could be planned and the Korean people assured of assistance.[6] Although Congress did not question the desirability of contributing to this program—assistance to civilians in Korea was currently being given by the UN Civil Assistance Command to which the United States Army was making contributions out of its regular Army appropriations[7]—it saw little point in providing additional funds at that time and,

[4] The notion that Israel was of "equal importance" to *all* the Arab States was strongly resented in the latter as "an insult and a dangerous principle." (See, for example, *New York Times*, May 29, and June 10, 18, and 26, 1951.)

[5] The nations to be assisted included Afghanistan, Burma, Ceylon, Formosa, India, Indochina, Indonesia, Korea, Nepal, Pakistan, the Philippines, and Thailand. Several of these had not received official grants from the United States in the past. Aid to Japan and the Ryukyus was being provided under the Occupied Areas Program discussed in Section B below.

[6] For a brief official discussion of "Political Problems and Economic Developments in Korea," see Department of State *Bulletin*, December 10, 1951, pp. 927-935; see also *United Nations Bulletin*, February 1, 1952, p. 115, and *The Nation*, February 2, 1952, p. 107.

[7] In October, the Department of Defense Appropriation Act, 1952 (Title III) provided $50 million for additional civilian relief in Korea.

although the authorization bill allowed $45 million, the appropriation act made no new funds available on the ground that the carry-over of some $50 million from previous appropriations was adequate for the time being.

For this area in general, whose strategic importance as a source of raw materials and of manpower was acknowledged by both the Administration and Congress, spokesmen for the Executive Branch stated that the most urgent considerations were those of raising consumption levels—some Senators agreed that the satisfaction of the more "urgent basic needs of these people is . . . vital to the security of the area and constitutes a fundamental part of American foreign policy"[8]—and of helping ". . . into being a state of affairs in which these friendly countries . . . can build the economic foundations of the political freedom they have already won."[9] Thus, most of the economic aid was to be for consumer goods and raw materials—as well as some technical assistance and capital goods of the Point Four variety.[1] Emphasis in the latter was to be on public administration, agriculture, health and sanitation, and the development of mineral resources.

In previous years, Congressional sentiment had been strong for huge aid programs to the Far East.[2] Some recurrence of this sentiment was expected and, as noted above, the Administration explained in some detail why only relatively small amounts of aid were being programmed for the non-European areas.[3] However, no serious question was raised in Congress as to whether Asia rather than Europe was the appropriate area for major United States assistance. In fact, the final law reduced the Administration's

[8] *Hearings on H.R. 5020, op.cit.*, p. 890.

[9] Address by Mr. Bissell, Acting ECA Administrator, on October 19, 1951, before the Far East America Council of Commerce and Industry, New York City (mimeographed release by the Economic Cooperation Administration).

[1] The Administration had also requested that, in order to obtain local currencies needed by the Government for various purposes in areas where the grant programs —and so the counterpart funds—were small, it be allowed to use specified amounts of appropriated funds to purchase such local currencies. The law as approved authorized that $10 million of the funds made available for the Near East and Africa and $25 million of those set aside for Asia and the Pacific could be so used, on condition that the dollars involved be used by the recipient for purposes agreed to by the United States. An additional $50 million from the total appropriation were permitted to be used to "acquire local currency for the purpose of increasing the production of materials in which the United States is deficient." (Mutual Security Act of 1951, Section 519.)

[2] See *Survey—1949*, pp. 43-46.

[3] See *Hearings on H.R. 5020, op.cit.*, pp. 892-894.

request for Asia and the Pacific by some 10 percent in keeping with its general economy drive.

For several years Latin America had been receiving small amounts of grant aid from the United States, mostly in connection with the technical assistance activities of the Institute of Inter-American Affairs and the program for eradicating hoof-and-mouth disease in Mexico. During the Fourth Meeting of Consultation of Ministers of Foreign Affairs of the American Republics, called by the United States during the early spring of 1951, several of the Latin American delegates complained that the United States was putting too much emphasis on military preparedness in Latin America and was not fulfilling its "commitments" for technical and economic assistance to the area. These officials argued that the most serious Communist threat in their countries was from internal subversion, which could best be met by faster and more diversified economic development.[4] The final resolutions of this conference, for which the United States voted, laid great stress on economic development as an essential factor in the concept of Hemisphere defense.[5] In its MSP proposals, submitted to Congress after this inter-American conference, the Administration asked for $22 million for Point Four assistance—a larger amount than had been spent in any previous year—but stated that more than three-fourths of this amount would be used to carry on existing projects; a few new projects were contemplated to help increase production of natural rubber and scarce materials, to improve transportation and communication facilities, and to assist in programming the utilization of borrowed funds, thereby improving the quality of applications for loans, especially from the International Bank.[6] The Administration emphasized that most of the funds scheduled for Latin America would go for technical assistance; the bulk of the capital goods needed would be provided through the area's own foreign exchange earnings supplemented by foreign private

[4] Some Congressmen were resentful of this attitude, believing that it carried with it the conviction that these countries were doing the United States a favor by rearming or accepting military aid. See, for example, the statement of Senator Hickenlooper in *Hearings on S. 1762, op.cit.*, pp. 404-405.

[5] For the text of the relevant resolutions, see Department of State *Bulletin*, April 16, 1951, pp. 610 ff. The Latin American delegates also attempted, unsuccessfully, to get the United States to undertake commitments to maintain the purchasing power of any dollar reserves they accumulated (see Chapter VI, Section C, below).

[6] For details on the proposed Latin American programs, see *Hearings on H.R. 5020, op.cit.*, pp. 1089-1104.

investment and public loans from the Export-Import Bank and the International Bank. Although the Senate Foreign Relations Committee reduced the Administration's request, practically the entire amount was restored on the Senate floor—where some Senators stated that the amounts proposed for this area were "shamefully" low in comparison with those for other areas,[7] and the final appropriation act provided $21 million.[8]

Such reductions as were made in the aid for areas other than Europe were reflections of Congressional concern over the ability of the American economy to bear the drain of these unilateral transfers and over the level of taxation required in the United States to finance them, rather than from any doubts that such foreign aid would strengthen the security of the United States. Table 1 below summarizes the general distribution of aid under the MSP as requested by the President and as finally appropriated by Congress.

TABLE 1

Appropriations for the Mutual Security Program for Fiscal Year 1951-1952
(millions of dollars)

Area and Purpose		*President's Request*	*Congressional Appropriation*[a]
Europe	— Military	5,293	4,819
	— Economic	1,675	1,022[b]
Spain	— Military and Economic	0	100
Near East and Africa	— Military	415	396
	— Economic	125	160
Asia and the Pacific	— Military	555	535
	— Economic	375[c]	237
Latin America	— Military	40	38
	— Economic	22	21
Total	— Military	6,303	5,788[d]
	— Economic	2,197	1,440
	— Undistributed	0	100
	Grand Total[e]	8,500	7,329

a) The President was authorized to transfer, within any area, up to 10 percent of the area's total funds from military aid to economic aid or vice versa, and was

(*Notes continued at bottom of next page*)

[7] See *Congressional Record*, August 30, 1951, pp. 11039-11041.

[8] In September, the Department of Agriculture Appropriation Act, 1952 allowed the use of an indefinite sum for control of hoof-and-mouth diseases of animals in Mexico; it also provided that $32.7 million of notes of the CCC, given to the Treasury to finance such operations through fiscal year 1950, be canceled.

The MSP authorization act provided that any unutilized funds under the various programs which had been subsumed under the MSP were to continue to be available. As of the beginning of fiscal year 1952, the total of such unexpended funds was nearly $8 billion, of which, however, all but $100 million had been allocated or committed, as shown in Table 2. Thus, $15.2 billion were available for expenditures during the period July 1, 1951 to June 30, 1952.

TABLE 2

Summary of Unutilized Foreign Aid, by Program, as of June 30, 1951
(millions of dollars)

Program	Total Unutilized*	Allocated or Committed	Unallocated or Uncommitted
European Recovery	1,688	1,589	99
Korea and Far East	273	272	1
Mutual Defense Assistance	5,899	5,899	0
Greek-Turkish Aid	12	12	0
Chinese Military Aid	2	2	0
Technical Assistance and Inter-American Aid	23	21	2
Total	7,897	7,795	102

* These data include appropriations and transfer authorizations but exclude contract authorizations.
Source: Department of Commerce, *Foreign Transactions of the U.S. Government* (Basic data through June 30, 1951), Washington, D.C., September 1951, p. A-12.

C. OTHER LEGISLATIVE ISSUES

(1) *Conditions on aid*

Throughout the hearings on the legislation many members of Congress expressed their conviction that if the aid were to accomplish its purposes certain new policy commitments should be made by the recipients and specific timetables of accomplishments

also authorized to transfer up to 10 percent of the amount specified for any one area to another area or areas.
b) Including $10 million specifically set aside to aid European migration.
c) Includes a request for $112 million for the United States contribution to the UN Korean Rehabilitation Program.
d) In addition, the Mutual Security Act of 1951 authorized the transfer of up to $300 million in "excess" military supplies.
e) Detail may not add to totals because of rounding.
Source: "The Mutual Security Program," President's Message to Congress, May 1951, and Mutual Security Appropriation Act, 1952.

should be met.[9] The Executive Branch was opposed to any detailed conditions or timetables being legislated, favoring a wide area of discretion by those administering the aid, and gave assurances that it would see to it that no country would be aided unless its "performance" was found to be "adequate."[1] However, in addition to the general requirement that the President find that the extension of aid would strengthen the security of the United States and promote world peace, the authorization law set forth specific eligibility requirements for military and economic aid as follows: "(*a*) No military, economic, or technical assistance . . . shall be supplied to any nation in order to further military effort unless . . . [it] has agreed to (1) join in promoting international understanding and good will, and maintaining world peace; (2) take such action as may be mutually agreed upon to eliminate causes of international tension; (3) fulfill the military obligations which it has assumed under multilateral or bilateral agreements or treaties to which the United States is a party; (4) make, consistent with its political and economic stability, the full contribution permitted by its manpower, resources, facilities, and general economic conditions to the development and maintenance of its own defensive strength and to the defensive strength of the free world; (5) take all reasonable measures which may be needed to develop its defense capacities; and (6) take appropriate steps to insure the effective utilization of the economic and military assistance provided by the United States. (*b*) No economic or technical assistance shall be supplied to any other nation unless the President finds that the supplying of such assistance will strengthen the security of the United States and promote world peace, and unless the recipient country has agreed to join in promoting international understanding and good will, and in maintaining world

[9] Some objections were raised against United States support of social reform measures in Europe which drained away capital and weighed heavily on rearmament programs. ECA witnesses agreed that these measures did make "it harder for them to finance . . . military activities" but argued that their effect "on any need or justification for help from us, is very slight, indeed" and that "they do not directly compete in most cases with their military efforts." (*Hearings on H.R. 5684, op.cit.*, p. 11.)

[1] As with similar attempts in other years, efforts in Congress to withhold aid from Britain so long as Ireland was partitioned were defeated, as were proposals that aid be denied to France as long as American businessmen were being discriminated against in Morocco. For an official French statement on the rights of Americans in Morocco, see Department of State *Bulletin*, December 17, 1951, pp. 978-984.

peace, and to take such action as may be mutually agreed upon to eliminate causes of international tension."[2]

Congress, as in previous years, stated without qualification its belief that the long-run solution of Europe's economic (and defense) problems demanded that the area unite or at least federate. There was little discussion as to specifically what this meant, but the Administration, while agreeing that a "unified Europe" was a desirable objective, again stated its conviction that "unification" should not be a condition for receiving aid. In 1950, Congress had stated in the law extending the Economic Cooperation Act that it was the policy of the people of the United States "to encourage the further unification of Europe" and in the 1951 Mutual Security Act this was amended to read "to further encourage the economic unification and the political federation of Europe."[3]

Without Administration approval, and over the strenuous objection of some who, in the words of Senator Taft, felt that it "was a most outrageous interference with the affairs of other nations," Congress also accepted the so-called "Benton amendment," aimed at encouraging free private enterprise abroad[4]—and so, it was reasoned, fostering greater production and increased productivity.[5] This provision stated that the Act should be so administered as "(1) to eliminate the barriers to, and provide the incentives for, a steadily increased participation of free private enterprise in developing the resources of foreign countries consistent with the policies

[2] Mutual Security Act of 1951 (P.L. 165) Section 511. According to the press, in practice some modifications in these "requirements" had to be made for at least Iran, which refused to agree to the specific wording proposed by the United States.

[3] The inclusion of "political federation" indicated a weakening of the 1950 opposition to placing anything political in an economic program. See Chapter VII for discussion of the activities of the United States in encouraging the economic unification of Europe during 1951.

[4] At the same time, as in earlier years, certain members of Congress expressed concern over the use of United States aid funds to help foreign industry compete with United States enterprise. (See *Hearings on H.R. 5020, op.cit.*, pp. 197-198; *Hearings on H.R. 5684, op.cit.*, pp. 78-79; and *Congressional Record*, January 31, 1951, p. 867.)

[5] During the Congressional consideration of the program, Administration officials reported that the unwillingness of certain American manufacturers to license their patented processes was constituting a "real drag on the production program abroad." (*Hearings on H.R. 5020, op.cit.*, p. 1364.) To alleviate some of these difficulties, Congress approved a provision which made it clear that the use of patented inventions, processes, etc., in the advancement of the purposes of the act would be "by and for the United States" and would thus come under the same procedures and protection as those requisitioned by the Government at other times for other purposes. Private industry spokesmen raised no objection to this provision.

of this Act, (2) to the extent that it is feasible and does not interfere with the achievement of the purposes set forth in this Act, to discourage the cartel and monopolistic practices prevailing in certain countries receiving aid under this Act which result in restricting production and increasing prices, and to encourage where suitable competition and productivity, and (3) to encourage where suitable the development and strengthening of the free labor union movements as the collective bargaining agencies of labor within such countries."[6]

(2) *Grants versus loans*

While the Administration anticipated a continuation of Government lending and to facilitate this was requesting, in separate legislation, that the lending authority of the EIB be increased,[7] its MSP proposals called for all the aid being extended as grants. But Congress once more showed a strong desire to provide part of the assistance on a credit basis.[8] Many in Congress argued that the "debt-paying capacity" of Europe at least was as great as the "tax-paying capacity" of American citizens, that the psychological effect of receiving aid on a credit basis was better than receiving it on a grant basis, and that any project which produced commodities which were commercially saleable was the appropriate subject for a loan.

Many Congressmen also argued that most of the aid proposed for capital as distinct from technical, assistance projects in the various *non-European* areas should be on a loan basis.[9] Those taking this view pointed out that many of the countries were currently earning substantial amounts of dollars and stated that,

[6] Mutual Security Act of 1951 (P.L. 165) Section 516.

[7] See Chapter III. In an effort to increase the amount of capital assistance available from international sources, the House Foreign Affairs Committee reported a provision that consideration be given to merging the International Monetary Fund and the International Bank with the aim of enlarging the latter's resources by some $2 billion which were being held idle by the Fund. The Administration argued that its inclusion was "inappropriate," and the provision was omitted from the final Act.

[8] See *Survey—1949*, pp. 10-11, for a review of this problem during the early discussions of the ERP. The arguments of the Administration in 1951 against extending aid on a credit basis were essentially the same as those offered in 1949 and so are not repeated here.

[9] They argued further that such loans preferably should come from private American sources or existing national and international governmental institutions rather than from a special new U.S. Government aid program.

in any case, aid in the form of loans would reduce the amount of aid requested by the countries, would create a better psychological relationship between them and the United States, and would result in a more efficient use of any funds provided. Administration spokesmen replied that repayment capacity did not exist in many of the nations at present, that many of the projects contemplated were not "productive" in the banking or loan sense, that many of the proposed undertakings were on a village scale and so did not lend themselves to foreign loans,[1] and that future borrowing capacity should not be impaired by extending what would in fact be "gift-loans." After much discussion, the Administration, however, finally stated that it would shift some of the capital items in the program to a loan basis rather than incur the displeasure of Congress.[2] The authorization act stipulated that, of the funds appropriated for economic assistance, "as great an amount (in no event less than 10 per centum) as possible shall be provided on credit terms."[3]

To encourage the movement abroad of private United States capital, Congress accepted the Administration's suggestion that the previous authority of ECA to extend investment guarantees to private investors in ERP countries and their dependent overseas territories be expanded so as to permit MSA to extend the guarantees to any area mentioned in the Act. This proposal was accepted with relatively little questioning, despite the fact that during the previous two years there had been considerable opposition to investment guarantees both in Congress and from private investors.[4]

(3) *Aid to escapees*

An amendment to the Administration's proposals, offered from the floor of the House and accepted without debate, authorized that up to $100 million of the funds for military assistance to Europe could be used to assist "any selected persons who are residing in or escapees from the Soviet Union, Poland, Czechoslovakia, Hungary, Rumania, Bulgaria, Albania, Lithuania, Latvia, and Estonia,

[1] See Chapter IV for a short account of the efforts of the International Bank to develop procedures for financing such small investments.

[2] For further discussion on this question of loans versus grants, see *Hearings on S. 1762, op.cit.*, pp. 585-591, 602-605, 611-623, 666-669.

[3] Mutual Security Act of 1951 (P.L. 165), Section 522.

[4] See *Survey—1949*, pp. 77-85, and *Survey—1950*, pp. 107-112.

or the Communist dominated or Communist occupied areas of Germany and Austria, and any other countries absorbed by the Soviet Union either to form such persons into elements of the military forces supporting the North Atlantic Treaty Organization or for other purposes, when it is similarly determined by the President that such assistance will contribute to the defense of the North Atlantic area and to the security of the United States."[5] The Soviet Union subsequently protested the provision, saying it was a violation of previous understandings that neither Government would engage in subversive activities against the other; it brought its protest before the UN, which body decided not to consider it.[6] Russia also sent a formal note of protest to the U.S. Government which was rejected by the latter.[7] No funds were spent for these purposes in 1951, but in March 1952 the President allocated up to $4.3 million to be used during calendar 1952 to "improve the reception and treatment and secure the resettlement of qualified people who escape from the Iron Curtain countries. . . ."[8] The press reported that most of the funds would be used for "resettling" such emigres in the armed forces of the North Atlantic powers, but there was nothing in official United States statements to support this view.

(4) *Migration*

Congress had empowered ECA in 1950 to encourage the migration of surplus manpower within and out of Europe. With the approaching end of the International Refugee Organization, both the Administration and many members of Congress believed that the United States should assume further responsibility for the problem of resettling European refugees and facilitating the emigration of Europeans to areas where labor was in relatively greater demand.[9] State Department spokesmen testified that they were not

[5] Mutual Security Act of 1951 (P.L. 165), Section 101 (a) (1).

[6] Department of State *Bulletin*, December 3, 1951, pp. 910-911, and December 24, 1951, p. 1010. For an appraisal of this provision, see the comments by James Reston in *New York Times*, December 9, 1951.

[7] Department of State *Bulletin*, December 31, 1951, p. 1056, January 7, 1952, pp. 28-35, and January 28, 1952, pp. 128-129.

[8] For the text of his letter, see *New York Times*, March 24, 1952.

[9] For a UN report on some of these problems, see "Methods of International Financing of European Migration," UN Doc.E/2019, June 18, 1951. See also *The Economist*, September 29, 1951, pp. 730-731.

prepared to commit the United States to any long-range migration and resettlement scheme—the International Labor Organization had proposed one—but did want funds to continue some of the work which was being done by the expiring IRO. The MSP authorizing act permitted up to $10 million of the funds for economic aid to Europe to be used for such purposes. However, ECA spokesmen stated before the appropriation committees that, given the permissive nature of the law and the cuts which had been made in their requests for economic aid, they probably would not use the funds for facilitating migration; thereupon Congress specified in the appropriation legislation that $10 million of the appropriations were to be earmarked and used for such purposes only.[1]

Implementation

a. MILITARY ASSISTANCE

Beginning in 1949, foreign military assistance by the United States was approached as a continuing long-term undertaking.[2] By the end of 1950, Congress had authorized over $7.2 billion for the Mutual Defense Assistance Program and, as noted above, additional authorizations for military aid during 1951 raised the total to some $13.3 billion.[3] Of this only $2 billion had been utilized by the end of the year, of which $1.5 billion were actually extended during the calendar year 1951. Because of certain shortages in the United States and the larger demands for domestic rearmament,

[1] At the United States sponsored Conference on Migration at Brussels during November and December, the United States delegation proposed a plan to transfer 115,000 persons from Europe at a cost of $34 million, using the above $10 million as its contribution. At this conference a "Provisional Inter-Government Committee for the Movement of Migrants from Europe" was formed, and the first meeting was held in December. An operating budget of over $14 million was approved, with contributions to be voluntary. It was not clear at the end of the year whether or not these steps would merely be the first in larger efforts to meet what many regarded as an acute European problem. (See *New York Times*, November 27, 1951; *United Nations Bulletin*, November 1, 1951, p. 324; and Department of State *Bulletin*, February 4, 1952, pp. 169-173.)

[2] See *Survey—1949*, pp. 32-39; *Survey—1950*, pp. 36-53, for a summary of the activities and policies during those years. For a periodic official report on the Mutual Defense Assistance Program, see the *Semiannual Report to Congress on the Mutual Defense Assistance Program*, Department of State, Washington, D.C. The reader's attention is especially directed to the *Fourth Semiannual Report to Congress on the Mutual Defense Assistance Program* (*H. Doc. No.* 352, 82d Cong., 2d *Sess.*) February 14, 1952, which includes a summary of the operations, objectives, and problems of the program through 1950 and 1951.

[3] These figures include the authority to transfer up to $1.0 billion of "excess" military supplies.

shipments decreased in the last quarter, as is shown in Table 3.[4]

TABLE 3

Military Assistance Grants Utilized, 1950-1951[1]
(millions of dollars)

		1951				
	1950	*Total*	*1st Quarter*	*2nd Quarter*	*3rd Quarter*	*4th Quarter*
Europe						
Military end-items	333	915	198	276	289	152
Other[2]	1	95	18	9	25	43
Near East and Africa[3]						
Military end-items	118	184	39	65	43	37
Other[2]	3	2	2	*	*	*
Asia and the Pacific[4]						
Military end-items	58	293	66	64	62	102
Other[2]	*	*	*	*	*	*
Latin America[1]	0	61	*	*	28	33
Total						
Military end-items	509	1453	302	405	422	324
Other[2]	4	97	19	9	25	44
Grand Total[5]	513	1550	321	414	447	368

* *Less than $500,000.*

1) Grants "utilized" represents shipments when goods are procured by U.S. Government agencies and cash payments by the Government when other methods of procurement are used. Excess equipment provided on a grant basis is included at original cost. Where such equipment is sold, the difference between the amount received for and the "standard value" of the items is included as a grant. Thus, in the case of Latin America, which received no aid out of appropriated funds, all the assistance was of grants in connection with sales of excess equipment.

2) This represents funds transferred to the ECA/MSA and used to finance the shipment of materials and equipment for expanding the production of military matériel in the recipient countries and for providing food for the Yugoslav army.

3) Includes military aid financed from funds provided for the Greek-Turkish Assistance Act of 1948 as amended.

(*Notes continued on next page*)

---

[4] As of January 8, 1952, the date of effectiveness of the requirements for eligibility for military aid (Section 511a), all nations concerned had met the conditions save Iran, from which military aid was withheld, pending an agreement.

A complete list, as of early 1951, of bilateral treaties on military, economic, and technical assistance, on security matters, and on commercial relations and tariffs with respect to countries scheduled to receive aid from the United States in fiscal year 1952 is given in *Hearings on H.R. 5684, op.cit.*, pp. 159-167. Agreements signed later in the year are recorded in Economic Cooperation Administration, *Thirteenth Report to Congress, Supplement*, Washington, D.C., 1951, and Mutual Security Administration, *First Report to Congress, Supplement*, Washington, D.C., 1952.

In his Budget Message on January 21, 1952, the President stated that deliveries under the program had been smaller than anticipated, partly because a large part of the production of United States military goods had been sent to Korea to meet the needs of American forces there,[5] and partly because of the time required to produce much of the so-called "long-lead time" equipment—i.e., such complex items as tanks, planes, heavy guns, etc. But expanding the production of military supplies in the United States was not the only difficulty, and later the President wrote that not "even a majority" of the difficult and complex problems posed by the "systematic creation of military strength in the free world"[6] had been solved.

The other major problems in implementing the program of building up "balanced collective forces" in the North Atlantic area during 1951 revolved around the interrelated questions of distributing the defense burden among the NATO countries, determining the ability of the various countries (especially the European members) to make additional sacrifices in favor of rearmament,[7] and incorporating German forces and military production potential into the defense of the West.

(1) *Size and distribution of the defense burden*

A great deal of time and effort was spent during the spring and summer in efforts to find a formula for "sharing the burden" of mu-

4) Includes small amounts of aid financed from funds provided for military assistance under the China Aid Act of 1948 as amended, and the China Aid Act of 1950.
5) Excludes administration expenses of $14 million in 1950 and $37 million in 1951.
Source: Compiled from data in Department of Commerce, "Foreign Aid," *Foreign Transactions of the U.S. Government* (Basic data through December 31, 1951) Washington, D.C., April 1952, Appendix Table 6.

[5] Although the President did not so state, large amounts of military matériel were also supplied to the various other United Nations forces fighting in Korea. Data on this military assistance are not available and are *not* included in the statistics in the present document on United States grant programs.

[6] *Fourth Semiannual Report to Congress on the Mutual Defense Assistance Program, op.cit.*, p. iii. For an official statement by Secretary Acheson of the position at the end of 1951, see Department of State *Bulletin*, January 7, 1952, pp. 3-7.

[7] *The Economist* (May 5, 1951, pp. 1024-1025) stated that because the United States was rearming so fast some of the European countries felt that they could afford to pursue less energetic mobilization programs.

tual defense—the so-called "burden-sharing" exercises.[8] Publicly available data indicate that these studies produced little in the way of firm bases for reaching mutual agreement on each country's rearmament program or guides to the distribution of United States aid. Difficulties were encountered in agreeing as to what defense expenditures were,[9] how to measure "burdens,"[1] and the relative ability of the various countries to bear them.

By the summer of 1951, it was unofficially reported that all the various NATO organizations had "planned themselves more or less

[8] Most of this work was done by the Financial and Economic Board, which was created as part of the NATO in late April. At that time, the NATO consisted, in major outline, of the Council, which was composed of Ministers and met infrequently, and the Council Deputies, under which were three separate groups, in addition to General Eisenhower's military headquarters: the Military Standing Group, which was concerned with strictly military problems and was located in Washington; the Defense Production Board, concerned with the actual procurement and production of munitions and located in London; and the Financial and Economic Board, responsible for studying and making recommendations on financial and economic problems arising in connection with the defense programs and on the best use of financial and economic resources in the member countries in support of the common defense effort. The Financial and Economic Board was located in Paris, where it was cooperating with the OEEC. (See Department of State *Bulletin*, May 21, 1951, pp. 810-812, for an official detailed statement on the NATO organization at that time.) Early in 1952 extensive organizational changes were made in the NATO with the aim of increasing the operating authority and efficiency of the organization. The North Atlantic Council, while continuing to hold periodic *ministerial* meetings, was to sit in permanent session. Twelve permanent representatives, one from each member, were appointed. Between ministerial meetings the new Council was to have authority to act on all matters—military, political, and economic—which were within the purview of the North Atlantic Pact. This Council was to have an international secretariat and would assume the functions previously performed by the Council Deputies, the Financial and Economic Board, and the Defense Production Board. The permanent representatives and the secretariat were both to be located in Paris, so as to be near other international agencies whose work was closely related to that of NATO, especially the OEEC.

[9] For example, should the cost of providing post exchange facilities to American troops be counted as defense expenditures when the troops of certain other countries did not receive such amenities; and how should account be taken of expenditures for, say, improved roads which were necessary for defense but which also were directly and immediately useful for the civilian sector of the economy?

[1] For example, many urged measuring the burden in terms of percentages of national income, but national income was not measured in the same way in the different countries, and, even if it were, production was not homogeneous and there were great differences in the physical ability of the various nations to supply the sorts of goods needed. Further, since national income varied greatly on a per capita basis some sort of progressive principle would have to be applied, and agreement on such rates was extremely difficult. In addition, the effects of increased rearmament varied greatly from country to country. Thus, in one country it was reflected primarily in higher internal prices while in another it was reflected in an adverse balance of payments; there were no agreed-upon criteria for assessing the relative burdens of such distinct phenomena.

to a full stop."[2] The Military Standing Group in Washington had decided what forces were "needed" on what dates. The Defense Production Board had made estimates of surplus capacity in Europe, but it had reportedly accomplished little in the way of getting European countries to speed up their own production or to specialize in certain arms production and to place orders among themselves. The Financial and Economic Board had analyzed the burdens of rearmament and their impact on the various economies, but their studies were unofficially said to be little more than an outline of the main problems that needed to be considered and did not prescribe coordinated action to ease the burdens.

In the meantime, officials of most European countries were insisting that, with the planned volume of United States aid,[3] it was not possible to reach the rearmament levels planned by the Military Standing Group without what was regarded as intolerable reductions in civilian consumption and investment.[4] The U.S. Administration—which had earlier decided that "it no longer seemed realistic to maintain the concept embodied in the Mutual Defense Assistance Act that economic recovery should be given clear priority over the effort to build military strength" [5]—was saying during the summer that, while it was aware of the difficulties and conscious of the great efforts being made, it was not satisfied with the current rate of rearmament in Europe.[6]

The Council of the NATO met in Ottawa during September.[7] It

[2] *The Economist*, November 10, 1951, p. 1098; see also issue of September 15, 1951, pp. 607-612.

[3] Secretary of the Treasury Snyder made it clear in September that there was no possibility of any American aid for the current fiscal year beyond that being provided by the Mutual Security Act and that he could give no promises as to amounts which the Administration might ask Congress to provide for later years.

[4] See, for example, *The Banker*, October 1951, pp. 211-218.

[5] Department of State, *Fourth Semiannual Report to Congress on the Mutual Defense Assistance Program, op.cit.*, p. 9.

[6] See, for example, *Third Semiannual Report to Congress on the Mutual Defense Assistance Program*, Department of State, Foreign Policy Series 59, July 1951, pp. 9-21. By the end of 1951, the NATO members as a group had lengthened the period of compulsory military service, European defense budgets were roughly double those of 1949, and military production of Western Europe was four times that of 1949 (Department of State *Bulletin*, August 13, 1951, pp. 272-276, and report by Secretary Acheson, February 29, 1952, reprinted in the *New York Times*, March 1, 1952).

[7] The meetings were, of course, held in closed session and few specific details of the discussion were released to the public. The texts of the official communiques issued at the Ottawa conference may be found in Department of State *Bulletin*, October 1, 1951, pp. 523-528.

was agreed at this meeting that the problem of reconciling "military requirements with political-economic capabilities" required that both aspects of it be examined by a single group and that agreement could be reached only if the work were done not just by "experts" but by persons of political prestige and authority. Therefore, a Temporary Committee of the Council was established to study and make recommendations for achieving "the most effective use of the resources of the member countries." The Committee included a representative from each of the member governments, but it subsequently was agreed that the United States,[8] United Kingdom, and French representatives (who became known as the "Three Wise Men") would actually prepare the report, subject to review by the full committee. The Temporary Council Committee report—the detailed assumptions on which it was based were not made public—was completed in December.[9] It was discussed, and its "plan of action" was adopted, by the North Atlantic Council at its meeting in Lisbon in late February 1952.[1]

The Committee stressed the necessity for "sound and healthy" economic and social "foundations" for each country and made recommendations (unpublished in detail) as to measures for encouraging "general economic expansion"—a 14 percent increase in total production by 1954 was the goal—preventing inflation, facilitating labor mobility, improving "the equitable distribution of the internal burden of defense" in each country, and for maintaining essential imports, "in particular by increasing the dollar earnings of European countries." During late 1951 and early 1952, President Truman transferred, under the provision cited above, $470

[8] Mr. Averell Harriman, later designated as Director of the Mutual Security Program, was appointed the American member of the group.

[9] The North Atlantic Council held a meeting in Rome in late November, but apparently no important decisions on economic and financial matters were taken since the report of "The Wise Men" was not completed. The press reported that the United States representatives were urged by the European delegates to use every possible avenue available under the Mutual Security Act to speed up the flow of aid for "economic" purposes and that the United States representatives were sympathetic to this request.

[1] The official summary of the report may be found in the Department of State *Bulletin*, March 10, 1952, pp. 368-370. The full text was not published; the summary given here also includes data published in the press, especially the *New York Times* issues for February 25 through 28, 1952.

This report concluded the work of the Temporary Council Committee and it was therefore disbanded, but it was agreed at Lisbon that annual reviews of the same type should be made so as to keep up-to-date a NATO-wide defense program which was "balanced, feasible, and economic."

million from military end-item assistance to "defense support" activities,[2] and the Administration also began to increase the volume of its purchases in Europe of military goods for Europe as a means of providing that area with "free" dollars.

While not specifically recorded in the official summary of the report, the press stated that the Committee found that the rearmament program previously planned by the military groups constituted a serious threat to the internal economic and political stability of Europe and that for 1952 the emphasis should be more on what was immediately possible than on long-term planning.[3] The United States was also urged to accelerate the provision of equipment authorized under the Mutual Security Program. The Committee studies showed that important savings could be made in military expenditure by eliminating waste and duplication, by eliminating "less essential defense activities," and by specializing production. Many specific but unpublished recommendations were made for increasing the rearmament efforts of individual countries, and specific new goals for 1952 were reported as agreed upon.[4] It was implied that these new goals were smaller than had previously been planned by the military groups but larger than most of the European Ministers of Finance previously had believed feasible.

The official summary of the report said nothing about the "burden-sharing" problem; and it appears that, in general, this "fair shares" approach by the NATO was, for the time being at least, to be abandoned in favor of simply trying to get each member to undertake as large a rearmament program as was feasible.[5] The

[2] See Department of State *Bulletin*, February 25, 1952, pp. 317-319.

[3] See *The Economist*, November 10, 1951, pp. 1089-1090. A "high-ranking military officer" was quoted in the *New York Times* (February 13, 1952) as saying: ". . . the Chiefs of Staff have taken a more conservative view of what the North Atlantic nations can do this year. In other words, the Military Committee has profited by the wealth of information given to it by the Temporary Council Committee in its report and it has also reexamined in that light its present capacity for actual military preparedness."

[4] The member nations agreed to provide some fifty divisions "in appropriate conditions of combat readiness" by the end of 1952, plus 4,000 operational aircraft in Western Europe and "strong naval forces." These do not include the contributions of Greece and Turkey or any contribution from Germany. The press later reported that only about one-half the combat divisions, including the six United States divisions in Europe, were to be "ready" with the remainder "in reserve." Provisional goals were also set for 1953 and 1954.

[5] For an official statement of the procedures employed during 1951 in determining the United States contribution to NATO, see *First Report to Congress on the Mutual Security Program, op.cit.*, pp. 14-18.

member countries did reach agreement at the Lisbon meeting in February 1952 on specific contributions to the costs of the construction of facilities (especially airfields) for the common use of NATO forces—the so-called infrastructure program: the United States, 42.8 percent; Britain and France, 13.2 percent each; with the rest apportioned among Italy, Belgium-Luxembourg, Canada, Denmark, the Netherlands, and Norway.[6]

Potentially more important was the Committee recommendation (accepted by the Council) that new and stronger attempts be made to achieve a "further development of NATO-wide supply planning," and that there be instituted a "system of NATO priority recommendations to assist in the allocation of equipment. . . ." In the first instance, this recommendation was directed toward the United States and was aimed at improving the "tie in" of United States-supplied end-items with existing and planned European production of military equipment. Some of the press[7] interpreted this decision more broadly to mean that a "coordinated arms program" was to be adopted in the sense that duplicate production be eliminated and materials be allocated to those nations which could produce a given item most efficiently. This in turn was interpreted to mean that no one country would produce all of its own requirements but each country would specialize on certain items needed for the whole North Atlantic arms market.[8]

While this "plan of action" covered a wider range of specific subjects than had previously been agreed upon by the signers of the North Atlantic Pact and did represent firm commitments by the executive branches of the various countries, many of the decisions were paper decisions in the sense that they still had to be implemented, and for some of them legislative action was required.

[6] *New York Times,* February 26, 1952.

[7] See especially *The Economist,* December 15, 1951, p. 1451, and December 22, 1951, p. 1516.

[8] In this connection it should be noted that, although Canada was placing large orders in the United States for military equipment, American authorities had through 1951 relied scarcely at all on Canada for military equipment for United States forces, despite the fact that it was reported that facilities existed there for such production. (See *The Financial Times* [Toronto], April 7, 1951, and *The Economist,* December 8, 1951, p. 1404.)

(2) *Discussion of an "Atlantic Community"*

Article 2 of the North Atlantic Treaty states that the members will ". . . encourage economic collaboration between any or all of them" and there was much talk, in general terms, at the September meeting in Ottawa on the concept and the desirability of developing an "Atlantic Community." In formal recognition by the members at Ottawa that their joint aim was building up the defense forces and "the no less important objective of a sound and stable economy necessary to support that effort," the Council of Ministers established a Ministerial Committee to study and recommend lines of future action toward developing the concept of the Atlantic community, with special reference to the Article 2.[9] This committee was composed of representatives from Belgium, Canada, Italy, the Netherlands, and Norway. It prepared an interim report for the November meeting of the Council in Rome, but the latter body directed that further study be made of the unpublished proposals. The text of the final report, "adopted" by the Council at its February 1952 Lisbon meeting, was not made public; but the official communique[1] stated that it "emphasized the importance of economic cooperation, the expansion and liberalization of trade, and the possibility of working out closer cooperative arrangements with other bodies, particularly the Organization for European Economic Cooperation." Particular attention was given to the desirability of encouraging the movement of labor among the European members.

The press[2] stated that the reference to liberalizing and expanding trade was included largely on the insistence of the Benelux countries. The NATO had in the past not dealt with these prob-

[9] "The committee was instructed specifically to make recommendations on the following matters:

"Coordination and frequent consultation on foreign policy, having particular regard to steps designed to promote peace.

"Closer economic, financial, and social cooperation, designed to promote conditions of stability and well-being, both during the period of rearmament and thereafter, within the North Atlantic Treaty Organization or through other agencies.

"Collaboration in the fields of culture and public information." (*Fourth Semi-annual Report to Congress on the Mutual Defense Assistance Program, op.cit.*, p. 35.)

[1] The communique issued by the NATO Council after its Lisbon meeting may be found in full in the *New York Times*, February 26, 1952, and in the Department of State *Bulletin*, March 10, 1952, pp. 367-368.

[2] See especially *New York Times*, February 27, 1952.

lems on the grounds that they were being handled by the GATT and the OEEC. The press also reported that in the full text of the report it was recognized—at United States and British insistence—that there were both difficulties and dangers in attempting to liberalize trade just *within* the North Atlantic community; the United States expressed concern over possible discrimination against it and Britain over the possible effects on her commercial relations with the Commonwealth. In view of the emphasis, noted above, given by the Temporary Council Committee report on economic matters, and accepted as part of its "plan of action" by the Council, and the fact that solutions to the economic problems required the participation of all the members, this Ministerial Committee was dissolved at the Lisbon meeting and its responsibilities transferred to the reconstituted Council.

The final communique of the February meeting of the Council stated, in a "Declaration of Aims," that the "partnership between the nations of the North Atlantic Treaty" was not for defense alone and that the Council looked forward to the time when the energies of the association could be concentrated less on defense and given more "to cooperation in other fields, for the well-being of their peoples and for the advancement of human progress." These were grand generalizations, and there is nothing in the public record to indicate that the United States was, as yet, anxious, or even willing, to define more precisely the concept of an "Atlantic Community" insofar as nonmilitary activities are concerned.

(3) *Admission of new NATO members*

For some time, the United States had been urging that Greece and Turkey, who for several years had been receiving military assistance from the United States, be invited to become full members of the NATO. The European members had several objections to so extending the North Atlantic Treaty Organization,[3] but at the September conference in Ottawa all agreed (under strong pressure from the United States) to recommend to their respective governments that the North Atlantic Treaty be amended to allow

[3] The more important being that the area to be defended would be too greatly extended, that the additional contribution to production would be small, and that United States aid would be spread thinner. For some other objections to the inclusion of Greece and Turkey on the part of the European members, see *The Economist*, July 7, 1951, pp. 5-6.

the admission of Greece and Turkey. The U.S. Senate so amended the Treaty in February 1952.[4]

(4) *Role of Germany*

A major obstacle in implementing the military assistance program during 1951 was the problem of reaching agreement on the role of Germany in the mutual defense efforts. After the outbreak of the Korean war, most United States officials—both in Congress and in the Administration—became convinced that the defense of the West required large and immediate German participation. The French were at first violently opposed to this,[5] but in October 1950, French Premier Pleven proposed that a European army, including German units, be created.[6] The core of this idea was that German troops and military production could be obtained without a danger of resurgent German militarism only if an army were created in Europe composed of units from several nations (including Germany) and placed under the control of a supra-national authority.[7] The December 1950 meeting of the NATO Council agreed that France should talk with the other members of the NATO and with the Germans on the problem of forming such an army. The discussions were among officials of France, Germany, Italy, Belgium, the Netherlands, and Luxembourg. The United States was represented by an "observer." The public record indicates that for some time the United States did not regard the idea as likely to be productive. By mid-1951, however, American officials, convinced that along this road lay the best possibility of

[4] The United States, along with France and the United Kingdom, also favored a revision in the Italian peace treaty so as, among other things, to remove certain of the restrictions on the size and composition of the Italian armed forces. Russia, the other signatory to the treaty, opposed such a revision, and no action was taken during 1951. (For details on this question, see Department of State *Bulletin*, October 8, 1951, pp. 563-570; October 22, 1951, pp. 648-649; and December 24, 1951, p. 1011.)

The press reported that the area covered by the Treaty had indirectly been expanded still further in February 1952 when the North Atlantic Council revised the "terms of reference" of the Supreme Commander, Allied Powers in Europe, to include Morocco and Tunisia—areas in which the United States was constructing a network of air bases. (See *New York Times*, February 25, 1952.) Any formal extension of the area would require the approval of the U.S. Congress.

[5] For their reasons, see *Survey—1950*, p. 51 and pp. 262-263.

[6] For Pleven's original statement, see Document No. 23, Ambassade de France, Service de Presse et d'Information, New York, October 1950.

[7] It was also planned that there would be "standardization" of equipment for all of the various units (see *New York Times*, February 25, 1952).

getting both German and French participation in the defense program, were saying "We are deeply concerned with the success of this . . . and we are doing all that friendly cooperation can do to help it succeed."[8] The public record is sparse on the forms which this "friendly cooperation" took. Certainly it included several speeches by American officials urging that the European Defense Community be consummated and many talks among American and German and French officials aimed at getting over specific obstacles. The United States supported the NATO Council statements at Ottawa and Rome, which "welcomed" the discussions in Paris on the European army and expressed "hopes" that a final agreement would be reached soon, and the Council statements after the Lisbon meeting that it had learned with "approval" of, and gave its blessing to, the various provisions of the plan. The encouragement by the United States went beyond this, however. American officials stated that they did not intend to "buy or force" German participation but that German agreement to participate in a European army was "an essential factor" in the replacement of the occupation statute with a contractual agreement, which would restore to the German authorities control over practically all of their internal and many of their external affairs[9] and ap-

[8] Secretary Acheson, in Department of State *Bulletin,* August 6, 1951, p. 205. See also statement by Lieutenant General Gruenther in *Hearings on H.R. 5020, op.cit.,* pp. 1513-1514.

[9] The terms of the contractual agreement had not been concluded at year's end; several, but not all, of the questions were settled in a series of ministerial meetings held in February 1952.

Discussions were held during the year on the settlement of the German external debts. The U.S. Government recognized that Germany would not be able to repay them in full and that any settlement should not undermine the stability of the German economy. At Potsdam it was agreed—and this was confirmed in an exchange of notes in March 1951 between the Allied High Commission and the Federal Government of Germany—that the German Government would assume responsibility for both the prewar and postwar Reich debts and that the claims of the United States, British, and French Governments arising from postwar economic assistance given by their countries to Germany would have priority over all the other external claims against Germany and the Germans. The three Allied Governments stated that they would be prepared to consider reducing the amounts of these claims on the condition that a "reasonable" settlement was made with respect to Germany's prewar external debts. During the summer and autumn a series of meetings were held between the officials of the four Governments, and an agreement was reached, "on the clear understanding that these concessions are conditional on the achievement of a satisfactory and equitable settlement of Germany's prewar debts," whereby the U.S. Government's claims of $3.2 billion were reduced to approximately $1.2 billion, to be paid in thirty-five equal annual installments at an interest rate of 2¼ percent; the United Kingdom claims of £201 million were

parently would result in a reduction of the occupation costs levied against Germany.[1]

To encourage the other five countries to agree to participate in a European Defense Community, the press reported, American officials were giving assurances that the proposed army would not be looked upon as a means of permitting the withdrawal of United States forces from Europe, or the creation of a "third force in Europe," but rather as a means of strengthening and developing an "integrated Atlantic Community."[2] The United States was unofficially reported as giving assurances that Germany, once her forces were rebuilt, would not be permitted to pursue nationalistic operations against the others. The details of these assurances were not made public, but the North Atlantic Council at its meeting in February 1952 did agree that each member would propose to its legislature that a "reciprocal security undertaking" be agreed upon between the NATO and the proposed European army. If the press is correct, probably the most important encouragement given by the Administration was its stressing, in talks with European officials, that Congress was not likely to be generous in appropriating aid for the next year if agreement were not reached on establishing a European army.

The discussions[3] among the six European nations went on throughout the year, and a tentative and partial agreement among

---

reduced to £150 million, to be paid in twenty annual installments with interest waived; and French claims of the equivalent of $15.7 million were reduced to the equivalent of $11.84 million, to be paid in twenty equal annual installments with interest waived. Discussions on the prewar claims were to begin in early 1952. (For further details, see Department of State *Bulletin*, December 24, 1951, pp. 1021-1022; and *The Economist*, December 15, 1951, pp. 1489-1490 and January 19, 1952, pp. 159-161.)

[1] On October 19, 1951, Congress, by a joint resolution, terminated the state of war with Germany, but this did not affect the status of the occupation since the rights of the occupying powers were not founded on the existence of a state of war as such. Terminating the state of war was regarded, however, as an important step in restoring German independence, and it also facilitated private economic intercourse between Germany and the United States. (See Department of State *Bulletin*, July 16, 1951, pp. 90-92, and November 12, 1951, p. 769.)

[2] See especially *New York Times*, January 22, 1952, and February 17, 1952.

[3] It is outside the scope of this document to trace the issues among the six proposed participants in the European army. For a discussion of some of these, the interested reader is referred to *The Economist*, especially July 14, 1951 and July 28, 1951, and to almost every issue during the period September 1951 through February 1952. The *New York Times* also carried extensive reports on these discussions, and the reader is further referred to the Department of State *Bulletin*, July 9, 1951, pp. 63-67, and August 13, 1951, pp. 272-276.

the experts was reached late in December. The details have not yet been published, and, indeed, many of them had not yet been settled; but the press reported that, even if agreement were finally reached, for many years at least it was to be something far less than the integrated European army under a supra-national authority which the French had originally proposed.[4] None of the parliaments of the six nations had ratified a treaty at the year's end, moreover, and until all had done so Germany would presumably not be contributing directly to Western defense.

(5) *Other area security arrangements*

In the Asia and Pacific area 1951 saw nothing comparable to the coordinated defense efforts which characterized the North Atlantic area, and the relatively small amounts of military assistance extended to several countries in the Far East were on a strictly bilateral basis.[5] However, a series of new defense ties was being formed during 1951 in the shape of a peace treaty with Japan and through "security treaties": with Japan, the Philippines, and Australia and New Zealand.[6] None of these had been ratified by the U.S. Senate by the end of the year, and in most respects they still had to be "translated into action."[7]

In explaining why the United States did not attempt to sign a single overall security treaty with the various Far Eastern and Pacific nations—comparable to the North Atlantic Pact and the Rio Pact, and frequently urged by members of Congress—John Foster Dulles, the chief United States negotiator on the treaties, wrote that (1) many of the countries in the area were unwilling, in view of World War II, to join with Japan in such a treaty; (2) many of the nations were unable or unwilling to agree (as specified in the 1948 "Vandenburg resolution") to "continuous and effective self-help and mutual aid"; (3) some of the nations had just won their independence and did not want to enter into security relationships of a formal variety with either the United States or

[4] See *The Economist*, January 5, 1952, pp. 2-4, for an unofficial account of the agreement.

[5] See *Survey—1950*, p. 53 for a brief account of military assistance to this area in 1950.

[6] For details on the treaties, see Department of State *Bulletin*, July 23, 1951, pp. 147-149; August 27, p. 335; September 10, pp. 422-425; September 24, pp. 495-497; and October 15, pp. 616-620.

[7] See Department of State *Bulletin*, January 7, 1952, p. 6.

Japan; (4) there was as yet no sense of "common destiny" among all the nations in the area; and (5) the United States should not assume such heavy commitments in view of its existing ones.[8] Nevertheless, these treaties do refer to the desirability of "the development of a more comprehensive system of regional security in the Pacific area."

The official record does not indicate whether any military assistance was provided to Australia, New Zealand, and Japan under the MSP during 1951, but it is known that such aid was given to the Philippines, with whom a military assistance agreement had been signed in March 1950. For the whole area of "Asia and the Pacific" military assistance extended during 1951 totalled $293 million, as shown in Table 3 above. Probably most of this went to Indochina, Formosa, the Philippines, and Thailand.

No regional security treaties were proposed with the Near East and Africa area[9] during the year, but in October the United States, joined by France, the United Kingdom, and Turkey, proposed that a Middle East Command be established.[1] Details had not been formulated by the end of the year, but the Command was projected as an integrated corporate defense enterprise whose major task in the immediate future would be one of planning the mutual defense of the area and of "coordinating" the requests of the various states in that area for assistance—advice, training, funds, and equipment—from the sponsoring states.[2] Military assistance actually extended the area during 1951 totalled $184 million, as is shown in Table 3. The bulk of this assistance was to Greece and Turkey, but, although details were not published, small amounts were sent also to certain of the other states in the area. In late

[8] John Foster Dulles, "Security in the Pacific," *Foreign Affairs,* January 1952, pp. 175-187. See this authoritative article for a lucid account of the substance of these treaties and in which important respects they differ from the North Atlantic Pact.

[9] As noted above, Greece and Turkey became members of NATO in early 1952.

[1] The text of this proposal may be found in Department of State *Bulletin,* October 22, 1951, pp. 647-648. Further details on the proposed Middle East Command may be found in the issues of October 29, 1951, p. 702 and November 19, pp. 817-818.

[2] Egypt was invited to become a founding member, but, as had been anticipated, it rejected the proposals. (The proposals were formally put forward in the midst of the dispute between Egypt and the United Kingdom over the former's unilateral abrogation of the 1936 Anglo-Egyptian treaty.) Nevertheless, the four original nations, together with Australia, New Zealand, and South Africa, were at year's end continuing their efforts to establish a Middle East Command.

December, Secretary Acheson said that the United States would be called upon for "further resources of leadership, and for a willingness to assume increasing responsibilities in this area."[3]

The political foundations for joint defense arrangements between the United States and the Latin American countries were laid in 1947 when the Inter-American Treaty of Reciprocal Assistance (the Rio Pact) was ratified. No military assistance under the Mutual Security Program was provided any of these countries during 1951, but in early 1952 the United States began negotiating with the individual Latin American states, looking toward the signing of bilateral military assistance agreements which would serve as the basis for providing aid.

b. EUROPEAN RECOVERY PROGRAM

In late 1950, in accordance with the emerging United States policy of concentrating its efforts as regards foreign aid on providing "strength for the free world," ECA announced that the main objectives of the European Recovery Program were being turned from "economic recovery" in the sense of previous years to (a) building defense against aggressors, (b) helping the European economies to become self-supporting in their military defense efforts, and (c) continuing to lay the base for further improvements in living standards.[4] In implementing this shift in objectives, criteria for extending aid were reported as changed during the first part of 1951 from the dollar imports needed to reach a viable balance of payments position by mid-1952 to those needed to meet the armament goals and to cushion the effect of the European economies from the effects of a diversion of their own resources to military purposes. The record shows that, in practice, although the total amount of aid declined and in a few instances increasing emphasis was placed on activities directly and immediately related to the mobilization program, the types of commodities and investments financed by ECA were not greatly different from those financed in the previous years.

ECA had "suspended" aid to the United Kingdom in December

[3] Department of State *Bulletin*, January 7, 1952, p. 5.

[4] For details on the ECA programs for Europe, the reader is referred to the quarterly *Report to Congress of the Economic Cooperation Administration* and to the various hearings on the Mutual Security Program cited at the beginning of this Chapter.

1950,[5] and during the first month of 1951 aid was similarly stopped to Ireland, Sweden, and Portugal.[6] These countries all, of course, continued during the year to receive aid which was in the pipeline. The total amount of grants actually extended by ECA to Europe during 1951 was $2.4 billion—a drop of 12 percent from 1950—and its distribution among countries varied greatly from the previous year. Several countries (Germany, Italy, Austria, Greece, Turkey, Iceland, and Sweden) actually received more aid in terms of dollars than in 1950. The largest total recipients were respectively Germany, France, and Italy, though France took a reduction compared with 1950. The United Kingdom, of course, suffered the largest absolute reduction, followed by Belgium-Luxembourg, France, the Netherlands, and Norway. Details of the aid provided by ECA to Europe from 1948 through 1951, according to countries, type of aid, and sources of commodities, are shown in Appendix Tables I and II.

Save for the large relative increase in coal shipments, the composition of commodities financed by ECA and actually shipped during 1951 was in almost the same proportion as in 1950: the categories of raw materials and semi-finished products accounted for slightly more than one-third of the total; food, feed and fertilizer accounted for somewhat less than a third; and fuel, and machinery and vehicles each represented a little less than one-fifth. Details are presented in Appendix Table III.

The trend toward greater procurement in the United States of ECA-financed commodities, which had been evidenced each year of the program, continued, with the United States supplying over three-quarters of the total goods, by value.[7] There was almost no change in the percentage of industrial commodities supplied by the United States sources (about 60 percent), but the proportion

[5] In February 1952, $300 million of the MSP funds transferred from "military" to "economic" purposes were earmarked to provide the United Kingdom with certain "defense support" items. (Department of State *Bulletin*, February 25, 1952, pp. 317-319.)

[6] The only direct aid which Sweden had received under the European Recovery Program was in the form of credits and conditional aid, and of the aid to Ireland and to Portugal only some 10 percent was in unconditional grants.

[7] The Economic Cooperation Act required that, wherever available, at least 50 percent of the ECA-financed shipments from the United States, by cargo, liner or tanker, be in United States bottoms; this provision was met during the year for all categories except tankers, whose rates had become so high in late 1950 that ECA invoked the "nonavailability" clause and no longer used United States-flag tankers.

of agricultural commodities coming from the United States rose from less than 85 percent of the total in 1950 to nearly 93 percent in the year under review.[8] In previous years Canada had been the largest offshore supplier of ECA-financed commodities, but during 1951 no Canadian agricultural products were purchased with ECA funds, with the result that her share of the total dropped from about 10 percent in 1950 to slightly more than 4 percent in 1951. The Latin American nations as a group supplied over 8 percent of the total, similar to previous years, while purchases from the participating countries themselves declined from about 4.5 percent of the total to just over 3 percent. The balance was furnished from other areas, largely the Middle East. Crude petroleum and petroleum products and nonferrous metals account for most of the offshore purchases under the program; the United States direct investments were important in many of these sources. The details of the sources of ECA-financed shipments are given in Appendix Tables II and IV.

ECA had begun a program of technical assistance in 1949 and during 1950 had placed increasing emphasis on this phase of its operations as existing capital equipment and labor in most areas became fully employed at the old techniques and as rearmament began to impinge on consumption and nonmilitary investments.[9] Its efforts to increase productivity in Europe were expanded during 1951, and in April it instituted a "Production Assistance Drive." This program, which attempted to elicit the direct support of management, labor, and consumers in Europe, was aimed at hastening the introduction of new machines, techniques, and organizational procedures and at obtaining a more "equitable" distribution of the fruits of the increased productivity. To ECA and to Congress this latter meant lower prices to the consumer, higher wages to the workers, and an "uprooting" of the "whole, cartelized, restricted

[8] In accordance with the law, ECA channeled to the United States market all requests for agricultural commodities declared surplus to domestic needs by the Secretary of Agriculture; during the entire program (to the end of 1951) $129 million of such items (only $6 million during 1951) were procured from *official* stocks compared to total requests approved for surplus products worth $3.8 billion. The Department of Agriculture also continued during 1951 to subsidize the purchase by ERP recipients of eggs, peanuts, grain, sorghums, flaxseed, and linseed oil held by the Government. The amount of such subsidized payments is not available. Apart from the ECA program, the Department of Agriculture donated surplus food stocks valued at $45.7 million to private welfare agencies for distribution abroad.

[9] See *Survey—1950*, pp. 25-27.

economy that has grown so deep-rooted in Europe. . . ."[1] ECA had anticipated that under this "drive" it might extend aid directly to foreign enterprises, obtaining agreement from the employers, workers, and consumers at the "village level" as to the use of the aid and the distribution of its benefits as among profits, wages, and prices. Many Congressmen favored this direct approach and shared the belief held by some ECA officials that it would be an effective way of winning labor from Communism and of shifting the European economy from one of "scarcity" to one of "expansion." Although few in Europe publicly questioned the general objectives of the program, there was opposition to the particular methods envisaged by ECA—for example, the Netherlands Government strongly objected to agreements between foreign governments and private Dutch firms—and the program had gained little momentum by the end of the year. The previous technical assistance program was continued, and total authorizations and expenditures exceeded those of the previous year with a marked shift recorded in assistance to increase industrial productivity and away from agricultural production, manpower utilization, public administration, and transportation and communications. Statistics of the technical assistance program are given in Appendix Table V.

During the first three years, an important part of ECA's program in Europe had been the partial financing of the establishment and/or modernization of specific industrial projects which it believed would result in one or more of the following: larger output, greater productivity, smaller imports, more effective utilization of manpower, and improved quality of product.[2] Authorizations for such projects, however, dropped off sharply during 1951[3]—being less than 15 percent of the previous year—in line with the new ECA position that the objectives of the European Recovery Program in the immediate future should come less through additional investment in plant and more through the "productivity drive"

[1] Statement by an ECA official quoted in *New York Times*, December 13, 1951. For details on this program, see *Hearings on H.R. 5020, op.cit.*, pp. 132, 156-157, and 447; and *Hearings on S. 1762, op.cit.*, pp. 78-90. Concern with cartels and the desirability of instituting a more extensive free private enterprise economy in Europe was also reflected in the so-called "Benton amendment," described in subsection e (1).

[2] See *Survey—1949*, pp. 24-28 and *Survey—1950*, pp. 27-29.

[3] Paid shipments of equipment and material under this program rose steadily during the year in fulfillment of previous commitments.

mentioned in the previous paragraph. Statistics on the industrial projects program are given in Appendix Table VI.

Each ERP recipient country was required to deposit in a special account amounts of its own currency—called counterpart funds—equivalent to the dollar cost of the ECA-financed goods and services received by it on a grant basis.[4] Five percent of these were set aside for use by the United States, and the remaining 95 percent were used by recipient countries for purposes agreed to by the United States and that country. Given the dollar aid, these counterpart funds do not constitute any increase in the real resources of the recipient country; in most cases they represent only a minor fraction of the total expenditure of the various governments; and their effects can be counteracted by the monetary and fiscal policies of the recipient government. Yet, ECA has believed that, to the extent that these funds were permitted to accumulate or were used to retire public debt held by the central bank, they played an important anti-inflationary role and that, even when spent, a considerable influence could be exerted through them over internal investments.[5] With the European Recovery Program tapering off during 1951, deposits of these funds totalled just over $2 billion equivalent, as compared with the equivalent of $2.7 billion in 1950. During 1951 approximately one-third of the new deposits were allowed either to accumulate or were used to retire government debt held by central banks and thus exercised an anti-inflationary effect; this compares with some four-fifths so used in 1948, one-half in 1949, and one-fourth in 1950. As compared with previous years, a much larger proportion of the expenditures was devoted to promoting manufacturing, especially of primary metals and machinery—vital to the rearmament program—and to the construction of public buildings and housing facilities. Withdrawals for the promotion of public utilities, agriculture, and relief were relatively smaller than in the previous year. Despite the authority to use counterpart funds outside the depositing country and the encouragement given in the Mutual Security Act to their use for developing the production of strategic materials, only $1 million

[4] Such deposits were also required for "drawing rights" utilized under the Intra-European Payments Scheme and for "initial credit balances" utilized under the European Payments Union as grants. See Chapter VII.

[5] See *Survey—1949*, pp. 28-31, and *Survey—1950*, pp. 29-30, for a brief account of the activities and policies regarding these funds during those years.

equivalent were so used in 1951. The volume of actual expenditures by the United States out of its 5 percent counterpart funds was not made public for the year, but a large portion was *committed* for the procurement and development of production of strategic and critical materials for the United States stockpile. Data detailing the 95 percent counterpart fund deposits and withdrawals and deposits and commitments of the 5 percent funds are given in Appendix Table VII.

In 1950, ECA had created a special "fund" for the purpose of facilitating the economic development of the dependent overseas territories of metropolitan Europe, with particular emphasis on projects which would contribute to Western defense and, especially, to expanding the production of strategic and critical materials.[6] During 1950, ECA had financed only dollar goods which were directly associated with the approved projects, but, on finding that shortages of many other types of equipment, materials, and supplies were a "major deterrent to a steady rise in the production of primary materials in most of these relatively underdeveloped territories," ECA during 1951 broadened its assistance to finance imports of "general types of commodities needed from the dollar area as well as specific items of equipment required in individual projects," thus making possible "a greater allocation of internal resources to priority projects."[7] In all cases, the ECA-supported projects dovetailed into activities being financed by the recipient territory and the mother country.

The rearmament program in Western Europe which began in 1950 makes arbitrary the selection of any given date for the end of the European Recovery Program. By United States law, and so officially, the program ended on June 30, 1952, but its character and some of its objectives changed in late 1950, and it expired administratively on December 30, 1951 when the United States

[6] See *Survey—1950*, pp. 30-32, for a brief account of this program; see also Mutual Security Agency, "The Overseas Territories in the Mutual Security Program," Washington, D.C., March 31, 1952. In addition to expenditures from this fund, some of the European countries themselves used free dollars and ECA-supplied dollars as well as local currencies (counterpart and otherwise) to facilitate the development of their overseas territories. ECA gave additional help via a special strategic materials program, which is discussed in Chapter VI, Section D, infra.

[7] Economic Cooperation Administration, *Thirteenth Report to Congress*, Washington, D.C., 1951, p. 47.

administering agency, the Economic Cooperation Administration, was dissolved as a legal entity, with many of its personnel and some of its authority being transferred to the new Mutual Security Agency. ECA itself stated that the Marshall Plan "passed into history" at the end of 1951,[8] at which time the United States had financed some $11 billion of goods and services to the ERP recipients.[9] Accepting this termination date, it is appropriate to record very briefly the accomplishments of the program.

The first and foremost objective set by the U.S. Government for the European Recovery Program was political: the prevention of the spread of Communism and the weakening of its influence in the recipient countries. The second major objective was that the program should result in the adoption by the European states of more liberal (that is, free-market) internal and international economic and financial policies and practices. In the words of the law, the policy was the "restoration or maintenance in European countries of principles of individual liberty, free institutions, and genuine independence."[1]

On the assumptions, rarely explicitly stated, that Communism has an especially strong appeal to those in poverty and distress and that extensive control of economic transactions would not appear as attractive as a free-market determination of the use of resources if the European economies were "vigorous and healthy," the two major objectives were to be achieved by "cooperative" (or "unified" or "integrated") efforts on the part of the European countries —aided by large-scale assistance from the United States—to (a) expand both agricultural and industrial production, (b) restore and maintain the "soundness of European currencies, budgets, and finances" (that is, internal price stability and "equitable" exchange rates), and (c) stimulate and facilitate the growth of international trade, both with one another and with other countries (especially a growth of exports to the dollar area) "by appropriate measures including reduction of barriers which may hamper such trade." These subsidiary objectives were to be achieved by mid-

[8] See Economic Cooperation Administration, *Press Release*, December 29, 1951, entitled "Marshall Plan Passes into History December 30 along with Economic Cooperation Administration"; or Department of State *Bulletin*, January 14, 1952, pp. 43-45.

[9] An additional $1 billion or so was in the pipeline.

[1] Economic Cooperation Act of 1948, Section 102.

1952 to such an extent that extraordinary assistance from the United States would no longer be necessary.[2]

The first major objective had been achieved if measured, as ECA officials have done before Congress, in terms of a decline in Communist representation in the various parliaments, known membership in the Communist party, and known Communists in the labor unions. On the other hand, Communism was still regarded as a major threat in some countries, especially France and Italy.[3] Only modest progress, however, had been recorded in reaching the second major goal. Many of the more drastic direct controls which had been imposed during or immediately after the war had been removed or relaxed, and in some countries, especially Germany, Italy, and Belgium, increasing emphasis was being placed by the governments—sometimes over the objections of important ECA officials—on monetary and credit policies rather than on direct controls. Still, throughout the ERP period the European economies were, in varying degrees, being subjected to a vast and intricate network of controls. And, under the impact of the rearmament program which began in late 1950, many of the decisions which had earlier been returned to a free-market determination were being reassumed by government authorities—just as they were in the United States.

Varying degrees of success were achieved with respect to the chief subsidiary objectives—expansion of output, creation and maintenance of internal financial stability, expansion and freeing of trade, and the development of a high degree of economic cooperation, or "integration," among the recipient countries. Great accomplishments were recorded in expanding output. The volume of European industrial production by the end of 1951 was officially estimated to be approximately 40 percent above 1938 and nearly

[2] This is an extreme condensation of the objectives of the program. Many less important objectives, including support of certain sectors of the United States economy, were also set up from time to time and the more important of them have been noted in the previous issues of this *Survey*. The reader wishing a more detailed statement should read at least the full text of the Economic Cooperation Act as amended each year, as well as the various Congressional committee reports which accompanied the proposed legislation. A thoughtful nonofficial presentation of the basic objectives of the program may be found in Ellis, H. S., *The Economics of Freedom,* Council on Foreign Relations, 1950, pp. 3-9.

[3] For more details on the ECA statements in 1951 describing the decreasing importance of Communism in the ERP countries, see *Hearings on H.R. 5020, op.cit.*, pp. 1350-1351.

65 percent above 1947.[4] These increases in output were accompanied by steady increases in productivity and declining unemployment. Agricultural output was nearly 10 percent above prewar when the Marshall Program ended and almost 25 percent above 1947, although per capita agricultural production was still slightly below 1938 because of the population increases. But these increases in output took place while Europe was receiving substantial amounts of American aid, and it was not demonstrated that they could be maintained without aid.

The record on the fight against inflation was much less impressive. As measured by wholesale price indices, most countries witnessed continuous increases (moderate, as compared with the postwar pre-ERP period) until shortly after the outbreak of war in Korea when the "creeping inflation" was greatly accelerated under the pressure of rearmament and soaring prices for many imported raw materials.

With respect to foreign trade, the accomplishments were notable, but a socially and politically acceptable level of imports without extraordinary assistance had not been achieved. Europe's total current account deficit was reduced from the equivalent of some \$5.3 billion in 1948 to \$2.1 billion in 1950, but, due in large part to the sharp rise in import prices, the deficit rose to an estimated \$3.8 billion equivalent in 1951.[5] In terms of volume, European exports increased by some 75 percent during the period 1948 through 1951,[6] but before the events in Korea introduced many new factors, Europe was finding it extremely difficult to find markets (especially

[4] These figures, which include Germany, are intended to convey only a broad indication of the magnitude of the improvement. There is, of course, a large margin of error in such aggregative statistics, and the record varies greatly from country to country and commodity to commodity. Thus, for example, German industrial production was only about 20 percent above prewar at the end of 1951 and European coal production was a little below the 1938 output. Detailed data on industrial output, foreign trade, and price movements in Europe may conveniently be found in the periodic reports of the Economic Commission for Europe, in the appendices to the Economic Cooperation Administration's quarterly *Report to Congress of the Economic Cooperation Administration* and in the Economic Cooperation Administration's monthly *Recovery Guides*, supplanted after November 1951 by the Organization for European Economic Cooperation, *General Statistical Bulletin* and *Foreign Trade Statistical Bulletin*.

[5] The gold and short-term dollar assets of recipient countries increased by \$3 billion in the period January 1, 1948 to June 30, 1951.

[6] These figures on foreign trade are only estimates and have been taken from *The Economist*, January 5, 1952, p. 9.

dollar markets) for many of her exportables. There were during the period some reductions in quantitative trade barriers, especially *within* Europe.

As regards intra-European economic cooperation—an objective seen as increasingly important by the U.S. Government—the progress was officially regarded as great, though it certainly was not spectacular. It is discussed in some detail in Chapter VII.

In sum, the major political objective of the program had apparently been achieved, and the salvage of the European economies from the postwar chaos had been accomplished in a shorter time and with less financial aid than had been anticipated when the program was begun. Most observers at the end of 1951 attributed to the impact of the post-Korean rearmament efforts the fact that as the ERP ended "Europe is still hungry for dollars; the overseas payment accounts of most countries are again markedly in the red; countries are still trying vainly to combat inflation; while the need to increase productivity is just as great as it was four years ago."[7] Although ERP was not intended to furnish the basis for rearmament, it could be claimed, as the Administration did, that the "European Recovery Program provided sufficient economic stability to promote the mounting of a larger European defense effort without, at the same time, destroying the economic and political foundations of European society."[8]

C. ECONOMIC AID TO ASIA AND THE PACIFIC

For reasons discussed above, the U.S. Government decided in 1951 that, as a part of its Mutual Security Program, the amount of economic aid to Asia and the Pacific should be increased although it would only indirectly strengthen the military build-up of the West. (The Occupied Areas Program for Japan and the Ryukyus was not legally incorporated into the Mutual Security Program and is discussed in Section B below; aid to countries in this area under the Point Four Program is discussed in the following chapter.) In previous years, aid to China and Korea had been important components of the Far Eastern aid programs, but in

[7] *The Economist*, January 5, 1952, p. 8. It is beyond the scope of this document to attempt to set out the reasons why all of the objectives sought by the United States in the European Recovery Program were not achieved.

[8] *Fourth Semiannual Report to Congress on The Mutual Defense Assistance Program, H. Doc. No. 352*, February 14, 1952, p. 8.

1950 aid to mainland China had ceased, and the proposed three-year aid program to Korea, which was begun in 1948, was abandoned in early 1951, with the U.S. Army assuming responsibility for furnishing emergency civilian relief supplies and the United Nations accepting responsibility for planning for Korean reconstruction.[9] Thus, in the year under review the civilian aid programs in this area were concentrated on Southeast Asia and, in particular, on Formosa, Indochina, the Philippines, Burma, Indonesia, and Thailand.

The basic objectives of the economic assistance program in Southeast Asia, said ECA, were the following: "(a) To regularize and increase production of food and promote full-scale restoration and expansion of trade relationships between the food surplus and food deficit countries. (b) To expand the capacity of the region to develop its resources of other essential commodities, including rubber, tin, oil, graphite, manganese, and abaca. (c) To help countries in the region to diagnose and deal with their most fundamental problems of economic development. (d) To assist the creation of social and economic conditions and institutions under which the people feel that their basic needs and aspirations are being satisfied by their own free and independent governments. (e) To promote confidence, good-will, and friendship for the United States on the part of the governments concerned and among the masses of the people. (f) To alleviate the impact of military aid programs in these countries where such programs are in operation."[1]

These programs, most of which were begun in 1950, were slow in getting under way, in part because of difficulties encountered in negotiating the required bilateral agreements, in part because of the necessity, in some cases, of establishing new United States supervisory missions in the countries which then required time to reach decisions as to the specific form the aid should take, and in part because of the time consumed in ordering and shipping equipment and supplies.[2] Most of the goods supplied, and programmed,

[9] For a summary of the United States aid programs to Asia in 1950, see *Survey—1950*, pp. 56-72.

[1] Economic Cooperation Administration, *Twelfth Report to Congress*, Washington, D.C., 1951, p. 64.

[2] For details of the programs in this area, see the quarterly Economic Cooperation Administration, *Report to Congress of the Economic Cooperation Administration,*

were for "maintenance of essential supplies"—meaning that in large part they took the form of consumers' goods, fertilizer, fuel, and raw materials and semi-finished products which the recipient countries were able to sell quickly, thus relieving certain acute hardships and increasing production, while providing the governments with local currencies. These internal sales served to counter inflation or to provide funds which were used to help carry out ECA-approved economic development programs. In addition to such commodities and many miscellaneous goods, small amounts of machinery and equipment were supplied for use in improving transportation, power, and other public utilities (and to a small extent manufacturing), as well as for promoting agriculture and the production of strategic and critical materials. A statistical breakdown of the shipments is given in Appendix Table VIII.

Of major importance policy-wise was the inauguration during 1951 of the new assistance program to the Philippines. In 1950 a special United States mission—the so-called Bell Mission—had studied the Philippine economic problem and in a strongly-worded report had advised a five-year program of United States aid *provided* that the Philippines carried out a long list of internal reforms.[3] After some delays, the Philippine Government agreed to accept and to implement these recommendations; in particular, it reformed the tax system in a way designed to expand Government revenues by 60 percent, approved a minimum wage law which more than doubled the previous wages of a "substantial" number of workers, and the legislative body passed a Joint Resolution promising to implement "certain social legislation" and "economic development" measures recommended by the Bell Mission. In no other country, with the possible exception of Greece, had the United States demanded such extensive internal reforms as a condition of receiving grant aid. Total economic aid extended to the Philippines during the year under this program was $5.2 million.[4] In addition, $12 million was provided under the expiring Philip-

and the *First Report to Congress on the Mutual Security Program*, Washington, D.C., December 31, 1951, pp. 28-35.

[3] See *Survey—1950*, pp. 69-72.

[4] The Philippine Government announced in 1951 that it held claims against the U.S. Government totalling $414 million arising out of events before, during, and after the war; these were compared with $95 million in outstanding long-term debt to the U.S. Government. (See International Monetary Fund, *International Financial News Survey*, June 15, 1951, p. 387.)

pine Rehabilitation Program[5] and small amounts were extended for medical care and treatment of Philippine veterans.[6]

d. ECONOMIC AID TO OTHER AREAS

Those countries in the Middle East and Africa and Latin America which had received aid under terms of the 1950 Act for International Development (Point Four) continued to receive such aid during 1951, but before the other countries in these areas could receive the economic assistance of this type as authorized in the Mutual Security Act of 1951, bilateral agreements had to be signed with the United States stating acceptance by the recipients of the conditions set forth in Section 511 (b) of the Mutual Security Act and quoted above. By the deadline of January 8, 1952, only Egypt and Iraq, among the countries to receive aid in these two areas, had failed to comply; Iran had balked, along with these two nations, at identifying itself with the Western anti-Soviet bloc, but a temporary agreement was accepted allowing aid to be initiated. Aid under the Point Four Program was slow in getting underway, however, and by the end of the year, only $22 million had actually been expended for the Near East and Africa (of which $16 million went to Israel) and $10 million (including some $3 million under the Institute of Inter-American affairs) for Latin America.[6a] The problems and activities under the Point Four Program are discussed in Chapter II.

The UN Palestine Refugee Program was expanded in 1950, with strong United States support, into a proposed relief and works program, designed to be a first step in long-range planning to de-

[5] As recorded in the *Survey—1950*, pp. 67-69, the Philippine Rehabilitation Program had been virtually completed by the end of 1950, but some payments were continued throughout 1951. By mid-year, the remaining reconstruction programs under the State Department were completed, with the exception of a few of the public roads projects which had been delayed by the activity of the Huks and the lack of local currency funds which were to be contributed by the Philippine Government. In view of these delays, the Administration requested that an extension of authority for one year be granted beyond June 30, 1951 and that $3 million be appropriated to liquidate existing contract authority. Congress granted the request, and with these funds the total program of the Philippine rehabilitation was completed. (See "Department of State Appropriations for 1952," *Hearings*, House of Rep., Subcommittee of the Committee on Appropriations, 82d Cong., 1st Sess., February-March 1951, pp. 496-507.)

[6] The Independent Offices Appropriation Act, 1952, provided $1.1 million for these purposes for fiscal year 1952.

[6a] In addition, the United States contributed $6 million to the UN technical assistance program and spent $3 million under Point Four Program in the Far East.

velop the area's resources, as well as to "reintegrate" the refugees. The program, calling for expenditures from all sources of the equivalent of $55 million, in the year ending June 30, 1951, was placed under the United Nations Relief and Works Agency for Palestine Refugees in the Near East (UNRWAPRNE).[7] Because most of the United Nations members did not make a contribution to the program and because of the relatively high cost for providing work relief as compared with furnishing simple relief, the public works aspect of the program was, for all practical purposes, abandoned during 1951—or at least postponed until plans for resettling the refugees could be agreed upon.[8] In December, the UNRWAPRNE presented a program to the UN General Assembly calling for contributions of $250 million equivalent by mid-1954, at which time it was planned that the refugees would be self-supporting. Of the total, $50 million were to be used for "relief" and $200 million for "reintegration" activities, the former becoming smaller over time and the latter involving grants to individual refugees to enable them to engage in economic activities which would be linked to the general economic development programs of the area.[9] In the UN debates on the resolution, the United States gave wholehearted support to the proposal,[1] and it passed with only Soviet bloc opposition. As noted above, the Mutual Security Program provided $50 million for assistance of Palestine refugees, both within the UN organization program and otherwise. During the calendar year 1951 the United States transferred $24 million to the UNRWAPRNE. The Mutual Security Program, as noted above, also made provisions for $50 million for resettlement and relief projects in Israel, but none of these funds had been spent during 1951.

[7] For a summary of these activities and citations of official sources through 1950, see *Survey—1949*, pp. 56-59, and *Survey—1950*, pp. 75-77.

[8] See Department of State, "Aid to the Palestine Refugees," Near and Middle Eastern Series 4, April 1951, pp. 12-14.

[9] See *United Nations Bulletin*, February 15, 1952, pp. 166 and 171-173 f.; and March 1, 1952, p. 223; and *New York Times*, December 12, 1951 and January 17, 18, 21, 23 and 27, 1952.

[1] See Department of State *Bulletin*, February 11, 1952, pp. 224-227.

B. *OTHER AID PROGRAMS*

Yugoslav Aid Program

Late in 1950 the Administration had authorized "stopgap assistance" of $31 million to Yugoslavia by allowing $15 million of the Export-Import Bank credit to be used for purchases of foodstuffs and $16 million of Mutual Defense Assistance Program funds to be used to provide food for the Yugoslav army. Shortly thereafter, Congress had approved a special law authorizing ECA to use up to $50 million of its previously appropriated funds to provide emergency relief—in the form of food—to Yugoslavia.[2] Of this latter amount, $12 million was used to reimburse Germany and Italy for food they had given to Yugoslavia, and the remainder was used largely to purchase surplus food stocks held by the CCC.[3] The final shipment of goods under this program was received in Yugoslavia in early August. Yugoslavia had agreed, as a condition of this aid, to facilitate the sale to the United States of strategic materials. The press reported that specific commitments were honored, even though they were at prices which had been set before the great increases of early 1951 and meant that Yugoslavia was losing many millions of dollars as compared to what she could have received in other markets.[4]

Yugoslavia continued to find herself in serious economic difficulties,[5] and in April President Truman authorized the use of another $29 million of MDAP funds to help meet the "consumption requirements" of the Yugoslav armed forces. In the same month the Yugoslav Government requested the United States and Britain to "underwrite" its foreign trade deficits during the period 1951-1954—it was stated that much of the deficit was the result of the Cominform blockade—sufficiently to allow Yugoslavia to obtain a loan of some $200 million from the International Bank.[6]

[2] See *Survey—1950*, pp. 54-56.

[3] Early in 1951, ECA granted $5 million of aid to Austria on condition that she fulfill the terms of her previous $10 million (equivalent) loan to Yugoslavia for machinery and industrial items.

[4] *New York Times*, June 10, 1951.

[5] For a recent brief general survey of the Yugoslav economy, see *The Economist*, October 20, 1951, pp. 926-927 and October 27, 1951, pp. 987-988.

[6] For a brief account of the developments of this request, see Halperin, E., "Arms for Yugoslavia?" *Swiss Review of World Affairs*, May 1951, pp. 10-11.

This request was discussed during the hearings on the MSP. A major obstacle in the eyes of United States officials to the granting of such "economic" aid was the fact that it would support Communist-type planning and what was regarded as uneconomic industrialization, but the Administration urged that the aid should be given and linked it, as it had in 1950, to keeping out of Russian hands the thirty-odd Yugoslav divisions. In June, after Yugoslavia had agreed to curtail its industrialization somewhat, the United States, Britain, and France agreed "in principle" to underwrite the Yugoslav deficit for the period ending June 30, 1952;[7] the United States share in fiscal year 1952 was unofficially reported to have been set at $60 million.[8] In November, after the Mutual Security Act had been approved, President Truman formally determined that the economic stability and military security of Yugoslavia were important to United States security and declared her eligible for military and economic assistance under the program.[9] Apparently no formal agreement between Yugoslavia and the United Kingdom, France, and the United States for granting aid to the former by the latter was signed. The United States "commitment" was being discharged under the November decision of the President out of MDAP funds transferred to ECA. During calendar 1951, Yugoslavia received a total of $92.3 million of grants from the United States, plus an undisclosed amount of military end-items.

Occupied Areas Program

The United States program for Government and Relief in Occupied Areas (GARIOA) had been a major component of official foreign aid in the years immediately following the war, but by the end of 1950 most of these activities in Europe had been taken over by ECA and the State Department. Those in Korea were being handled by new and special United States and United Nations programs, and the amount of assistance to Japan and the Ryukyus

[7] The three aiding nations also agreed to seek an alleviation of the service charges on Yugoslavia's external debts for the next few years.

[8] *Hearings on H.R. 5020, op.cit.*, p. 400. See *New York Times*, June 15, July 6, and 26, and August 26, 1951, for unofficial reports on this three-power agreement, which was apparently not a formal one.

[9] See Department of State *Bulletin*, November 19, 1951, p. 826, and *New York Times*, November 15, 1951, for further details.

was declining in the face of the rapid Japanese economic recovery.[1] In preparing the federal budget proposals for fiscal 1952, the Administration included some $150 million for the program in Japan and the Ryukyus. Before going to Congress to defend this request, however, the Administration decided (in view of the preparations for signing a peace treaty with Japan) to alter its previous practice of requiring Japan to provide, without reimbursement, all the yen needed by the United States occupation forces[2] in favor of a procedure whereby one half of such yen, would be purchased by the United States with dollars. The new policy was put into effect on July 1, 1951, and these earnings, plus the foreign exchange being earned from other sources, led the Administration to conclude that economic aid to Japan could be terminated.[3] Therefore, the Administration requested Congress to provide only $27 million for a GARIOA program in the Far East. Two-thirds of this amount was for economic aid to the Ryukyus, which, the Administration testified, would need external financial assistance for a long time. Most of the rest was to be used for the "reorientation" programs in Japan and the Ryukyus, and the balance was for dollar administration expenses.[4] The House appropriated only $5.2 million, arguing that the Executive Branch had overestimated the requirements of the Ryukyus and their capacity to absorb aid and that the United States administration costs could be greatly reduced. The Senate restored most of the cut and the final act appropriated $22.5 million for the fiscal year 1952. During the calendar year 1951, grants extended to Japan totalled $247 million and the Ryukyus $6 million, but during the last quarter aid amounted to only $11 million and $2 million respectively.

[1] See *Survey—1949*, pp. 39-43, and *Survey—1950*, pp. 64-66, for a summary of the GARIOA programs during those years.

[2] These had been at the rate of the equivalent of about $300 million per year during 1949 and 1950.

[3] For a detailed discussion on the GARIOA program, see "The Supplemental Appropriation Bill for 1952," *Hearings, Part 2*, House of Rep., Subcommittee of the Committee on Appropriations, 82d Cong., 1st Sess., June 1951, pp. 371-417; and "Supplemental Appropriations for 1952," *Hearings on H.R. 5215*, U.S. Senate, Committee on Appropriations, August and September 1951, pp. 77-232. For a late 1951 statement on "Economic Outlook for Japan," see Federal Reserve Bank of New York, *Monthly Review*, December 1951, pp. 174-176.

[4] Japan paid the local currency costs of administering the GARIOA program. Included in the Administration's request was $136 thousand for dollar administration costs of the military government organization in Trieste.

Economic aid to Germany and Austria was provided under the European Recovery Program and its successor, the Mutual Security Program, and the United States was a member of the Allied High Commission in these two countries. In addition to its various control operations and more or less normal counselor and diplomatic activities, the Commission also carried out certain recreation, health, education, and propaganda, etc., programs. The Executive Branch requested Congress to appropriate $28.9 million for United States expenses in these matters. Congress finally appropriated $26.25 million, justifying the reduction on grounds that the proposed activities in some cases duplicated those for which the State Department was receiving funds in other appropriations.

International Children's Emergency Fund

Despite the opposition of the United States, which wanted long-term and continuing arrangements made, the United Nations General Assembly voted late in 1950 to continue for three more years the emergency International Children's Emergency Fund.[5] After the vote, the United States delegation stated that Congress would be asked to provide funds for continuing the work. Early in 1951, the Administration asked Congress to appropriate $12.5 million—the authorization had been approved in 1950—to be made available to the ICEF during the spring, that is, during the 1951 fiscal year. The Administration reported that it still supported a permanent United Nations program covering all child welfare work and that plans for this would go forward, although under the terms of the recent UN resolution no such program could be set up during the fiscal year. Congress was urged to make the contribution not only for humanitarian reasons but also because to refuse to do so might lead the rest of the world to believe that the United States was interested only in the problems of children in the war-devastated areas and not of those who lived in economically poor and underdeveloped regions, which areas were scheduled to receive increasing attention under the Program during the next three years.[6]

The House originally appropriated only $4 million, and this on

[5] See *Survey—1949*, pp. 54-55, and *Survey—1950*, pp. 72-73, for a summary of United States policies and activities with respect to the ICEF in those years.

[6] For a record of the official statements on the program, see "Third Supplemental Appropriation Bill for 1951," *Hearings, Part 2*, House of Rep., Subcommittee of the Committee on Appropriations, March 1951, pp. 362-393.

condition that the United States contribution be no more than one-third of the total contribution, as compared with 72 percent in the past. Before the Senate Committee, the State Department strongly urged that the amount be increased in order that the proposed United Nations program not be curtailed and that the percentage contribution not be specified, pointing out that while the United States was attempting to restrict to one-third its contributions to the United Nations administrative budget, it had in the past been willing to contribute a larger percentage to the budgets of the various United Nations emergency agencies. The Senate bill appropriated $7.5 million. In conference this was reduced and the final law provided $5.75 million and did not contain any specific restrictions on the percentage contribution of the United States.[7]

In August, the President requested Congress to authorize the appropriation of an additional $12 million for fiscal 1952. The Senate approved the request, with no restrictions on the percentage contribution by the United States, but no action was taken on it by the House during the year. The ICEF had established a budget of the equivalent of $30 million for fiscal year 1952, but at the end of the year had allocated only $10 million, since the remaining $20 million had not yet been collected.[8] During 1951, the United States contributed $5.8 million to this UN child welfare program.

International Refugee Organization

In 1950, Congress had exacted from the State Department a categorical statement that the latter would request no funds for contribution to the International Refugee Organization after June 30, 1951.[9] The IRO continued to operate, at a reduced rate,

[7] Even so, the conference report stated that the conferees were agreed that the United States contribution should not exceed one-third of the total. Such statements are not law, but the chairman of the House Appropriations Committee expressed the hope that its "significance will not be overlooked." (*Congressional Record*, May 21, 1951, pp. 5655-5656. See also pp. 5638-5639.)

[8] For an official record of the past activities and future plans for the ICEF, see "Final Report of the First Executive Board," December 1946 to December 1950, ECOSOC, *Official Records*, 12th Session, Supp. No. 3, E/1908 E/ICEF/160, January 27, 1951; "Report of the Executive Board," ECOSOC, *Official Records*, 13th Session, Supp. No. 14, June 28, 1951; and *United Nations Bulletin*, December 15, 1951, pp. 540-542.

[9] See *Survey—1949*, pp. 55-56, and *Survey—1950*, pp. 74-75, for a discussion of United States policies and activities vis à vis the IRO during those years.

throughout 1951 on funds that had previously been made available (United States payments to the IRO during the year were $8.3 million). By the end of the year, many of the remaining refugees were placed under the protection of the United Nations High Commissioner's Office for Refugees, which had been established on January 1, 1951. The latter office—whose operating funds came from the United Nations general budget—has responsibility for providing "international protection" for refugees and for seeking "permanent solutions" for refugee problems, but it has no facilities for caring for or resettling refugees in the manner of the IRO.

There were many groups in the United States during the year which urged that large contributions be made by the Government to continue the resettlement and emigration of refugees. They based their position on humanitarian considerations and also on the grounds that the remaining refugees constituted potentially dangerous political forces in many foreign countries and that resettlement would cost less than the "needless" expenditures it would otherwise be called upon to make. The Government, however, showed no intention of reviving IRO or of establishing a similar organization. As noted above, Congress had provided funds for continuing the program of helping to care for and to resettle the Arab refugees in Palestine and for helping Israel to meet its immigration problems. With respect to other refugees, Congress did set aside $10 million of the MSP appropriation for aiding migration from Europe. This would help only a small portion of the refugees previously under the care of the IRO.[1] It should also be noted in this connection that the Displaced Persons Act expired on December 31, 1951; some 300,000 displaced persons had entered the United States under this authority.

C. *TOTAL UNITED STATES GOVERNMENT GRANTS*

Total United States Government foreign grants are shown by program and area of destination in Table 4. Attention is called to the fact that ECA aid extended on a credit basis is not included in this table.

[1] For further details on the refugee problem, see Department of State *Bulletin*, June 11, 1951, pp. 952-953; September 24, 1951, pp. 502-504; January 14, 1952, pp. 50-52; and January 28, 1952, pp. 121-123; the *United Nations Bulletin*, September 15, 1951, p. 257; and "Department of State Appropriations for 1952," *Hearings*, House of Rep., Subcommittee of the Committee on Appropriations, 82d Cong., 1st Sess., March 1951, pp. 652-654.

I. GRANT PROGRAMS

TABLE 4

United States Government Foreign Grants, 1951[a]

(millions of dollars)

By Program			*By Area*	
Military End-Item Assistance[b]		1492.3	ERP Europe	3313.2
Defense Support—European Recovery[c]		2398.2	Other Europe	92.3
Defense Support—Asia and the Pacific[d]		152.6	Near East and Africa	232.8
Defense Support—Near East and Africa		2.3	Asia and the Pacific	784.2
Occupied Area of Japan		253.3	Latin America	76.5
Korean Relief Aid[e]		65.3	Unallocable[i]	101.7
Yugoslav Food Aid[f]		92.3	Total	4600.8
Technical Cooperation				
Technical Cooperation Administration	31.5			
United Nations	6.0			
Institute of Inter-American Affairs	3.4	40.9		
Philippine Rehabilitation				
Private Claims	1.2			
Public Reconstruction	10.8	12.0		
Palestine Refuge Relief[g]		24.2		
International Refugees		8.3		
Child Welfare		5.8		
Other[h]		53.3		
Total		4600.8		

a) In most instances these data represent shipments where goods are procured by the U.S. Government agencies and cash payments by the Government where other methods of procurement are used. Includes ECA-owned counterpart funds spent for administration and other services of benefit to the countries concerned in an amount of $45.3 million in Europe and $3.9 in Asia and the Pacific. Dollar costs for administering all aid programs are included. ECA aid extended on a credit basis is not included here but in Table 7.

b) Consists of MDAP shipments of $1,481 million (including $37 million for administration), $8.7 million under the former Greek-Turkish Program, and $2.6 million to China (Formosa).

c) Consists of ECA/MSA shipments of $2,354.3 million, ECA shipments under the former GARIOA program of $3.9 million, and $40 million out of MDAP funds transferred to ECA, other than to Yugoslavia, and $0.4 million of economic and technical aid by the State Department.

d) Consists of $152.4 million of ECA/MSA economic and technical assistance and $0.2 million of MDAP funds transferred to MSA.

e) Civilian relief supplied by the Army.

f) Consists of $55 million of MDAP funds and $37.5 million out of the 1950 Yugoslav Emergency Aid Program expended by State Department and ECA.

g) Consists of $8.2 million by State Department under 1950 appropriation and $16 million under MSP.

h) Consists of Department of Agriculture donations of surplus food stocks valued at $45.7 million, $5.3 million of aid to Mexico for eradication of hoof and mouth disease, and $2.3 million of aid to Chinese and Korean students in the United States.

i) Consists of expenses of administering military end-item assistance and technical cooperation assistance, donations by the Department of Agriculture (see note h), and contributions for international refugees and child welfare.

Source: Department of Commerce, "Foreign Aid," *Foreign Transactions of the U.S. Government,* Washington, D.C., April 1952, Appendix Table 6.

These data are gross aid and exclude the returns on grants and reverse grants which during 1951 amounted to $140 million, of which about $117 million were counterpart fund deposits reserved for United States use and $23 million arose out of the value of returned lend-lease vessels. Thus, net disbursements under the official grant programs amounted to $4,461 million during 1951, about 7 percent more than during 1950.

D. *MISCELLANEOUS GOVERNMENT UNILATERAL TRANSFERS AND RECEIPTS*

Miscellaneous unilateral transfers (mostly pensions, settlement of various claims, and disvestments by the Alien Property Custodian) totalled $103 million in 1951, compared with $87 million in 1950. Unilateral receipts were only $22 million, excluding reverse grants and returns on grants mentioned above.

When net miscellaneous transfers of $81 million are added to net disbursements under the grant programs, the net unilateral disbursements of the U.S. Government during 1951 totalled $4,542 million.

E. *PRIVATE REMITTANCES*

Private charitable remittances (personal and institutional, in cash and in kind) are estimated to have made a net contribution of $405 million to financing the 1951 surplus in the United States balance on current account. This volume continued a downward trend in such remittances since the war; it was composed of payments of $435 million and receipts of $30 million.

To encourage private gifts, ECA continued to subsidize ocean transportation costs of relief packages sent to a few ERP countries and India by individuals and/or by voluntary nonprofit relief agencies. The amount of such subsidies in 1951 was only $2 million, or less than half that in 1950.

II · POINT FOUR PROGRAM

THE Point Four Program—originally and broadly defined by President Truman as "a bold new program for making the benefits of our scientific advances and industrial progress available for the improvement and growth of underdeveloped areas"—in the minds of many people outside the Government had come by the end of 1950 to be a catch-all label to describe all the expanded economic activities and policies of the United States vis-à-vis the so-called underdeveloped areas.[1] In this broad sense, the program encompassed the various operations of ECA in Asia and in the dependent overseas territories of metropolitan European countries, the technical and capital assistance programs for all except the European area under the Mutual Security Program (discussed in Chapter I) and a large part of the lending activities of the Export-Import Bank and of the International Bank (discussed in Chapters III and IV).

The program had been given specific and more restricted legislative reference during 1950 in the Act for International Development, which stated that it was in the interest of the United States to engage in a program of "promoting the development of economic resources and productive capacities of underdeveloped

[1] Official documents provide little in the way of an agreed-upon or careful and explicit definition of an "underdeveloped" area or of "economic development," but in the minds of many Congressmen and officials of the Executive Branch the former apparently meant those countries with low per capita incomes and the latter involved raising per capita incomes. For working purposes, the underdeveloped areas usually included Latin America, Africa, the Middle East, and the Far East, excluding Japan and Communist areas.

For selected bibliographies on the economies of underdeveloped countries and their plans and problems, see the "Point Four" *Series issued by the Division of* Library and Reference Series, Department of State. Also, a very detailed and comprehensive study of the *Formulation and Economic Appraisal of Development Projects* was published by the UN (Sales No. 1951.II.B.4, vols. I and II) from lectures delivered at the Asian Centre on Agricultural and Allied Projects at Lahore, Pakistan, during October-December 1950. See also Department of State, "Brazil: Plans for National Development," Inter-American Series 43, July 1951.

A study of "The Pattern of Overseas Development in World War II; Its Significance for the Present," was made by H. Mendershausen, *Economia Internazionale,* Agosto 1951, pp. 745-771.

areas."[2] The Government expected the program to serve the interests of the United States in various ways, the more important being that it would (a) expand the sources of urgently needed raw materials,[3] (b) help prevent these areas from succumbing to or embracing Communism,[4] (c) facilitate the establishment of "representative and responsible governments [which] by their nature contribute toward world peace,"[5] and (d) develop overseas markets for United States goods. The Act recognized that such a program would call for the extension by the United States of both technical knowledge and capital investment.[6] It made specific provision for the U.S. Government to finance and organize the transfer of technical assistance and authorized it to cooperate with various international organizations in technical assistance programs but stressed that capital assistance was to come primarily from private sources and that the Administration should direct its efforts to encouraging private foreign investment.

Some of the policy issues concerning the Point Four Program

[2] See *Survey—1950*, pp. 89-97 for a summary of the more important provisions of the law and of the Congressional debates on it.

[3] Representatives from the underdeveloped countries frequently took exception to concentrating their development activities on expanding the output of strategic materials, arguing that it would leave them with "unbalanced" economies and that the future market for such goods was likely to be a temporary one. They insisted that "industrialization" must be a major part of their development programs.

[4] U.S. Government officials apparently did not question the assumption that economic development would serve to weaken the appeal of Communism to the peoples of the underdeveloped countries, but even if the Administration had any doubts on the point it probably would not have revealed them publicly.

[5] Secretary Acheson, "What Is Point Four?" Department of State, Economic Cooperation Series 30, February 1952, p. 7; see also "The Mutual Security Program for Fiscal Year 1952," *Committee Print*, House Committee on Foreign Affairs and Senate Committee on Foreign Relations, 82d Cong., 1st Sess., 1951, p. 8. For a convenient abstract of some Congressional views, see "The Point Four Program and International Politics," *Congressional Digest*, January 1952.

Many of the expressions of United States policy on measures for economic development were voiced in the UN debates on the subject in the Economic, Employment and Development Commission, the Economic Committee of ECOSOC, ECOSOC itself, the Second (Economic and Financial) Committee, and the General Assembly; for details see the relevant documents of these bodies.

[6] Significantly, the State Department also asserted that, "There is a considerable element of straight political basis in offering a country, friendly to us, when other countries adjoining it are getting a large program, a small program of assistance, so they can feel we are interested in that country." Congress, however, objected to such a use of United States public funds, and Senator Lodge replied that the "goodwill" obtained by such "political" expenditures "is very limited." (See "Mutual Security Act of 1951," *Hearings on S. 1762*, U.S. Senate, Committees on Foreign Relations and Armed Services, 82d Cong., 1st Sess., July-August 1951, pp. 659 and 665.)

were examined during 1951 within the U.S. Government, and discussion on many of them took place in the United Nations. The major issues during the year centered around (a) the extent to which financing of economic development should come from domestic and from external sources, (b) the relation of technical to capital assistance, and (c) the adequacy of existing sources of external aid and the degree of reliance on public or private sources.

A. *EXTERNAL FINANCING OF ECONOMIC DEVELOPMENT*

While always maintaining that the bulk of the resources (real and financial) for development programs must come from within the underdeveloped areas themselves, the Executive Branch issued a series of statements late in 1950 urging that the volume of external aid from the United States for both technical and capital assistance to such areas be greatly expanded.[7] During 1951, the Administration found that its position with respect to external assistance was more generous than that of Congress but much more stringent than that of the underdeveloped countries, which considered that the volume of aid projected by the Administration was insufficient to accomplish even its limited objectives, much less their own. The debates in Congress over the amount of United States aid to such areas are summarized in Chapter I.

In the various UN debates and discussions during the year, the United States delegates not only reiterated their earlier statements that by far the largest portion of the cost of economic development programs in the past had been, and in the future should be, represented by the use of internally produced goods and services but also stated that the recent increases in demands and prices for many of the raw materials which these areas produced was providing them with sufficient foreign exchange to meet a large part of the costs of imported goods and services required for their economic development.[8] This thesis was contested by the delegates

[7] See *Survey—1950*, pp. 118-123.

[8] Several members of Congress took the position that in view of their large current foreign exchange earnings the underdeveloped areas should finance even the technical services received from the United States. They only grudgingly accepted the Administration's argument that, unless such services were provided free by the United States, not many United States technicians would in fact go out because officials in the underdeveloped areas were extremely relucant to hire American technicians at salaries many fold their own.

of most of the underdeveloped countries, who stressed repeatedly, in general terms, the "desirability" and "necessity" of larger and steadier flows of foreign capital into their countries.[9] They argued, relying heavily on the United Nations *World Economic Report, 1949-1950,* that their internal incomes were so low that they could not accumulate sufficient domestic savings to carry out "needed" investment programs at "desired" rates and that any increased foreign exchange earnings in the near future were needed to provide consumer goods.[1]

Pursuant to a United States-supported UN resolution in 1950, the Secretary General appointed a group of five experts "To prepare, in the light of the current world economic situation and of the requirements of economic development, a report on unemployment and under-employment in the under-developed countries, and the national and international measures required to reduce such unemployment and under-employment."[2] The United States delegates were worried at the time that the experts might concentrate their study on "the requirements of economic development," especially on the need for external financial assistance, rather than on specific problems of employment, and for this reason they seriously considered opposing the resolution. The experts submitted their report in April 1951, significantly entitled "Measures for the Economic Development of Under-developed Countries."[3] As the United States delegates had feared, the report emphasized

[9] At the same time, they were insistent that such capital must be accompanied by guarantees protecting the recipients' political and economic sovereignty and, thus, gave substance to some of the dilemmas which Assistant Secretary of State Thorp had stated late in 1950 were confronting the Point Four Program. (See *Survey—1950,* pp. 118-120.)

[1] *The Economist* (June 2, 1951, pp. 1277-1278) noted that the world-wide shift in the terms of trade against the industrial and toward the raw material-producing countries had served to expand the foreign exchange earnings of the latter, but it also observed that the earnings were distributed unevenly among those countries and that probably much of these increased earnings were not likely to go into internal economic development since their ownership tended to be concentrated in the hands of a small group who could be expected to use a large part of them for increased "luxury" imports and for investments abroad.

During the year the United Nations Secretary General issued a "Report on the Relation of Fluctuations in the Prices of Primary Commodities to the Ability of Under-developed Countries to Obtain Foreign Exchange," UN Doc.E/2047.

[2] ECOSOC Resolution 290 (XI).

[3] UN Doc.E/1986.U.N.Pub. Sales No.:1951.II.B.2. Their recommendations may be found also in the *United Nations Bulletin,* June 1, 1951, pp. 513-518. The five experts were from Chile, India, Lebanon, United Kingdom, and the United States. Only the Lebanese member was a government official.

the overall problems of economic development and laid great stress on the need for external capital assistance, as discussed in Section C below. Although half of the specific recommendations referred to actions which the governments of the underdeveloped countries themselves should take to hasten their economic development,[4] only one referred directly to the problem of internal financing.[5] During the summer, the United States delegates in the Economic, Employment, and Development Commission criticized the experts' report for paying too little attention to specific problems of unemployment and underemployment; for overstressing the contribution to economic development which could and should be made by external investment; and for overlooking the improved foreign exchange position of many of the underdeveloped areas.[6]

Later in the year, the question of methods of financing economic development was discussed at length in ECOSOC[7] and the Second (Economic and Financial) Committee of the UN. On the basis of these deliberations and resulting resolutions, the General Assembly, in early 1952, approved a three-part resolution [520 (VI)] on "Financing of Economic Development of Under-developed Countries." In the General Assembly, the United States delegation voted for that part which, *inter alia*, requested the Economic and Social Council "To continue its studies on the problem of

[4] The experts recommended that the governments of the underdeveloped countries "take vigorous action to remove the obstacles to free and equal opportunity" of their peoples; "prepare a programme . . . for the improvement of public facilities by capital investment"; "prepare a programme of education and research," particularly for agricultural extension services, industrial training, and for the training of scientists and administrators; take measures to improve their "efficiency" in production, distribution, and finance; establish a central economic agency to plan and carry out development programmes; and "survey the prospects . . . and announce its programme for expanding employment" and for "increasing agricultural yields."

[5] It recommended that governments of the underdeveloped countries "Prepare programmes to stimulate domestic savings, including the extension of savings institutions and measures involving taxation; and, in order to ensure that capital moves into the most productive uses, establish a development bank and an agricultural credit system, and if necessary, take other measures for influencing the direction of investment, such as credit controls, foreign exchange controls, or licensing of buildings or capital extensions." (Recommendation 8.)

[6] See, for example, UN Doc.E/2006 E/CN.1/86, June 7, 1951.

[7] For general reviews of ECOSOC deliberations, see *United Nations Bulletin*, September 15, 1951, pp. 250-256; October 1, 1951, pp. 286-293; October 15, 1951, pp. 330-331; and December 15, 1951, pp. 495-501 and 543-544; see also *World Today*, November 1951, pp. 489-498; and *International Conciliation, No. 474*, Carnegie Endowment for International Peace, October 1951, pp. 460-472.

financing the economic development of under-developed countries"; and "Within the framework of existing institutions, to pay particular attention to the problems presented by the financing of non-self-liquidating projects and, generally, by the establishment of a regular flow of international public capital"; and "To consider additional methods of increasing the international flow of public funds for the economic development of under-developed countries." It also approved that section of the General Assembly resolution which, among other things, invited the International Bank "to continue to expand its lending operations keeping in mind the special situation of under-developed countries with low levels of annual *per capita* income." But it was in the minority in voting against the first section of the resolution, the important clause of which requested the Economic and Social Council to prepare "a detailed plan for establishing, as soon as circumstances permit, a special fund for grants-in-aid and for low-interest, long-term loans to under-developed countries for the purpose of helping them, at their request, to accelerate their economic development and to finance non-self-liquidating projects which are basic to their economic development."[8] The debate on this question of creating a new international institution to extend grants and loans is discussed in Section C below.

B. *TECHNICAL ASSISTANCE*

United States Bilateral Program

The 1950 Act for International Development (known in Congress as AID) emphasized that the Point Four Program was essentially one to provide technical assistance[9] and that projects needing foreign capital should attract it from private sources. The first Technical Assistance Agreement under the Act was signed

[8] For the complete text of this resolution, see UN General Assembly, *Official Records: Sixth Session,* Supplement No. 20 (A/2119), New York, 1952. For convenient summaries of all the resolutions on economic development problems approved by the General Assembly in its Sixth Session, see *United Nations Bulletin,* February 1 and March 1, 1952, pp. 118-128 and 225-227 f., respectively.

[9] The previously operating programs of the Institute of Inter-American Affairs were continued, and in November the IIAA was placed under the Technical Cooperation Administration and made its regional arm for programs in Latin America. On these programs, see Iverson, K. R., "Progress of the Institute of Inter-American Affairs—Point IV in Action," Department of Commerce, *Foreign Commerce Weekly,* April 9, 1951, pp. 3 f.

with Iran on October 19, 1950, and by the beginning of 1951 agreements had been signed also with Ceylon, Paraguay, Brazil, Liberia, Panama, Nicaragua, and India.[1]

When the Administration presented its request for approximately $79 million for Technical Cooperation Administration expenditures during fiscal year 1952,[2] the major questions raised by Congress concerned the character of existing and planned projects and the proportion of their cost to be financed by the recipients. The Administration spokesmen testified that over 50 percent of the costs of each project covered by an agreement was provided by the aid recipient and that in some cases it was over 90 percent. As to their character, TCA Administrator Bennett testified that almost all of the agreements which had been signed concentrated on such basic projects as improved health and sanitation facilities, land improvement, locust control, water development, and good roads campaigns. He chose to refer to the United States activities as a "grass-roots" program of sending United States technicians into the field to "help-do" and "help-teach" individuals.[3]

With respect to the provision by the United States of commodities, rather than services, under the Technical Cooperation Program, he argued that emphasis should be placed on providing relatively simple modern tools to replace the primitive ones being used in these areas. He did state that some more elaborate capital goods from abroad would be needed to implement the programs for improving transportation and communication facilities, for financing certain "village" manufacturing industries which were being encouraged, and for those projects which were designed to increase the production of raw materials needed by the United States and her allies. It was urgently necessary, he testified, that efforts

[1] See *Survey—1950*, pp. 95-100, for a summary of the criteria and procedure for extending technical assistance under this Act.

[2] This included the $48 million for the Near East and Africa; $18 million for Latin America; $0.5 million for Afghanistan, Ceylon, and Nepal; $12 million for contributions to the UN technical assistance program; and $1 million for contributions to the Organization for American States. In addition to this, some $6 million for administration of the aid was to come from the Mutual Security Program funds requested for Europe, while ECA (later MSA) was to provide technical assistance to India, Iran, the Far East, and Europe from MSP funds. These latter programs, however, were not a formal part of the Point Four Program. ("The Mutual Security Program," *Hearings* [on H.R. 5020 and H.R. 5113], House of Rep., Committee on Foreign Affairs, 82d Cong., 1st Sess., June-July 1951, p. 1430.)

[3] See also his "The Engineer and Point Four," Department of State *Bulletin*, July 16, 1951, pp. 107-111.

be intensified by the underdeveloped countries themselves to mobilize existing internal capital funds for investment in local enterprises, but he also believed that some foreign capital beyond that provided under the Technical Cooperation Program was needed now to take advantage of the "opportunities" and "needs" which could not be financed by the small amounts of investment funds available locally. He went on to say, however, that large-scale inflows of foreign capital were precluded until the internal markets for locally produced goods had been enlarged and that at such time private capital investments would be profitable and should be relied upon to fill the requirements.[4]

This report was precisely what many in Congress apparently wanted to hear, especially those who in 1950 had expressed fear that the Point Four Program was launching a big, new "give-away," and few in Congress questioned the desirability of continuing such a "shirt-sleeve, grass-roots" program.[5] Largely because of the smaller dollar expenditures involved and because of the greater appeal of a program directed toward helping poverty-stricken *individuals* learn how to improve their physical well-being, both houses of Congress expressed more sympathy for this "technical assistance" type of aid than for that requested by ECA for the underdeveloped countries. In the appropriations for fiscal year 1951-1952, the Administration's request for funds to continue the program of the Technical Cooperation Administration was reduced by only $5 million. During calendar year 1951, the Technical Cooperation Program was accelerated and bilateral agreements were signed with Afghanistan, Bolivia, Chile, Colombia, Costa Rica, Cuba, Dominican Republic, Ecuador, Egypt, Eritrea, Ethiopia, Haiti, Honduras, Iraq, Israel, Jordan, Lebanon, Mexico, Nepal, Pakistan, Peru, Saudi Arabia, Uruguay, and the United Kingdom (on behalf of its dependent overseas territories), raising the total of

[4] See *Hearings on H.R. 5020. op.cit.*, pp. 1430-1463, for more detail on some of these points. See also Boris, G. (French Alternate Delegate to ECOSOC), "Assistance Technique et Point IV. Origines, Principes et Buts," *Politique Étrangère*, December 1950, pp. 533-550.

[5] Several members of Congress did voice concern over land-tenure conditions in many of the aided areas and expressed hope that the program, in some undefined way, might work toward a more "equitable" distribution of ownership. As noted in the final section of this chapter, the United States sponsored a resolution before the UN General Assembly, which was approved in early 1952, urging certain land reform measures on the various member countries.

"Point Four General Agreements" signed to thirty-one at year's end. By the end of the year over 216 specific projects were under way, 619 United States technicians and experts were serving abroad, and 372 foreign technicians were studying in the United States. Total expenditures under the program during the year were only $41 million, of which $3.4 million were by the Institute of Inter-American Affairs, $6 million were transferred to the United Nations for its technical assistance program, and $0.4 million were transferred to the Organization of American States; over half of the remainder went to Israel.

United Nations Program

The United States had played an initiating and major role in 1949 and 1950 in encouraging the United Nations and its various specialized agencies to expand their technical assistance activities.[6] Contributions from member governments (including those from the United States) were slow in coming in, and operations under this program began only during the last quarter of 1950. They were on a modest, but accelerated, scale during 1951.[7] The UN Technical Assistance Board, responsible for the day-to-day supervision of the program and for coordinating the activities of the various United Nations specialized agencies, reported that there were several factors which limited the extent of the UN opera-

[6] See *Survey—1949*, pp. 71-74, and *Survey—1950*, pp. 100-101, for a summary of United States participation in the UN technical assistance programs during these years; for a summary covering the first part of 1951, see Department of State, "Technical Assistance under the International Agencies," International Organization and Conference Series I, 16; August 1951.

In addition to the "expanded" program, the United Nations also continued to carry out a program which was started before the United States Point Four Program. This "regular" program is much smaller than the "expanded" program and is directed to three fields: training and public administration, advisory social welfare services, and to some extent economic development.

The International Monetary Fund and International Bank for Reconstruction and Development also provide considerable technical assistance to their members, but these are financed out of their regular operating budgets and are not usually included in the literature on the United Nations program.

[7] One of the more interesting UN technical assistance projects was the United Nations mission to Bolivia which, in effect, was scheduled to constitute for five years a sub-cabinet of that Government to supervise the country's development program. For details, see *Report of the United Nations Mission of Technical Assistance to Bolivia*, UN Sales No. 1951.II.B.5.; see also Lepawsky, A., "The Bolivian Operation: New Trends in Technical Assistance," *International Conciliation, No. 479*, March 1952. For data on another mission, see the *Report of the UN Economic Mission to Chile, 1944-1950*, UN Sales No. 1951.II.B.6.

tions, the more important being that (a) many types of projects which the Technical Assistance Board said would likely qualify for assistance were not proposed by potential recipient governments because they involved basic reforms in established practices which these governments regarded as unwanted; (b) some governments were not prepared to make adequate use of the experts requested, or expected results too soon, or underestimated their own responsibilities; and (c) there was a shortage of capital needed to support the technical assistance projects.[8]

Many of the delegates from the underdeveloped countries expressed dissatisfaction with the size and scope of the United Nations program and most of them stated that technical assistance was of little value to their countries unless it was accompanied by large amounts of capital assistance. The United States delegates responded that their Government was favorably impressed with the record of activity and the types of projects begun and planned, and repeatedly emphasized that, in their view, technical assistance was not of secondary importance but in many cases was a prerequisite to the effective use of capital assistance.[9] At the Thirteenth Session of the Technical Assistance Committee (which has general policy, supervisory, and review authority over the Technical Assistance Board) the United States delegate stated that his Government believed that even more emphasis than in the past should be placed on programs for encouraging savings and for educating and training local personnel, especially in the fields of health improvement, agricultural extension work, and fiscal practices. He also recommended that attention be given to setting up carefully selected pilot plants and that, to make the demonstration and training projects more effective, somewhat larger amounts of supplies and equipment should be provided than had been in

[8] For details on the operations of these programs of the Technical Assistance Board, see the Second and Third Report of the Technical Assistance Board to the Technical Assistance Committee, UN Docs.E/1911, January 24, 1951; E/2054, July 19, 1951; and E/2054/Add.1/Rev.1, August 7, 1951. See also the *United Nations Bulletin*, August 15, 1951, pp. 154-156 and January 1, 1952, pp. 15 f., and the record of the Meeting of the Technical Assistance Committee in early February 1951: UN Docs.E/TAC/SR.6-12, February 26-March 3, 1951; and the "Second Report of the Technical Assistance Committee," UN Docs.E/1920 and E/1920/Add.1, February 17 and February 28, 1951.

[9] See, for example, UN Doc.E/CN.1/SR.122, p. 7.

the past.[1] The Committee subsequently issued a report incorporating these suggestions. The Economic and Social Council in turn passed a resolution approving the work of the Technical Assistance Board, and on January 12, 1952 the General Assembly overwhelmingly adopted a resolution "noting" the progress of the program, welcoming the Technical Assistance Committee recommendations for greater emphasis on training and demonstration projects and pilot plants, and urging member governments to contribute for the next year's program amounts at least equal to those pledged ($20 million equivalent) for the first eighteen months of the program. Expenditures under the expanded UN program in 1951 were estimated at the equivalent of $10 million, raising the total since its beginning to some $11 million.

C. *CAPITAL ASSISTANCE*

In the United Nations debates the representatives of the United States, along with most of the other historically capital-exporting countries, accepted, "in principle," the desirability, over the *long run* of an expansion in the flow of capital from the more to the less developed areas. But there was sharp disagreement between them and the delegates from the potential capital-receiving countries as to (1) the relative role of public and private sources and (2) the desirability and feasibility of increasing *public* assistance in the immediate future, particularly through a new international institution. The difference in viewpoints on these questions was the basis for widespread pessimism as to the value of the September ECOSOC session and for the United States delegate's characterization of it as "constructive, though sometimes tedious and bitter."[2]

Encouragement of Private Foreign Investment

During 1951, the U.S. Government continued to emphasize that private foreign investment should be the major source of external capital assistance for the developing countries. In its policy of encouraging such investment, it concentrated on the extension of investment guarantees, negotiation of tax conventions and invest-

[1] For details of these statements, see UN Doc.E/TAC/SR 13–20, and UN Doc. E/2102, August 29, 1951.

[2] See *New York Times*, September 22, 1951, for further comment.

ment treaties, and efforts to gain a more favorable "climate" abroad for United States private capital—through both bilateral negotiations and by pressure in the United Nations upon the developing countries to assume more responsibility for enticing foreign capital.[3]

a. INVESTMENT GUARANTEES

During 1949 and early 1950, the Administration had placed much emphasis on the role that investment guarantees—commitments by government agencies, in return for a fee, to purchase for dollars foreign currencies representing certain specified receipts from approved private direct investments abroad—could play in expanding private direct foreign investment. Under the Economic Cooperation Act, Congress had granted, and later expanded (most importantly, to cover *compensation* in dollars for loss of ownership through war—but not "war damage"—confiscation or nationalization) the authority of ECA insofar as investments in ERP countries were concerned, but it had refused to authorize the Export-Import Bank to extend such guarantees on investments in other countries.[4] By late 1950, the Administration, in view of the need to obtain Congressional approval of what was regarded as more pressing legislation, of the need for more experience under ECA guarantees, of the opposition to guarantees by the business community, and of its own growing conviction that in the current international political situation (but not necessarily in the longer run) guarantees would have little effect on private investment, had abandoned its efforts to get Congressional support for the Export-

[3] In this emphasis on private investment, the U.S. Government had the support of the business community. See, for example, the various speeches before the National Foreign Trade Convention, as reported in the *Commercial and Financial Chronicle*, November 8, 1951, and the articles on obstacles to foreign investment and investment guarantees in the issues of August 23 and August 30, 1951. See also the statements of the position of the International Chamber of Commerce presented in its *Brochures* 145, 146, 155, 158, and 161, during 1951, and the report of its XIIIth Congress in *World Trade*, July-August 1951; and the recommendations of businessmen as reported by the National Industrial Conference Board in "Obstacles to Direct Foreign Investment," *Technical Papers No. Two*, April 1951, and *Business Record*, July 1951.

[4] See *Survey—1949*, pp. 77-82 and *Survey—1950*, pp. 107-112, for a summary of the policies and activities with respect to investment guarantees during those years.

Import Bank program and did not resubmit its proposals to the first session of the 82d Congress.[5]

During the hearings on the Mutual Security Program,[6] however, several members of Congress showed interest in widening the geographic coverage of the guarantees extended by ECA. For the reasons noted above, Administration spokesmen were not enthusiastic about such an expansion at that time, but Congress included in the Mutual Security Act of 1951 a provision which authorized the ECA/MSA to issue guarantees, under the terms and conditions established in the earlier legislation, to new private direct investments in *any* area to which assistance was authorized under the Act.

During the year and for the first time, two guarantee contracts were signed covering the risk of expropriation and confiscation; both were on investments in Berlin.[7] But the total amount of investment guarantees issued during 1951—$8.5 million covering nine projects—were less than half that recorded in 1950. Previous guarantee contracts were reduced by $1.7 million, leaving a total of guarantees outstanding at the end of the year of only $31.4 million. No disbursements had been made on any of these investment guarantees. As described in previous volumes of this *Survey*, the law also authorized the extension of informational media guarantees which insure the convertibility into dollars of the local currency earnings of publishers and producers from their informational media exports. Most of those issued have been for films, books, and periodicals sent to Germany. Such contracts signed during the year totalled $3.9 million. From the beginning of the program in 1948 through 1951, $11.7 million of such guarantees had been issued. The equivalent of $5.4 million in foreign currency receipts had been converted into dollars by ECA, compared with fees charged of less than $0.2 million. Most of these foreign currencies so acquired were being used (or held) to cover certain expenditures of the U.S. Government abroad. After taking into account cancella-

[5] The so-called Rockefeller report of March 1951, *Partners in Progress*, had recommended that Congress appropriate a fund of $100 million to guarantee transfers of currency returns from private investments abroad.

[6] See *Hearings on H.R. 5020, op.cit.*, pp. 193-195, and 373-378.

[7] For statements on the importance of "silent expropriation" through German labor laws, see *New York Times*, February 5 and March 21, 1951.

tions and expirations, only $4 million of such contracts were outstanding at the end of 1951.

b. TAX REFORMS AND CONVENTIONS

The business and financial community of the United States had for several years insisted that the burden of taxes levied, by the United States and foreign countries, on earnings from foreign investments was a serious deterrent to increased capital flows out of the United States. To meet some of these problems, the Administration has for several years been negotiating tax conventions with foreign countries. Such conventions—usually two are signed, one with respect to the income taxes and one with respect to taxes on estates and inheritances—were aimed at eliminating double taxation, by allowing a credit against the domestic taxes for those paid to a foreign country, and at preventing fiscal evasion. During 1951, negotiations on such conventions were carried out with Switzerland, Colombia, Uruguay, Israel, and Finland, but only two (with Switzerland) were signed. However, in September the Senate, which had taken no action on these matters since 1948, ratified twelve of the tax conventions which had been signed during 1946 through 1951.[8] Thus, at the end of the year, conventions relating to taxes on income with ten foreign countries and conventions relating to taxes on inheritances and estates with five countries were in effect. An income tax convention with Belgium (signed in 1948) and the estate and inheritance convention with Switzerland (signed in 1951) had not been ratified at year's end. A calendar of these tax conventions as of December 31, 1951 is given as Appendix Table IX.

To provide some additional relief from taxation of foreign income, Congress, in the Internal Revenue Act of 1951, granted some of the 1950 requests of the President.[9] The law reduced to 510 consecutive days out of eighteen months the foreign residence requirement for the exemption from United States federal personal income tax on income earned abroad, and it also reduced from a "majority

[8] For an analysis of these conventions, their terms, and the recommendations of the Senate committee which considered ratification, see *Congressional Record,* September 17, 1951, pp. 11668-11700. On the Swiss convention, see Department of State *Bulletin,* June 4, July 23, and October 8, 1951, pp. 907, 145, and 575, respectively.

[9] For a summary of his requests, see *Survey—1950,* p. 116.

to "at least 10 percent" the minimum amount of voting stock which must be held by a domestic corporation in a foreign subsidiary if the former is to be entitled, with respect to dividends received, to obtain a credit against United States taxes for taxes paid to a foreign government.[1] Congress did not, however, approve the 1950 request of the President to postpone taxation of income earned by branches abroad until it was brought home, as was already allowed in the case of subsidiaries. This relief was one of the major reforms desired by the business community, and the Administration placed a similar bill before Congress in 1952.

C. INVESTMENT TREATIES

In an effort to provide a more favorable climate for private investors abroad, the U.S. Government also continued during 1951 to negotiate treaties of friendship, commerce and navigation (or economic development)—often referred to as "investment treaties"—which attempt to define how businessmen may operate in each other's country. In recent years the United States has been making a special effort to include provisions which will assure potential investors that they would receive nondiscriminatory treatment, reasonable opportunity to manage their properties and to withdraw both earnings and capital, and prompt and adequate compensation for any property expropriated.[2] The Administration saw its program of negotiating treaties of this type as "an integral part of this country's policy for the furtherance of liberal principles of trade and economic relations in general, and particularly for creating throughout the world conditions favorable to economic development."[3] During the year, the Executive Branch was reported as engaging in "active" negotiations for such treaties with some half dozen countries, and, in addition, it successfully completed negotiations with Colombia, Denmark, Ethiopia, Greece, and Israel, bringing to nine the number of such treaties signed since 1945. None of these was ratified by the Senate during the year. A calendar of prewar and postwar treaties in effect as of the end of 1951 is given as Appendix Table X.

[1] For unofficial discussions of this tax relief as a support for the Point Four Program, see *New York Times*, September 12 and October 21, 1951.

[2] See *Survey—1949*, pp. 86-88 and *Survey—1950*, pp. 113-116 for more details on these provisions.

[3] Department of State *Bulletin*, May 7, 1951, p. 746.

d. REMOVAL OF OBSTACLES TO PRIVATE FOREIGN INVESTMENT BY FOREIGN GOVERNMENTS

Both the Executive and the Legislative Branches of the Government reiterated during 1951 their belief that much of the encouragement of private capital flow should come from the capital-importing countries.[4] During the hearings on the Mutual Security Program, several Congressmen recommended that the removal of restrictions and obstacles to foreign private investment be made a condition for receiving United States aid. The Administration opposed such a policy, arguing, among other things, that many foreign countries were already taking steps to encourage foreign investment,[5] that such conditions were not attached to aid being currently provided, and that in the long run the Mutual Security Program would, by increasing security and strengthening the economies (and so the balance of payments positions) of these countries, result in a removal of many of the obstacles.[6] Congress acceded to the Administration's wishes on this question but did insert in the final Act a provision, the so-called Benton Amendment, discussed in Chapter I, Section C above, making the extension of aid conditional on certain general actions being taken by the foreign countries to foster free-private enterprise.

In the United Nations, United States representatives repeatedly stressed that the underdeveloped countries must assume greater responsibility for encouraging private foreign investment. They stated that it was useless for the United States to take the initiative in providing investment guarantees and negotiating tax and investment treaties, as various United Nations reports had urged, unless such action were generally welcomed and facilitated by the other countries. The United States delegates offered a draft resolution in connection with the methods of financing economic development which stated that the governments of underdeveloped coun-

[4] For an example of the support given this position by private groups, see National Planning Association, "Private Investment in Underdeveloped Countries," *Special Report No. 30*, February 16, 1951.

[5] For action taken by a few countries, see International Monetary Fund, *International Financial News Survey*, February 16, 1951, p. 249; June 1, 1951, p. 370; August 17, 1951, p. 54; and November 16, 1951, p. 164.

[6] See "Mutual Security Appropriations for 1952," *Hearings on H.R. 5684*, U.S. Senate, Committee on Appropriations, 82d Cong., 1st Sess., October 1951, pp. 143-146 and 153-154.

tries "seeking to attract foreign capital"[7] should examine their domestic laws and administrative practices with a view to removing deterrents to private capital inflows and should provide "adequate assurances" for private investors with respect to operations, management and control of their enterprises, remittances of earnings and withdrawals of capital, protection of their property and persons, compensation in the event of expropriation, and nondiscriminatory taxation. They also recommended that such countries develop means for informing potential investors of investment opportunities and, as a means of attracting and absorbing foreign capital, that they expand domestic programs of "mass education" and technical training, initiate "meaningful measures" of land reform, and attempt to increase social mobility. While accepting "in principle" these responsibilities, the representatives of most of the underdeveloped areas made it clear in the debates that in their view large-scale foreign public aid was necessary *before* conditions attractive to private investors could be created through these domestic measures and that, in any case, they much preferred capital assistance from public rather than private sources.[8] One delegate, whose views reflected those of many of the underdeveloped countries, went so far as to say that the problem was not one of such countries creating a favorable atmosphere for private foreign capital but rather it was "whether the industrialized countries . . . were able to ensure the well-being of the great majority of the peoples of the world or, more generally, whether the Western way of life gave them promise of such well-being."[9]

The final ECOSOC resolution[1] on means of financing economic development did incorporate the above recommendations of the United States on domestic measures for encouraging inflows of foreign private capital. The resolution also stated that governments

[7] In a sense this qualification begs the question, for most of the underdeveloped countries did not fall in this category, seeking rather to avoid having to import any *private* capital. During the debates of the Second Committee, the South African representative expressed mild shock at the widespread distrust of private capital evidenced in the statements of the underdeveloped countries' delegates. (See UN Doc.A/C.2/SR 164, December 11, 1951.)

[8] See, for example, UN Docs.E/AC.6/SR 111, p. 9, and A/C.2/SR 153, November 27, 1951.

[9] Economic and Social Council, *Official Records*, Thirteenth Session, 503rd Meeting, August 15, 1951, p. 208.

[1] ECOSOC Resolution 368 (XIII). The text of this resolution may be found in the *United Nations Bulletin*, September 15, 1951, pp. 250-256.

had the right "to take any appropriate safeguards necessary to ensure that foreign investment is not used as a basis for interference in its internal affairs or national policies," and the capital-exporting countries were urged to impress upon their private foreign investors the importance of (a) "adhering to proper standards of conduct in the operation of their foreign enterprises, and in particular having due regard to the economic and social welfare of the capital-receiving countries," and (b) "ensuring, wherever feasible, opportunities for participation of nationals of the under-developed countries in the administrative and technical services in industry, and for their training."

Pressure for Greater Public Assistance

The United States, along with the majority of the other members of the United Nations, had formally recognized in late 1950 that the flow of private capital was not likely to be adequate to "meet the financial needs of the economic development of the underdeveloped countries and that those needs cannot be met without an increased flow of international public funds."[2] In March 1951, the so-called "Rockefeller Report" recommended that "the United States take the initiative in creating an international finance corporation, as an affiliate of the International Bank, with authority to make loans in local and foreign currencies to private enterprises without the requirement of government guarantees and also to make non-voting equity investments in local currencies in participation with private investors," and support "the prompt creation of a new International Development Authority," operating under management contract with the International Bank for Reconstruction and Development, to help finance projects of basic development and public works that "cannot be financed entirely on a loan basis."[3]

The April 1951 report on measures for economic development by the United Nations experts picked up the two themes and rec-

[2] See text of a portion of the General Assembly resolution in our *Survey—1950*, pp. 106-107.

[3] *Partners in Progress*, A Report to the President by the International Development Advisory Board, Washington, D.C., March 1951, pp. 72-73 and 84. See also comments on this report by Felix Belair, Jr., in *New York Times*, March 18, 1951, and the report on comments by Mr. Rockefeller and on the attitudes of some of the private bankers toward it in the *New York Times*, March 21 and 13, 1951.

ommended unqualifiedly that institutions similar to the Export-Import Bank be established by other industrialized countries, that the International Bank "aim at" an annual lending of $1 billion for economic development,[4] and that "the United Nations should establish an International Development Authority to assist the under-developed countries in preparing, co-ordinating, and implementing their programmes of economic development; to distribute to under-developed countries grants-in-aid for specific purposes; to verify the proper utilization of such grants; and to study and report on the progress of development programmes." It was more cautious with respect to an international finance corporation, recommending only that "the United Nations should explore the possibility of establishing an international finance corporation to make equity investments and to lend to private undertakings operating in under-developed countries."[5]

a. INTERNATIONAL FINANCE CORPORATION

The United States delegates and those of many other potential capital-exporting nations agreed on the desirability of studying the creation of an international finance corporation, believing that it could help expand the area open to private enterprise, circumvent the obstacles encountered by the International Bank that government guarantees had to be obtained even for loans to private enterprises, help mobilize domestic savings and investment, and possibly stimulate private foreign investment. The United States, in a draft resolution before ECOSOC, incorporated a provision recommending the exploration of the possibility of establishing such an agency and the International Bank stated that the proposal should be sympathetically studied.[6] The potential capital-receiving countries were not insistent on the establishment of such an organization, but they readily agreed to a further study of the matter, and a provision was included in the final ECOSOC resolution on "Means of Financing Economic Development" requesting "that the possibility be explored" (by the International Bank and ECOSOC) of establishing an international finance corporation. Thus the matter rested at year's end.

[4] The International Bank replied that such a policy was not feasible.
[5] UN Doc.E/1986, pp. 94-95.
[6] For details, see UN Docs.E/CN.1/SR 111 and 120.

b. INTERNATIONAL DEVELOPMENT AUTHORITY

The creation of an International Development Authority to help plan programs of economic development and to provide some of the capital financing (through grants and/or long-term low-interest loans) for basic non-self-liquidating development projects was much favored by the delegates of the underdeveloped countries, but was strongly opposed by the representatives of the countries which have historically been exporters of capital.[7] The discussions on this issue—carried on throughout the last half of the year in the UN Economic, Employment and Development Commission, the Economic Committee of ECOSOC, ECOSOC itself, the Second (Economic and Financial) Committee of the General Assembly, and the General Assembly itself—revolved around the questions of whether existing financing organizations and their resources were adequate and appropriate and of whether basic non-self-liquidating projects should be financed by foreign grants as well as loans.[8]

On the last question, the United States spokesmen were adamant in their position that, although grants were appropriate in a few cases and some were available from the United States (and from some European countries to their dependent overseas territories) on a bilateral basis, they should be extended for "special" cases only, and that they should not be a "normal and lasting" practice. In this stand, they had the support of the delegates from most of the other capital-exporting countries, and a Canadian delegate called specific attention to the fact that Canada's own development was accomplished during the past fifty years without grant aid. Many of the representatives of the underdeveloped countries were equally insistent in their position that some of the non-self-liquidating projects which were needed and desired in their countries could be undertaken only if foreign aid on a grant basis were provided since, they stated, the income levels and debt-servicing

[7] Proposals for a similar authority and fund had been offered, and opposed by the United States, in 1949 and 1950. See *Survey—1949*, pp. 75-76 and *Survey—1950*, p. 104n.

[8] In the discussion, the United States insisted that even low- and slow-yielding projects would be more readily financed by loans if undertaken in conjunction with well-balanced development programs (UN Doc.E/2007/Add.2, July 2, 1951).

capacities of most such countries were so low that they could not hope to receive sympathetic consideration of requests for loans. They were equally insistent that the amounts of loans needed were greater than those currently available and expressed a strong preference for the additional aid being extended through a new international (rather than national) institution.

On the question of whether a new international lending organization was needed, the United States delegates insisted that existing loan resources were adequate and that most, if not all, of the functions of the proposed International Development Authority could be carried out by existing national and international organs.[9] Moreover, United States officials stressed that since rearmament had first call on the West's resources, "the limiting factor on the rate of economic development . . . is likely to be, not the general lack of means of financing development programmes, but rather the scarcity of certain critical materials and of equipment necessary to implement such programmes."[1] United States spokesmen also emphasized that, in practice, the proposed International Development Authority would, under existing conditions, have to rely almost entirely on the United States for funds—it pointed out that many of the other UN members had found it difficult to pay their pledges to the relatively small technical assistance program—that the United States itself was not currently prepared, in view of the amount of resources it was devoting to the rearmament of herself and her allies, to make contributions to such a development fund, and that the U.S. Government would not support the creation of a new international organization which would in fact not be truly international. For these reasons, the United States delegates (supported, among others, by those from the United Kingdom, France, Canada, and Australia) argued that, while there might at some time in the future be a need for such a special development fund and/or authority, even a discussion or study of it at this time was ill-timed and ill-advised since such action would

[9] Supporters of this position again pointed out that the volume of International Bank loans to individual areas was not larger because it had received relatively few carefully prepared and justified requests and because of the inability of certain members to make available for unrestricted lending even their 18 percent contribution to the Bank. (See Chapter IV, Section A.)

[1] UN Doc.E/2007/Add. 2, July 2, 1951, pp. 1-2.

raise hopes and expectations which would be disappointed and might retard current international assistance and cooperation activities.

The delegates of most of the underdeveloped countries contested these statements in general and in detail. They repeated that their experience had been that the "ability to repay" of their countries was so low that they were not in fact eligible for loans from the International Bank or other existing institutions. As to the inability of the more developed countries to provide additional quantities of funds and capital goods, it was clear that many of the underdeveloped countries simply did not believe this. In any case, they argued that the emphasis (of the United States in particular) on rearmament and economic aid to Europe was misplaced since the primary, and in the long run the most important, problem facing the world was that of the economic development of the underdeveloped countries, that substantial progress here was essential to peace, and that any further postponement would be "enormously dangerous."[2] Several of the delegates criticized United States officials for having talked for many years in expansive terms about international development and for now objecting even to the study of concrete and specific proposals which were designed to do something about it.

In the face of the concerted opposition of the major industrialized nations to the proposal, representatives of the underdeveloped countries stated that, even if it were impossible to establish such a fund at once, at least some "positive action" should be taken at this time by the United Nations in the way of preparing new plans for meeting the problem of economic development when the re-

[2] For a summary of their arguments, as given in the General Assembly debate, see *United Nations Bulletin,* February 1, 1952, pp. 126-128; the United States position is reported in detail in the Department of State *Bulletin,* December 17, 1951, pp. 989-994.

In the discussion of the physical availability of capital goods for economic development, the underdeveloped countries urged that the industrialized countries should agree to provide high export priorities for capital goods and should take measures to assure that the prices of their exports were "equitable." The United States representatives believed that adequate attention was being given to these problems in the GATT and elsewhere (including the United States export priorities system—discussed in Chapter VI) but it nonetheless supported a General Assembly resolution, approved in early January 1952, which urged the creation of conditions whereby underdeveloped countries could more readily acquire, at equitable prices, machinery, equipment, and industrial raw materials, in return for their exports. (See *United Nations Bulletin,* February 1, 1952, p. 119, for details of this resolution.)

armament crisis was over. This was desirable, they said, in order not only to avoid delays later in implementing the program but also to "ripen public opinion" in the developed countries for making contributions to the fund and to restore faith in the United Nations by the "man in the street" in the underdeveloped countries. Even if implementation were delayed, they argued, this would not "disillusion" people in the underdeveloped countries for they were already disillusioned, indeed desperate.

The United States was defeated on this issue. On January 12, 1952, the General Assembly passed a resolution, with the United States and fifteen other countries voting against it, asking the Economic and Social Council "to submit at the next regular session of the General Assembly a detailed plan for establishing, as soon as circumstances permit, a special fund for making grants-in-aid and for low-interest, long-term loans" to help the underdeveloped countries accelerate their economic development.[3] As noted above, the General Assembly also passed, with United States support, a companion resolution asking the Economic and Social Council to continue its studies of the problem of financing economic development out of existing resources and other means of "increasing the international flow of public funds" for economic development.

The year under review brought into sharp focus, but did not bring solutions for, the major policy issues which the State Department

[3] The sharp division in this debate between those who would be asked to contribute and those who would receive prompted *The Economist* (January 19, 1952, p. 150) to state that the proposal was doomed "to remain indefinitely in the blueprint stage," and provided "the clearest example yet of the unreality of so many UN debates on economic aid for backward countries."

In addition to the resolutions on economic development which are referred to in this chapter, the United Nations General Assembly in early January 1952 approved two others. One asked the Economic and Social Council to promote studies of programs for the rapid industrialization of the underdeveloped countries, paying attention not only to financial, fiscal, technical, and social organization problems of the to-be developed countries, but also to the roles which the relatively developed and the relatively underdeveloped countries could play; it also asked that concrete proposals for solutions to some of these problems be submitted to the Assembly. Another resolution requested the Economic and Social Council to make a study of the various ways in which the productivity of people "everywhere" could be increased by the application of existing technical and scientific knowledge and to recommend ways of making the results of such studies available to underdeveloped countries. Details on these resolutions may be found in the *United Nations Bulletin*, January 15, 1952, pp. 75-76.

had said confronted the Point Four Program as the year began: how to insure that the aid was effectively used without subjecting the United States to charges of "imperialism," particularly in Communist and Socialist propaganda; how to reconcile the United States desire to have private enterprise assume major responsibility with the existing mistrust of private enterprise on the part of many of the underdeveloped countries due to past exploitation, real and alleged; how to resolve the rearmament demands on resource use and allocation in all countries with the wishes of the poorer countries quickly to diversify their economies and improve their living standards.[5] Indeed, the discussion on economic development in the United Nations during 1951 showed, or perhaps just high-

[4] There was an increasing awareness, but little public discussion, during 1951 of the obstacles to economic development presented by political instability, together with inefficiency and corruption of local governments in the underdeveloped areas. United States authorities did conclude that land tenure reform in many of the underdeveloped areas was a necessary condition for the success of the Point Four Program; they presented a resolution in the United Nations, which with certain amendments was approved by the United Nations General Assembly in February 1952, urging the member governments to provide, among other things, for more equitable "systems of land tenure and greater returns to tenants working the land." (For texts of these resolutions, see *United Nations Bulletin*, October 1, 1951, p. 287; and February 1, 1952, p. 123. For a summary of the United States position, see Department of State *Bulletin*, September 17, 1951, pp. 467-475; October 22, 1951, pp. 660-664; December 17, 1951, pp. 998-1000; and January 14, 1952, pp. 63-66.)

United States spokesmen in the United Nations also supported a resolution directing that study be continued on the problem of the effects of the distribution of income on economic development. The problem presented by the increase in population which seemed likely to result from the great emphasis on improving health and sanitation facilities under both the bilateral technical assistance programs and the United Nations program received some attention in the discussions of the Economic, Employment and Development Commission, but the members could come to no agreement on the interdependence of population growth and the use of economic resources. United States delegates strongly urged that the problem of population growth and its effect on economic development should be given specific and extensive study by ECOSOC, particularly with a view to determining its effect on *per capita* incomes and living standards. (Prior reports by the Gray and Rockefeller groups paid no attention to this problem.) Both philosophic and religious factors were cited by representatives of the underdeveloped countries as ones placing the problem outside the scope of ECOSOC. They also argued that the size of population was not necessarily a deterrent to the desired development. (UN Doc.E/CN.1/SR 126, June 12, 1951, pp. 19-24.) The Commission had before it certain documents of the UN Population Commission concerning the relation of economic and social factors and population growth (UN Doc.E/CN.1/85, May 24, 1951), but it concluded in its report only that ECOSOC "should keep the relationship between population growth and economic development under study as a matter of importance." (Paragraph 21 of the Report of the Sixth Session of Economic, Employment and Development Commission, ECOSOC, *Official Records: Thirteenth Session*, Supl. No. 2, June 7, 1951.)

[5] For a more detailed statement of these "dilemmas" as seen in late 1950, see *Survey—1950*, pp. 118-120.

lighted, that there was a growing rift between the developed and the underdeveloped countries as to the feasible pace of development, the prerequisites of foreign assistance, and the amount and manner of the extension of aid, and that, on the surface at least, the program was a more fertile source of friction than harmony in the international economic and political relations between the United States and the so-called underdeveloped countries. Still, there was some evidence that the position taken by representatives of the latter in the United Nations debates was an extreme one (often intended for home consumption) and that in discussions which were not so fully publicized these and other responsible officials took a more moderate view as to what is feasible in their economic development and in the amount and form of foreign financing.

Part of the differences expressed publicly in the United Nations resulted from the lack of agreement within the U.S. Government as to the precise scope of Point Four.[6] By linking both economic and technical assistance in the Act for International Development and in many public speeches of officials, by loosely associating the program with the Mutual Security Program and with loans by the EIB and the International Bank, and by the publication of such documents as the Gray report and the Rockefeller report, potential recipient nations were encouraged to press for an expansion of capital assistance. Some members of the State Department were at year's end attempting, in the light of the pressure in the UN, to restrict the program to technical assistance—an approach closely in line with Congressional sentiment in 1951. In particular, in a speech on January 25, 1952, on "What is Point Four?" Secretary Acheson stressed that, so far as the U.S. Government was concerned, it was principally a technical assistance program. But, in his message to Congress presenting the 1952 Mutual Security Program, President Truman stated that "Point Four means technical assistance at work, and it also means the supplies and equipment that are needed to put new techniques into effect." It may be concluded that the Administration had not—three years after the first

[6] There was, for example, disagreement within the Administration as to whether the 1950 Act for International Development (see *Survey—1950*, pp. 94-96) restricted the provision of "supplies and equipment" by the U.S. Government under the program to those necessary simply to carry out demonstration and training projects.

statement by President Truman on the program—agreed on the scope of Point Four. At the same time, the Administration regarded the Point Four Program as an increasingly important element in the nation's foreign policy. In his "State of the Union" message to Congress in January 1952 President Truman said: "There is nothing of greater importance in all our foreign policy. There is nothing that shows more clearly what we stand for and what we want to achieve."[7]

[7] *H. Doc. No.* 269, 82d Cong., 2d Sess., January 9, 1952, p. 5.

III · LOANS AND INVESTMENTS

After having made large amounts of foreign loans immediately following the war, the Administration concluded in mid-1947 that, except for Export-Import Bank lending, official foreign aid should be primarily in the form of grants rather than on a credit basis. It argued (a) that most foreign countries would have serious difficulties in the foreseeable future in financing their "essential" dollar imports, let alone servicing dollar debts, and (b) that any large increase in Government loans would seriously prejudice foreigners' ability to attract private American capital in the future. Congress, while anxious to reduce the amount of Government foreign lending and to encourage private capital outflows, nonetheless insisted in 1948 and 1949 that a portion of the aid under the European Recovery Program should be extended on a credit basis. The result of these considerations, together with increasing repayments on past loans,[1] was that official lending continued, but the *net* outflow fell from nearly $4 billion (excluding official contributions to the International Bank and Fund) in 1947 to only $159 million in 1951, as is shown in Table 5.

As noted in the preceding chapter, the U.S. Government has for several years insisted that the bulk of investment capital from the United States should come from private sources and has attempted, principally by investment treaties, tax conventions, and investment guarantees, to "improve the climate" abroad for private investors. These measures had not been adequately tested because of the deteriorating international political situation, and although the net long-term private capital outflows since 1946 have been at annual rates of between $750 million to over $1.1 billion—higher than any year since 1928—a large part of this was in petroleum investments which were tapering off sharply at the end of 1950, and the preliminary estimates for 1951 placed such long-term outflows at some $400 million below the previous year.

[1] For details on payments on principal and interest during 1951 and future years, see Plybon, C. W., "Payments on Foreign Indebtedness to the United States Government," *Survey of Current Business*, January 1952, pp. 18-20.

TABLE 5

Net United States Capital Outflow, 1946-1951[a]

(millions of dollars)

Year	*Total as a Percentage of Exports of Goods and Services*[b]	*Total*[c]	GOVERNMENT *Long-term*	GOVERNMENT *Short-term*	PRIVATE *Long-term*[c]	PRIVATE *Short-term*
1946	21	3381[d]	3262[d]	—250	59	310
1947	23	7956[d]	6849[d]	108	810	189
1948	10	1750	973	—87	748	116
1949	7	1256	474	173	796	—187
1950	10	1481	127	37	1168	149
1951[p]	5	1053	140[e]	19	781	113

p) Preliminary.
a) Excludes Government grants, unilateral transfers, and private remittances.
b) *In calculating these percentages, subscriptions to the International Bank and* Fund and net purchases of Bank debentures by private sources (notes c and d) have been excluded.
c) *Includes net purchases of debentures sold or guaranteed by the International* Bank of $243 million in 1947, $7 million in 1948, $20 million in 1949, $1 million in 1950, and $147 million in 1951.
d) *Includes subscriptions to International Bank and Fund of* $323 *million in 1946,* and $3062 million in 1947.
e) The discrepancy of $26 million between this figure and that of $114 million calculable from Table 7 below is due to the inclusion in the latter of commercial bank loans made at the risk of the Export-Import Bank, which operations resulted in a net inflow of $23 million, and to the exclusion of such operations in the above figure. The remaining $3 million is due in part to rounding and probably to some miscellaneous net outflows from the Reconstruction Finance Corporation to finance abaca production, not included in Table 7.

Source: Department of Commerce, *Survey of Current Business,* Washington, D.C., June 1950, pp. 11-18; June 1951, pp. 18-21; and March 1952, pp. 16-17. It is to be noted that the Department of Commerce has made important revisions in the data for the years 1947-1950 and therefore figures for these years differ from those given in our *Survey—1950,* p. 125.

A. *UNITED STATES GOVERNMENT LOANS AND CREDITS*

In 1951 the Administration, while asking Congress to increase the lending authority of the Export-Import Bank, maintained its position that most official foreign assistance should take the form of grants. Again Congress insisted that some of the "economic" aid provided under the foreign aid programs (discussed in Chapter I) should be on a credit basis and that the emergency food aid to India should be in the form of a loan. Still, *net* long-term loans by the Government during the year were less than 4 percent of the total official foreign aid extended; this was a slightly higher percentage than in 1950, only one-half that of 1949, and a tenth of that reported for the first three postwar years.

Long-Term

a. EXPORT-IMPORT BANK

During 1951 the Export-Import Bank authorized new loans aggregating $244.2 million, less than half the amount recorded during the previous year; actual disbursements (including those of agent banks) were $204 million, just slightly in excess of the disbursements during 1950. As Table 6 shows, principal repayments and collections on interest and commissions were almost equal to the disbursements, with the result that the Export-Import Bank made practically no net contribution to financing the United States export surplus.

TABLE 6

Export-Import Bank Operations, 1934-1951

(millions of dollars)

	New Credits Authorized	*Authorizations Expired or Cancelled*	*Loans Disbursed by EIB & Its Agent Banks*	*Principal Collected by EIB & Its Agent Banks*	*Interest and Commissions Collected*	*Amounts Outstanding Dec. 31*
By Area—1951						
ERP Europe	50.0[a]	na	0.8	87.9	43.5	1487.6
Other Europe	0	na	15.4[b]	2.7	5.5	187.4
Latin America	111.0	na	128.7	39.1	16.0	459.2
Middle East and Africa	41.4[c]	na	46.5	2.5	2.6	111.9
Asia and the Pacific	41.1	na	11.8	2.2	0.5	46.3
Canada	0.7[d]	na	0.9	0	0.1	3.3
1951 Total	244.2	29.6	204.1	134.5	68.2	2295.9[e]
By Period						
1950	565.8	37.0	199.9	160.0	64.4	2219.5
1949	241.0	19.4	184.8	143.7	60.9	2179.6
1948	138.3	325.9	428.9	261.1	57.3	2138.5
1947	614.1	23.5	824.5	95.5	}	1970.7
1946	1211.0	122.7	1036.5	40.1	} 85.8	1241.7
1934-1945	2308.5	438.3	555.8	310.5	}	245.3
Cumulative Total, Dec. 31, 1951	5322.9	1128.9	3434.5	1145.5	336.6	

a) Germany only.
b) Yugoslavia only.

(*Notes continued on next page*)

As in previous years, Latin America received more of the new authorizations than any other area, but for the first time since 1948 a Western European nation (Germany) received a loan from the EIB. Of the total authorizations, $110 million went to Germany, Japan, and Colombia to finance the purchase of raw cotton, an operation which was in keeping with the original purposes of the EIB and which pleased many in Congress from the southern states since, in line with well-established policy for all Export-Import Bank loans, purchases under these loans were to be made in the United States. Nearly all the rest of the new authorizations dovetailed with the Point Four Program: many of the loans to Latin America were for such basic development projects as roads, irrigation, water supply, railroad electrification, cement production, etc., and nearly $77 million of the total were designed to expand the production of strategic materials. Important in the last category were a uranium project in Africa and tungsten, sulfur, manganese, and ferromanganese projects in Latin America. The loans for tungsten production in Peru and Bolivia carried the significant provision that a part of the production from the aided mines would be offered for sale to the United States Emergency Procurement Service, with the proceeds to be used to repay the loan.

Because of the large amount of authorizations made during 1950, the EIB's uncommitted lending authority was reduced to just over $500 million in early 1951, and the Administration considered it necessary to hold this amount as reserve against some unforeseen international emergency which might call for quick and large extraordinary financing from the United States. Early in 1951, the President therefore asked Congress to increase the Bank's lending authority by $1 billion (to $4.5 billion) and to extend the life of the institution from June 30, 1953 to June 30, 1958. EIB officials and other Administration spokesmen testified[2] that the new lend-

c) Includes South Africa loan authorization of $35 million.
d) Increase in previous authorization.
e) Includes a $7 million loan participation by another agency.
Sources: Compiled from Export-Import Bank of Washington, *Twelfth* and *Thirteenth Semi-annual Report to Congress,* 1951 and 1952; and Department of Commerce, "Foreign Aid," *Foreign Transactions of the U.S. Government* (period ending December 31, 1951) Washington, D.C., April 1952, Appendix Tables 8–11.

[2] See "Export-Import Bank Act Amendments," *Hearing on S. 2006,* U.S. Senate, Committee on Banking and Currency, 82d Cong., 1st Sess., August 28, 1951.

ing authority would be used mostly for two main purposes. The first was to aid in expanding the production of strategic materials abroad. It was planned that the Munitions Board or another such agency would approve these projects. It was anticipated that some of these loans would involve a greater repayment risk than the Bank had been willing to assume in the past.[3] In such cases, EIB officials testified, the Export-Import Bank would probably require some special supervisory authority, such as the appointment of a manager satisfactory to it. The second was to assist in the economic development of the Philippines (to which the United States was officially committed),[4] in the reconstruction of Japan, and in the economic development of the Middle East where, the Administration stated, the "situation will probably develop into a demand for some good lending."[5]

Congress raised no serious objections to the Administration's proposal. The legislators were impressed by, and were unanimous in their praise of, the financial record of the EIB, which, at the end of 1951, showed an earned surplus since its inception in 1934 of some $262 million[6] and less than 1/100 of one percent of its loans written off as "uncollectible." Several members of Congress did express concern over the influence exerted by the State Department on the Export-Import Bank's activities. Mr. Gaston, the Chairman of the EIB Board of Directors, asserted that the Bank

[3] Especially risky lending by the EIB was authorized in Section 302 of the Defense Production Act of 1950, as amended in 1951. Under it the EIB was allowed to extend credits (to be "certified" by a defense agency) for the production abroad of unusually essential materials in projects where there were associated risks which would preclude the Bank from lending under the provisions of its own Act. The EIB reported during the year that it was considering allotting $10 million of its funds for the development of essential materials under this authority, and, in November, the Defense Production Administration certified a credit of $202,000 for the construction of two sisal processing plants in Haiti. These loans were not made in 1951, and details as to the responsibility assumed by the "certifying" agency were not available. However, the Munitions Board had "approved" half of the EIB's loans for strategic materials made during the year.

[4] See *Survey—1950*, pp. 69-72, and Chapter I above. Pursuant to the so-called Quirino-Foster agreement of late 1950, the U.S. Government sent a delegation to the Philippines to study the feasibility of loan aid, and in January 1952 the Export-Import Bank authorized a $20 million loan.

[5] *Hearing on S. 2006, op.cit.*, p. 19. The Administration stated that development loans to the Middle East would be made only after or coincident with land reforms.

[6] Gross receipts less operating expenses and interest payments to the U.S. Treasury, at the rate of 1-7/8 to 2 percent, on its funds. If the EIB had paid interest equal to the cost of the funds to the U.S. Treasury, its earned surplus through 1951 would have been $166 million.

made no loans which the State Department found undesirable on political grounds, but that the State Department could not, and had not attempted to, force the EIB to make a loan which the latter found economically "unsound." He also testified that if the State Department believed that a loan was politically desirable the Bank would examine the economic aspects of it carefully to see if it could be justified within the Bank's terms of reference. This reply satisfied most of the questioners, and the Administration's proposal was passed by the Senate without debate and was later approved by the House.

b. ECA LOANS

Overriding Administration objections, Congress in 1948 and 1949 specified that a part ($1,150 million) of the aid authorized for the European Recovery Program should be extended on a loan basis, and in 1950 it authorized a $62.5 million loan to Spain. The Administration has always regarded these as "fuzzy" loans,[7] and during the hearings on the Export-Import Bank legislation in 1951, Mr. Gaston, the senior officer of that institution, argued that Congress should in the future extend aid either as "clean gifts or clean loans" since gift-loans impaired the quality of other official lending. Other Administration spokesmen also opposed the extension of aid under the Mutual Security Program on a loan basis, but, as noted in Chapter I, Congress did specify in the Mutual Security Act of 1951 that at least 10 percent of the "economic" aid should be extended in the form of a credit.

Most of the ERP aid set aside by Congress for extension on a credit basis had been utilized by the end of 1950, but during 1951 some $60 million were disbursed and three loans were authorized: one to Belgium (the Belgian-Congo) of $15.5 million, and two to Portugal, totalling $9.2 million. In addition, ECA extended a loan to Norway of the equivalent of $24 million, of which part was in dollars and the rest was 5 percent counterpart funds accumulated in Germany, Denmark, France, and Norway itself. As a part of its program for expanding the production of strategic

[7] The Export-Import Bank is ECA's agent in extending these loans, but the countries to receive them and the terms, which were very lenient (see *Survey—1949*, p. 91 for a brief review of the terms), were determined by ECA, after consultation with the National Advisory Council.

materials abroad (see Chapter VI), ECA also disbursed an equivalent of $25 million, approximately two-fifths in dollar loans from a "special reserve fund" and the rest in loans of 5 percent counterpart funds. *None of the appropriations under the Mutual Security* Act of 1951 had been extended on a loan basis during the year. By the end of 1951, specific credits totalling $48.5 million had been committed to Spain under the 1950 loan authorization, but only $17 million of these had actually been disbursed.

c. INDIA EMERGENCY FOOD LOAN

Late in 1950, the Indian Government requested the U.S. Government for a long-term loan to purchase 200 million tons of wheat, urgently needed because of the recent drought, floods, earthquakes, and locust plagues.[8] There was considerable sentiment in the Senate and throughout the United States for helping India, and the usual procedures were reversed when, in January 1951, the Senate Committee on Foreign Relations asked the President to submit to Congress an Indian aid proposal. In mid-February, the President sent a message urging that assistance be provided to India both for "humanitarian" reasons and as a means of supporting democratic institutions there. He proposed, however, that the aid be on a grant basis and that only half the request be provided immediately, with the balance to be extended only if a United States mission found it necessary.

In defending his proposal,[9] Administration spokesmen urged that Congress regard it as a relief measure and not take into consideration existing differences between Indian and United States policy over the threat of world Communism in general and the war in Korea in particular. Although they did not wish to require specific political concessions from India, many Congressmen asserted that the political and humanitarian aspects could not be dissociated—all agreed that a major purpose of the aid was to fight Communism and some believed that aid should not be given to any country

[8] For details of the request and its background, see "Staff Memorandum of Information on India Emergency Assistance Act," *Committee Print,* House of Rep., Committee on Foreign Affairs, 82d Cong., 1st Sess., May 17, 1951.

[9] See "India Emergency Assistance Act of 1951," *Hearings on H.R. 2692 . . . and H.R. 3017,* House of Rep., Committee on Foreign Affairs, 82d Cong., 1st Sess., February 1951. For further details on this program, see *H. Rpt. No. 185,* 82d Cong., 1st Sess., March 5, 1951; S. *Rpt. No. 297,* 82d Cong., 1st Sess., April 26, 1951. These documents are the source of most of the information contained in this section.

which opposed United States foreign policy with respect to Communism. Tempers in Congress were heated on this issue and were periodically fired by statements of Indian officials which were critical of United States policy toward Russia and China and which asserted that India would reject aid "with any political strings attached to it."[1] These political considerations were in large part responsible for the five-month delay in approving the aid bill, but in the final vote the majority of Congress concluded that the program would serve United States foreign policy objectives.

With respect to the "humanitarian" aspects of the program, several of the legislators argued that a government had no "right" to have "humanitarian instincts" as regards foreign areas and that taxation to provide funds for charitable foreign activities could be justified only if they promoted the "general welfare" of the grantor country—a result which they doubted would accrue in this case. A minority saw in the aid proposal the establishing (or strengthening) of a precedent that the United States should provide gifts to any country suffering a "deficiency" in consumption and that, in the case of India, the problem of food shortages was perennial. This aspect of the issue, along with other reasons noted below, led to a move in Congress to provide the aid on a loan rather than on a grant basis.

The Administration urged that the aid should be extended as a grant, rather than as a loan, because (a) the funds were to be used for consumer goods and not to increase productive (and hence repayment) capacity; (b) India's foreign debt paying capacity was already burdened with large amounts of British investment as well as International Bank loans and foreign currency purchases from the International Monetary Fund; (c) a loan would reduce India's ability to borrow abroad for economic development purposes, which development was necessary if she were to remain a democratic and independent country.[2] Sentiment in Congress, however,

[1] *New York Times*, May 2, 1951.

[2] The Administration also argued that a grant program was preferable since it would result in a counterpart fund deposit which could be used to improve production and provide for more adequate internal distribution of locally produced agricultural goods. It should be noted here, though the point was not raised by those members of Congress favoring the loan, that in the first instance at least aid in the form of a loan would have the same result as far as providing the Indian Govern-

was strongly in favor of a loan. Several arguments were presented: India originally had asked for a loan and Nehru had subsequently stated he would prefer a loan; a loan would show "confidence in India's future"; there was no provision for such a grant in the proposed budget; and undesirable precedents would be established if the aid were in grant form. After much debate, the final law provided that the aid—in the form of food grains or equivalents up to a value of $190 million during the period ending June 30, 1952—should be in the form of a loan and extended under terms similar to those that ECA and the National Advisory Council had set for ERP aid extended on a credit basis.[3]

In view of the great demand in the United States for strategic and critical materials,[4] many in Congress urged that the law specify that repayment should be in the form of certain materials produced in India. The Administration opposed this on the grounds that the United States was already purchasing as many of such commodities as were available from India, and some members of Congress argued that the Government's bartering grain for strategic materials would run counter to the commercial policy of the United States of supporting private trade. The final law, while not making repayment in such commodities mandatory, did "direct" the Administrator of the program to obtain, as far as possible, "immediate and continuing transfer of substantial quantities" of strategic and critical materials from India.[5] The Administration reported late in the year that negotiations for increasing the flow of such materials to the United States were proceeding satisfactorily.

Congress specified in the law that the loan was to be used only

---

ment with rupees for internal development was concerned. There would be one important difference: *in the case of a grant United States officials would have some* authority over the particular uses to which such rupee funds could be put, while in the case of a loan no such supervision could be exercised by the United States. This was reportedly one consideration in India's decision to ask for the aid on a loan basis.

[3] In most cases, ECA loans had provided that the principal is repayable in thirty-five years starting in June 1956 and interest is 2½ percent per annum, with payments waived until 1952. They also contain provisions for postponement of the payments and for an alteration of terms.

[4] See Chapter VI, Section C.

[5] The law also authorized that up to $5 million of any cash repayments on the loan before 1957 could be used for the instruction and training of Indian students, technicians, etc., and for exchanging scientific and technical books and materials between the two countries.

to purchase United States grains.[6] The "tying" of the loan was not designed, as similar tying has often been, to protect United States producers; indeed, there was some fear that the Indian purchases might be harmful to the United States economy by forcing grain prices, and so meat prices, up. Rather, it was done to prevent India from purchasing the grain in (and so supplying dollars to) Russia or China. The law also specified that at least 50 percent of the wheat should be carried in United States bottoms.[7]

The India Emergency Food Act was approved on June 15, and ten days later the first shipment of grain was made. By the end of 1951 some $106 million of wheat and grain sorghums had been shipped under the program.

d. LEND-LEASE AND SURPLUS PROPERTY CREDITS

No attempt was made by the State Department during the year to settle the Chinese lend-lease account, but negotiations did finally begin with Russia in January. The United States had earlier estimated that Russia should pay $1.3 billion for the reimbursable part (civilian supplies valued at $2.6 billion) of wartime lend-lease shipments.[8] During the 1951 talks, the U.S. Government offered to scale down the payment to $800 million. Russia offered $300 million, which the United States found unacceptable. Russia at first also refused to return any more of the many naval and merchant ships and boats loaned it under the lend-lease authority (over two-thirds of those originally lend-leased were still subject to

[6] The law stated that the terms of the aid, with respect to protecting the American economy, were to be in accord with the stipulations in the Economic Cooperation Act of 1948, as amended. For a statement of all the specific provisions which would be applicable, *see S.Rpt. No. 297, op.cit.*, pp. 11-12. The law also provided that some of the funds could be used—similarly to some ECA funds—to pay ocean freight on relief parcels sent to India by individuals or private nonprofitable charitable organizations in the United States. In July, the Indian Government agreed to allow these packages to enter duty-free and to pay inland transportation costs on such packages.

[7] In its original presentation, the Administration had stated that shipping would be short and that loan funds should be provided to "de-mothball" and reactivate some one hundred liberty ships to transport the grain. Such expenses, it was said, would be recouped in part by the transport costs—to be borne by India from its own funds—and in part by the freight charges on return cargoes. The act authorized the RFC to help finance any reactivations which the President found necessary. During the year, the President did authorize the reactivation of eighty-nine ships.

[8] The postwar lend-lease pipeline credit of $223 million extended to Russia in October 1945 was in arrears of interest during 1951, but principal repayments are not scheduled to begin until 1954.

return in the view of the United States), but at the end of the year it had returned two ice-breakers. At the beginning of 1952, the U.S. Government stated that it would submit its claims against Russia to the International Court of Justice.[9]

During 1951, the initial repayments on the war account settlements (lend-lease, surplus property, and certain other war and postwar transfers) were due from France and Britain. France had been paying interest since 1947 and made its first principal repayment on July 1, 1951—interest and amortization together amounted to $30.6 million and similar yearly payments are due through 1980. Britain's initial war account settlement payment was made on December 31, 1951, with amortization and interest amounting to $19.2 million; the same amounts are due annually through the year 2000. Total principal repayments[1] by *all* countries on lend-lease credits amounted to $28.4 million during the year and interest collected to another $21.9 million. Total principal repayments and interest collections by *all* countries on the postwar surplus property credits (including small amounts arising from sales of surplus property located in the United States which were under the jurisdiction of the General Services Administration) totalled $38.2 million and $17.6 million respectively.

e. OTHER LOANS AND CREDITS

The final repayment installment of the 1941 Reconstruction Finance Corporation loan of $425 million to Britain was made in September 1951, four years ahead of schedule. This repayment returned to the United Kingdom the one billion dollars of collateral—mostly marketable securities of United States enterprises—which had been pledged for the loan.[2] Britain also decided not to request a waiver of interest payment on the 1946 loan from the U.S. Treasury of $3,750 million[3] and paid just over $119.3 million, of

[9] On the entire negotiations during the year, see Department of State *Bulletin*, April 23, 1951, pp. 646-648; July 23, 1951, p. 145; and January 21, 1952, pp. 86-89.

[1] During the year some $2.3 million of previously established lend-lease credits were recorded in the official statistics as "utilized"—mostly by Latin American countries.

[2] For some interesting facts on the background of this loan, see Jones, J., *Fifty Billion Dollars*, New York: Macmillan Co., 1951, pp. 472-477. For current comment, see *The Economist*, July 7, 1951, p. 47.

[3] For comment on the desirability of invoking the waiver, see *Barclay's Bank Review*, November 1951, pp. 67-69, and *The Economist*, December 1, 15, and 22, 1951, pp. 1353, 1485-1486, 1517, and 1543; and *The Statist*, December 15, 1951, p. 758.

which $75 million was interest and $44.3 million principal amortization. Yearly payments are to continue at this figure through the year 2000, with increasing portions being for principal repayment.

The U.S. Government disbursed during the year $13.1 million under the $65 million interest-free loan which Congress had authorized in 1948 for helping to finance the building of the permanent headquarters of the United Nations in New York. Congress had specified that repayments were to start in 1951 and be completed not later than 1982; a $1 million repayment was made during the year. Repayments of principal and interest on other outstanding loans—the 1950 Philippine refunding operation, the Maritime Administration ship sales, small payments by Canada on a Reconstruction Finance Corporation loan—amounted to only $23.7 million of principal and $6.4 million of interest during the year.

f. TOTAL GOVERNMENT LONG-TERM

Data on the total long-term U.S. Government loans and credits, by program and area, are given in Table 7. Excluded from the total outstanding are the World War I debts, as of January 1, 1952, of $11.5 billion principal plus $5.1 billion of due and unpaid interest.

(*Footnotes to table on facing page*)

* Less than $500,000.

† Detail may not add to total due to rounding.

a) "Utilized" means cash disbursements for loans and value of goods delivered under the various property credits, or principal amount of mortgages received or sales contracts, or billings. For ECA loans these data are "amount of aid extended on a credit basis" and differ from "disbursements" as reported by the EIB; this discrepancy apparently arises because ECA frequently pays for and ships goods prior to determining whether they will be classified as "grants" or "credits."

b) Principal collected represents the payments received and applied to the reduction of outstanding indebtedness.

c) Interest and commissions collected represent the payments actually received.

d) Outstanding indebtedness represents utilizations from beginning of program through 1951 less principal repayments.

e) In "outstanding loans" is included a participation of $7 million by another agency.

f) Loans of silver bullion by the U.S. Government to be repaid in kind.

g) Australia, British Guinea, British East Africa, Canada, Jamaica, New Zealand, Southern Rhodesia, Union of South Africa, and United Nations.

Source: Department of Commerce, "Foreign Aid," *Foreign Transactions of the U.S. Government*, Washington, D.C., April 1952, Appendix Tables 8 through 11.

Note: Because of changes in Department of Commerce data for 1950 and a different area breakdown, the above table is not comparable with Table 15 in our *Survey—1950*, p. 133.

TABLE 7

Long-Term Foreign Loans and Credits of the United States Government, by Program and by Area, 1951

(millions of dollars)

	Utilized[a]	*Principal Collected*[b]	*Interest & Commissions Collected*[c]	*Outstanding Indebtedness Dec. 31, 1951*[d]
BY PROGRAM				
A. *Current and Active Programs*				
Export-Import Bank:				
Direct[e]	222	130	68	2253
Through agent banks	−18	5	—	43
Economic Cooperation Administration:				
European recovery	60	0	0	1116
Deficiency materials	25	*	*	38
Indian loan	106	0	0	106
Spanish loan	17	0	*	17
State Department:				
United Nations Building loan	13	1	—	57
B. *Completed or Nearly Completed Programs*				
Treasury Department:				
British loan	0	44	75	3706
Lend-lease credits:				
Current credits	0	7	*	47
Credit offsets to grants	0	21	22	1213
Lend-lease silver[f]	0	0	—	291
Surplus property credits	2	37	17	946
Philippine funding	0	4	*	32
Maritime Administration	0	20	6	155
Defense Department—China	0	0	0	20
Reconstruction Finance Corporation	0	44	3	66
General Services Administration	0	2	*	16
Total	428	314	192	10119
BY AREA				
ERP Participants:				
United Kingdom	0	97	88	4701
France and possessions	16	44	46	2009
Netherlands-Indonesia	0	42	8	438
Italy	1	26	8	331
Other	58	32	10	775
Other Europe	32	5	10	505
Asia and Pacific	118	16	3	586
Near East and Africa	50	3	2	174
Latin America	128	47	16	500
Other and Unallocated[g]	25	2	*	99
Total†	428	314	192	10119

(*Footnotes on previous page*)

Short-Term

U.S. Government short-term assets had increased by a *net* of only $19 million during the year. Nothing is known by the Department of Commerce about the sources of these flows beyond the fact that they represent changes in the short-term holdings of various Government agencies which conduct overseas operations; accumulations of unexpended 5 percent counterpart funds under the aid programs compose a significant portion.

B. *PRIVATE FOREIGN INVESTMENT*[4]

As during 1950, attempts of the U.S. Government to encourage an expanded outflow of private foreign investments were not effective in the short run, and the net outflow of private funds declined sharply during 1951, compared with 1950, as several postwar investment projects were completed and speculative outward movements declined.

Long-Term

Preliminary estimates of the *net* outflow of private long-term capital show a decline from the record outflow of nearly $1.2 billion in 1950 to less than $0.8 billion in 1951, with the reduction being divided evenly between portfolio and direct investments, as shown in Table 8. At $268 million, *net* long-term portfolio investments[5] by the United States were less than three-fifths the amounts reported

[4] For further details on United States foreign investment during the year, see Department of Commerce, *Survey of Current Business*, Washington, D.C., January 1951, p. 23; September 1951, p. 24; October 1951, pp. 7-14; December 1951, pp. 9-10, and 12-14; and March 1952, p. 21; and *Foreign Commerce Weekly*, April 28, 1952, pp. 3-5 f. See also "United States Private Investments," in Chase National Bank, *Latin American Business Highlights*, New York, March 1952, pp. 1-8. These documents are the source of most of the information given in this section.

[5] "Portfolio" investments are defined by the U.S. Department of Commerce as all private long-term investments except "direct" investments, which in turn are identified as "enterprises in one country controlled by investors in another country or in the management of which foreign investors have an important voice; these are

during 1950,[6] but they were still much larger than during any other postwar year. The bulk of the outflow consisted of purchases in the

TABLE 8

Net Outflow of Private Long-Term United States Capital, 1946-1951
(millions of dollars)

Year	*Total Outflow*	*Direct Investment*	*Portfolio Investment*
1946	59	183	−124
1947	810	724	86
1948	748	684	64
1949	796	786	10
1950	1168	702	466
1951p	781	513	268

p) Preliminary.
Source: Department of Commerce, *Survey of Current Business*, December 1951, p. 12 and March 1952, p. 21. Data for 1948-1950 have been revised by the Department of Commerce and differ substantially from those given in Table 16 of our *Survey—1950*.
Note: Portfolio investments consist of the holdings of miscellaneous foreign securities which do not involve controlling interest by the American investor. Direct investments represent the extension of American business into foreign countries and consist largely of foreign branches and subsidiaries of United States companies. Included in the portfolio data are net purchases of debentures sold or guaranteed by the International Bank of $243, $7, $20, $1, and $147 million respectively in 1947, 1948, 1949, 1950, and 1951.

United States of $147 million of bonds sold by the International Bank and purchases of new issues of Canadian provincial and municipal bonds. The Department of Commerce states that the latter were induced by the credit restrictions in that country which resulted in raising interest rates there more than similar restrictions raised them in the United States. There was also some evidence that American lenders were encouraged to invest in

usually branch establishments or corporations in which the foreign parent company owns 25 percent or more of the voting stock. Holdings of United States residents other than those of the controlling interest are also included in the value of direct investments abroad."

[6] Revised Department of Commerce estimates place the total net portfolio investments by the United States in 1950 at $466 million, of which about $325 million went to Canada. The purchases in 1950 were largely of outstanding issues of the Canadian Government (rather than new issues of provincial and municipal authorities as in 1951) and were in large part regarded by both Canadian and United States officials as the result of speculation over an upward revaluation of the Canadian dollar. The Canadian dollar did subsequently rise, but little if any of the 1950 outflow had returned to the United States by the end of 1951.

Canadian securities because of the possibility of an appreciation of the Canadian dollar, which in fact did occur. (In early 1952 the Canadian dollar was at a small premium over the United States dollar.) Beginning in May, the Government of Israel attempted to float a $500 million bond issue in the United States, but the sales during 1951 amounted to only $50 million. Despite the fact that only Canada and Israel sold new dollar issues in the United States in 1951, the Department of Commerce noted a "generally improved market" for dollar bonds in 1950 and 1951, part of which was reflected in the large debenture sales by the International Bank. The rate of return[7] for private portfolio investments during 1950 was estimated to average about 3 percent. Estimates for the year 1951 have not yet been made, but it is probable that they were approximately the same.

The slump in *net* outflow of direct investments was such as to reduce it to the lowest level since 1946. A large (but as yet unspecified) part of the 1951 outflow went to Canada, while the amounts—both absolutely and relative to the previous year—which went to the Middle East and Latin America declined sharply with the completion of many of the major postwar oil expansion programs there. In fact, during the last quarter there was a net inflow of direct investments from Latin America. The Department of Commerce has reported that it was not yet possible to conclude whether the decline in direct foreign investments was merely a temporary phenomenon or was the beginning of a trend. It noted that this decline was not paralleled by investments in United States domestic industries—either as a whole or for those particular industries, petroleum and mining, which account for the bulk of the postwar direct foreign investments—and that the high rate of domestic investment indicated a continuing demand for additional raw materials. On the other hand, it recognized that the increasing political tensions, the continued movements toward nationalization of foreign (and domestic) production facilities abroad, and the action by some foreign governments to restrict the controls over their investments by foreign owners, may have constituted increasing deterrents to American foreign investment. The average rate of

[7] The ratio of income received (interest plus dividends after payment of foreign taxes) to the market value of securities and face or stated value of other components.

return[8] on all private direct investment during 1950 was estimated to be about 15 percent. This varied greatly from industry to industry, being higher for petroleum and much lower for public utilities, but, on the average, it was probably little, if any, higher than the rates of return on comparable domestic industries. Data for the rates of return during 1951 are not yet available, but there is no evidence to suggest that they departed greatly from those recorded during the previous year.

Although there was a slump in direct investment capital outflows in both 1950 and 1951, *reinvested earnings* (undistributed profits of foreign incorporated subsidiaries) in 1950 were estimated at $443 million—slightly higher than 1949—and probably increased in 1951, though data on the latter year have not yet been published. As a result, during 1950 the amount added to United States equity in direct investments abroad (taking into account *both* new capital outflows and reinvested earnings of subsidiaries) was more than $1.1 billion, as it had been in each year since 1946. The Department of Commerce states that it is probable that the net additions were near this level during 1951, raising the total value of American private direct investments abroad to over $14.5 billion. The net additions to private United States direct investment abroad during each of the postwar years through 1950, distributed according to areas of investment and major industries, are given in Table 9, together with the total value of such investments as of the end of 1945 and 1950.

In 1950, for the first time since the end of World War II, the additions to the value of manufacturing investments abroad were greater than those to petroleum investments. It is probable that there were further large reductions in net additions to petroleum investments during 1951.[9] Most of the increased investment since the war in manufacturing has been by reinvested earnings although there was some increase in capital outflows during 1950 and 1951

[8] Ratio of earnings (undistributed profits of subsidiaries plus dividends, interest, and branch profits after payment of foreign taxes) to the book value of the investments as reflected on the books of the foreign enterprises at the beginning of the year.

[9] In fact, the capital flow was reversed for some petroleum companies as foreign enterprises turned over to the American parent company larger portions of their sales proceeds which were no longer needed for expansions.

TABLE 9

Net Additions to Private United States Direct Investments Abroad, 1946-1950[a]

(millions of dollars)

Area and Industry	*Total Value as of Dec. 31, 1945*	*Net Additions During* 1946	1947	1948	1949	1950	*Total Value as of Dec. 31, 1950*
Area:							
Canada	2527	136	143	290	263	491	3850
American Republics	2999	147	559	528	565	267	5065
ERP Countries	1689	79	119	132	114	139	2272
ERP Dependencies	264	27	101	107	65	−3	561
Other Europe	329	4	4	−13	17	8	349
All Other Countries	561	92	185	197	188	230	1453
Total	8369	485	1111	1241	1212	1132	13550
Industry:							
Petroleum	1538	231	577	635	683	408	4072
Manufacturing[b]	2671	183	317	380	280	411	4242
Distribution	671	69	78	103	56	88	1065
Mining and Smelting	1064	−2	47	31	78	106	1324
Agriculture[c]	518	27	40	56	10	3	654
Public Utilities	1357	−80	−9	20	20	30	1338
Miscellaneous	550	57	61	16	85	86	855
Total	8369	485	1111	1241	1212	1132	13550

a) The small differences between "net additions" and the sum of "net outflows" plus "reinvested earnings," as given elsewhere in this *Survey*, is due to "other factors," including some allowance for revaluation of assets due to changes in exchange rates.
b) Includes paper and pulp enterprises.
c) Includes fishing enterprises.
Source: Department of Commerce, *Survey of Current Business*, January 1951, p. 22 and December 1951, p. 13. The Department of Commerce has made revisions in data for 1947-1949 causing discrepancies with those given in Table 17 of our *Survey—1950.*

for such investments. Most of the investments in the petroleum industry, on the other hand, were new United States funds and reinvested earnings of branches, as distinct from reinvested earnings of subsidiaries. While investments in other industries have been much smaller, those in mining and smelting have risen in recent years, especially in Canada; and, as a result of the increasing demand in both the United States and Western Europe for strategic and critical materials, there were during 1951 several major development projects under way or committed which led the Department of Commerce to conclude that the amount of private investment by the United States in these industries probably was even higher in 1951 and will continue to increase in the near future.

Area-wise, the outstanding development during 1950 was the great increase in total direct investments by the United States in Canada and the sharp decline in Latin America. This shift was the result primarily of the virtual completion of the postwar expansion of the petroleum facilities in Venezuela, on the one hand, and, on the other hand, the expanded petroleum and mining ventures in Canada, together with increased manufacturing and distribution facilities there. It is probable that this shift continued in 1951.[1]

Short-Term

Private short-term capital (foreign bank deposits held by United States banks on their own or customers' account) flowed out of the United States during 1951 to a net amount of $113 million. Gross outflows averaging around $50 million per quarter went to Latin America during the year, almost all in the form of United States commercial credits, but they were offset in part by the repatria-

[1] Most of the above data have been on a *net* basis and little current information is available on long-term private foreign investments in the United States; it is known, however, that for many years the volume of United States investments abroad have been growing by much larger amounts than the value of foreign investments in the United States. Foreign investments in the United States, in contrast with United States investments abroad, have been concentrated in portfolio investments, as is shown by the fact that since the war about 60 percent of United States payments to foreigners on investment income account was on that type. It appears that, since the war, there has been some reduction in foreign holdings of United States corporate stocks (portfolio investments) and that the expansion in the equity of foreigners in direct investments in the United States has been almost entirely accounted for by the retention in the United States of the earnings of such foreign-controlled companies. During 1951, however, there were net purchases of $120 million by foreigners of United States corporate stocks (mostly by the United Kingdom and Switzerland) but corporate bonds were *sold* in a net amount of $20 million. Foreign direct investments in the United States are concentrated in the insurance industry, mainly in fire and marine underwriting, but are also important in the petroleum and alcoholic beverages industries. Ownership of foreign investments in the United States is concentrated in the Western European countries (especially England, Switzerland, and the Netherlands) and in Canada. Income-wise, over 70 percent of all United States payments since the war have been to the ERP countries as a group and some 18 percent has been to Canada.

As of the end of 1951, total United States investments abroad (long- and short-term, private and government) were estimated at $36.1 billion as against foreign investments in the United States of $21.2 billion.

For recent official accounts of foreign investments in and by the United States, which have been heavily drawn on in this chapter, see Pizer, S., "Income on International Investments of the United States," *Survey of Current Business*, October 1951, pp. 7-14, and Pizer, S., "Recent Developments in U.S. International Investments," *Foreign Commerce Weekly*, April 21, 1952, pp. 3-5 f.

tion, mostly during the third quarter, of short-term capital from Europe, especially a reduction in American short-term holdings of pounds sterling, and the Export-Import Bank financed reduction in claims on Argentina. Apparently there were only relatively small amounts of speculative movements of United States short-term capital of the sort which had taken place during the last half of 1950 with the aim of taking advantage of anticipated currency revaluations during that period.

IV · INTERNATIONAL FINANCIAL RESOURCES: THE BANK AND THE FUND

A DOMINANT role is played by the U.S. Government in determining the policies and activities of the International Bank and the International Monetary Fund by virtue of the large voting strength of the U.S. Executive Directors and the fact that the bulk of the operations of both institutions have been in United States dollars. During 1949 and 1950 the International Bank had concentrated most of its activities on providing loans for the "basic" development of the so-called underdeveloped countries, and its objectives were seen by most as supporting those of the Point Four Program. Actual gross disbursements, however, were small, totalling only the equivalent of $142.8 million during those two years. In various United Nations discussions, United States delegates in 1950 had supported the Bank in its resistance to proposals that the latter's lending power be greatly expanded and that it assume responsibility for maintaining a stable flow of international investment. At the same time, American officials encouraged the other Bank members to make available, for lending by the Bank, larger amounts of their own currencies.

The U.S. Government during 1950 had been the most ardent supporter of the policies of the International Monetary Fund, which may be characterized as a most careful husbanding of its resources (not a single loan was made during the year); opposing flexible exchange rates and multiple exchange systems; fostering a progressive removal of exchange restrictions; and maintaining a single price for gold, with all supplies (except those for bona fide industrial, professional, and artistic purposes) being held as official monetary reserves. On most of these policies there was strong and growing opposition from other members.[1]

[1] Membership in both the Bank and the Fund was raised to fifty during 1951, with the signing of the Articles of Agreement by Sweden. (The total was raised to fifty-one in early 1952 with the admission of Burma, increasing the Bank's sub-

A. *THE INTERNATIONAL BANK*[2]

Lending Policies and Operations

As in the previous year, the U.S. Government was satisfied with both the level of operations and the lending policies of the International Bank during 1951. This year the governments of most of the other member countries also expressed general satisfaction, but, as evidenced by the United Nations debates discussed in Chapter II above, the governments of many of the underdeveloped countries believed that the Bank should greatly expand the volume of its loans for "economic development" and should broaden the scope of its operations.

As to the *amount* of loans, the Bank, with the full support of United States officials, repeatedly stressed that the effective limitations were those imposed by factors outside the control of the Bank and were not the result of a shortage of funds[3] or an unwillingness of the Bank to "accelerate the speed of development in member countries." As previously, it stressed the failure of the applicants adequately to prepare and support specific projects and programs which were "feasible" from the Bank's point of view, keeping in mind its responsibility for stimulating the flow of private capital and the necessity of its maintaining the "integrity" of its lending operations, which integrity, including repayment potentialities, was essential if it was to raise additional funds. The Bank also replied to those urging a larger volume of loans that such

---

scribed capital to the equivalent of almost $8.5 billion.) Applications for membership by Japan, Jordan, Indonesia, and West Germany were under consideration at year's end.

[2] The main sources for this section are: International Bank for Reconstruction and Development, *Sixth Annual Report*, Washington, D.C., 1951; International Bank for Reconstruction and Development, *Summary Proceedings*, Sixth Annual Meeting of the Board of Governors, Washington, D.C., 1951; the periodic press releases of the International Bank (frequently published in the weekly International Monetary Fund, *International Financial News Survey*, Washington, D.C.); and Black, E. R., "The World Bank at Work," *Foreign Affairs*, April 1952, pp. 402-411.

[3] In an effort to expand the resources of the Bank and incidentally to activate the International Monetary Fund, Congressman Javits proposed a merger of the two institutions. His proposal was accepted by the House but went no further. See *Congressional Record*, September 13, 1951, p. 11487. For an unofficial study of the appropriateness of the two organizations for meeting many current problems, see Crick, W. F., "International Financial Relations: Some Concealed Problems," *International Affairs* (London), July 1951, pp. 297-305.

suggestions frequently ignored the fact that the volume of capital goods that could be "effectively utilized for development" was strictly limited by the shortage of local capital necessary to supplement it, by the lack of local entrepreneurs and technicians,[4] and by the absence of basic facilities such as power and transportation.

Although the Bank stated that its operations had not yet been impeded seriously by the nonavailability of capital goods in the face of rearmament programs in the industrialized countries, it foresaw that this might well be a serious obstacle if the amount of loans were greatly expanded. In a move designed to ease supply difficulties due to physical shortages, the Bank established a unit in its organization to investigate the availability of capital goods and to help borrowers find alternative sources. United States officials asserted that the underdeveloped countries could "hardly be expected to supply basic commodities [especially raw materials needed for rearmament], without some reasonable return in equipment and machinery that will enable them to raise their own standard of living,"[5] but at the same time they stressed that the rearmament program was sharply reducing the amount of many types of capital goods which the United States could provide for economic development in the rest of the world.

The Bank's president asserted, but did not detail, that suggestions that "new ways must be found to increase many times over the amount of intergovernmental loans for development purposes" not only ignore "the frustration and bitterness a country invites when it shoulders an obligation greater than it can afford" but also "distract developing countries from concrete objectives" and "can do great harm to the orderly progress of development."[6] More concretely, the Bank pointed out that many of the underdeveloped countries which had been granted loans in the past had made such slow use of them as to raise concern over the appropriateness of

[4] The Bank continued its activities in the form of technical assistance to members on such diverse matters as control of materials and manpower, road maintenance, surveys of local resources, monetary and fiscal policies, procurement methods, bond issues, corporate organization, budgeting and accounting—both firm and national, etc. These activities dovetailed with those under the United States Point Four Program.

[5] International Bank for Reconstruction and Development, *Summary Proceedings*, *op.cit.*, p. 7. See Chapter VI, Section A, for a statement of United States policy with respect to export priorities.

[6] *Summary Proceedings*, *op.cit.*, p. 6.

the specific projects and programs which the Bank had already approved. The relevance of this conclusion is indicated in the righthand column of Table 10 below, in which disbursements *through 1951* on loans granted by the Bank *through 1950* are calculated as a percentage of such loans.

The U.S. Government and the Bank agreed with the underdeveloped countries that the Bank should concentrate on loans to underdeveloped areas and, as Table 10 shows, all the 1951 loans

TABLE 10

International Bank: Loans Granted and Disbursed, 1947-1951

(millions of U.S. dollar equivalents and percentages)

	LOANS GRANTED[a]		LOANS DISBURSED		*Disbursements thru 1951[b] on loans granted thru 1950*
Country	*1951*	*Total 1947-1951*	*1951*	*Total 1947-1951*	*(in percentages)*
Australia	0	100.0	36.9	36.9	37
Belgium (and Belgian Congo)	70.0	86.0	0.7	12.8	80
Brazil	(d)	105.0[d]	28.7	75.5	72*
Chile	1.3	17.3	1.6	7.5	47*
Colombia	18.9	29.9	5.6	10.4	70*
Denmark	0	40.0	0	40.0	100
El Salvador	0	12.5	3.4	3.4	27*
Ethiopia	1.5[c]	8.5	2.0	2.0	33*
Finland	0	14.6	4.2	10.6	73
France	0	250.0	0	250.0	100
Iceland	3.5	3.5	0.7	0.7	—
India	0	59.8	10.2	45.0	75*
Iraq	0	12.8	0.1	0.1	1*
Italy	10.0	10.0	0	0	—
Luxembourg	0	11.8	0	11.8	100
Mexico	0	60.1	13.8	30.7	51*
Netherlands	0	215.8	1.7	211.4	98
Nicaragua	5.3[c]	5.3	0.1	0.1	—
Paraguay	5.0[c]	5.0	0	0	—
Thailand	0	25.4	3.7	3.7	15*
Turkey	0	25.4	0.7	0.7	3*
Union of South Africa	50.0	50.0	10.8	10.8	—
Uruguay	0	33.0	4.0	4.0	12*
Yugoslavia	28.0	30.7	0	2.7	100*
Total	193.5	1212.4	128.9	770.8	75

* Commonly considered as an underdeveloped country in United Nations debates.

a) Excluding cancellations as of December 31, 1951. Prior to cancellations the total amount of loans granted was $1231.8 dollars.

b) Total disbursement less $14.3 million of disbursement in 1951 on loans granted in 1951 ($2.7 million to Colombia; $0.7 million to Iceland; $0.1 million to Nicaragua; and $10.8 million to the Union of South Africa).

(*Notes continued on next page*)

granted were to the less highly developed areas or in connection with programs in such areas. In 1950, the Bank had stated that "whenever feasible" it would be glad to help finance "national development programs" rather than just individual projects, to make some local currency loans, and to provide assistance to small borrowers by lending to national development banks which in turn would lend to individuals.[7] These lending policies developed slowly in 1951. The Bank did not help organize, as it had in 1950, any new development banks or consortium of existing banks to facilitate lending to small private borrowers.[8] Most of the loans during 1951 followed the earlier practice of being for specific "basic" projects and to meet direct foreign exchange costs: thus loans were extended for agricultural machinery, implements, and processing plants in Paraguay, Nicaragua, and Iceland; electric power projects in South Africa, Colombia, and Iceland; highway construction and other transportation facilities in South Africa, Colombia, and Nicaragua; and telephone and telegraph facilities in Ethiopia and Brazil. Importantly, several of these loans were made for projects within a broader development program, and

c) As of December 31, 1951 part or all of these loans still required action of the borrower and/or member government before becoming effective.

d) A 1949 loan of $75 million was increased by $15 million in January 1951. The International Bank does not regard this increase as a new loan.

Source: Compiled from data given in International Monetary Fund, *International Financial Statistics*, January 1952, p. xv.

---

[7] See *Survey—1950*, pp. 143-145.

[8] During the year, however, the Bank "sympathetically" studied—but issued no official reports on—a proposal, originally made by the International Development Advisory Board (the so-called Rockefeller group) and mentioned in Chapter II above, to establish an International Finance Corporation. It was suggested that this Corporation would be financed by government subscription and would make equity investments in private undertakings in member countries without government guarantees.

Another new development involving the Bank was its attempt to find a "practical proposal" for settlement of the conflict between British and Iranian authorities over the latter's nationalization of the Anglo-Iranian Oil Company. With the encouragement of both Britain and Iran, the Bank presented a program under which the Bank would manage the properties, hire operating and supervisory personnel, sell the oil produced to the Anglo-Iranian Oil Company at a price mutually agreed upon by Iranian and British interests, and hold a portion of the proceeds in escrow pending a final settlement of the dispute. Iran insisted that the Bank should not hire any British subjects to operate the properties, that it should manage the properties in "Iran's interest," and that it should be able to sell part of the production on the world market; Iran also objected to the suggested method of determining the price for sales to the Anglo-Iranian Oil Company. This position was rejected by the Bank and/or the British, and the talks were "adjourned" in late March 1952.

other projects in the same programs were under consideration for financing by the Bank.

Three of the 1951 loans were of special interest, however, in the sense of being radically different from earlier operations and as possibly pointing the way toward more flexible policies. For the first time, the Bank made two loans (to Iceland and Yugoslavia) not in dollars but in a series of European currencies. The loan to Yugoslavia was also unusual because of its departure from the general practice of lending to underdeveloped countries only for such "basic" items as improving agriculture, power, transportation, and communication facilities[9] in that it also included funds to provide equipment for coal mining, extraction and processing of nonferrous metals, and manufacturing. This broad industrialization program was made possible by the "underwriting" by the United States, United Kingdom, and France of the current account deficits of Yugoslavia arising out of consumer goods imports, as mentioned in Chapter I. The loan to Italy was not only designed to assist in financing a broad national development program in the Southern part of that country by providing funds to pay for some of the imports directly associated with the program, but, in line with a policy announced in 1950,[1] the agreement also provided that some of the dollars made available could be sold to the Bank of Italy for lire to help meet a portion of the local currency costs. This procedure was designed to minimize the internal inflationary effect of the program and to meet some of the *indirect* foreign exchange costs. The loan to Belgium-Belgian Congo was also for a broad basic development program but was especially significant because it took the form of two loans: one of $40 million to help finance the foreign exchange costs for specific projects in the Congo and another for $30 million to Belgium to help meet the impact on the metropolitan country of the diversion of exports to the Congo and

[9] In 1947 and 1949 the Bank had loaned large amounts to several Western European countries for reconstruction of industrial facilities, but through 1951 it made almost no loans for industrial purposes in the underdeveloped countries (save through the industrial development bank it helped establish in Turkey) on the grounds that improvements in agriculture and such basic facilities as power, transportation, etc. were prerequisites to industrialization and that industrial undertakings were usually the special province of the private entrepreneur who, in turn, often found it difficult or undesirable to borrow from the Bank since all the Bank loans require the guarantee of the borrower's government. Presumably the problem of the private entrepreneur did not arise in the case of Yugoslavia.

[1] See *Survey—1950*, p. 145.

possible increase in imports from other areas resulting from its assistance in helping to finance the development program in the dependent overseas territory.

One objection raised by some of the borrowing countries during 1951 was that they were required to repay loans not necessarily in the currency which was disbursed to them by the Bank but rather in the currencies which were taken from the Bank's resources,[2] either for disbursement directly to the borrower or to purchase other currencies which in turn were disbursed to the borrower. In particular, the Bank used some of its available United States dollars not only for direct disbursement to the borrowers but also to

TABLE 11

International Bank: Currencies Disbursed and Repayable, as of December 31, 1951

(millions of dollars or equivalent)

	Disbursed to Borrowers						Repayable
Currency	*1947*	*1948*	*1949*	*1950*	*1951*	*Total*	*Total to Dec. 31, 1951*
U.S. dollars	297.9	170.7	58.2	56.9	94.2	677.9	738.9
Canadian dollars	2.0	0.8	5.1	12.2	15.0	35.1	17.6
Belgian francs	0.3	19.7	1.6	1.7	2.4	25.7	2.1
Swiss francs	—	7.7	0.4	2.3	2.3	12.7	8.1
Pounds sterling	—	—	1.9	1.1	12.2	15.2	2.8
Swedish kroner	—	—	0.2	0.6	1.7	2.5	—
French francs	—	—	—	0.1	0.8	0.9	1.0
Netherlands guilders	—	—	0.5	—	—	0.5	—
Danish kroner	—	—	—	—	0.2	0.2	0.2
Italian lire	—	—	—	—	0.1	0.1	0.1
Total	300.2	198.9	67.9	74.9	128.9	770.8	770.8

Source: International Monetary Fund, *International Financial Statistics,* January 1952, p. xv.

purchase another member's currency for disbursement; in the latter case, as well as in the former, the borrower was required to repay in United States dollars. The extent of this practice is shown in Table 11. This practice was a consequence of the Bank's policy of not "tying" loans,[3] but some of the borrowers stated that it placed an "unnecessary" demand on their dollar resources, reduced their

[2] The Bank is thus not required to take a long or short position on any currency.

[3] The Bank's Articles of Agreement prohibit its tying the use of any loan funds to purchases in a particular country, but only the United States and a few other countries have allowed unrestricted use of their 18 percent contributions. The majority of members which had released their currencies did so in conjunction with a specific program of purchases by the borrowers in the former countries.

ability to repay loans, and, consequently, lowered their credit standing with the Bank. Bank officials defended this practice, so did the British Governor of the Bank, who said that it was one consequence of the disequilibrium in the world's balance of payments and of the fact that there were but few countries (particularly the United States and Canada) which were in a position to export capital even though other countries might be able to produce some of the capital goods.

Marketing Operations and Financial Resources

To meet its need for loanable funds[5] the Bank relied, during 1951 as it had in the previous year, largely on the sale of its own securities.[6] Two issues of dollar bonds, totalling $150 million, were successfully floated in the United States capital market,[7] raising to $400 million the amount of such debentures outstanding. In 1948, and again in 1950, the Bank had borrowed a total of approximately $10.6 million equivalent by selling its own Swiss franc bonds to a group of Swiss banks; in 1951 it placed another 50 million francs (equivalent to some $11.3 million) of such securities in Switzerland but this time sold them through public offerings. For the first time, the Bank also sold in 1951 an issue of sterling bonds. The total was small—£5 million—and was accompanied by assurances to the United Kingdom Treasury that the sterling would not be convertible but would be used only for loans to be disbursed in sterling.[8]

The Bank, encouraged by the United States, continued to press the other members to consent to the use by the Bank of that portion of the Bank's paid-up capital represented by the 18 percent local currency contributions, arguing that many of the borrowing

[4] See International Bank for Reconstruction and Development, *Summary Proceedings*, Sixth Annual Meeting of the Board of Governors, Washington, D.C. 1951, p. 35.

[5] As of the end of 1951, the Bank had available liquid resources of the equivalent of $83.5 million over and beyond its loan commitments.

[6] Repayments of previous loans were still small, totalling only the equivalent of $4.5 million in 1951 and $8 million since the inception of the Bank. The Bank's operations during the year resulted in a net interest income of $15.5 million plus $6.7 million in commissions on loans. These funds were transferred respectively to the General Reserve and Special Reserve accounts, raising them to $50 million and $23.7 million at year end.

[7] The first issue was also listed on the Paris Bourse; apparently only a few were sold there.

[8] For some British editorial comment, see *The Economist*, May 19, 1951, p. 1188, and *The Statist*, May 19, 1951, p. 663.

countries were more able to repay in nondollar currencies, that the extension of loans to them which were desirable and economic from the standpoint of total creditworthiness might otherwise be prevented, and that the Bank should become increasingly international. France authorized an additional $24.0 million of its contribution to be so used, and Canada another $7.5 million; Italy $1.1 million; Denmark $0.95 million; Netherlands $0.5 million; and Norway $0.1 million. By the end of 1951, twenty-nine of the fifty members of the Bank had given such permission.

The Bank has also, from time to time, replenished its loanable funds by selling borrowers' obligations. Such sales from its portfolio have been small, totalling only the equivalent of $33.4 million as of the end of 1951, although the United States position in the early development of the Bank was that this would be one of the major devices for reviving private capital movements. Less than the equivalent of $5 million of such obligations were sold in 1951, but nearly $4 million of this were sales made *without* the Bank's guarantee. The Bank's experience had been that the private capital markets showed little interest in purchasing long-term obligations held by the Bank but were ready to purchase short maturities even without the Bank's guarantee. In 1951 the Bank did directly facilitate some private long-term capital flows from the United States by cooperating with eight private American financial institutions in loans to the Government of South Africa, with the private lenders supplementing the former's loan with $10 million to be used for purposes closely related to those being financed by the Bank.

B. *INTERNATIONAL MONETARY FUND*[9]

Lending Policy and Operations

In 1950, U.S. Government representatives had publicly urged that the Fund conserve its resources until such time as their use

[9] The most important official sources on Fund policies and activities during 1951, and the source of most of the information given here, are: International Monetary Fund, *Annual Report, 1951*, Washington, D.C., April 1951; International Monetary Fund, *Second Annual Report on Exchange Restrictions*, Washington, D.C., April 1951; see also its weekly *International Financial News Survey* and its monthly *International Financial Statistics*, and the various mimeographed *Documents* prepared for and issued subsequent to the Sixth Annual Meeting of the Board of Governors of the International Monetary Fund held in Washington in September 1951.

might be more effective in achieving its basic objectives, and they stated that loans should not be made to countries suffering a "fundamental disequilibrium." During that year not a single loan was made, giving rise to complaints by many members—but not the United States—that the Fund was serving no useful purpose.[1] In an attempt to take a more positive approach to the problems of the use of its resources in the "present world monetary situation," the Executive Directors approved a proposal in May 1951 whereby members who, in consultation with the Fund, carried out agreed-upon programs aimed at achieving the Fund's objectives—in particular, internal monetary stability, adoption of "realistic" exchange rates, simplification of multiple exchange rates, and relaxation of exchange restrictions and discrimination—would be assured that the Fund's resources would be made available to them, on a temporary basis, if the Fund determined that the implementation of such agreed-upon programs required such assistance. This procedure was to be in addition to, and without prejudice to, the previous procedures and policies as to the use of the Fund's resources.

Several members had serious objections to this proposal—as well as to the previous policies—many of which were voiced at the September meeting of the Board of Governors. Some stated that the new proposal was so generally and obscurely worded as to give inadequate assurance that funds would be made available even if the approved policies were inaugurated and that it was "out of touch with reality"; others protested the "adjudicial" nature of the action taken by the Executive Directors and raised again the issue that the *spirit* of the Fund Agreement was that members have a more or less automatic right to use the Fund's resources.[2] The

[1] By the end of 1951, the Fund had made net sales of dollars to twenty-two members aggregating some $80 million *less* than the total amount of gold and dollars paid in by all members, excluding the United States, as subscriptions to the Fund. Only nine countries had borrowed (net) more than their own gold and dollar subscriptions; two-thirds of these purchases "in excess" went to only two countries, India and the United Kingdom.

[2] Some members, notably Australia and South Africa, argued that in many of the Fund's decisions the majority—in numbers but not in voting power—was overruled and urged that the Executive Board adopt a "nonpolitical and impartial approach" in making policy decisions. (That an intergovernmental organization could be either nonpolitical or impartial—in the sense of not guarding national interests—is a contradiction in terms and in fact.)

United Kingdom Governor stated[3] that using the Fund's resources as a lever to encourage removal of exchange restrictions was inappropriate; that the Fund should be prepared, under defined principles, to intervene with its resources to prevent price inflation, to achieve stability of exchange rates, and even to help tide over the rearmament difficulties of members; that the relevant test for loans should be the "credit-worthiness" of the borrower; and that the Fund's resources should be regarded as a second line of reserves for the members.

The U.S. Government strongly supported the Fund's new proposal and its general lending policies. Secretary Snyder stated that "credit-worthiness" was one, but only one, of the relevant criteria for borrowing from the Fund; that under the Articles of Agreement the Fund's resources could not be regarded simply as a second line of reserves since they were available only for short-term balance of payments difficulties and that before approving any drawing the Executive Directors must assure themselves that there was a good prospect of early repayment; that the Fund was aware of the problems faced by many countries but careful study had shown that in many cases the advantages of removing exchange restrictions outweighed the advantages of their retention;[4] and that the United States itself had been and was providing dollars to foreign countries to achieve certain objectives, but that an automatic right to use the Fund's resources would not necessarily speed the progress toward the Fund's objectives and that "the Fund, apart from its objectives, is no Fund at all."[5]

No country applied during the year for loans under the new proposals, and during the last quarter of the year the question of the future use of the Fund's resources was, under the leadership of the new Managing Director Ivar Rooth, being actively studied. No

[3] The speech setting forth his argument was not made public, but it was reported in several sources. See especially *The Statist,* September 15, 1951, pp. 318-319; *The Economist,* September 15, 1951, pp. 640-641; *The Bankers' Magazine,* October 1951, p. 266; and *The Banker,* October 1951, pp. 219-220.

[4] The Netherlands Governor made the point that removal of exchange restrictions on international transactions means little so long as large portions of a nation's foreign trade are carried out directly by the Government and/or private importers are required to obtain an import license.

[5] For the text of Secretary Snyder's report, see International Monetary Fund, *Fund Document No. 25, Sixth Annual Meeting of the Board of Governors,* Washington, D.C., September 12, 1951.

changes in policy had been announced by the end of the year, but consideration was being given to the Fund's assuming more initiative in offering its resources, granting special emergency short-term loans to members not eligible to make drawings under existing policies, aiding members (especially in Latin America) in financing their foreign payments arrears, and helping to finance trade between Latin America and Europe.

The Fund made only three currency sales during 1951; all under its previously established policies and procedures. In January the equivalent of $28 million in pounds sterling were sold to Brazil, and in November and December two sales totalling $6.6 million in U.S. dollars were made to Iran. During the year ended April 30, 1951, the Fund's total income was the equivalent of $2.7 million and over the same period its total expenditures were $4.6 million, resulting in a decrease in its net capital for the year of $1.9 million.

The Fund, again with United States blessings, continued to express concern over the long-term nature of some of its earlier loans (currency sales) and to encourage members who had purchased currency from it in the past to repurchase their own currencies and so maintain the revolving character of the Fund's resources. As of December 1, 1951, the Fund established a new series of charges for the use of its resources; as compared to the previous charges, the new ones were lower on loans outstanding for a very short time and higher for loans outstanding for longer periods.[6] At the same time, the Fund reduced the period of time for which it would hold a member's currency before requiring that consultations be held for reducing such holdings, and consideration was being given to imposing a requirement that repurchases must, in any case, be made within a specified time period. During the year, and before the new charges went into effect, the Fund repurchased the equivalent of $46.6 million of members' currencies.[7] As shown in Table 12, this was a larger amount than in any previous year; it exceeded, as it had in 1950, the amount of loans made, but it was still true

[6] A detailed presentation of the old and new charges may be found in International Monetary Fund, *International Financial Statistics*, Washington, D.C., November 1951, p. vi.

[7] Some of these repurchases were voluntary—that is, they were not specifically required by terms of the Fund's Articles of Agreement.

that many of the Fund's previous loans in effect had become long-term.[8]

Foreign Exchange Rate Policy

a. EXCHANGE RESTRICTIONS

The United States has consistently supported the Fund in its efforts to get other members to relax their exchange restrictions. Both the Fund and United States officials were increasingly cautious in their public statements on this policy during 1951. In April the Fund had asserted that "many countries are in a position to undertake substantial removal of discrimination and relaxation of nondiscriminatory restrictions and to make significant progress toward convertibility."[9] But in their *Annual Report*, released in September, the Executive Directors chose to quote as "still sound" a more qualified statement from the April report that "it is the view of the Fund that, if countries have favorable balance of payments conditions and are experiencing increases in their reserves providing a reasonable basis of exchange stability, it is in their interest, and in that of the international community, to relax or remove restrictions unless such action would produce conditions justifying the intensification or reintroduction of those restrictions."[1]

In its *Annual Report*, the Fund recognized that there were many impediments to any prompt relaxation of restrictions. Not only were some members still suffering underlying structural balance of payments difficulties, which limited their ability to relax restrictions, but also the rearmament efforts of some members were resulting in a deterioration in their balance of payments and reserve positions. The Fund also recognized that some countries would want to retain restrictions in order to maintain or build up their reserves to insure that funds would be on hand to pay for rearmament-needed imports. The Executive Directors expressed much concern over the mounting inflationary pressures which they saw

[8] For an unofficial appraisal of the Fund's activity through 1951, see Bareau P., "Is It Good-Bye to Bretton Woods?" *The Three Banks Review*, March 1952, pp. 3-18.

[9] International Monetary Fund, *Second Annual Report on Exchange Restrictions*, *op.cit.*, p. 14. See this report for a detailed description of the exchange restrictions imposed by each of the member countries as of early 1951.

[1] *Annual Report, 1951*, pp. 58-59.

TABLE 12

International Monetary Fund Exchange Transactions, 1947-1951
(millions of U.S. dollar equivalents)

	1947[a]-1949	1950	1951	Total
Currency Sold	*783.4*	*0*	*34.6*	818.0
U.S. dollars	766.0	0	6.6	772.6
British pounds	6.0	0	28.0	34.0
Belgian francs	11.4	0	0	11.4
Currency Bought	*783.4*	*0*	*34.6*	818.0
Australian pounds	20.0	0	0	20.0
Belgian francs	33.0	0	0	33.0
Brazilian cruzeiros	37.5	0	28.0	65.5
British pounds	300.0	0	0	300.0
Chilean pesos	8.8	0	0	8.8
Costa Rican colones	1.3	0	0	1.3
Czechoslovakian korunas	6.0	0	0	6.0
Danish kroner	10.2	0	0	10.2
Egyptian pounds	3.0	0	0	3.0
Ethiopian dollars	0.6	0	0	0.6
French francs	125.0	0	0	125.0
Indian rupees	100.0	0	0	100.0
Iranian rials	0	0	6.6	6.6
Mexican pesos	22.5	0	0	22.5
Netherlands guilders	75.3	0	0	75.3
Nicaraguan cordobas	0.5	0	0	0.5
Norwegian kroner	9.6	0	0	9.6
Turkish liras	5.0	0	0	5.0
Union of South Africa pounds	10.0	0	0	10.0
Yugoslav dinars	9.0	0	0	9.0
Gold[b]	6.1	0	0	6.1
Currency Repurchased	*2.3*	*30.8*	*46.7*	79.8
U.S. dollars	1.4	21.3	31.0	53.7
Gold	0.9	9.5	15.7	26.1
Currency Resold	*3.6*	*30.8*	*46.7*	79.8
Belgian francs	0.9	20.7	0	21.6
Chilean pesos	0	0	3.4	3.4
Costa Rican colones	0.9	1.3	0	2.2
Egyptian pounds	0	8.5	0	8.5
Ethiopian dollars	0	0.3	0.3	0.6
Lebanese pounds[c]	0	0	0.9	0.9
Mexican pesos	0	0	22.5	22.5
Nicaraguan cordobas	0.5	0	0	0.5
Norwegian kroner	0	0	9.6	9.6
Union of South Africa pounds	0	0	10.0	10.0

a) The IMF began operations in March 1947.

(*Footnotes continued on next page*)

as a major factor in the retention (or increase) of exchange restrictions and noted that members would require a more extensive use of exchange restrictions if they chose to combat such inflation by direct controls rather than by monetary and fiscal methods. Still, the Fund stressed that for many countries the balance of payments justification for existing restrictions was no longer valid, and that while there were, in some cases, security grounds for maintaining certain restrictions, the advantages of relaxing restrictions during a period of rearmament were impressive: a more efficient use of economic resources and an increase in the supply of goods for domestic consumption and investment. At the meeting of the Fund's Board of Governors in September, many members not only expressed great pessimism over the possibility during the foreseeable future of relaxing restrictions but also gave some evidence of being impatient with the Fund for devoting so much of its time and energies to the problem. United States Secretary of Treasury Snyder, however, defended the objectives—while recognizing that prospects of achieving them were remote—and the Fund's activities.

Although some countries relaxed certain exchange restrictions during the early part of the year, many strengthened or reimposed them during the last half and, on balance, there were probably more restrictions at the end than at the beginning of the year. An outstanding exception was the action by Canada (blessed by the Fund[2]) in removing all exchange controls as of December 1951.

The Fund continued its policy of urging those of its members

---

b) Sold by Norway in 1948 in exchange for U.S. dollars. Article V, Section 6a of the Agreement of the International Monetary Fund provides: "Any member desiring to obtain, directly or indirectly, the currency of another member for gold shall, provided that it can do so with equal advantage, acquire it by sale of gold to the Fund."

c) Repurchase obligations of members are not restricted solely to cases where purchases have been made by a member from the Fund (Article V, Section 7). In the case of Lebanon, it was required, because of increases in its monetary reserves, to repurchase its own currency so as to reduce the Fund's holdings of Lebanese pounds to 75 percent of that country's quota.

Source: International Monetary Fund, *International Financial Statistics*, Washington, D.C., January 1952, p. xi.

---

[2] In 1950 the Fund had "accepted" the decision by Canadian officials to abandon the fixed par value of the Canadian dollar.

having multiple exchange rates to unify them as quickly as possible,[3] but, while there were many changes in individual systems, the Fund reported that for the world as a whole there was no pronounced trend toward a decrease in such practices.[4]

The Fund Agreement specifies that member countries still retaining certain exchange restrictions[5] in March 1952 must consult with the Fund as to their retention. The Fund expressed the cautious hope that these consultations would result in some relaxations[6] but also stated that it was aware that many countries would find it necessary to maintain exchange restrictions for the time being.

b. PAR VALUES AND EXCHANGE RATES

Finland, Pakistan, and Sweden established initial par values for their currencies during 1951, and the Fund concurred in the depreciation proposed by Paraguay and Yugoslavia[7] for their respective currencies. None of these actions raised major policy issues.[8] In 1949 and 1950 the Fund had accepted, with reference to Peru and Canada, that there were circumstances where fixed rates were inappropriate and had in these cases recognized government

[3] For a theoretical treatment of certain aspects of multiple exchange rates, see Schlesinger, E. R., "Multiple Exchange Rates and Economic Development," International Finance Section, *Studies in International Finance*, Princeton University Press, May 1952.

[4] One particularly interesting action by the Fund with respect to multiple exchange rates was its approval of the devaluation in Colombia's "coffee buying" rate of exchange to be followed by progressive devaluation in this rate over the forty following months until it reached the buying rate which applied to all other exchange proceeds. (See International Monetary Fund, *International Financial News Survey*, November 2, 1951, p. 141.)

[5] Those inconsistent with Article VIII, Sec. 2, 3, or 4.

[6] The most important single case would be that of the United Kingdom; it was unofficially reported that the British Government would look upon the talks as a time merely for "informing" the Fund that their restrictions would not be removed. Contrarily, the United States and Canada were reported as viewing the time as one in which members would "ask permission" to retain the restrictions. (See *The Banker*, October 1951, p. 222.)

[7] The depreciation of the Yugoslav dinar by over 80 percent was in conjunction with the efforts of the Fund and Bank to make the economy of that country viable and to increase its exports (see *The Economist*, January 5, 1952, p. 16, for critical comments on this policy).

[8] In July, the U.S. Treasury signed a new Stabilization Agreement with Mexico which represented a continuation of the dollar-peso exchange rate stabilization arrangements between the two countries initiated in 1941. Under the agreement, the United States Stabilization Fund undertakes, until June 30, 1953, to purchase Mexican pesos up to the equivalent of $50 million if necessary.

decisions to have a fluctuating rate on the specific understanding that a par value would be established "as soon as circumstances warrant."[9] In their 1951 *Annual Report,*[1] the Executive Directors took note of the continuing interest in fluctuating-rate systems and argued that such systems were not "a satisfactory alternative" to the par value system—except in "occasional and exceptional circumstances where a country concludes that it cannot maintain *any* par value for a limited period of time, or where it is exceedingly reluctant to take the risks of a decision respecting a par value"—since (a) "There is no such thing as a 'natural' level for the rate of exchange of a currency," and the "proper" rate depends upon the various financial, economic, and monetary policies followed by many countries; (b) it takes a considerable length of time for any economy to adjust to a given rate and therefore "in the short run changes in the exchange rate provide no test or a very poor test of basic economic interrelationships" and that it is impossible to determine whether a rate is "correct" unless it is maintained for an extended period; (c) movements of fluctuating rates are "significantly affected by large speculative transfers of capital"; and (d) fluctuating rates do not give sufficient weight to the interests of other nations. No additional countries instituted fluctuating rates during 1951, and the Fund successfully discouraged Brazil from establishing a free market, alongside the official market, designed to legalize dealings in foreign notes and coins and encourage the inflow of foreign capital.[2]

In the spring of 1951, the Economic Commission for Europe had proposed, in the face of existing worldwide inflationary tendencies and the deterioration in European terms of trade, that European currencies be appreciated,[3] and there had been much talk in the

[9] France, Italy, and Thailand also had fluctuating rates, but the first had been opposed by the Fund and the last two countries had never established a par value for their currencies with the Fund.

See *Annual Report, 1951, op.cit.,* p. 40, for the intricate legal formulation by which the Executive Directors can recognize, without "approving," a departure of a member from the par value system.

[1] Pp. 36-41.

[2] See International Monetary Fund, *International Financial News Survey,* August 31, 1951, p. 65.

[3] Economic Commission for Europe, *Economic Survey of Europe in 1950,* Geneva, 1951, pp. 157-164.

For a theoretical discussion of some of the issues in currency appreciation during an inflationary period, see Hinshaw, R., "Currency Appreciation as an Anti-Inflationary Device," *Quarterly Journal of Economics,* November 1951, pp. 447-462,

press[4] of an upward revaluation of sterling.[5] Secretary of the Treasury Snyder expressed strong opposition to this so long as the United States was supplying large amounts of assistance to these countries, and a Governor of the Fund stated that the majority of its members were "strongly of the opposite view." Much of the public talk on appreciation then ceased. In its 1951 *Annual Report*, the Fund repeatedly expressed great concern over the severe inflationary pressures arising out of the rearmament programs and the consequent pressure on many of the members' balances of payments.[6] It went on to state, however, that a widespread currency appreciation in Europe was not a "suitable" means of dealing with these inflationary problems since such action would provide a strong upward impetus to world market prices in terms of dollars and would weaken the competitive position of Europe's exports and might result in a greater outlay for imports.[7] The Fund concluded that, since most of the sources of inflationary pressure were internal, they should be combatted primarily by internal methods (preferably fiscal and monetary) rather than by attempting to transfer these pressures elsewhere by an upward revolution of exchange rates.[8]

---

and the "Comments" on the article by Harrod, R. F., Hirschman, A. O., and Hinshaw, R., in the February 1952 issue of the same journal.

[4] For some current unofficial comment on the proposals for appreciation, see the *New York Times*, May 6 and 31, June 4, 6, 7, 9, 11, September 24, and October 1, 1951; *The Banker*, July 1951, pp. 7-27, and December 1951, pp. 351-356; *The Bankers' Magazine*, July 1951, pp. 1-4; and Kent, T. W., "1947 Comes Again," *Lloyd's Bank Review*, October 1951, pp. 1-18.

[5] For an essay holding that the 1949 sterling devaluation was a mistake and that sterling should be revalued upward, see Harrod, R. F., "The Pound Sterling," *Essays in International Finance No. 13*, International Finance Section, Princeton University, February 1952.

[6] The December 1950 United Nations resolution on international full employment (detailed in *Survey—1950*, pp. 161-166) recommended, among other things, that each government "furnish the Secretary General . . . with quantitative estimates of the main elements of the balance of international payments that it proposed to attain by 1954. . . ." Many members, including the United States, during 1951 submitted answers to questionnaires on their balance of payments policies and practices through 1951 (see *Balance of Payments Trends and Policies, 1950-1951*, UN Sales No.: 1951.II.D.3.), but the Economic and Social Council, because of the unsettled international conditions and lack of adequate statistics, temporarily relieved the Secretary General of responsibility for making a long-run study of the members' balances of payments.

[7] Pp. 33-36.

[8] The Fund continued to extend to its members technical help during the year. This largely took the form of studies and advice on such problems as the financial aspects of economic development programs, the processes of inflation in member

Gold Policy

From its establishment, the Fund, again with the strong support of the U.S. Government, has discouraged external sales of gold at premium prices on the ground that such sales tend to go into private hoards, thus not only reducing the proportion of the total gold supplies available for international monetary reserves but also directly or indirectly involving exchange dealings at depreciated rates and so disturbing the existing exchange relationships of its members. In pursuit of this policy, the Fund had attempted to specify the conditions under which the gold-producing nations could sell gold at premium prices so as to insure that such sales were for bona fide industrial, professional, or artistic purposes and not for private speculation or hoarding. Since 1949 the policy had been under severe attack by some of the members, especially South Africa,[9] and during 1951 there was a large increase in the volume of international gold transactions at premium prices and a decline in the proportion of newly-mined gold entering official monetary reserves. Gold production, outside the United States and Russia, has been estimated at some $760 million during 1951. Of this, only about $160 million went into official monetary reserves, with the remaining $600 million going into industrial uses, or private hoards, or otherwise accounted for.[1]

In the face of this, the Fund Executive Directors in March directed the staff of the Fund "urgently to elaborate, after consultation with the countries concerned, more effective methods than existing ones"[2] for implementing the established policy. Several members—especially South Africa, Canada, and Australia—subsequently urged that the Fund's policy be changed so as at least to generalize the conditions under which approved sales at premium prices could take place. Although official details are not available,

countries, monetary and credit policies, operational and policy problems of commercial and central banks, foreign exchange controls, and balance of payments conditions. The Fund also continued its program of training, in Washington, selected nationals of member countries in balance of payments techniques and in interpretation of monetary and economic data.

[9] See *Survey—1949*, pp. 122-127 and *Survey—1950*, pp. 158-161 for a summary of the Fund and United States gold policies during those years.

[1] "International Flow of Gold and Dollars," *Federal Reserve Bulletin*, Washington, D.C., March 1952, p. 230.

[2] *Annual Report, 1951*, p. 74. See also *New York Times*, March 8, 1951.

it has been reported that considerable pressure was applied on the Fund (and the United States) during the September meetings of the Board of Governors to alter the policy, and Secretary of the Treasury Snyder was reported as saying that, while his country supported the policy, it could not control the actions of other nations.[3]

Shortly after this meeting adjourned, the Fund issued a new gold statement reaffirming its previous policy and urging members to support it but stating that study had shown that it was "impracticable to expect all members to take uniform measures" to achieve the objectives of the Fund's policy and that therefore it was leaving "to its members the practical operating decisions involved in their implementation."[4] In announcing the new decision, the Fund's Managing Director stated that the only effective way of stopping private gold hoarding and removing premium prices was for member governments to pursue such internal fiscal and monetary policies as would give people confidence in their currencies and that supplementary controls by the Fund could attack only symptoms and not causes.[5]

Members were thus left free to handle their external gold sales as they saw fit, and the Fund anticipated that some countries which had not previously done so would now sell gold at premium prices. Some observers interpreted the new policy as a defeat for the Fund and an abdication of its authority.[6] Certainly, the policy had not been successful, and the Fund was no doubt glad to abandon it.

Following the Fund's announcement, South Africa stated that it would continue to allow its miners to make premium gold sales but would limit these to 40 percent of current production. Southern Rhodesia and West Africa followed suit. Canada and Australia

[3] See *The Statist*, September 22, 1951, p. 355.

[4] International Monetary Fund, *International Financial News Survey*, October 5, 1951, p. 109.

[5] The United States simultaneously announced that it concurred in the Fund's statement but that it planned to continue its policy of maintaining the present dollar price for gold and of limiting international transactions to those of central monetary authorities.

For an unofficial essay defending the United States policy with respect to the price of gold, see Kriz, M. A., "The Price of Gold," *Essays in International Finance, No. 15*, International Finance Section, Princeton University, July 1952.

[6] See, for example, *The Banker*, November 1951, pp. 290-294.

announced that they would permit some such sales[7] (no specific limitation was set on the amounts), but the former specified that any producers doing so must forego the domestic subsidy[8]; most producers chose to receive the subsidy. The free-market price of gold dropped an average of about $2 an ounce on the Fund's announcement, but, despite larger sales, part of this drop had been regained at year's end, when prices were frequently quoted at around $39 per ounce.

TABLE 13

Foreign Gold Transactions by the United States, 1951
(net purchases (+); net sales (−))
(millions of dollars)

Country	*First half*	*Second half*	*Year*
ERP Countries (other than United Kingdom)	−191	+36	−155
United Kingdom	−480	+950	+470
Other Europe	—	—	—
Union of South Africa	+13	+39	+52
Canada	−10	—	−10
Latin America	−164	+38	−126
Asia	−26	−31	−57
Egypt	−45	−31	−76
Bank for International Settlements	−34	+4	−30
Total	−937	+1005	+68

Source: Board of Governors of the Federal Reserve System, *Federal Reserve Bulletin,* Washington, D.C., March 1952, p. 230.

The large net outflow of gold which the United States experienced in foreign transactions during 1950 continued at an annual rate of nearly $3.5 billion during the first quarter of 1951. The outflow began to fall rapidly during the second quarter, the movement was reversed in the third quarter, and the net inflow was at an annual rate of nearly $3 billion during the last three months. With this reversal in flows, the unofficial speculation that the United States might raise its gold price faded away. As Table 13 shows, for the year as a whole there was a small net inflow. The transactions of the United Kingdom dominated the United States

[7] For all five countries sales were to be made against U.S. dollars, except that in South Africa the premium over the official dollar-gold price was accepted in other currencies.

[8] During March and May 1951 the Fund had concurred in two changes in the Canadian gold subsidy program. For details, see its *Annual Report, 1951,* pp. 73-74.

purchases and sales, and, in effect, the large net amount of gold sold by the United Kingdom to the United States was in turn purchased from the United States by the rest of the world. For the year, the United States made significant purchases only from the United Kingdom, the Union of South Africa, Colombia, and Uruguay, with net sales (or minor purchases) being recorded for all other countries. As of the end of the year, United States official gold stocks were valued at $22.9 billion—almost two-thirds of the world's gold reserves, excluding those of Russia, on which data are not available.

The Fund and EPU

The Fund had been, to say the least, unenthusiastic as to the desirability of establishing the European Payments Union, and the U.S. Government had not been of one mind in the matter, with ECA energetically pressing the European countries to establish such a regional payments arrangement and the U.S. Treasury expressing concern lest the Union conflict with the responsibilities and objectives of the Fund. Fund officials finally did participate in the discussions during the formative stage of the Union and, when agreement was reached in mid-1950 establishing the Union, it was also agreed that close cooperation and consultation between the two organizations was "desirable." Details as to the precise nature of the relationship between the two were left for further study. In their 1951 *Annual Report*, the Executive Directors of the Fund reported only that the Fund and EPU Managing Board were still considering the problem and that the Fund would continue to "study" the effects and significance of the Union's operations on the payment positions of the Fund's members. The various reports issued during the year by the EPU Managing Board and the OEEC made no mention of the Fund, and the question of the relationship between the two organizations was unresolved at year's end. At the September meeting of the Fund's Board of Governors, at least one Governor took occasion to point out that, while the Fund was providing almost no financial assistance to its members, EPU was extending credit to its members on a large scale and was an active and constructive force in international financial affairs.[9]

[9] See Chapter VII below for details of EPU's accomplishments and difficulties during the year.

United States officials admitted during the year that the Fund had not been able to play the role anticipated for it when it was established in 1947, but they reaffirmed their faith in the validity and desirability of the Fund's objectives, asserting that these objectives should be used as guides even in the storm of current problems since "there would never be another conference called that could plot a new course if we abandoned this one."[1]

[1] International Monetary Fund, *Fund Document No. 25, Sixth Annual Meeting of the Board of Governors,* September 12, 1951.

V · RECIPROCAL TRADE AGREEMENTS PROGRAM

THE Reciprocal Trade Agreements Program has been the heart of United States commercial policy since 1934. During 1950, the policies of the immediately preceding years were—by and large—vigorously pursued. Although the Administration abandoned attempts to gain Congressional approval of the ITO Charter, the Executive Branch gave notice that it would ask approval of measures designed to make United States participation in the General Agreement on Tariffs and Trade (GATT) "definitively effective," and Congress already had been asked to approve measures designed to simplify American customs administration. The United States also participated in two sessions of the Contracting Parties to the GATT held during 1950. As the year under review began, the United States was also taking part in a third round of tariff negotiations under the GATT, but the problem of maintaining foreign markets for American exports while reducing official aid, which had seemed so important a year before, had faded into the background under the impact of the free world's rearmament programs.

With security considerations beginning to dominate all of the nation's international economic affairs, the strategic aspects of commercial policy—especially problems of stockpiling, export controls, and the international allocation of scarce materials—began to take precedence over the Reciprocal Trade Agreements Program as such. Further, the acceleration of rearmament intensified most of the previous obstacles to the program, and many new ones were introduced as the United States and the rest of the free world increasingly abandoned free-enterprise economies in favor of state planning and direct controls. Still, the program remained as the core of the nation's long-term commercial policy. The basic legislation under which it had been carried out was due to expire in June 1951. In considering its extension, Congress had the opportunity to reassess past policies and to debate the role of the program during a period of partial mobilization; it took the former but not the latter opportunity.

A. *EXTENSION OF THE TRADE AGREEMENTS ACT*[1]

Both the Gray *Report*[2] and the Council of Economic Advisers' *Annual Economic Review*[3] urged that the Reciprocal Trade Agreements Act be renewed for at least three years and that, as an emergency measure, legislation be sought authorizing temporary unilateral reductions in import restrictions on goods in short supply as long as the emergency conditions continued. In presenting the Administration's program to Congress, President Truman did not request any special or new authority for meeting cases where trade barriers conflicted with the mobilization effort but asked only that the existing legislative authority be extended in unamended form for three more years. In presenting the case for a simple renewal of existing authority, Administration spokesmen stressed that the tariff reduction program as then conceived would be almost completed once the Torquay negotiations were finished and that the next three years would be largely a period of adjusting and consolidating past concessions—but the possibility of some new negotiations was not ruled out.

The Administration only briefly presented the program as aiding directly the nation's rearmament effort—both by the deflationary effect of larger imports and as a means, through closer contacts and larger trade, of "uniting and fortifying the free world against aggression."[4] Secretary Acheson argued that American efforts to expand world trade supported one of the main purposes of the rearmament program of the United States and its allies: that is, of creating conditions in the world under which all countries could ". . . without fear of aggression, pursue the uninterrupted, normal, fruitful intercourse between nations. Trade is one of the most

[1] The most important primary sources of information are: "1951 Extension of the Reciprocal Trade Agreements Act," *Hearings on H.R. 1612*, House of Rep., Committee on Ways and Means, 82d Cong., 1st Sess., January 1951; and "Trade Agreements Extension Act of 1951," *Hearings on H.R. 1612, Parts 1 and 2*, U.S. Senate, Committee on Finance, 82d Cong., 1st Sess., February-March 1951.

[2] *Report to the President on Foreign Economic Policies*, Washington, D.C., November 10, 1950, p. 15.

[3] Washington, D.C., January 1951, p. 123.

[4] Secretary Brannan, *Hearings on H.R. 1612, Part 1, op.cit.*, pp. 64 and 71. See also W. G. Brown's statement, *ibid., Part 2*, pp. 1165-1166.

important and most fundamental elements."[5] Administration spokesmen also maintained that the program not only aided Europe's recovery but also helped it to earn dollars to replace grant aid.

None of these strategic and "current" arguments were pursued in detail, and the Administration's statement that the next three years would be largely ones of consolidation implied that trade liberalization was not regarded as of major short-run strategic importance.[6] The Executive Branch chose rather to base its case for continuing the program mainly on the general, familiar, and pre-Korean bases of contributing to "building the kind of world trading system in which competition, equality of opportunity, and private enterprise can have their best opportunity to survive and develop," as a "symbol of United States determination to lead in the cooperative effort to expand world trade,"[7] and as a means of giving the rest of the world confidence in American leadership. It was also stated that the program was consistent with and supported the United Nations, the Point Four Program, and the expansion of private foreign investment. The assertion that it operated to enlarge the market for United States agricultural products found a receptive audience among many of the members of Congress representing the rural areas. The Administration did not discuss the question of whether a rearming world, with its state planning, direct controls, and discrimination, was so fundamentally inconsistent with the underlying assumptions of the trade agreements program in its wide aspects that any attempt to implement it was bound to failure.[8]

The Administration was supported before the Congressional

[5] *Ibid., Part 1,* p. 4.

[6] It is perhaps noteworthy that none of the defenders of the freer trade policy argued its strategic aspect in the sense of attempting to show that the comparative advantages of the United States were especially great in almost all the major branches of production which are most vital to a mobilized or garrison economy.

[7] *Hearings on H.R. 1612, Part 1, op.cit.,* pp. 3 and 5.

[8] See *ibid.,* pp. 14 ff., for Secretary Acheson's statement, in the face of contrary Congressional views, that some state trading was not incompatible with the practice of free private enterprise in general, that arrangements had been and could be worked out under the GATT and otherwise by which state trading "is carried out under principles which are consistent with the free enterprise system"; and that "considerable progress" had been made in ridding foreign countries of trade restrictions.

committees by such diverse and powerful groups, among others, as the United States Chamber of Commerce, American Farm Bureau Federation, Congress of Industrial Organizations, and the American Federation of Labor, as well as many civic groups. Extension of the Act was opposed in general and in principle by many individual business interests but by only a few private organizations (notably the American Tariff League) which based their opposition on the assertion that the effect of the program had been to do great injury to American industry. Some of these agreed that in the past the program had perhaps been "needed" in order to maintain exports but that this was no longer the case since other measures, especially official foreign aid of one kind or another, were being employed to maintain exports.[9]

A more interesting, though not new, challenge to some of the basic concepts of the program was provided by the argument that wages in many foreign countries were not rising *pari passu* with productivity and were relatively lower in terms of output than in the United States, with the result that American industry was being faced with "unfair" competition. Some private spokesmen suggested once again that an effective way of protecting United States labor and producers from this "exploited" labor abroad would be to offset the cost differential by imposing a *flexible* United States tariff, equal to "the difference between the cost of an article at the port of entry and the cost of production of the same article in our country."[1] Senator Malone was an ardent proponent of "equalization" of costs to gain both "fair and reasonable competition," but Congress showed little inclination to consider his specific proposals.[2] There was no serious danger of Congress

[9] The ECA program came in for criticism on the ground that it was being used to "crucify" American industry by building up competition in Europe and in third markets.

[1] *Congressional Record,* January 31, 1951, p. 843. This proposition was the governing principle for the Tariff Commission until suspended by the Trade Agreements Act of 1934.

[2] See *Congressional Record* (1951), pp. 1631-1642, 2563-2564, 2868-2869, 4435-4452, 5262-5264, 5317-5319, 5557-5561, 5626-5636 *passim,* 6023-6028, 10770 ff., and A3167, for details of the argument. Early in the year Senator Malone had introduced a bill (S. 981) whose object was to authorize such an approach and which also would have returned to Congress, already far behind in its schedule of work, much of the detailed responsibility for foreign trade policy. No action was taken on this measure, nor on one introduced by Senator Anderson (S. 220) which

abandoning completely the Reciprocal Trade Agreements Program.

Nevertheless, in both the hearings and debates there was much Congressional sentiment that the tariff concessions granted in recent years had harmed both the national and many individual interests in the United States.[3] Some argued in particular that, with respect to the national interest, damage had been suffered because the program was not in fact a reciprocal one; the American tariff reductions, they maintained, were in essence unilateral in view of the nontariff restrictions on imports maintained abroad. Supporters of the program tended to minimize this aspect, noting that tariff concessions would become more meaningful when conditions abroad were such that restrictions imposed for balance of payments reasons could be taken off, and did not attempt to take the affirmative position that such a unilateral reduction was perhaps called for by the postwar conditions in both the United States and foreign countries. Both Congress and private spokesmen expressed greater concern over the harmful effects of tariff concessions suffered by individual producers, and most of the discussion on extending the act revolved around the specific questions of providing greater protection to domestic enterprise by (a) writing an escape clause into the law, (b) inserting a peril points clause, (c) providing additional protection to agriculture, (d) withdrawing previous concessions to Communist nations; and (e) introducing a caveat on American participation in the GATT.[4]

Escape Clause

The standard escape clause—permitting any party to a trade agreement to modify or withdraw a concession which it finds has caused or threatens to cause serious injury to domestic producers—has been included (at first as a matter of administrative practice and later by terms of Executive Orders[5]) in all *new* trade agreements signed by the United States since 1943 and is a part of the

had some points in common. A sliding-scale plan for tariffs was also proposed by the Emergency Lead Committee for various metals (*New York Times*, March 11, 1951).

[3] The point was made that the Administration had used its authority under the Act only to lower and never to increase the 1930 tariff rates.

[4] For a statement in Congress supporting the Administration's position on these issues, see *Congressional Record*, January 31, 1951, pp. 857-864.

[5] Executive Order 9832, February 25, 1947; Executive Order 10004, October 5, 1948; Executive Order 10082, October 25, 1949.

GATT. In what the press reported was an effort to forestall Congressional criticism, the Administration had insisted in the summer of 1950 that the clause be inserted in the 1936 agreement with Switzerland.[6] However, there were still several pre-1943 agreements which did not include the clause and some Congressmen insisted that it be inserted in all existing agreements. The Administration opposed this action, arguing that where the clause had not been included the important parts of the agreement frequently merely bound the United States duties (or absence of them) on noncompeting agricultural products such as coffee and cocoa, in return for duty reductions on American exports, and so the inclusion of the clause might well prove more harmful to American exporters than its omission would to domestic producers. Further, it argued, a mandatory requirement that the clause be inserted would cost the United States dearly since the other country would insist on concessions in return and would know that the United States negotiators were operating under a legislative order. Despite these objections, Congress amended the Trade Agreements Act to require the President to take action "as soon as practicable" to insert the escape clause in existing agreements and to report to Congress every six months on such action as he had taken.[7]

Of greater policy significance was the desire of many private persons and members of Congress to make it easier for domestic producers to obtain relief under the escape clause and to increase Congressional authority over the day-to-day operations of the trade agreements program.[8] At the time of the discussion (early

[6] See *Survey—1950,* pp. 186-188 for a brief account of the operations under this clause during 1950.

[7] In his first report (*H. Doc. No. 328,* January 14, 1952, reprinted in Department of State *Bulletin,* January 28, 1952, pp. 143-148) the President stated that clauses, in conformity with the law, were contained in all but six agreements. Of these six agreements, that with Turkey was being terminated since Turkey was a new signatory to GATT and that with Venezuela was being renegotiated and the new agreement was "likely" to include the escape clause. A Subcommittee of the Interdepartmental Committee on Trade Agreements had been set up to formulate proposals with respect to the inclusion of the clause in the remaining four trade agreements—with Ecuador, El Salvador, Guatemala, and Honduras.

[8] Among the many producing groups requesting Congress to provide greater protection through the escape clause and the peril point procedure were the following: fruits and vegetables, wool, coal, watches, fountain pens and mechanical pencils, paper and pulp, meat, cotton, woven wire netting, feldspar, mushrooms, clothespins, lead, glass and china, pottery, fisheries, bookbinding and publishing, photoengravers, hats and millinery, shoes, gloves, furs, aluminum, copper, lead, zinc, cement, lime

1951), the Tariff Commission had received only twenty applications for relief and had invoked the clause only once.[9] The Administration presented this record as evidence that extreme care had been taken in negotiating trade agreements so as not to injure domestic producers, but several members of Congress interpreted the data to mean that procedures under the clause had been unfavorable to domestic producers.

After much emotional discussion,[1] the House amended the Act by inserting an escape clause provision designed to extend greater protection to domestic producers than was being provided under the current practices of the Administration. Any producer of "like or directly competitive products" claiming serious injury (in fact or threatened) was to be entitled to a full investigation and a public hearing by the Tariff Commission. Evidence of "serious injury or a threat thereof" was defined as "a downward trend of production, employment and wages in the domestic industry concerned, or a decline in sales and a higher or growing inventory attributable in part to import competition."[2] If the Commission found no serious injury or threat of such, it was required to make a public report of its finding.

Many members of the House believed that the Tariff Commission could not administer the escape clause effectively so long as the Commission was closely tied to State Department policy via its participation in the Trade Agreements Committee. Therefore, the House-approved measure specified that the Tariff Commission was no longer to participate in the Trade Agreements Committee.

When the measure was sent to the Senate, the Administration argued against these amendments. Its spokesmen stated that, as passed by the House, full investigation and public hearings were required regardless of the flimsiness of the case presented; that, as a result, attention of the already overworked Tariff Commission staff would be diverted from the more meritorious cases, and that the Tariff Commission was legally bound to find "injury" if the

---

and gypsum, chemicals, matches, clay tile, wallpaper, greenhouse vegetables, potatoes, and bicycles.

Not all these complainants could argue that they had been injured by tariff reduction, for some represented commodities on which the tariff had been bound; these and others simply argued that the existing (nonreduced) tariffs were injuriously low.

[9] See *Survey—1950*, p. 187.

[1] See, for example, *Congressional Record*, February 7, 1951, pp. 1077-1121.

[2] H.R. 1612, section 7(c).

"conditions" cited in the law were present even if such conditions did not in fact lead to injury.[3] The chairman of the Tariff Commission testified that it was his opinion that the escape clause as approved by the House would so widen possible action that it would require a termination or renegotiation of United States membership in the GATT; in particular, he stated, the General Agreement clause required an increase in imports as a condition for starting the escape clause procedure.

The Executive Branch made it clear that it was not opposed to the principle of the escape clause, asserting that protection was not "vicious" or "evil" if done "soundly" and "correctly." It argued, however, that the clause as presently applied by the Administration was adequate and that the House provision was "unworkable." In recognition of the strong Congressional sentiment for facilitating the obtaining of relief under the clause, Administration spokesmen did not insist that no clause be inserted in the law but urged that at least the House proposal be modified by (a) allowing the Tariff Commission to continue to sit with the Trade Agreements Committee, thus giving the latter group the benefit of the Commission's counsel, (b) eliminating the mandatory requirement of a public and full investigation of every complaint of injury, (c) merely listing the factors which might indicate injury but not specifying that they were "evidence of injury," (d) requiring that an "essential" finding, if injury were to be declared, be that imports had increased relatively to domestic production, and (e) providing that relief be given only to injury sustained as a result of concessions granted in a trade agreement.[4]

[3] The chairman of the Tariff Commission testified that the House bill's criteria of evidence of injury were considered by the Tariff Commission under existing procedures but that the existence of such conditions did not mean *prima facie* that the injury had been or would be sustained. He also stated, that under the existing law, relief could be given only if increases in imports were the result of concessions but that the conclusion usually drawn by the Commission was that if a concession exists it is in part responsible for any increase in imports. (*Hearings on H.R. 1612, Part 2, op.cit.*, pp. 1320-1330 and 1356-1394.)

[4] This argument was presented by the Administration in the face of insistence by some members of Congress that the escape clause be so broadened that domestic producers suffering injury from import competition be given relief in the form of an increased tariff or imposition of a quota even if there had been no concession in a trade agreement (see *ibid.*, pp. 1002-1003).

Another procedure which may be followed when escape from injury is desired and there is no concession on the item under a trade agreement is exemplified in the attempt to provide relief to the Pacific Coast tuna fish industry from Japanese competition. The House passed a bill (H.R. 5693), after a favorable report from the

As finally approved by both Houses, some of the Administration's requests were honored, but Congress did make it easier procedurally to obtain relief from tariff concessions and effectively reassumed a greater degree of indirect supervision over the administration of the escape clause. Representatives of the Tariff Commission were permitted to continue to sit with the Trade Agreements Committee as the Administration had requested. The Commission was required to make an investigation and hold public hearings not only, as before, where it has reason to believe that serious injury or threat of injury existed but also when so directed by the Senate Committee on Finance and/or the House Ways and Means Committee. In making its determination of whether injury has been sustained or is threatened as a result of imports arising out of a reduction or binding of a duty (or other concession) under the Trade Agreements Act the Commission was required to "take into consideration a downward trend of production, employment, prices, profits, or wages, in the domestic industry concerned, or a decline in sales, an increase in imports, either actual or relative to domestic production, a higher or growing inventory, or a decline in the proportion of the domestic market supplied by domestic producers."[5] If, after full investigation, the Commission decides that no modification of tariff concessions is required, it must, as it previ-

Ways and Means Committee (*H. Rpt. No. 1153*, October 12, 1951), imposing a duty of three cents per pound on imported tuna fish, fresh or frozen. The duty was to remain in effect until April 1, 1953, during which time the Tariff Commission was charged with making a study of the competitive position of the American tuna fish industry and the Secretary of Interior with making a long-range study—both to be reported to Congress by January 1, 1953. The State Department was reported as appreciating "the unique nature of the situation, the temporary character of the duty, and the basic studies which are to be undertaken." (*Congressional Record*, October 15, 1951, p. 13491.) The domestic tuna fish fleet was said to be tied up almost completely because of the low price of imported tuna, and the duty was said to give the minimum amount of relief necessary to activate the fleet. The measure was sent to the Senate Committee on Finance; it did not report it during the 1951 session but it was scheduled for early consideration in 1952.

An additional means of obtaining an increase in tariff is provided under Section 336 of the Tariff Act of 1930 which allows petitions to the Tariff Commission for review of the rate necessary to equalize foreign and domestic cost of production. Only two applications were presented in 1951 and both were denied and dismissed, indicating that this procedure is not important in providing tariff relief.

[5] P.L. 50, Section 7, 82d Cong., 1st Sess. For an example of the data submitted to the Tariff Commission by an industry requesting relief, see that presented by the American Watch Association for the Commission's "Investigation Number 4, under Part III of Executive Order 10082," U.S. Tariff Commission, Washington, D.C., 1951.

ously had in practice, publish the conclusions and the "findings." If injury is found, the Commission, as before, must make a report to the President, who is to take appropriate action in the area of duties, quotas, or other modifications of the trade agreement to prevent or remedy the injury. In addition, the new law provides that if the President does not take action within sixty days he must make a report to the appropriate committees of both Houses.

Peril Points

Intermingled with the debate on the escape clause was the question of the so-called "peril points" procedure. Congress had introduced this provision in the 1948 extension of the Trade Agreements Act. It required the President to inform Congress whenever he proposed reducing a tariff rate below the minimum, as determined by the Tariff Commission, necessary to avoid serious injury to a domestic industry. The clause was repealed in 1949[6]—both opponents and supporters of it usually agreed that it provided more protection than the escape clause—but the increasing number and vehemence of complaints by domestic producers of injury and inadequate relief under the escape clause led in 1951 to a majority of the Congress supporting reinstatement of the clause.

The proponents in the House argued that the effective operation of the provision (as with the escape clause) required that the Tariff Commission no longer participate in the Trade Agreements Committee so that its decisions and recommendations would not be influenced by the State Department and so that the Trade Agreements Committee would be provided with competent, expert, nonpartisan information for guidance in tariff negotiations. They supported the provision also with the claims that producers of strategic defense items (minerals and wool were most frequently named) would not be further injured by tariff concessions and that serious cutbacks in employment would be prevented. Several Republican members broadened the base for their position by stating that they had received a mandate from the voters in the last Congressional elections to regain some of the Congressional powers which had in the past been delegated to the President and that the peril points clause was one means of curtailing

[6] See *Survey—1949*, p. 155.

Presidential authority and restoring more power over trade and tariffs to the Legislative Branch.[7]

In reply to the criticism on the floor that the clause was fundamentally a return to narrow protectionism and served to concentrate attention on the short-run welfare of specific domestic industries rather than on the broader and longer-run national and international considerations, some of the Congressional advocates of the clause maintained that, after all, the President could authorize concessions below the peril points when he deemed it in the national interest but that he would have to explain why. Some other supporters of the clause were not prepared to concede so much and stated that in practice Congress would not allow the peril points to be exceeded.[8]

Administration spokesmen testified in the hearings that the clause was both unnecessary and undesirable. Secretary Acheson stated that it was *unnecessary* because the Administration accepted the doctrine that "no American industry or agriculture or segment thereof would be seriously injured under the Act,"[9] and because there were other safeguards in the escape clause and in the authority to impose quotas for the protection of agriculture.[1] The fact that "relief" had been granted in only a few cases under these procedures was taken by some Congressmen to indicate their inadequacy, and they stressed that the escape clause was available only after the determination of actual or potential injury and then only by a lengthy procedure.[2]

The Administration and its supporters in Congress maintained that the peril points provision also was *undesirable* on several counts. They argued, in general, that it introduced new rigidities into a program where considerable flexibility was necessary if ne-

[7] See especially *Congressional Record,* February 7, 1951, pp. 1082-1096.

[8] *Ibid.,* pp. 1079-1085.

[9] *Hearings on H.R. 1612, op.cit.,* p. 15.

[1] Section 22 of the Agricultural Adjustment Act.

[2] Several Congressmen questioned the genuineness of the stated Administration policy of protecting American producers, and, in this connection, asked for information on the extent to which the concessions granted at Annecy in 1949 went below the peril points determined by the Tariff Commission in accordance with the 1948 Act. The Administration replied that such information was confidential because publication of the points would irritate foreign countries as a result of their not having been given all that United States negotiators could have offered and that such reactions would weaken the Administration's hand in future bargaining. Some Congressmen considered this a "very offensive" reply which implied that members of Congressional committees could not keep a secret.

gotiations were to be successful and that it would in fact provide more protection and so was inconsistent with the overall foreign economic policy of the United States and with its efforts to get the Western European nations to increase their dollar exports, to severely restrict their trade with Eastern Europe, and to integrate their economies.[3] More particularly, the opponents of the proposal stated that: (a) the determination on peril points would be made without the benefit of facts developed in actual negotiations, meaning that inadequate attention would be given to the interrelationships of domestic and foreign industries and of exports and imports; (b) the Trade Agreements Committee would lose the benefit of consultations with the Tariff Commission on policies to be followed; (c) it was, as a matter of practice, impossible to determine with precision a point at which concessions would result in injury and, since it must be on the basis of *estimates* of *possible* effects, the point selected would be higher than necessary because the Tariff Commission would be under pressure to "play it safe"; and (d) there would be little room left for effective tariff negotiation with other countries—if negotiators went below the established point the Administration would be criticized by domestic interests and if they did not go to this point the other party to the tariff negotiation would find the Administration's position unreasonable.

These objections were not strong enough to overcome sentiment for the provision, and the House passed the amendment reinstituting the peril points by the substantial majority of 225 to 168. Before the Senate Committee on Finance, Acheson argued the same points as had been presented on the House floor and quoted with approval a press editorial which stated that "the philosophy underlying the 'peril point' amendment, however, is the philosophy of a country cowering in its corner and unwilling to put its great system of free enterprise to the competitive test."[4] Neither the Administration's arguments nor this quotation received a warm reception in the Senate Committee; and the Administration, bowing to the inevitable, formally requested that, if the peril point clause were to be retained, at least the Tariff Commission should be allowed to continue on the Trade Agreements Committee.

[3] See, for example, *Congressional Record,* February 7, 1951, p. 1098.
[4] *Hearings on H.R. 1612, Part 1, op.cit.,* p. 7.

On the Senate floor there was no questioning of the desirability of the clause, and it was accepted without debate.[5] The final Act did allow the Tariff Commission to continue to participate in the Trade Agreements Committee, but it reinstituted the peril points provision, requiring a determination by the Tariff Commission (with the advice of other departments) of the minimum point below which a tariff reduction was likely to cause injury to domestic industry. If the Administration proposes any tariff concession or modification which goes below this point, the Act requires the President to notify Congress.

Protection of Agricultural Products and Furs

For many years, most conflicts between domestic agricultural policy and foreign economic policy have been resolved in favor of the former.[6] The extension of the Trade Agreements Act in 1951 provided another occasion for increasing the protection of American agriculture. Some Congressmen expressed much concern over the fact that certain agricultural products were being imported at a time when identical products were being purchased by the Commodity Credit Corporation under the agricultural price-support program. The House amended the Act to provide that a concession or reduced tariff should be suspended with respect to any item subsidized under the price-support program whenever the "sales price" of the imported commodity after duty was equal to or lower than the price-support level.

During the Senate Committee consideration of the House bill, the Administration argued that the amendment must not be allowed to stand for it would destroy the Reciprocal Trade Agreements Program and would not accomplish the results aimed at, namely, prosperity of the farmers. Executive Branch spokesmen maintained that this clause would make it impossible for the Government to make binding tariff concessions and that, as a result, trade agreements as they were known simply could not be negotiated. The Secretary of Agriculture bore the brunt of the

[5] It is to be noted that although the Senate devoted three days to the Trade Agreements Act, in fact it did little more than listen during this period to Senator Malone talk in favor of the "flexible-fee" system for the promotion of "fair and reasonable competition" noted above.

[6] See *Survey—1949*, pp. 160-162; *Survey—1950*, pp. 199-206; and Section F, below.

Administration's case in this discussion. Neither he nor his Congressional examiners questioned the desirability of the price-support program or the assumption that it should take precedence over the Reciprocal Trade Agreements Program.[7] The Secretary argued rather that the amendment would require a suspension of trade agreement concessions even when the increased imports were temporary and would fall off in a short time without impairing the price-support operations or causing serious injury to domestic producers; that any reciprocal automatic cessation of concessions by others (which retaliation must be anticipated) would damage United States agricultural interests more through curtailing exports than they would be aided by the reduced imports, since exports far exceeded imports and the bulk of the importing countries abroad tended to be high-cost producers as compared with the United States, with the result that a given formula would operate more quickly for them;[8] and, further, that speculation on a wide scale would be invited to take advantage of duty fluctuations. Secretary Brannan asserted that the United States was getting along fine with its various agricultural programs and that an analysis had shown that American farmers would have received almost no benefit if the proposed amendment had been in force in 1949 and 1950. In any case, he stated, domestic agricultural interests could be more effectively protected by recourse, if necessary, to the other "safeguards" which were available, particularly the escape clause and import quotas.[9]

The Committee on Finance deleted the amendment, but gave as its reason that it believed the clause impossible to administer. It observed, however, that the existing Trade Agreements Act limited the power of the Administration to employ import quotas in pro-

[7] Although price supports and tariffs were sometimes seen as alternative means of subsidizing agriculture (see statement of Senator Wherry in *Congressional Record*, May 22, 1951, p. 5739), agricultural interests were not averse to the employment of both measures.

[8] It was never clear from the discussion whether the Secretary was referring to exports of the same items as those imported being more important or exports of other agricultural products on which concessions had been received. He stated, however, that he had never suggested, and would resist, the United States granting import concessions on one agricultural product in order to obtain concessions on another (Senate *Hearings on H.R. 1612, Part 1, op.cit.*, p. 75). In this position the Secretary of Agriculture was in opposition to the established policy of the Administration.

[9] Import quotas are permitted under Section 22 of the Agricultural Adjustment Act, under the Sugar Act, under various Articles, notably XI and XX, of the GATT, and under P.L. 590, 81st Cong., 2d Sess.

tection of agriculture, as provided under Section 22 of the Agricultural Adjustment Act, by specifying that no action under the section should be in conflict with obligations under a trade agreement or under GATT. Therefore, it proposed an amendment stating that no trade or other international agreement ("heretofore or hereafter entered into by the United States") shall be applied in a manner "inconsistent with the requirements" of Section 22.[1] This amendment was incorporated into the final law. Additional protection to agricultural products classed as "perishable" was also provided in an amendment designed to speed up action under Section 22 and under the escape clause procedure.[2]

Efforts in 1949 to impose special restrictions on the importation of furs had been rejected by Congress. The problem of increasing imports and decreasing markets for domestic fur producers was raised again in both Houses in 1951, and the Senate accepted an amendment to restrict imports of certain specified furs to 25 percent of domestic production. In the Senate-House conference on the measure, this clause was stricken, but the law as approved required the President to prevent, as soon as practicable, the importation of several specified furs from Russia and Communist China.[3]

When President Truman signed the extension Act, he lauded Congress for reaffirming the United States determination "to expand trade by the reduction or elimination of barriers and thus to build up the strength of the free world." But in the same message he criticized the action of Congress in reassuming responsibility for details of commercial policy: "I am very much concerned at the fact that some of these new provisions single out particular types of products for special consideration. One of the basic principles of the trade agreements program, repeatedly enunciated in

[1] Some Senators argued that even stronger provisions were needed to protect agriculture.

[2] See *Congressional Record,* May 23, 1951, pp. 5805-5808, for a statement of how this amendment came into being. Under this amendment the President was empowered to take action under Section 22 immediately and without prior investigation. Investigation by the Tariff Commission under the escape clause was required in those cases to be completed within twenty-five days, as compared with the one year allowed in ordinary escape clause cases.

[3] In August 1951 a bill (H.R. 5284) was introduced to prohibit the import of certain additional furs, but the proposal was not considered by Congress.

In December, United States fur manufacturers complained of the rising cost of furs due to the ban on imports from Russia, asserting that the restriction was purely protectionist since no other imports from Russia and China were embargoed. (*New York Times,* December 9, 1951.)

the Congress, is that the Congress should confine its legislative mandate in this field to general principles. The dangers of reverting to product-by-product legislation in the field of tariffs are obvious."[4]

Withdrawal of Concessions to Communist Areas

Increased protection of fur producers was made easy by the fact that most of the competition came from Communist-dominated countries. The increasing sentiment to curtail trade with Communist-oriented countries showed itself primarily in efforts to restrict exports to these nations (see Chapter VI, Sections A and B). But it was also reflected in the introduction of at least seven concurrent resolutions in the House early in the year which would have restricted imports from these countries by requiring the President to rescind any existing trade agreements with Communist-controlled countries. The House committee considering the extension of the Trade Agreements Act did not report out such a provision, but an amendment offered from the floor prohibiting the universalization of concessions[5] to those nations—publicly determined by the President to be dominated by the governments or organizations controlling the "world Communist movement"[6]—in any future trade agreement with other countries was accepted by the House. Congressional discussion on this issue was not distin-

[4] For the full text of his statement, see Department of State *Bulletin*, July 2, 1951, pp. 16-17.

[5] Many of the concessions extended to Russia and its satellites came about under the multilateralization of the unconditional most-favored-nation clause contained in the trade agreements entered into by the United States. The Trade Agreements Act of 1934 provides for this extension of benefits: "The proclaimed duties and other import restrictions shall apply to articles [which are] the growth, produce, or manufacture of all foreign countries whether imported directly or indirectly. . . ." The law also authorizes the President to suspend the application of this provision to the goods of any country "because of its discriminatory treatment of American commerce or because of other acts or policies which in his opinion tend to defeat the purposes" of the Act. (Section 350 of the Tariff Act of 1930, as amended in 1934, 19 U.S.C.A. Sect. 1351.)

Many Congressmen vented a critical impatience with the State Department when one of its spokesmen testified that the Department had no plans, and saw no reason, for restricting the universal application of the most-favored-nation treatment. Subsequently, the State Department did state that it was possible for security reasons that a broad and vigorous attack on the whole problem of trade with Communist countries might be needed but not a "halfway measure" such as the above amendment by the House. For a discussion of East-West trade issues see Chapter VI, Section B below.

[6] Presumably the words "world Communist movement" excluded Yugoslavia.

guished by a severe analytical approach.[7] Many of those who supported the provision did so on the ground that it was "obviously wrong" to trade with, or grant concessions to, countries which were directly or indirectly killing American soldiers in Korea. In addition, many favored the amendment on the grounds that many of these concessions had been granted by the United States on a unilateral rather than reciprocal basis.

Before the Senate Committee, the State Department maintained that if the problem were one of injury to domestic producers a remedy existed under the escape clause. Executive Branch spokesmen also testified that the amendment as approved by the House probably would not reduce the volume of trade with these countries[8] but that it would violate existing treaties with Poland and Hungary and the trade agreement with Czechoslovakia under the GATT and that, in general, it would be an irritant to political relations without producing the desired commercial results. The State Department insisted that it was undesirable to open the United States to charges of such treaty violation, especially since the United States had repeatedly made the same charge against the Soviet Union. In recognition of strong Congressional sentiment for some such new clause in the law, the State Department urged that, at the least, the President should not be required to determine publicly which countries were "Communist-dominated"; that the clause should be made to apply only when the President "determines such action would further the national security of the United States";[9] and that provision should be made whereby concessions might be suspended—rather than withdrawn—so that they could be restored quickly if it appeared that the foreign country was moving away from Communism.

Although the Senate Committee seemed impressed at the time by some of the Administration's arguments, it subsequently proposed a broadening of the provisions of the House amendment to include both past and future agreements. The House concurred and the final law read as follows:

"As soon as practicable, the President shall take such action as

[7] For an extreme example of the emotional content of the discussion, see *Congressional Record,* January 31, 1951, p. 869.

[8] The implicit argument seems to have been that the Communist countries would simply absorb any increase in the United States tariff.

[9] *Hearings on H.R. 1612, Part 2, op.cit.,* p. 995.

is necessary to suspend, withdraw or prevent the application of any reduction in any rate of duty, or binding of any existing customs or excise treatment, or other concession contained in any trade agreement entered into under authority of section 350 of the Tariff Act of 1930, as amended and extended, to imports from the Union of Soviet Socialist Republics and to imports from any nation or area dominated or controlled by the foreign government or foreign organization controlling the world Communist movement."[1]

Caveat on GATT

In late 1950, the State Department had announced that the ITO Charter would not be resubmitted to the 82d Congress but that Congress would be asked to approve the creation of certain permanent administrative machinery to permit the GATT to operate efficiently.[2] The mood of Congress in early 1951, however, was one of increasing hostility to such generalized undertakings, and no such legislation was proposed by the Administration. But Congress insisted on expressing its views on the GATT.[3] Several members objected to Czechoslovakia's receiving benefits under it and others complained that by virtue of membership in GATT the United States had accepted certain restrictions on its own commercial policy. More important were the frequent assertions that several of the commercial policy provisions of the ITO had been incorporated

[1] P.L. 50, Section 5, 82d Cong., 1st Sess.

[2] See *Survey—1950,* pp. 172-177 and 181 for a summary of the developments which immediately preceded this decision to abandon the ITO. Under leading questioning, Secretary Acheson stated in unqualified terms, in 1951, that it was his firm policy that the ITO would *never* be resubmitted to Congress. (See *Hearings on H.R. 1612, Part 1, op.cit.,* pp. 10-13.) He also elaborated a bit on the reasons for abandoning the ITO: "The support which we hoped would develop for the ITO did not develop; and, on the contrary, a great deal of opposition developed for it and it seemed a fruitless effort to go forward with it." Only Liberia had previously unconditionally ratified the Charter; the Australian and Swedish parliaments had ratified it conditional on the United States and, in Australia's case, the United Kingdom taking similar action. Following the United States decision to drop the ITO, all the other signatories abandoned their efforts to obtain legislative ratification of the Charter. It should be recorded here that some of the principles embodied in it were finding expression in other international undertakings, e.g., the GATT and certain aspects of the International Materials Conference, the Schuman Plan, and in the ECOSOC deliberations and resolutions, etc.

[3] Almost the entire volume of Part 2 of the Senate *Hearings on H.R. 1612, op.cit.,* is devoted to discussion of the GATT, with Mr. Winthrop G. Brown, Director of the Office of International Trade Policy of the State Department, presenting the Administration's position. This volume is a valuable source of detailed, official information on the General Agreement.

into the GATT although Congress had not been given an opportunity to approve these principles. Administration spokesmen maintained that authority for everything the United States had agreed to under the GATT was provided in the Trade Agreements Act and under the executive power of the President, but many Congressmen believed that some of the actions taken by the Contracting Parties went beyond that which Congress had—or at least thought it had—specifically authorized. To make certain that the Administration recognized that Congress did not consider it had given its approval to all the policies followed under the GATT, the following caveat was written into the 1951 extension of the Trade Agreements Act: "The enactment of this Act shall not be construed to determine or indicate the approval or disapproval by the Congress of the Executive Agreement known as the General Agreement on Tariffs and Trade."[4]

B. *CUSTOMS SIMPLIFICATION*

As a part of its trade agreements program in the broad sense, the Administration has been attempting for several years to simplify United States tariff administration and customs procedures. Certain reforms could be and were undertaken without changes in the law, but many of the reforms urged by importers, desired by the Administration, and necessary to fulfill United States obligations under GATT required new legislation.[5] An Administration-sponsored measure for customs simplification was sent to Congress in May 1950 but was not acted upon by that session of Congress. An identical measure was reintroduced in the 1951 session.[6] This measure was discussed at length, amended, and finally approved by the House, but the Senate took no action on it during the year under review.

The Treasury Department had primary responsibility for drafting this complex and technical measure and bore the brunt of justifying the specific provisions before the House Committee on Ways and Means. The Department of State presented the Ad-

[4] P.L. 50, 82d Cong., 1st Sess., Section 10.

[5] See *Survey—1950*, pp. 190-194 and *Survey—1949*, pp. 131 and 159.

[6] H.R. 1535. Various other bills relating to particular aspects of customs administration were offered by members of Congress but were later incorporated in the bill which was returned by the committee to the floor of the House (H.R. 5505).

ministration's case for customs simplification in general.[7] The latter case was based largely on the ground that unnecessary impediments to the free world's dollar exports should not be continued at a time when the United States was extending financial aid and urging greater economic and political cooperation among these countries. State Department spokesmen argued that capricious and arbitrary treatment of imports led to retaliation and friction and that the bill was a "costless way of adding to the good-will of the nations of the free world and to fruitful and friendly trade between them."[8] They also stated that, as a general principle, any protection which the country wished to give domestic producers should be open and apparent and not via administrative procedures. While maintaining that it was not the intent of the measure to reduce tariff levels or relax protection against foreign "dumping," they admitted[9] that customs simplification probably would increase trade and decrease protection.

As in the debate on extending the Trade Agreements Act, some Congressmen charged that this measure was an attempt by the Administration to bring in Congressional approval of the GATT by the back door. State Department spokesmen denied this, asserting that the Administration would support the bill even if GATT did not exist; however, they stressed that the measure was consistent with GATT and if approved by Congress would make it easier for the Administration to obtain through GATT the application by other countries of the same procedures, thus eliminating some of the arbitrary and discriminatory regulations frequently facing American exporters. The House committee was specifically told, however, that approval of the bill did not mean approval of the GATT and, in fact, that the United States needed to make at least two additional legislative changes before the GATT could

[7] The major 1951 primary sources of information on United States policy regarding customs simplification are "Simplification of Customs Administration," *Hearings on H.R. 1535*, House of Rep., Committee on Ways and Means, 82d Cong., 1st Sess., September 1951, and *Congressional Record*, October 15, 1951, pp. 13442 ff. See also Ostroff, N., "Customs Reform: Character and Purpose of Proposed Legislation," Department of Commerce, *Foreign Commerce Weekly*, May 8, 1950, pp. 8 ff.

[8] *Hearings on H.R. 1535, op.cit.*, p. 610.

[9] It is to be noted that the correct verb here is "admitted" and not "affirmed." During these hearings in the late summer of 1951, the Administration was very much on the defensive vis-à-vis Congress with respect to the policy of increasing world trade—especially United States imports.

be made "definitely effective": one was revision of its copyright laws,[1] and the other was removing the export prohibition on tobacco seeds.[2] But the Executive Branch did not think the present was a propitious time to press for these two measures. Indeed, further evidence that this was a year of retreat by the Administration—in the face of a critical Congress—as respects its oft-repeated long-term commercial policy objectives, was supplied by the State Department testimony that it was not pressing for approval of GATT and had "not been thinking recently about the problem of getting the GATT definitely approved."[3]

To avoid any suggestion that they were approving GATT by passing the customs simplification measure, the majority of the House eliminated several of the provisions in the Administration's measure which were similar to articles of GATT but which were not obviously desirable in the sense of lowering the costs of customs administration without reducing protection.[4] The House gave wholehearted approval to the committee amendment that "the enactment of this act shall not be construed to determine or indicate the approval or disapproval of the Congress of the executive agreement known as the General Agreement on Tariffs and Trade."

The measure itself was long, technical, and complicated, covering a wide variety of items, ranging from such important matters as methods of valuation to such relatively unimportant things as correction of errors. The most important and controversial provisions related to the method of valuing imports.[5]

[1] A bill for this purpose was before the Judiciary Committee of the House but no action was taken by it in 1951. See *Survey—1950*, p. 199n, for a statement of the problem.

[2] No bill was before Congress on this measure although State Department spokesmen stated that the Administration expected to present such a measure at some time in the future since the prohibition was unrealistic and ineffective, mainly because enough seeds could be carried in one's hip pocket to start a plantation.

[3] *Hearings on H.R. 1535, op.cit.*, p. 640.

[4] The House committee itself had deleted more than half the volume of the original measure. The National Council of American Importers testified before the House committee that the Administration's measure was a long step toward needed reforms but that even the Treasury proposals should be expanded and added to. (See *Hearings on H.R. 1535, op.cit.*, p. 260.)

[5] Space does not permit detailed treatment of all the provisions. The House did accept the Treasury's recommendations for reducing the penalties for nonfraudulent declarations, for simplifying and reducing the special marking requirements on imported goods, for liberalizing the value of goods which travelers could bring back into the United States duty-free and for small-value imports sent in as gift parcels, for liberalizing the effective rates of duty on commingled imports, and for using

The Administration's proposal was, with respect to determination of the value of imports subject to *ad valorem* duties, to abolish "American selling price" as a basis and replace the use of "foreign value" or "export value," whichever is higher, by the universal application of "export value," whenever it was ascertainable.[6] The Administration favored these changes on the grounds that they would (a) eliminate many costly delays and increase the administrative efficiency of the Customs Bureau, since "foreign value" was difficult to determine, (b) make United States practices consistent with the "logical" and "realistic" provisions of the GATT, (c) provide a commercially realistic and equitable procedure for customs valuation, and (d) do away with the present practice of "arbitrary and unreasonable additions to the ordinary value of some imported merchandise."[7]

The House accepted—as did even the American Tariff League—the deletion of "foreign value" in favor of "export value" as the primary basis for valuing American exports. The major debate on valuation procedures revolved around the question of abolishing "American selling price" as a base. This particular criterion had been imposed by Congress to permit effective duties in excess of 100 percent of export value while still maintaining the general Congressional policy of not legislating *rates* in excess of 100 per-

International Monetary Fund certified par values, where such existed, for currency conversion purposes. The United States had pressed in the GATT for equal treatment by all signatories of domestic and imported products, and the House accepted the Treasury proposal to abandon the processing tax on certain imports of oil-bearing substances in favor of import duties designed to provide the same protection as previously existed to domestic fat and oil producers, but rejected the Treasury proposal to remove certain discriminatory internal revenue taxes on imported distilled spirits.

The Administration's proposal to change the criteria for imposing anti-dumping duties, designed to make the law consistent with the intent of GATT and certain practices of the Customs Bureau, was rejected by the House on the ground that it would decrease protection. Such duties were of no practical significance since the only existing "finding" of dumping—wool knitted berets from France—was revoked during 1951. The House did accept the Administration's proposal that injury—actual or threatened—be a precedent condition for imposing countervailing duties.

[6] If "export value" were not ascertainable—the Treasury testified it could be calculated in 95 percent of the cases—then "United States value," "comparative value" and "constructed value" ("cost of production") were to be used in turn.

[7] *Hearings on H.R. 1535, op.cit.*, p. 21. The Treasury made the point that not only was "foreign value" extremely difficult to determine but frequently the use of "foreign value" for identical products led to discrimination among supplying countries. For additional comment, see Savell, I., "The Value Dilemma," *American Import and Export Bulletin*, October 1951, pp. 837-838.

cent.[8] For some years, Congress had restricted the application of this valuation base to coal-tar and organic chemical products. The Treasury argued for elimination of this procedure on the grounds that it was inconsistent with the GATT, that tariff theory required that the basis of valuation for duty purposes should be the value of the product imported, and that arbitrary valuations should be eliminated so that the tariff schedule would be more indicative of the actual level of protection. In order not to result in an effective reduction in duties for the products affected, the Treasury proposed that the import duties on them be raised; it estimated that on some products the duties might have to be raised up to 300 percent of export value. The domestic chemical industry[9] and some Congressmen argued that the Tariff Commission simply could not in practice find a tariff structure which would compensate for the loss of protection under the existing valuation procedures inasmuch as the latter reflected current changes in domestic prices and no tariff schedule based on export values could do so. The majority of the House were convinced that the Treasury's proposals would lower the protection to the chemical industry, and they therefore rejected the proposal that the "American selling price" basis for valuation be eliminated.

The bill, as reported by the Committee, was passed without extensive debate and was then referred to the Senate Committee on Finance. That group took no action during 1951, and it was placed well down on the Committee's calendar at the beginning of the 1952 session.

C. *TARIFF NEGOTIATIONS AND TRADE AGREEMENTS*

Torquay Tariff Negotiations

The third round of tariff negotiations under the GATT took place at Torquay, England, from September 28, 1950 to April 21, 1951.[1]

[8] For a brief discussion of certain other practices which result in effective *ad valorem* duties far in excess of the published rates (to 1,000 percent and over), see *Hearings on H.R. 1535, op.cit.*, pp. 150, 154, 190, and 191.

[9] See *ibid.*, pp. 322-344, and the *Commercial and Financial Chronicle*, September 20, 1951, p. 18.

[1] For official accounts of the problems and results of the Torquay negotiations, see especially Department of State, *Analysis of Torquay Protocol of Accessions, Schedules, and Related Documents: General Agreement on Tariffs and Trade*, Com-

A brief account of the major policies and issues during the first several months was given in the immediately previous volume of this *Survey* and need not be repeated in detail here.[2] The major deterrents to reductions of trade barriers during the negotiations were reported to have been the following: many of the relatively nonpainful concessions had already been granted at Geneva and Annecy; the United States was bound by the Trade Agreements Act to grant concessions only on a reciprocal basis and could reduce rates to not more than one half those in effect in June 1945—for many items this had already been done; some of the low-tariff countries desired to obtain reductions from the high-tariff countries in return for merely binding their rates; several of the European members had lowered their quantitative restrictions on imports as part of the OEEC-ECA trade liberalization program[3] and so could no longer grant tariff concessions and then offset their effect by direct controls; a general feeling of uncertainty as to the economic effects of rearmament with a resulting reluctance to introduce additional possibly upsetting forces by lowering import barriers; a reluctance to engage in new negotiations at a time when some members had stated their intention of modifying or withdrawing previous concessions; and, very important, a strong determination by Britain and some of the Commonwealth countries to maintain their imperial preferences.[4]

Many of those who had hoped that these negotiations would put an impressive capstone on the previous attempts at Geneva and Annecy to lower tariff barriers and reduce preferences throughout the world regarded the results of Torquay as disappointing. Out of a maximum of 630 possible pairs of negotiations, only 147 in-

---

mercial Policy Series 135, May 1951; Department of State *Bulletin*, June 11, 1951, p. 934; Department of Commerce, *Foreign Commerce Weekly*, May 28, 1951, p. 4 ff., and MacGowan, H.R., "The Reciprocal Trade Agreements Program," *Foreign Commerce Weekly*, July 30, 1951, p. 3 ff. For some unofficial accounts, see D'Anna, F. Coppola, "Lights and Shadows of the Torquay Conference," Banco di Roma, *Review of Economic Conditions in Italy*, May 1951, p. 183 ff.; Alexandrowicz, C. H., "International Trade and Tariffs at Torquay," *World Affairs*, April 1951, pp. 211-221; *New York Times*, March 12, March 30, March 31, and April 2, 1951; *The Statist*, May 19, 1951, p. 669 ff.; and *The Economist*, May 19, 1951, p. 1149.

[2] See *Survey—1950*, pp. 182-186.

[3] See Chapter VII.

[4] For an official account of the difficulties encountered at Torquay, see Interim Commission for the International Trade Organization, *GATT in Action*, Geneva, January 1952, pp. 9-11.

volving 34 countries[5] were completed, and almost no progress was recorded in dismantling the structure of British imperial preferences. Still, the results were not negligible.

The accession of Germany was an important achievement, especially since in the previous two rounds many members had refused to negotiate tariff concessions on commodities—particularly chemicals—for which Germany had before the war been the main supplier until Germany herself participated. While the number of bilateral agreements was no greater than that reached at Annecy in 1948, the number of concessions was almost double. The importance of this shrinks somewhat in view of the fact that most of the concessions were of smaller magnitude than the previous ones; but, on the other hand and to the extent the new concessions were on products whose duties had previously been lowered, it *may* be that a smaller reduction from an already reduced duty is more significant than a large reduction from a higher one.

Another major accomplishment of the meetings was that, after certain adjustments, the concessions granted at Geneva and Annecy were extended for another three years; that is, until January 1, 1954. Before agreeing to this, sixteen countries (not including the United States) had given notice of intention to withdraw or modify certain of their earlier concessions. In most of the cases in which such action was taken, compensating concessions were granted for those withdrawn or modified. No retaliatory withdrawals were made. Some observers suggested that this modification of concessions without retaliation was the greatest success at Torquay since in effect it amounted to a "customs truce"—or something like it. The State Department reported that the modifications were not on the whole detrimental to United States interests, even though many of them did deal with concessions previously granted the United States and some were deliberate protectionist measures, it being expected that, in addition to specific compensations given for the withdrawals, in many cases the reimposed restrictions on manufactured goods would be offset by corresponding increases in imports of semi-manufactured products, parts, and raw materials. The United States did not make any withdrawals or modi-

[5] Of the countries present at Torquay, Burma, Syria, Liberia, and Nicaragua did not conclude any negotiations.

fications as a condition for agreeing to the three-year extension of the earlier concessions.[6]

The United States successfully completed negotiations with seventeen countries,[7] including all of the new countries which were participating in the GATT negotiations for the first time except the Philippines, with which an agreement under the GATT was interdicted by the Philippine Trade Act of 1946. The United States did not undertake negotiations with eleven of the participants. Negotiations with the United Kingdom, Australia, New Zealand, India, and Cuba were attempted but were unsuccessful. The failure to reach an agreement with the first three was especially regretted by the United States delegation since the issue on which the discussions foundered was primarily one of reducing imperial preferences—long a major goal of American foreign economic policy. With the exception of Canada,[8] all the Commonwealth countries at Torquay (including the colonies for whom the United Kingdom spoke) stood firm on their "contractual rights" in maintaining "contractual preferences."[9]

For the United States, the most important successful negotiations, from the point of view of volume of trade covered, were those with Germany and Canada, followed by those with Peru,

[6] It did, through the regular process of negotiation at Torquay and in the light of others' modifications, raise existing duties on three minor imports. (See Department of State *Bulletin*, June 11, 1951, p. 934.) Later in the year it raised the duty on another small import because of its inadvertent inclusion in a category of goods on which concessions had been granted at Torquay (see Department of State *Bulletin*, November 19, 1951, p. 828). As noted above, in passing the Customs Simplification Act of 1951, the House voted to reimpose duties on certain oils and their raw materials as a means of eliminating domestic processing taxes; however, these would not increase the tax burden borne by the imports.

[7] "New" countries: Austria, West Germany, Korea, Peru, Turkey. Countries previously members of GATT: Belgium, Luxembourg, Netherlands, Brazil, Canada, Denmark, Dominican Republic, France, Indonesia, Italy, Norway, Sweden.

[8] For one view of Canada's position on imperial preference, see *Bankers' Magazine* (London), October 1951, pp. 270-271.

[9] Official details on negotiations on this issue are not available. The press reported that Britain had been more concerned with maintaining preferences than with obtaining the rather considerable reductions the United States was prepared to offer on a large variety of goods. The negotiations went far enough, it was reported, to show that the United Kingdom itself was reluctant to lower preferences even to the extent the Commonwealth countries would permit, thus contradicting the previous assertions by Britain that its reluctance was based solely on Commonwealth insistence on continuing their protected status in the British market. (See *New York Times*, March 31, 1951.)

Austria, Turkey, France, and the Benelux group. Through direct negotiations, the United States obtained concessions (lower rates and bindings) on exports to the seventeen countries valued at slightly over $1 billion in 1949. In addition, via the most-favored-nation clause, concessions were obtained on another $100 million of exports as a result of the concessions exchanged by other participants. Altogether, these concessions covered about 20 percent of the value of United States exports during 1949 to the countries negotiating at Torquay. In exchange, the United States bound or reduced duties on imports valued at about $500 million in 1949.[1] The Department of Commerce reported that the excess of concessions obtained over those granted was in part accounted for by the fact that there were several abnormalities in United States export trade in 1949 which served to swell the apparent value of the concessions obtained. Also, it stated, the difference was partly the result of acceding countries "paying for benefits accruing from United States concessions granted at Geneva and Annecy, as well as at Torquay."[2]

The Torquay Protocol was originally left open for signature until October 21, 1951,[3] and on June 2 President Truman issued a proclamation putting the concessions into effect so far as the United States was concerned vis-à-vis the others who signed. Only twenty-nine of the thirty-seven countries who had negotiated at Torquay had signed by the October date, and an extension until

[1] In terms of value of imports in 1949, duties were reduced less than 25 percent on $156 million of imports, by between 25 and 35 percent on $104 million, by between 36 and 50 percent on $160 million. Duties were bound on $24 million and duty-free bindings were agreed to on $34 million of imports in 1949.

For the Tariff Commission's analysis of the "Operation of the Trade Agreements Program," see its various reports so titled, covering the periods June 1934 to April 1948, Second Series, No. 160; *Second Report,* April 1948 to March 1949, No. 163; and *Third Report,* April 1949 to June 1950, No. 172; an analysis of operations at Torquay is in process.

[2] MacGowan, H. R., "The Reciprocal Trade Agreements Program," *Foreign Commerce Weekly,* July 30, 1951, p. 4. Under the established United States procedure of "generalizing" its concessions, the "new" countries had in effect already received the benefits of American concessions granted at Geneva and Annecy. By acceding to the GATT at Torquay they did obtain a "legal" title to past concessions granted by the United States but it would not appear that this was a strong bargaining point in the arsenal of the United States negotiators.

[3] It was decided that the Torquay schedule should prevail in case of conflict with concessions granted at Geneva and Annecy. Uruguay, which had participated at Annecy and been approved for accession but had not signed, again participated at Torquay and the Contracting Parties decided that she should be allowed to sign the Torquay protocol after first signing the Annecy protocol.

December 31, 1951 was granted to Brazil, Chile, Denmark, Nicaragua, the United Kingdom, and Uruguay; until March 31, 1952 to Korea; and to May 22, 1952 for the Philippines.[4] Denmark and the United Kingdom signed in December, and Brazil announced its intention of applying at least certain of the concessions as of late January 1952.

During 1951, therefore, the United States via the Torquay negotiations had added to its calendar of trade agreements ones with Germany and Austria and had revised previously existing agreements with Belgium, Luxembourg, the Netherlands, Brazil, Canada, Denmark, Dominican Republic, France, Indonesia, Italy, Norway, and Sweden. The prior bilateral agreements with Peru and Turkey were superseded. Lebanon and Syria, who had acceded to the GATT during the 1947 negotiations, withdrew—and so terminated their trade agreements with the United States—as of February 25 and August 6, 1951, respectively. A calendar of United States Reciprocal Trade Agreements as of the end of 1951 is given in Appendix Table XI.

Other Changes in the United States Trade Agreements

In addition to the negotiations at Torquay, the United States altered some of its existing trade agreements by bilateral negotiations. In 1950, the United States had agreed to a one-year's waiver of certain provisions in its 1936 agreement with Costa Rica so as to permit the latter to apply multiple exchange surcharges on certain imports from the United States. In April 1951, Costa Rica decided that, in view of the continuing acute imbalance in its accounts with the United States, it could not in the foreseeable future meet the terms of the trade agreements; it was therefore terminated by mutual consent.[5] The State Department reported that the existing United States tariff on all items under the terminated agreement would continue in effect since the same or lower rates and bindings were included in other agreements and would be extended to Costa Rica under the practice of generalizing concessions to all (non-Communist) countries.[6]

[4] *United Nations Bulletin*, November 1, 1951, p. 384.

[5] Department of State *Bulletin*, April 23, 1951, p. 662.

[6] Essentially the same result occurred for many of the products formerly covered under the trade agreement with Mexico which was terminated in 1950 (see *Survey—1950*, pp. 188-189). There were strong complaints in Congress during 1951 that the

In July, the United States accepted the request of Venezuela to renegotiate its 1939 agreement with the United States. No final action had been taken by the end of the year, but the United States petroleum industry had agreed in the hearings before the Trade Agreements Committee that a 5¼ cent a barrel duty reduction on certain petroleum products would not injure domestic interests.[7] China had withdrawn from the GATT in 1950, and most of the concessions negotiated directly with her at Geneva in 1947 were withdrawn by the United States during that year. Some of the concessions, however, because of the interest of other countries in them via the most-favored-nation clause, were the subject of further consultations between the United States and the interested countries. In December 1951, the State Department announced the completion of these consultations, which left certain of the concessions in operation among the GATT members and others were terminated as of January 25, 1952.[8]

As discussed above, the Trade Agreement Extension Act of 1951 required the President to withdraw any concessions provided under the Trade Agreements Act to Communist-dominated countries. Of the affected countries, only Czechoslovakia had a formal reciprocal trade agreement with the United States, and since this was by virtue of membership in the GATT its suspension is discussed in Section D below. Clauses providing for a contractual right to concessions with reference to Russia, Bulgaria, and Rumania were contained in special bilateral commercial agreements (not classified as reciprocal trade agreements)[9] and in treaties of "friendship, commerce and consular rights" with respect to Hungary and Poland.[1] There were no contractual obligations with respect to the other Communist-dominated countries.

Torquay negotiations merely returned to Mexico many of the concessions granted under the terminated treaty without the United States obtaining anything in return from Mexico.

[7] *New York Times,* October 3, 1951. See Department of Commerce, *Foreign Commerce Weekly,* September 10, 1951, p. 23, or Department of State *Bulletin,* September 10, 1951, pp. 433-436, for the announcement of the Trade Agreements Committee concerning the negotiations and hearings.

[8] Department of State *Bulletin,* December 17, 1951, p. 977.

[9] For details on the signing of the agreements and their termination provisions, see Department of Commerce, *Foreign Commerce Weekly,* July 30, 1951, p. 28; October 15, 1951, p. 27; and December 10, 1951, p. 27.

[1] The United States attempted to cancel only the most-favored-nation clause of the Polish agreement, but since Poland did not reply to this proposal, the United States gave notice that the entire treaty would be terminated.

During June and July, the President notified Russia, Rumania, Bulgaria, Hungary, and Poland that the most-favored-nation clause in the various bilateral agreements with them would be terminated in accordance with the terms set forth in the agreements.[2] The suspension of concessions to Rumania was effective in July,[3] that to Bulgaria in October, and those to Russia and Poland in January 1952. After January 4, 1952 the only concessions in effect under these treaties were those with Hungary, which were not terminable until July 1952.

On August 1, 1951, the President proclaimed that the reductions in rates of duty made in trade agreements should be suspended as of September 1, 1951 in the case of a list of nations and areas as to which such withdrawal would not on that date conflict with any international obligations. (That is, the "generalized" extensions of most-favored-nation treatment should be withdrawn from the cited countries and areas.) He then notified the Secretary of the Treasury that concessions should be withdrawn on trade with Albania, Communist Indochina, Communist Korea, Kurile Islands, Latvia, Lithuania, Outer Mongolia, Rumania (since the contractual commercial agreement had been terminated by that time), Southern Sakhalin, and Tanna Tuva. Imports, unless otherwise embargoed, could still be brought in from these areas but only at the statutory duties stated in the Tariff Act of 1930.

Action under the Escape Clause

By the end of 1950 only twenty applications had been filed for relief under the escape clause; of these only one (on fur felt hats and hat bodies)[4] had been granted and four had been deferred or investigations were pending. Of these, one was withdrawn during 1951, two were denied or dismissed, and for the other—hatters' fur—relief was granted.[5] In his proclamation on this case, the President announced intention to require periodic review of all modifications under the escape clause to prevent "various adverse

[2] Termination dates were thirty days to one year from date of notification. See Department of State *Bulletin*, July 16, 1951, p. 95-96, and December 3, 1951, pp. 913-914 for details.

[3] Rumania still received, however, the benefits from the United States practice of "generalizing" its concessions. These were withdrawn as of September 1, 1951.

[4] See *Survey—1950*, pp. 186-188, and footnote 9, p. 173 below.

[5] For details of the relief granted, see Department of State *Bulletin*, January 21, 1952, pp. 96-97.

effects" resulting from their retention over too long a period—namely, that other countries might retaliate, that consumer prices might be raised unnecessarily, and that American foreign policies might be hindered by denying foreign nations the opportunity to earn dollars for recovery and mutual defense.

During 1951, reflecting the encouragement given to import-competing firms by the new escape clause, applications were submitted for relief from imports of watches, motorcycles, blue-mold cheese, spring clothespins, ground-fish fillets, wood screws, bicycles and parts, garlic, and glacé cherries, but no decision had been reached on them by the Tariff Commission by the year end.

D. *SIXTH SESSION OF THE CONTRACTING PARTIES*

In addition to the tariff negotiating conferences, the Contracting Parties to the GATT also meet from time to time in "sessions" to discuss, and sometimes to take action on, broad policy issues as well as specific problems which have arisen under the Agreement. The Sixth such Session was held at Geneva from September 17 through October 26, 1951.[6] Significantly, in part a reflection of the growing importance of GATT as a consequence of the demise of the ITO, an unusually large number of Ministers attended. The Session not only brought out serious inconsistencies in United States policies but also led many observers to conclude that several of the basic GATT principles were being increasingly violated by the various members.

Suspension of United States-Czechoslovakian Concessions

In late July, the Administration denounced Czechoslovakia for numerous acts of "ill will" and, pursuant to the 1951 amendment to the Trade Agreements Act requiring withdrawal of any concessions to Communist-oriented countries,[7] declared its intention of virtually ending economic relations with her. Of the Communist-dominated countries, only Czechoslovakia was a member of the GATT, and Washington notified Prague of its intention of requesting a complete dissolution of United States-Czechoslovakian obli-

[6] See *Survey—1950*, pp. 177-181 for a summary of the Fourth and Fifth Sessions.

[7] Congress later passed a Concurrent Resolution stating its belief that all trade relations with Czechoslovakia should be terminated in retaliation for the imprisonment of the American newspaper correspondent, William N. Oatis.

gations under the General Agreement. It was apparent before the Sixth Session began that the European Contracting Parties disliked this action by the United States, which several of them regarded as unilateral. The Assistant Secretary of State for Economic Affairs went to Geneva to present the American case. He stated that the United States considered that the proposed action was justified since political developments made effective implementation of the Agreement impossible and since the trade concessions which had been granted the United States by Czechoslovakia had been nullified by the use of other controls.[8] Mr. Thorp worked hard, and successfully, at Geneva to win from a critical audience acceptance of his Government's request. He said that the proposed measure affected only the relations between the two countries and not those between either of them and the other Contracting Parties; that the United States would not attempt to quash the Czechoslovakian-initiated complaint against the earlier American withdrawal of concessions on felt hats;[9] that the case was an "exceptional" one, did not set a precedent, and was the outgrowth of "total incompatibility" between the two countries;[1] and that the other countries were not being requested to take sides on the issue. As a mild means of expressing their disapproval of the United States position, the other members forced a delay in the voting and

[8] The latter was no doubt true, but it was also true of many of the concessions granted the United States by several of the other GATT members. The Czechoslovakian case was regarded by the United States as different in two respects: direct controls over trade applied to all items and most of these controls were applied *after* the trade agreement was concluded.

[9] In 1950 the President, under the escape clause, had withdrawn the 1947 concessions granted on imports of certain felt hats and hat bodies. Czechoslovakia had protested this action, and the question was referred to a GATT inter-sessional Working Party. The report of this group—presented at the Sixth Session—stated that there had been some "adverse effects" on the United States hat industry by the increased imports after the concessions had been granted but that these effects appeared to be only temporary. The report also said that there was no evidence that the United States had violated its obligations under the GATT but advised that the situation be kept under review with the aim of restoring the concessions as soon as possible. The Contracting Parties approved the report, and the United States delegate said that the U.S. Tariff Commission had the matter under review and would take "appropriate" action in the future. (See Department of Commerce, *Foreign Commerce Weekly*, December 31, 1951, p. 27, and *Report on the Withdrawal by the United States of a Tariff Concession under Article XIX of the General Agreement on Tariffs and Trade*, Geneva, October 1951, UN Sales No. GATT/1951-3.)

[1] For a text of Mr. Thorp's statement, see Department of State *Bulletin*, October 15, 1951, pp. 622-624. See also Department of State *Bulletin*, November 19, 1951, p. 830, for other details on this issue.

thus dashed American hopes for a quick and quiet disposal of the issue. Approval was finally given—by a surprising vote of 24 to 1, with 4 abstentions—but in the form of a "declaration" rather than a "resolution" so as to honor the American request without committing the other parties to an "approval" of the American position.[2]

On October 2, the U.S. Government announced that as of November 1 its trade concessions to Czechoslavakia would be withdrawn; that is, the 1930 tariff rates on imports would apply. Three weeks later Czechoslovakia announced that it was raising its duties on United States goods.

United States Import Quotas

The United States fared less well on the question of the new and stringent quotas on certain dairy products which Congress had legislated earlier in the year (see Section F below). Several of the GATT members filed strong protests during the Sixth Session against this measure, stating that they had not been imposed for balance-of-payments reasons—the justification for quantitative restrictions used by other countries—but for purely protectionist purposes and were thus in violation of the GATT. The Netherlands delegate accused the United States of "nullifying" and "impairing" both a solemn international agreement and the vigorous efforts undertaken by the Dutch people and their Government, in complete accordance with the Marshall Plan, to become independent of outside financial assistance. He emphasized that the United States action would seriously deter the efforts of European exporters to cultivate American markets. Several of the other affected countries openly threatened to take reprisals if the quotas were not removed.[3]

The United States representatives implicitly recognized, as they had explicitly stated before the Congressional committees, that the law was in conflict with the GATT and had resulted in injury to several of the Contracting Parties. They reported that these quotas did not reflect a basic change in American policy and that the Ad-

[2] Michael Hoffman reported in the *New York Times* (September 27, 1951) that the form of the approval and the delays were a demonstration that the Contracting Parties were "unlikely to accept many more unilateral actions by the United States . . . without an open split."

[3] See *New York Times*, September 25, 1951.

ministration gave high priority to their repeal by Congress.[4] The other Contracting Parties found that the United States had violated the GATT and, while urging those members most affected to wait and see whether Congress would repeal the provision before imposing retaliatory measures, also found that compensatory action under Article XXIII would be in order. Denmark delayed signing the Torquay protocol until late in the year, and the press interpreted this as a protest against the quotas.[5]

Dollar Import Restrictions by Belgium

The United States delegation had an opportunity to put the pinching shoe on another's foot when Belgium announced in September that it was imposing certain import restrictions on dollar imports in order to redirect her imports to European sources in her effort to reduce her large EPU surplus.[6] The United States, Canada, and Cuba strongly attacked the Belgian action as a protectionist measure designed to shield European goods from Western Hemisphere competition and so not in accord with the nondiscriminatory clauses of the GATT and a violation of the rules for imposing import restrictions as provided in Articles XI and XII, since Belgium's overall balance-of-payments position was improving. The Belgians insisted that the measures were in the nature of exchange restrictions and were authorized under Article XV of the General Agreement.[7] The United States position was *unofficially* reported to have been weakened in that its representatives in Paris concerned with the EPU had supported the Belgian restrictions.[8] The conference finally decided not to press for any formal action at that time in the hope that the restrictions might be removed in the near future, but the State Department recorded its concern over the possibly adverse impact of the Belgian action on the future development of the GATT.[9]

[4] The Senate in January returned for "further study" a Banking and Currency Committee repeal bill in view of recent sharp declines in the prices of various agricultural commodities. (*New York Times*, January 31, 1952.)

[5] *New York Times*, December 22, 1951.

[6] See Chapter VII for a discussion of the EPU and Belgium's position in it. Details of the measures taken by Belgium may be found in Canadian Department of Commerce, *Foreign Trade*, October 13, 1951, pp. 529-530.

[7] See *New York Herald Tribune*, "Monthly Economic Review," Paris, November 5, 1951.

[8] *New York Times*, September 23, 1951.

[9] Department of State *Bulletin*, November 19, 1951, p. 831.

Continuation of Quantitative Restrictions

The GATT (notably Article XX) permits the "temporary" imposition of quantitative import restrictions by members under certain specified conditions. The Agreement stipulated that, as a general rule, these were to be removed not later than January 1, 1951, but provisions were included for an extension of this time, and during 1950 a one-year extension was granted. The agenda for the Sixth Session included the item of a further extension. The issue was not whether there should be an extension (practically all countries, including the United States, were agreeable to some extension) but rather whether it should be for a limited or an indefinite period. The United States, strongly supported by Canada, Cuba, India, and South Africa, urged the former; the final decision, reached by "general agreement," was to grant a two-year extension.[1]

Article XII of the GATT permits the use of quantitative restrictions for balance-of-payments reasons, and during the Sixth Session the Contracting Parties "examined" and "reviewed" the practices and techniques being used by the various member countries. This was merely a "stock-taking" operation, and individual governments were not asked to justify their actions. In their subsequent report,[2] the Contracting Parties noted that for certain countries the impact of rearmament, especially by worsening their terms of trade and creating new internal inflationary pressures, was causing serious balance-of-payments difficulties; they concluded that "Countries cannot all move at the same pace, but a number, particularly those whose trade and payments position is improving as a result of recent developments, should be able to take definite steps toward the further relaxation of the restrictions and the reduction of discrimination." In November, shortly after the session ended, however, Britain, faced with a continuing sharp decline in her reserves, announced her intention of imposing additional quantitative restrictions to reduce her imports. This action was referred to a Working Committee of the Contracting Parties to consider

[1] The United Nations Office at Geneva, *Press Release GATT/66,* October 29, 1951.

[2] *The Use of Quantitative Import Restrictions to Safeguard Balances of Payments,* October 1951 (Sales No. GATT/1951/2). For a summary of this report, see *United Nations Bulletin,* February 1, 1952, p. 125, and *New York Times,* January 16, 1952.

whether it constituted an *intensification* of restrictions and so required consultation between the United Kingdom and the other Contracting Parties.[3] This Committee, however, with United States agreement, decided to let the whole question slide for the time being, since, among other considerations, provisions in both GATT and the Articles of Agreement of the International Monetary Fund required that, in any event, consultation with the United Kingdom on the discriminatory aspect of import restrictions would be required in 1952.[4]

The public was given no evidence that the problem of quantitative restrictions on the export side was discussed, although earlier in the year the International Monetary Fund, along with others, had stated that export controls were "becoming increasingly important determinants of the composition, volume, and direction of international trade."[5] As discussed briefly in Chapter VI following, there were those in the United States who argued that the United States export controls were not discriminatory in the GATT sense, since they were designed to promote Western defense objectives and were not intended to be protectionist.

Administration of the GATT

When announcing in late 1950 that Congress would not be asked again to approve the ITO Charter, the State Department said that it would suggest to other GATT members that there be created "the necessary administrative machinery, including a small permanent staff," to permit the GATT to operate efficiently and that Congress would be asked to approve this agency and United States participation in it.[6] In light of the strong Congressional reservations on the GATT noted earlier in this chapter, the Administration did not broach the subject to Congress in 1951. Nevertheless, at the Sixth Session the United States delegates urged the creation of such machinery. The British delegation, along with certain others, demurred (for reasons noted below), and officially

[3] There was no official formal discussion during the Sixth Session of the discriminatory aspects of the Schuman Plan since it had not yet been approved but a working party was asked to study the draft Treaty.

[4] For further discussion of this point, see *GATT in Action, op.cit.*, p. 17.

[5] International Monetary Fund, *Annual Report, 1951*, Washington, D.C., July 1951, p. 64.

[6] See Department of Commerce, *Foreign Commerce Weekly*, January 8, 1951, p. 25, for the text of the official statement.

the Session merely noted the importance of having some kind of intersessional machinery, established an *ad hoc* committee to so function until the next session, and asked the Executive Secretary to consult with the UN Secretary General as to possible arrangements.

Other Major Agenda Items

Four new members—West Germany, Peru, Turkey, and Austria—were formally received as Contracting Parties during this Session, and the deadline for signature of the Torquay Protocol was extended for certain other countries. A French plan to reduce customs duties among members by an additional 30 percent over the next three years was heard; it was referred to a special committee which was to study the technical details and methods of application with the aim of submitting a report to the next session. The Contracting Parties did, however, approve certain measures for the conduct of tariff negotiations outside a full-scale GATT conference; they drew up a draft convention designed to facilitate the importation of commercial samples and made recommendations for simplifying certain customs formalities and documentary requirements for imports.[7] Both the draft convention and the recommendations were submitted to member governments for study, it being planned that their comments would be examined at the Seventh Session, scheduled for 1952.

Norway proposed that the Contracting Parties incorporate into the GATT those articles of the ITO Charter dealing with employment and levels of economic activity. The position of the United States delegation has not been published, but it is clear that in 1951 Congress would have objected strongly to such action. The proposal received the support of the United Kingdom. Others, agreeing in principle with the Norwegian contention that "the principles of commercial policy should not be practiced indefinitely without regard to the principles of employment and economic activity" as laid down in the ITO Charter, doubted that a piecemeal amendment of the GATT was desirable.[8] The Session

[7] See Department of Commerce, *Foreign Commerce Weekly*, January 21, 1952, p. 5 f. This convention and these recommendations grew out of a study by the Contracting Parties of some resolutions adopted by the International Chamber of Commerce.

[8] *Press Release GATT/66, op.cit.*

took no formal decision on the Norwegian proposal—Norway did not press for a decision at that time—but a "measure of agreement" was recorded on the view that since the ITO was not likely to come into force a constitutional session of the Contracting Parties should be called at a later date for a thorough reexamination of the GATT.

General Support of the GATT Principles

The debates and discussion at the Sixth Session were not widely publicized, but it appears from the somewhat meager information available that support of the GATT by several members was waning rapidly. Especially important was the attitude of the British Government. Sir Hartley Shawcross delivered a speech at the Session which was regarded by some as "tantamount to a provisional notice of withdrawal from GATT."[9] He said that the United Kingdom must give serious consideration to how far the disadvantages of the GATT in restricting preferences were outweighed by the advantages of trade promotion. The seriousness of the British concern was evidenced in their opposition to the creation of any new permanent secretariat to service the GATT until that organization had been subjected to a broad and detailed "review." At the closing meeting the chairman of the Session stated that a general review of the GATT was to be expected in the near future.[1]

The United States was the strongest advocate of the past success and future potentialities of the GATT. But there were many who saw in the record of the Sixth Session indications that the United States was in danger of losing the leadership role in the general field of international commercial relations. Its failure to ratify the ITO Charter, the failure to legislate what the Administration originally had regarded as a necessary underpinning for the GATT, the caveats on GATT discussed above which were entered during the year by Congress, the imposition of the cheese quotas, the action with respect to the trade agreement with Czecho-

[9] *The Economist*, September 29, 1951, p. 763.

[1] The European correspondent on economic affairs for the *New York Times* stressed in his reports his own conclusion that any general revision of the GATT at that time would bring results much more to the liking of those dedicated to state trading and rigorous controls and planning than to those supporting the principles of nondiscriminatory multilateralism. (The reader is referred to the many articles with Michael Hoffman's by-line in the *New York Times* during the period September 15 through October 1951.)

slovakia, and the use of the escape clause on fur felt hats were reported as shaking the faith of other governments in the ability or willingness of the United States to honor either specific agreements or general policies when the price at the moment was deemed "politically too high" or when even minor and isolated domestic economic hardships resulted. But the problem of leading the world toward more liberal commercial policies was seen by some to be dependent on more basic considerations than these. Although rarely discussed publicly, the point has been made that a rearming world means state planning, direct controls, and discrimination and that these conditions are fundamentally incompatible with an international commercial policy of a single, nondiscriminatory, world-wide trading system where the movements of goods, services, and capital among nations are directed by individuals.

E. *MISCELLANEOUS ENCOURAGEMENT OF IMPORTS*

In addition to the tariff reductions discussed above, the United States engaged in several other activities directly designed to increase imports.[2] ECA, with the help of other branches of the Government, continued its previous efforts to encourage European dollar exports, and at least one new device was used—the highly advertized exhibition and sale of consumer items from one foreign country in major department stores throughout the United States. The most successful of these was the "Italy Comes to Macy's" and to Kaufman's, etc.

No international trade fairs were held during the year, but plans were going forward to hold the Second International Trade Fair in Chicago during the spring of 1952. In October 1951 Congress passed a law authorizing the President to invite the States of the Union and foreign countries to participate in it. Several "world trade fairs" and "expositions" and "shows" were held;[3] these are distinguished from "international trade fairs" in that the latter are essentially large-scale exhibitions of samples from many countries for the benefit of commercial buyers while the former are intended to appeal primarily to the general public and frequently

[2] See *Survey—1950*, pp. 194-197, for a summary of these miscellaneous activities during 1950.

[3] For details, see Department of Commerce, *Foreign Commerce Weekly*, March 26, April 9, 16, 26, and 30, May 21, June 4, and October 22, 1951.

are restricted to one group of commodities or the products of a single foreign country.

The President also proclaimed that May 20-26 would be observed as World Trade Week and during this period, as in previous years, both the Department of Commerce and various Chambers of Commerce throughout the nation presented programs of various sorts dedicated to convincing the public of the importance to the United States of increasing both imports and exports.

Following the 1950 amendments to the Celler Foreign Trade Zone Act, which permitted limited manufacturing and exhibiting in the zones,[4] there was a great increase in the zones' operations.[5] An official study of their operations during the year found them being used at full capacity and in need of further expansion. The final report of this study was not published during the year, but the press stated that the Foreign Trade Zones Board of the Department of Commerce would recommend that the zones be physically expanded by authorizing manufacture and, especially, exhibition at centralized locations outside the present limits of the zones while remaining under zone jurisdiction.[6] Such expansion is permitted by the existing law.

F. CONFLICTS BETWEEN TRADE AND AGRICULTURAL POLICIES

The year 1951 again witnessed serious conflicts and inconsistencies between the nation's agricultural and international trade policies. The general practice of previous years was continued whereby most of such conflicts were resolved in favor of the agricultural policies. The protection provided American farmers by tariffs has been discussed in Section A above;[7] this section will

[4] See *Survey—1950*, p. 194.

[5] See Carr, A. B., "Foreign-Trade Zones Prepared to Meet New Trade Conditions," and Forbes, F. P., "New Business Created by Use of Foreign-Trade Zone Privileges," Department of Commerce, *Foreign Commerce Weekly*, November 12, 1951, pp. 3 ff., and 5 ff., respectively.

[6] *Foreign Commerce Weekly*, May 28, 1951, p. 26, and *New York Times*, August 26, 1951.

[7] One action on tariffs not discussed previously and which provides an instance of consistency of agricultural and trade policies was the 1951 removal of the duty on baler twine. The case is also interesting in that it showed that a resumption by Congress of detailed determination of tariff rates would consume enormous amounts of time and involve a return to pork-barrel practices on these matters. (See the debates and discussion in "Free Importation of Baler Twine," *Hearings on H.R.*

therefore be confined to a survey of direct import controls and export subsidies.[8]

Direct Import Controls

a. FATS AND OILS

During the Second World War and through 1948, direct import controls on fats and oils (excluding petroleum products) and rice and rice products were used by the United States to implement the international allocations of these scarce commodities made by the International Emergency Food Committee. Beginning in early 1949, however, the authority of the President to restrict the imports of such goods by subjecting them to import licenses was continued on the ostensible grounds of facilitating an "orderly liquidation of temporary surplus stocks" controlled by the Government[9] but, in fact, also as a form of unvarnished protection for American farmers. Under this authority a virtual embargo had been placed on all such imports through 1949 and most of 1950, but late in the latter year, as shortages began to develop and the Government's stocks declined, several of the affected goods were removed from control.[1] The legislation (Second War Powers Act) under which these controls had been imposed expired in mid-1951. However, the Defense Production Act of 1950 contained a section (101) which

1005, House of Rep., Committee on Ways and Means, 82d Cong., 1st Sess., July 1951; and *ibid.,* U.S. Senate, Committee on Finance, 82 Cong., 1st Sess., October 17, 1951; *H. Rpt. No. 771,* 82d Cong., 1st Sess., July 27, 1951; and *S. Rpt. No. 1050,* October 19, 1951; and *Congressional Record,* September 13, 1951, pp. 11491 ff., September 14, 1951, pp. 11630-11638, and October 20, pp. 13996-13997.)

Supporters of the measure argued that the existing duty was a violation of the general principle that farm supplies and equipment should enter duty-free. They also stressed the current shortage of twine and the resultant hardship on farmers. Domestic twine producers and their Congressional supporters argued that the shortage was temporary and that a removal of the duty would place the American farmer at the "mercy" of foreign twine producers. The Congressional supporters of the Administration and farm organizations were numerous enough to pass the measure by large majorities in both Houses despite the arguments of protectionists that it would set yet another precedent for removal of tariff duties.

[8] For an official statement of the effect of trade policies on agriculture, see Department of State, "American Agriculture and World Trade," Commercial Policy Series 137, September 1951.

[9] See *Survey—1950,* pp. 201-202, for a statement of the relationship between these particular controls and the GATT.

[1] See *American Import and Export Bulletin,* March 1951, p. 225, for details on the commodities decontrolled in early 1951 and those kept under control.

authorized the reduction of imports by direct controls when such imports were deemed harmful to national defense interests, and the Secretary of Agriculture announced in June that quotas on imports of flaxseed, flaxseed screenings, linseed oil and rice and rice products would be continued under that authority. This action was justified by the Secretary on several bases: to prevent the diversion to the United States of commodities urgently needed by her rearming allies; to encourage domestic production and reduce American dependency during a possible war period on foreign sources; and to relieve the burden on the rearmament-taxed transportation and distribution systems of the United States.[2]

The Administration did not propose any new legislative authority, but when Congress was considering the 1951 revision of the Defense Production Act an amendment was offered from the floor of both Houses to add a new section explicitly authorizing import quotas on fats and oils[3]—specifically mentioning, among others, "butter, cheese and other dairy products"[4]—until June 30, 1953. These quotas were to keep out such imports as were found to "(a) impair or reduce the domestic production of any such commodity or product below present production levels, or below such higher levels as the Secretary of Agriculture may deem necessary in view of domestic and international conditions, or (b) interfere with the orderly domestic storing and marketing of any such commodity or product, or (c) result in any unnecessary burden or expenditures under any Government price-support program."[5] Congressional opponents emphasized that the amendment was inconsistent with the Reciprocal Trade Agreements Program, but its

[2] Department of Agriculture, Production and Marketing Administration, *Press Release U.S.D.A. 1605-51*, June 29, 1951.

[3] As "necessary for the protection of the essential security interests and economy of the United States in the existing emergency in international relations." In reply to those who protested that the usual "hearings and careful consideration" on the amendment had not been held, the Senate proponents asserted that such hearings and consideration were not necessary since the proposal was identical to the previous legislation (in the Second War Powers Act). This statement shaded the truth a good bit since the earlier legislation did not include cheese and did not have the same criteria for imposing import controls.

[4] The amendment (Sect. 104 of the Defense Production Act) lists: fats and oils (including oil-bearing materials, fatty acids, and soap and soap powder, but excluding petroleum and petroleum products and coconut and coconut products), peanuts, butter, cheese and other dairy products, and rice and rice products.

[5] *Congressional Record*, June 28, 1951, p. 7588.

supporters, stressing the threat of imports to domestic dairy producers,[6] were in the majority and both Houses approved the measure.

While the Defense Production Act was in conference, Secretary of State Acheson and Secretary of Agriculture Brannan wrote letters to Congress requesting the deletion of this import control rider. The latter stated that it was unnecessary since adequate protection could be provided under Section 101 of the Defense Production Act, Section 22 of the Agricultural Adjustment Act, and under the escape clause provision of the Trade Agreements Act as extended in 1951.[7] Secretary Acheson wrote that the amendment should be stricken because of possible retaliation against United States exports, especially agricultural products; because it would constitute a reversal of the general position of the United States on international commercial policy; and because it would reduce foreign dollar earnings at a time when the United States was extending financial assistance to foreign countries.[8]

These objections were not heeded and the amendment became law. Three weeks later the Secretary of Agriculture "found" that uncontrolled imports of several of the commodities named would have one or more of the effects cited in the law and therefore prohibited imports of peanuts, peanut oil, butter, butter oil, and nonfat dried-milk solids for domestic consumption.[9] He also placed imports of cheese and casein on a per country quota basis—imports during the first seven months of the year having already filled the quotas established.[1]

[6] Domestic dairy interests were reported instrumental in the introduction of the amendment, and, indeed, to have helped draft it. They argued that the 50 percent reduction in the duty on butter agreed to at Torquay would have the effect of permitting foreign butter to be delivered in the United States at well below the United States support price, that greater imports would mean a higher cost for the price-support program and that dairymen—suffering a dairy cow population decline during the past five years—needed additional protection.

The main basis for protection of cheese was to support the war-expanded domestic production of blue-mold cheese.

[7] See *Congressional Record,* September 7, 1951, p. 11242.

[8] See *Congressional Record,* July 30, 1951, p. 9359. Later, Administration spokesmen testified that, because of the cheese quota, foreign aid to Europe would have to be increased if American exports were to be maintained.

[9] Defense Food Order No. 3 which restricted these imports is given in full in the *American Import and Export Bulletin,* September 1951, pp. 680-682.

[1] Department of Commerce, *Foreign Commerce Weekly,* August 27, 1951, p. 21. Attention may be drawn again to the fact that for several years ECA had been encouraging Europe to expand its cheese exports to the United States. Lest any believe

President Truman immediately requested Congress to repeal this amendment on the grounds that it was unnecessary for the protection of domestic producers and ran counter to the established Reciprocal Trade Agreements Program. Before the Senate committee considering the President's request, State Department spokesmen enlarged on Acheson's earlier objections, stressing the danger of retaliation,[2] the loss of dollar earnings by America's allies with consequent deprivations for foreign countries and harmful effects on United States exports, the weakening of United States efforts to reduce trade barriers throughout the world, and the probability that it would open the United States to charges that it did not "practice what it preached." Department of Agriculture spokesmen stressed that the interest of American agriculture as a whole was greater in exports than in competing imports and that attention should be concentrated on the whole industry, not just individual sectors which suffered import competition.[3] In the meantime, protests had been received from several foreign countries—particularly on the cheese import restrictions since most of the other commodities had previously been under import control —and, as noted in Section D above, severe criticism was directed toward the United States during the Sixth Session of the Contracting Parties to the GATT.

Several influential private groups—including not only various export interests and cheese importers but also the American Farm Bureau Federation and the National Farmers Union—supported repeal of the rider, primarily on the grounds of possible retaliation which would limit United States agricultural interests and conflict with general trade policy. Important sectors of the American press published strong editorials condemning the law.[4] The

that it was only ECA which found Congress working at cross purposes to it in these matters, it should be noted that American officials in Japan had for some time been particularly active in rejuvenating the Japanese fishing and fish-canning industries—both for internal Japanese consumption and for export—but as their exports of tuna became competitive with the West Coast industry, efforts were made in Congress to raise the rates of duty on this item, as discussed in the footnote on page 149, and proposals were also made in Congress to impose import quotas on tuna.

[2] Supporters of the proposal discounted this on the ground that the existence of United States aid would deter retaliatory measures.

[3] See "Defense Production Act Amendments of 1951," *Hearings on . . . S. 2104, Part IV*, U.S. Senate, Committee on Banking and Currency, 82d Cong., 1st Sess., August-September 1951, pp. 2959 ff.

[4] See especially *Barron's*, New York, September 17, 1951, and the *New York Times*, September 15, and September 22, 1951.

National Milk Producers Federation, which had helped draft the amendment, urged its retention largely on protectionist grounds, and the National Renderers Association (dealers in edible fats and oils) argued that the United States should not give money to foreigners and at the same time let foreign goods displace domestic commodities. The dairy industry argued that the 1949 devaluations and ECA's European export drive justified special restrictions on imports.

The Senate Banking and Currency Committee later voted to repeal the amendment,[5] but the Senate itself decided not to debate the bill during that session[5a] and the House Committee voted to defer action until the 1952 session.

b. SUGAR QUOTAS

By terms of the Sugar Act of 1948, the U.S. Government exercizes a cartel-like control over sugar imports with the aim of protecting domestic producers by guaranteeing them a specified portion of the domestic market.[6] Although the existing law was effective through 1952, in early 1951 the Administration asked Congress to approve certain amendments.[7] The most important were to extend the Act until 1956 and to increase the fixed quotas assigned Puerto Rico and the Virgin Islands. Despite the fact that, as in several previous years, the statutory quotas assigned continental producers exceeded their production, the increases in the quotas assigned Puerto Rico and the Virgin Islands were at the expense of Cuba. The Administration was not yet prepared to follow the 1950 recommendations of the Gray *Report* that ". . . the *growth* of the domestic industry should not be encouraged except in limited cases where security reasons may be clearly involved."[8]

[5] See S. *Rpt. No. 790*, September 20, 1951, 82d Cong., 1st Sess.

[5a] In January 1952, the Senate returned the repeal measure to Committee "for further study," in view of price declines in various agricultural products.

[6] See *Survey—1949*, pp. 161-162, and *Survey—1950*, p. 203.

[7] For details, including a history of the United States sugar policy and programs, see "Extension of Sugar Act of 1948," *Hearings on H.R. 4521*, House of Rep., Committee on Agriculture, 82d Cong., 1st Sess., June 1951; *H. Rpt. No. 810*, 82d Cong., 1st Sess., August 8, 1951; *S. Rpt. No. 648*, 82d Cong., 1st Sess., August 20, 1951; and *Congressional Record*, August 13, 1951, pp. 10095-10109, and August 22, 1951, pp. 10707-10726.

[8] *Report to the President on Foreign Economic Policies*, Washington, D.C., November 10, 1950, p. 87.

Administration spokesmen said that their proposal would help restore prewar relationships in United States sugar import trade and was also a means of aiding the Puerto Rican and Virgin Islands economies while avoiding direct financial assistance. They also stated that because of an increase in total sugar imports, the absolute volume of Cuban exports to the United States would still be greater than during the immediately previous years.[9] During the Congressional debate, a few expressed concern over the continued subsidization of domestic sugar producers, but these statements were answered with several long speeches citing the virtues of import quotas as a means of protecting domestic interests. Opposition to the measure was only token, and it was approved by large majorities.[1]

[9] The Department of Agriculture's original (December 1950) estimate of the total amount of sugar "needed to meet the requirements of consumers" during 1951 was eight million tons. In June this was increased by a quarter of a million tons, but in October, in an effort to bolster declining prices, it was cut back to 7.9 million tons; in November the Office of International Trade in the Department of Commerce was authorized to relax export controls on sugar.

[1] Although the U.S. Government pursues a cartel-like policy with respect to sugar, it has for many years opposed international cartels, public or private, on the grounds that they restrict trade, reduce production, frustrate the efforts of underdeveloped countries to develop particular industries, retard the introduction of new techniques and so cut down on productivity and, in general, restrain increases in living standards. In 1951 the United States delegation to the UNECOSOC presented a draft resolution on "restrictive business practices" by private or public enterprises.

In presenting this document, the United States spokesmen in effect argued that the principles set forth on these matters in Chapter V of the dormant ITO Charter should be implemented. Except for the Soviet and satellite delegations, there was little opposition expressed to the objective sought by the United States; some argued, however, that a piecemeal approach to reviving the Havana Charter was undesirable, and others said that the question of cartels was more properly placed under the purview of GATT. The final resolution was substantially as proposed by the United States. UN members were asked to take measures, individually and collectively, to prevent private and public business practices affecting international trade which limit access to markets, restrain competition, or foster monopolistic control of markets whenever such practices adversely affected trade, production, economic development of underdeveloped areas or standards of living. An *ad hoc* committee was established to prepare a report on the cartel problem and to recommend to ECOSOC before 1953 measures to be incorporated into an international agreement on cartels, with its work to be based on the policies and principles embodied in Chapter V of the Havana Charter. The UN Secretary-General was directed to consult with other UN specialized agencies and to make a report to the Council as to the organization which could best implement the proposed international convention. (See United Nations Economic and Social Council, *Official Records*, 13th Session, 546th Meeting, September 11, 1951, pp. 609-612; Department of State *Bulletin*, August 13, 1951, p. 277; October 8, 1951, pp. 590-596; and reports in the *New York Times*, September 10, 12, 13, 14, 1951, and *The Statist*, October 13, 1951, pp. 472-473.)

C. TARIFF AND OTHER QUOTAS

Tariff quotas, prescribed in the Tariff Act of 1930, as amended, and allowed under the GATT, were continued on whole milk, cream, butter, certain kinds of fish, white (or Irish) potatoes, and walnuts.[2] The quota was raised slightly on fish because of increased consumption during the year and that on white potatoes (other than "certified seed") was increased from 60 million to almost 250 million pounds. Tariff quotas were imposed on petroleum and petroleum products aggregating 3.4 billion gallons per year.[3]

There were no changes in the absolute quotas on buttons, cigars, tobacco, coconut oil, cordage and rice imposed under the Philippine Trade Act of 1946. An increase of 1.5 million pounds was allowed in the quota on long-staple cotton imposed under the authority of Section 22 of the Agricultural Adjustment Act,[4] but other import quotas under the same authority remained unchanged during the year; these latter were on wheat, wheat flour, cotton, and cotton waste.[5] Under a continuing investigation of imports of tree nuts, the Tariff Commission in late 1951 found that imports of almonds were occurring, or were likely to occur between October 1, 1951 and September 30, 1952, under conditions and in such quantities as to render ineffective the marketing program of the Department of Agriculture. By a Presidential proclamation in December, an additional duty was imposed on imports of certain types of almonds in excess of a specified amount.[6]

Export Subsidies

The U.S. Government continued during 1951 to subsidize exports of various agricultural commodities.[7] Details for the year are

[2] For current details on these quotas, see the monthly issues of the *American Import and Export Bulletin.*

[3] The petroleum quotas were allocated 59.4 percent to Venezuela, 18.7 percent to the Netherlands or its territories, and 21.9 percent to other countries. (*American Import and Export Bulletin,* February 1951, p. 123; April 1951, p. 311; and May 1951, p. 400.) The same percentage allocations were proclaimed to be applicable for 1952 (Department of State *Bulletin,* January 21, 1952, pp. 92-93).

[4] See *American Import and Export Bulletin,* September 1951, p. 720.

[5] See *Survey—1950,* pp. 202-203.

[6] See *Federal Register,* December 11, 1951, p. 12413, for details.

[7] See *Survey—1950,* pp. 204-205, for a brief account of the various legal bases for such subsidy payments.

not available,[8] but it appears probable that the amount of such payments was less during 1951 than in the immediately preceding years since purchases of agricultural products of ERP participants from aid funds were declining and the stocks of many of the commodities held by the Commodity Credit Corporation were lower than in previous years. There was, however, no change in the established policy of subsidizing the export of agricultural products declared by the Secretary of Agriculture to be in surplus to domestic needs under the various agricultural price-support programs.

[8] See, however, *American Import and Export Bulletin,* September 1951, p. 723, for an account of a proposed new program for subsidizing the export of apples and winter pears.

VI · STRATEGIC ASPECTS OF COMMERCIAL POLICY

As THE political differences between the United States and Russia became more intense, more generally recognized, and more sharply defined, and as the threat of war with Russia increased, the long-term commercial policy objectives embodied in the Reciprocal Trade Agreements Program were not only altered and violated, in ways discussed in the previous chapter, but the whole program was frequently overshadowed by what may be called the strategic aspects of commercial policy. These policies and activities—including export controls, restrictions on East-West trade, stockpiling, and international commodity arrangements, and involving dependence on state planning and direct controls over international economic affairs—were seen by most observers as short-term problems but of dominant importance. Where they conflicted with the long-term goals of the trade agreements program, the latter gave way. Some of these strategic policies had been pursued rather mildly for several years, but they increasingly became the center of attention in late 1950 and in 1951.

A. *EXPORT CONTROLS*

In May 1951, Congress extended (unanimously and without amendment or debate) for one more year—to June 30, 1952—the authority of the Government to control exports,[1] emphasizing that "export controls are an integral part of the defense mobilization program" and that "there would seem to be no basis for assuming that we will be able in the next few years to relax our controls on strategic exports."[2]

[1] The Export Control Act of 1949. See *Survey—1949*, pp. 169-172, and *Survey—1950*, pp. 206-212, for a brief account of the major postwar issues and changes in policy with respect to export controls through 1950.

[2] *H. Rpt. No. 318*, 82d Cong., 1st Sess., April 12, 1951, p. 4. For other primary sources on export controls, see especially the quarterly reports by the Secretary of Commerce, *Export Control*; Borton, J. C., "Current Developments in Export Control," *Foreign Commerce Weekly*, March 26, 1951, pp. 3 ff.; and S. *Rpt. No. 944*,

The controls were used for many purposes during the year. As in the immediate post World War II period, they again were used extensively as a device for preventing an "excessive" drain of scarce materials from the United States—from the point of view of inflationary pressures and of supplies needed for rearmament production. During the year, some commodities were removed from the control list, but a net of 150 new commodity classifications[3] were placed under control (that is, placed on the Department of Commerce's "positive list of control commodities" and so requiring a license for export), raising the total at year's end to 925. Most of the new listings were stated to have been for reasons of "short supply." In addition, quantitative export quotas were placed on many goods, the more important being on certain forms of sulphur, aluminum, copper, brass, bronze, molybdenum, nickel, zinc, and coke; a "closed" export quota (allowing no exports, except to Canada) was imposed on a few items.[4]

Because of an increased demand from friendly foreign nations for many United States exports, the export control machinery was also used for allocating controlled items among the various claimants[5] and for helping to implement the allocation recommendations of the International Materials Conference, discussed in Section D below. In mid-year a statement on the "Foreign Allocations Policy" of the U.S. Government was prepared.[6] This statement said that with respect to scarce resources which the United States devoted to foreign needs the allocations should be on the basis of the contribution of such resources to: (a) military production of the free world, (b) increased production of strategic and critical

---

Committee on Interstate and Foreign Commerce, Subcommittee on Export Controls and Policies, 82d Cong., 1st Sess., October 12, 1951.

[3] These figures refer to Bureau of Census export classifications. As of December 31, 1951, there were 1565 separate commodities listed.

[4] During the year the quotas and controls on cotton exports which had been imposed in 1950 were removed in light of the large increase in the current crop.

[5] During most of the year at least, ECA collected "requirements" data for countries receiving aid from it, and the Office of International Trade (OIT) of the Department of Commerce prepared such data for all other countries. These sets of data were then sent to an inter-agency committee which established specific export quotas against which the Office of International Trade issued export licenses. For a discussion of OIT's procedure, see *Congressional Record*, October 8, 1951, pp. 13024-13026.

[6] For text see Armstrong, W. C., "The International Materials Conference," Department of State *Bulletin*, July 2, 1951, pp. 29-30. See also Borton, J. C., "Current Developments in Export Control," *op.cit.*

materials required by the United States and her allies, (c) maintenance of minimum essential civilian consumption, (d) reduced future dependence upon United States military and economic assistance, (e) lessened dependence of the free nations upon supplies from Soviet bloc countries, and (f) "prevention of political deterioration in nations or areas essential to the combined strength of the free world."[7] The statement went on to say that after the above requirements of "high essentiality" had been met, both for the United States and foreign countries, the allocations of any remaining supplies by the United States (including allocations to American consumers) should take into account the effects upon the civilian economy of each nation's contributions toward the common defense, with the object of bringing about "an equitable distribution of the resulting burdens and sacrifices." It noted that the last principle was difficult to apply in practice and that the objective ruled out any mechanical formula or any mere leveling out of consumption.

A major purpose of the export control program in 1951, as well as in the previous year, was to prevent the export of items to potential enemies which might contribute to the latters' military might.[8] Exports to Soviet-dominated countries had been severely restricted during 1950, and during the year under review the controls were continued and in some cases tightened. Early in the year a requirement was imposed that an export license be obtained before shipment of *any* goods to Soviet bloc countries.[9] The ef-

[7] In December the press reported that the criteria for export of controlled commodities were tightened so as to include only shipments for direct defense needs, some essential raw material production, or support of basic economic services and production. (*New York Times*, December 2, 1951.)

[8] For discussion of the shipment of strategic items to Soviet areas and China during 1950, see "Export of Strategic Materials," *Hearings*, House of Rep., Subcommittee of the Committee on Interstate and Foreign Commerce, 81st Cong., 2d Sess., September 1950; "Investigation of Shipments to Communist China," *Hearings*, U.S. Senate, Subcommittee of Committee on Interstate and Foreign Commerce, 81st Cong., 2d Sess., October-November 1950; "Export Controls and Policies," *Hearings Pursuant to S. Res. 365 (81st Cong.) and S. Res. 56 (82d Cong.)*, U.S. Senate, Subcommittee on Export Controls and Policies of the Committee on Interstate and Foreign Commerce, 82d Cong., 1st Sess., *Part* 2, February 2, 1951, and *Part* 3, May 16 and June 14, 1951; and *Congressional Record*, July 18, 1951, pp. 8523-8525 as an example of Congressional opinion on the subject.

[9] "Soviet bloc" countries and areas included the following: Albania, Bulgaria, Czechoslovakia, Estonia, Hungary, Latvia, Lithuania, North Korea, Poland and Danzig, Rumania, Russia, Mainland China, Manchuria, Southern Sakhalin, Kurile Islands, and Tanna Tuva.

fectiveness of this action in restricting trade is witnessed by the decline in United States exports to these countries to less than $4 million in 1951 from $72 million in 1950 and from nearly $700 million in 1947. To prevent evasion of United States and foreign export controls via transshipments, the requirement of an export license was extended to cover all commodities of foreign origin destined for Soviet bloc countries which moved in transit through United States ports, foreign trade zones, or were manifested to the United States.[1] To strengthen these controls further, the U.S. Government required that foreign importers of any United States licensed exports give assurances that the items purchased would not be transshipped to Soviet-controlled areas,[2] and, as the year ended, arrangements were being worked out among the United States, Canada, and several Western European countries whereby the government of the importing country would assume responsibility for preventing the shipment of controlled items to other than their licensed destination.[3]

United States exports were greater in 1951 than in 1950, and the Department of Commerce concluded that, although controls had reduced some shipments, they had not "stifled" exports. The controls had, however, altered the direction of many exports and some noted that this was "discriminatory" and so contrary to established American commercial policy. Late in the year a Congressional committee took note of this "seeming inconsistency." It wrote: "From a theoretical viewpoint, export controls are just as objectionable as import controls in that they equally divert trade from channels in which they would flow normally under the influence of supply and demand. Upon examination, however, this seeming inconsistency has one all-important point of departure from what could be branded a discriminatory and restrictive policy. This lies in the fact that the adoption of export controls by the United States

[1] This measure was an extension of the controls applied for security reasons during late 1950 over all in-transit shipments destined for mainland China, North Korea, Hong Kong, and Macao and over "positive list" commodities to Russia and her European satellites.

[2] For some examples of the penalties imposed for violation (frequently a barring from United States export trade), see Department of Commerce, *Foreign Commerce Weekly*, October 1, 1951, p. 10, and *New York Times*, October 4, 1951 and December 28, 1951.

[3] See Secretary of Commerce, *Export Control* (Eighteenth Quarterly Report), Washington, D.C., February 1952, pp. 2-3, for a brief description of the mechanism.

is not couched primarily in terms of national interest, but the program of export controls has been pressed by the United States as a significant part of the total western defense program. . . . Distinction between export controls predominantly for national interests as opposed to those instituted to promote western defense objectives must be continually stressed."[4]

There was much less criticism in Congress of the administration of the export control activities in 1951 than there had been during the previous year. A Senate subcommittee specifically concerned with export controls stated that the United States controls were "sufficiently extensive" and "almost completely effective" and that the administration of them had been, on the whole, commendable. But it stressed that "any appraisal of the over-all effectiveness of controls on the export of strategic and critical materials from the United States to the Communist areas would be incomplete unless seen in relation to concurrent activities of this nature carried on in Western Europe, the Far East, and elsewhere by United States agencies and by other governments."[5]

B. *RESTRICTION OF NON UNITED STATES EAST-WEST TRADE*

Since the end of World War II there has been much disagreement in United States Governmental circles as to the precise policies which should be adopted toward aiding, directly or indirectly, countries under, or deemed likely to come under, the domination of the Soviet Union. By early 1947, all direct official aid to the Soviet bloc countries had been terminated by the U.S. Government, but Western European officials and the U.S. Administration continued to stress the desirability of restoring the prewar trade patterns and levels between Eastern and Western Europe and between Western Europe and Asia. In particular, the Administration joined with officials of the future ERP countries in emphasizing the need to expand East-West trade as a condition for making Europe self-sustaining.[6] Despite these arguments

[4] S. *Rpt. No. 944,* Committee on Interstate and Foreign Commerce, 82d Cong., 1st Sess., October 12, 1951, p. 9.

[5] S. *Rpt. No. 944, op.cit.,* pp. 1 and 2. See Appendices A through D of this report for details on shipments from foreign countries to Communist areas and measures taken abroad to restrict them.

[6] See the Committee of European Economic Cooperation, *General Report,* Volume I, Department of State, European Series 28, September 1947, pp. 41-49, and

that East-West trade was highly advantageous to Europe and to the United States, some Congressmen in 1948 expressed uneasiness over the fact that by virtue of such trade Russia and its satellites received goods of strategic value from the West. In its plans for Marshall Aid, the Administration agreed, as had been the practice under the post-UNRRA and Interim Aid programs, that no assistance should be extended under ERP to a country exporting military items to Communist countries. But Congress was also concerned with the strategic value of some nonmilitary exports, and it inserted in the 1948 Economic Cooperation Act a provision that "The Administrator is directed to refuse delivery insofar as practicable to participating countries of commodities which go into the production of any commodity for delivery to any nonparticipating European country which commodity would be refused export licenses to those countries by the United States in the interest of national security."[7] This directive applied only to goods used in the further production of exports considered "strategic" by the United States and under export license by it. The ability of aid recipients to substitute domestic resources for imported materials and to attest that no aid goods were going into the "prohibited" exports made it difficult for the Administration to obtain full compliance with the spirit of this provision, though the State Department and ECA did make strenuous efforts to get the ERP countries to apply export controls parallel to those in the United States.

Congress was not satisfied with the results and, shortly after the outbreak of the war in Korea, the Senate approved a measure requiring the Administration to cut off economic assistance to countries shipping "strategic" items (whether containing aid goods or not) to Soviet bloc countries.[8] The Administration pressed hard for its deletion on the ground that such a near-embargo would weaken the West more than the East, and in the conference with the House a weaker provision was inserted and became law. Under it, the National Security Council was given discretionary authority to cut off

"Outline of European Recovery Program," *Committee Print* (Information Submitted by the Department of State to the Senate Foreign Relations Committee), 80th Cong., 1st Sess., December 19, 1947, pp. 97-114. For two nonofficial statements at that time emphasizing the importance of restoring East-West trade, see Diebold, W. J., Jr., "East-West Trade and the Marshall Plan," *Foreign Affairs*, July 1948, pp. 709-722 and *The Economist*, July 19, 1947, pp. 91-93.

[7] P.L. 472, Section 117 (d), 80th Cong.

[8] See *Survey—1950*, p. 210.

economic aid (military aid was exempted from the law) when it determined that the aid recipient was shipping goods to Russia or to its satellites of such types as to be detrimental to the national security of the United States. No aid was terminated under the authority of this law—a record which some Congressmen thought proved the Administration to be delinquent since, they stated, East-West European trade had increased in the last half of 1950.

Many in Congress during 1951 believed that the U.S. Government should apply whatever pressure it could to eliminate *all* exports from the West to the Soviet bloc; others, who were not prepared to go this far, thought that "mandatory" (not just permissive) legislation should be passed to force the U.S. Administration to cut off *economic* aid to countries shipping "strategic" items to the East.[9] One of the most thoughtful statements by the Administration during these discussions was that given by H. F. Linder, a State Department official. He stated that the real objective of export restrictions was "to increase the strength of the free world relative to that of the Soviet world. . . . We will not accomplish this by following the simple and clear-cut course of embargoing everything." He emphasized that each export item must be examined with reference to the items imported against it and that a decision as to relative advantage required "expert technical advice, accurate information, and careful economic and political judgment."[1] But

[9] See, for example, the discussions in "The Supplemental Appropriation Bill for 1952," *Hearings, Part 2,* House of Rep., Subcommittee of the Committee on Appropriations, 82d Cong., 1st Sess., June 1951, pp. 326-336; and "Supplemental Appropriations for 1952," *Hearings on H.R. 5215,* U.S. Senate, Committee on Appropriations, 82d Cong., 1st Sess., September 1951, pp. 324-342.

[1] See "Defense Production Act Amendments of 1951," *Hearings on S. 1397,* U.S. Senate, Committee on Banking and Currency, 82d Cong., 1st Sess., pp. 357-379. See also a subsequent speech by Mr. Linder in Department of State *Bulletin,* November 12, 1951, pp. 759-762.

The Administration also argued that rather than embargo everything, the United States should try to help West Europeans to gain the most from the trade and to drive the hardest bilateral bargain possible. (See "Mutual Security Program Appropriations for 1952," *Hearings, Part 1,* House of Rep., Subcommittee of the Committee on Appropriations, 82d Cong., 1st Sess., September 1951, p. 399.) On various facets of the Eastern side of East-West trade, see Milenkovic, V., "Eastern European Foreign Trade an Instrument of USSR," *Review of International Affairs* (Belgrade), October 24, 1951, pp. 9-10, and "Czechoslovak Trade Fits Soviet Grand Plan," *Swiss Review of World Affairs,* October 1951, pp. 13-14; see also *ibid.,* May 1951, pp. 5-7 and September 1951, pp. 15-17 for other observations on East-West trade problems.

The effectiveness of the restrictions of East-West trade were reported to be evidenced by the attempts of Czechs to get vital goods "at any price" and by

Congress insisted on a broader directive, and an amendment (sponsored by Senator Kem and approved unanimously by the Senate) was added to the Third Supplemental Appropriation Act, 1951, prohibiting the extension of economic or financial (nonmilitary) assistance—during any period in which the armed forces of the United States were actively engaged in hostilities while carrying out any decision of the United Nations Security Council—to any country which exported to Russia or its satellites "arms, or armament, or military matériel, or articles or commodities which . . . may be used in the manufacture of arms, armaments, or military matériel, or shipment of which to the Soviet bloc is embargoed by the United States. . . ."[2] The Secretary of Defense was required to certify which articles were included in the above categories. Continuation of aid despite shipment of cited items was allowed, provided such exceptions to the general rule were determined by the National Security Council to be "in the security interests of the United States." Congressional discussion of the amendment showed that those sponsoring it considered that practically *all* materials were "war materials" when a country was at war and that the United States was at war with Communism. That is, the spirit, if not the letter, of this provision was that nearly all trade between the East and the West should cease.

In his message on signing the bill containing the Kem amendment, President Truman asked Congress to replace it with "improved legislation." He did not quarrel with the purposes of the provision but said that in its present form it suffered several major defects. First, he believed this "over-simplified approach" was "clearly wrong" since the problem of trade between the Soviet bloc and the free world was "a matter of evaluating, in terms of relative importance, what the free world gets from the bloc for what it must give in return." Second, the amendment replaced cooperation with coercion and "our experience so far shows that effective controls can be accomplished by cooperation." Third, by cutting off aid to friendly countries the United States might hurt itself more than it hurt Russia since such action "could strike a death blow at the tremendous defense effort in which the free nations are now

their increasing inability to remit hard currencies. (See *New York Herald Tribune*, "Monthly Economic Review," Paris, December 10, 1951, p. 3.)

[2] P.L. 45, 82d Cong., Section 1302.

engaged." He therefore urged that new legislation be enacted, designed not "blindly to cut off as much trade as possible, but to cut off trade only when such action will add to the security of the . . . free world"; and to take account of the value to the United States of the greater "strength for freedom which our economic aid brings about."[3]

Upon passage of the Kem amendment, the Secretary of Defense sent the ECA Administrator a list of commodities comprising thousands of items which aid recipients would have to refrain from exporting to Russia or its satellites if they were to qualify for continued aid.[4] In view of the wide scope of commodities involved, the Administration asserted that it might be impossible for even the friendliest of countries to qualify for aid from the United States.[5] Since the amendment became effective fifteen days after signature, a blanket interim exception was granted to all aid recipients in order to permit the Administration to make an analysis of the situation country-by-country. The Administration stated that this general exception was to be superseded as rapidly as possible by individual determinations.[6] Subsequently, the National Security Council received (and honored) certifications from twenty-five foreign countries that they were not shipping to the Soviet bloc any of the prohibited commodities. For another thirty-six countries currently receiving aid from the United States, the National

[3] For the text of the President's statement, see Department of State *Bulletin*, June 25, 1951, pp. 1027-1030, or *New York Times*, June 3, 1951.

[4] The Defense Department did not compile a new list but sent five lists already existing: (1) Presidential Proclamation 2776, enumerating the items within the categories of arms, ammunition and implements of war, (2) two lists prepared by the Atomic Energy Commission, (3) the Department of Commerce "Positive List," (4) a supplemental list of the Department of Commerce, and (5) the Department of Defense stockpile list. These lists comprised items, besides military matériel, ranging from heavy industrial equipment, to clothing, medicines, and condiments. (See *New York Times*, June 8, 1951.)

[5] Government officials were reported as saying that aid to all countries except Yugoslavia (which had a complete embargo on exports to Russia) would have to be stopped. For an estimate by an informed reporter of some of the resultant effects on the trade and aid to various countries, see *New York Times*, June 11, 1951.

[6] For the statement by the National Security Council justifying this interim general exception, see "Report by the National Security Council regarding An Interim General Exception under Section 1302 of the Third Supplemental Appropriation Act, 1951," dated June 14, 1951 (mimeographed). For a shorter statement, see *New York Times*, June 16, 1951.

Security Council granted specific exceptions,[7] it being felt that "on balance" such exceptions were "in the interests of United States security."[8] Thus, no aid was suspended under the provisions of the law.[9]

Immediately after the blanket interim exception was granted, many in Congress attacked the Administration for having circumvented the purposes of the law. They asserted that the debate on the provision showed clearly that it was meant to be mandatory, that the exception clause was meant to be applied only to individual commodities (not whole countries or groups of commodities), and that it was included only upon the Administration's urgent request and its representation that in specific cases certain commodities ought to be shipped to Russia because of the very special value of goods received in return.[1]

At the same time, violently adverse reactions to the amendment were received from many of the European countries likely to be affected by it. The press reported that European officials were baffled and irritated by this shift in policy from mutual cooperation in control of East-West trade to dictation by the United States.[2] Some expressed concern that it would lend credence to the Communist propaganda concerning American "interference." European officials were reported as being distressed at this evidence of lack of confidence by Congress in the European governments and the implication that Congress believed itself a better judge of potential gains and losses from trade than the people engaged in it. The Senate Subcommittee on Export Controls and Policies reported that objections in Europe to an acceptance of United States

[7] None of the countries granted such exceptions were known to be shipping arms, ammunition, implements of war, or atomic energy materials to the Soviet bloc.

[8] Three other countries—Argentina, Ceylon, and Guatemala—were receiving aid from the United States, but action had not been taken by the National Security Council on them by the time the Kem amendment was repealed, and so they were still covered by the original general interim exception.

[9] For the official National Security Council report on its actions, see "Report by the National Security Council Regarding a Review of its Determinations under Section 1302 of the Third Supplemental Appropriation Act, 1951," dated November 5, 1951 (mimeographed).

[1] See *Congressional Record*, July 18, 1951, pp. 8524-8529.

[2] See especially *New York Times*, February 24; April 15 and 30; May 13 and 23; June 6, 15, and 20; July 17, 22, and 25; August 7, 1951.

export control policy "usually stem from internal political problems, such as organized Communist troublemaking, special economic-interest groups which possess organized political power, and critical economic problems. The latter might be classed generally under (a) dependency on eastern markets as a trade outlet for goods which are not generally marketable in the west or (b) dependency on the east as a source of key raw materials and some manufactured goods. Not to be neglected are the very real problems faced in terms of payment difficulties, the dollar gap, and price differentials. In addition there are the various psychological factors affecting trade with the east as exemplified in the case of Eastern and Western Germany. Public opinion or the degree of public interest in or resistance to certain policies is an important factor."[3]

The Administration itself favored a policy of mutual negotiation for control over East-West trade, and it had some support from the Senate subcommittee studying export controls.[4] The subcommittee noted, however, that there were vast differences in the controls and policies being pursued by the various countries and that there remained a large field for cooperative endeavor in achieving "minimum standards" of performance. It concluded that continued insistence by the United States on adoption of its particular export control measures had reached a point of diminishing returns and that emphasis should be turned toward means of removing or reducing the underlying reasons for policies or operations which allowed what Congress considered was an undesirable flow of materials to Soviet-dominated areas. Among the measures it advised were: (a) "An aggressive effort to provide, seek out, or otherwise make available alternate markets and alternate sources of supply for those goods for which western nations are dependent on the east and for which their bargaining power consists largely in ship-

[3] S. *Rpt. No. 944, op.cit.*, p. 10.

[4] The subcommittee reported that for some time representatives of the principal North Atlantic Treaty countries and United States officials had maintained regular contact and discussion on these matters through a Committee on Security Export Controls in Paris. It recorded that the National Security Council stated that substantial agreement had been achieved with respect to embargoes on all items agreed to be of primary strategic significance and that the differences between the United States list and the international list were deemed to be very small and reflected differences of judgment as to the strategic importance of certain items. The subcommittee, however, felt that the results obtained by these discussions were less than completely satisfactory.

ping items of admitted strategic significance." (b) The establishment of methods ". . . for continuing evaluation, demonstration, and implementation of the policy of increasing to the maximum degree the differential of strength between the Soviet bloc and the west, to the advantage of the west." (c) ". . . a thorough, painstaking, and completely informed evaluation of the balance of value in commodity exchanges," and (d) "Positive efforts to mobilize the support of public opinion and establish a proper psychological setting for controls. . . ."[5]

In the meantime, in order to provide the "improved legislation" requested by the President, a *House* Subcommittee of the Committee on Foreign Affairs (under the chairmanship of Congressman Battle) studied for three months other measures for curbing East-West trade.[6] This Committee received the advice of the Departments of State and Defense whose spokesmen took the position, for reasons noted above, that a sweeping embargo on East-West trade forced on aid recipients would have undesired effects,[7] and that certain strategic items, but not armaments or munitions, might under certain conditions be exported profitably to the East.

The resulting House bill (H.R. 4550) stated that—in order to increase the strength of the United States and its allies, to impede the ability of possible enemies to conduct military operations, and to assist nations under domination of foreign aggressors to reestablish their freedom—it was United States policy to apply an embargo on the shipment of specified war-potential items[8] to any nation threatening the security of the United States and that no military, economic, or financial assistance should be extended to any

[5] S. *Rpt. No. 944, op.cit.*, pp. 10-11.

[6] For its report, see "Control of Exports to Soviet Bloc," *Committee Print*, Report on H.R. 1621 and H.R. 1939, 82d Cong., 1st Sess., June 7, 1951.

[7] One effect not mentioned above which was considered highly undesirable by the committee was that such an embargo, by increasing their interdependence, would consolidate even further the Eastern European countries with Russia. (See *H. Rpt. No. 703*, 82d Cong., 1st Sess., July 16, 1951, pp. 11-12.) The State Department later minimized this possibility. (See "Mutual Security Program Appropriations for 1952," *Hearings, Part 1*, House of Rep., Subcommittee of the Committee on Appropriations, September 1951, p. 404; see *ibid.*, pp. 388-406 for a discussion of East-West trade in general.)

[8] Arms, ammunition, implements of war, atomic materials, petroleum, transportation materials of strategic value, and "items of primary strategic significance used in the production of arms, ammunition, and implements of war." The bill directed the Administration to determine which specific commodities fell into these categories.

nation unless it applied a similar embargo. An exception to the suspension of aid was authorized in any case where the aid recipient shipped certain of the embargoed items,[9] and the President determined—and immediately reported such determination to Congress—that there were present "unusual circumstances" which indicated that the cessation of aid would be clearly detrimental to the security of the United States. With respect to *other items*, the bill directed that the Administration should negotiate with all aid recipients for their undertaking a program for controlling exports of such items as, in the judgment of the Administration, should be controlled in order to strengthen the free world and to offset acts which threaten the peace. All aid from the United States was to be terminated when the President determined that a recipient country (a) was not "effectively cooperating" with the United States in these matters, or (b) was failing to provide the United States sufficient information to determine whether it was so cooperating.[1]

The letter of this bill was more stringent than the Kem amendment, which it replaced, in three important respects: (a) it provided that "military" as well as "economic" aid should be suspended to nations shipping embargoed items to the Soviet bloc; (b) its duration was not limited to the period in which United States armed forces were engaged in hostilities while carrying out a decision of the United Nations Security Council; and (c) it permitted no exceptions to the general rule with respect to trade in arms, ammunition, implements of war, and atomic energy materials. On the other hand, it was generally regarded as a more liberal measure since the spirit of the bill was that the Administration should have considerable discretionary authority in providing exceptions to the general rule for other than the war-potential items mentioned above.[2]

[9] Petroleum, transportation material of strategic value, and "items of primary strategic significance used in the production of arms, ammunition, and implements of war."

[1] The President was also directed to invite all non-aid-recipient nations to cooperate in controlling exports to the Communist-dominated countries, and the Administrator of the Act was required to make a continuing study of the administration of export controls by foreign governments and to make periodic reports thereon to Congress, recommending action where appropriate.

[2] It was on this issue of discretion that most of the debate hinged. The distrust of a majority of Congress of the way in which the State Department would ad-

Neither the House nor the Senate questioned the desirability of attempting to curb the trade of aid recipients with the East. The Senate Foreign Relations Committee considered the bill and approved it within twenty minutes.[3] Those who favored a stronger measure took up almost all of the time used to debate the bill in Congress. Their arguments, often emotional and frequently referring to the necessity of keeping faith with the Americans "whose blood has been spilled in Korea," in essence were that the situation demanded that practically all trade between the West and the East be stopped and that specific provisions should be inserted so that the State Department, which they believed reluctant to impose those sorts of conditions on foreign aid, did not administer the measure.[4] The Congressional supporters of the measure justified it on the grounds that it did provide an embargo on arms exports and authorized the shipment of other "strategic" items only if the free world received more—in economic strength and political unity—than the Soviet bloc nations. (Members of neither the Administration nor Congress tangled, in public at least, with the many problems of establishing working criteria for determining which trade would add greater relative economic strength and political unity to the West than to the East.)[5] They emphasized that the aid-recipients were already severely restricting the exports of many items and that the United States could not obtain the results it hoped for by forcing its "flat judgments" upon other friendly nations. They stressed that a major readjustment of "free-world supplies" would be required if Western Europe's imports, especially of coal, timber, and grain, from the East were cut off,[6] and

minister the law caused it to place authority for administration in the office of the Director for Mutual Security.

[3] It should be noted that this did not indicate cursory consideration of the issues since the committee had previously had before it a good many measures of similar import and had discussed them at some length during previous years.

[4] See *Congressional Record*, August 27, 1951, pp. 10877-10891 and 10914-10988.

[5] See Sir Hartley Shawcross, "Britain Needs Trade with East," *Commercial and Financial Chronicle*, September 6, 1951, p. 21, and *New York Times*, August 16, 1951, for British arguments for continuing trade. See also *S. Rpt. No. 944, op.cit.*, pp. 11-12, and the *New York Times*, June 10 and August 6, 1951 for some views that a complete embargo on trade would damage the West more than the East. For a study on "Recent Developments in Trade Between Eastern and Western Europe," see Economic Commission for Europe, *Economic Bulletin for Europe*, Second Quarter, 1951, Geneva, October 1951, pp. 49-66.

[6] An editorial in *Fortune*, August 1951, pp. 68-69, argued that the Kem and Battle measures were only half a policy since neither made provisions for insuring that

they argued that if East-West trade were stopped the United States would have to supply the goods which Western Europe no longer received from her Eastern neighbors if the defense effort were to be maintained.[7]

The bill, in essentially the same form as prepared by the House Committee and summarized above, was finally approved on October 26 as the Mutual Defense Assistance Control Act of 1951. Relatively little criticism of the law was printed in the United States; but many in Europe, while regarding it as an improvement over the Kem amendment, found it objectionable.[8] Among their objections were: First, the method of bringing pressure to bear on Europe was distasteful—infringing the spirit of tact, trust, generosity, and mutual partnership which had characterized American aid—particularly when the allies were already doing most of what the United States appeared to desire; that is, the law implied that America's allies were either disloyal or incapable of deciding themselves the balance of gain and loss in trade with Communist countries. Second, all-out economic warfare (as they felt was implied in the law and desired by some Congressmen) was not yet appropriate. Third, rigid interpretation of the Act could cause friction and suspicion among nations of the free world.

Since the law was in effect only during the last two months of 1951, no official reports on its operations or assessment of its effect were published by the Administration during the year, but a Senate subcommittee reported, after a brief visit to Europe in January 1952, that the restriction of East-West trade was imposing significant and important handicaps on production in the Iron Curtain countries.[9]

Western Europe gained the goods from other sources that it lost in trade with the East. The editors emphasized that until an adequate policy of substituting Western goods for Eastern supplies was worked out, the U.S. Government must temporize with Communist trade. See also *New York Herald Tribune*, "Monthly Economic Review," Paris, August 6, 1951, p. 5, for a report on some of the problems of finding alternative sources of supply.

[7] In legislating the aid program discussed in Chapter I above, Congress apparently did not take into consideration the effects of curtailing East-West trade.

[8] *The Economist* published several editorials on it from the point of view of aid recipients; see especially the issues of August 25, 1951, pp. 431-433 and September 1, 1951, pp. 488-490.

[9] "Export Controls and Policies in East-West Trade—II," *Committee Print*, U.S. Senate Subcommittee of the Committee on Interstate and Foreign Commerce, 82d Cong., 2d Sess., February 18, 1952, pp. 12-14.

Note on United Nations Embargo

During the early part of 1951, the United States urged the United Nations to take nonmilitary as well as military action to support its Korean policies. An Additional Measures Committee was established in February to consider means which might be employed, and a Subcommittee on Economic Sanctions later reported that embargoes on particular commodities of primary importance to the enemy should be imposed by UN member states. In order to show Congressional support for this proposal and to strengthen the hands of United States delegates to the UN, Congress in mid-May passed a concurrent resolution requesting the UN to place an embargo on the shipment to Communist China of arms, ammunition, and all other materials which might add to the warmaking potential of that country.

The UN General Assembly passed on May 18, by a vote of 47 to 0 (Russia and its satellites stated that the action proposed was illegal and did not participate in the discussions or voting) a resolution recommending that every state "apply an embargo on the shipment to areas under the control of the Central People's Government of the People's Republic of China and of the North Korean authorities of arms, ammunition and implements of war, atomic energy materials, petroleum, and items useful in the production of arms, ammunition and implements of war."[1] The resolution was only a recommendation and left it to the individual states to determine whether they would adopt the embargo and, if so, on what specific commodities. However, nations supporting it were requested to report action within thirty days. By mid-July thirty-nine countries had reported their compliance; about half of them considered that they already were controlling exports sufficiently to require no new measures, while others adopted new legislation or administrative methods to implement the purposes of the resolution.[2]

[1] Department of State *Bulletin*, May 28, 1951, p. 849. The text of the resolution passed by the Additional Measures Committee, which was accepted almost verbatim by the General Assembly, and additional comment by the Committee may be found in the *New York Times*, May 15, 1951.

[2] See UN Doc. A/1841, July 12, 1951, and Doc. A/1841/Add. 1-5; see also *United Nations Bulletin*, August 15, 1951, p. 150. The resolution also requested the Additional Measures Committee to continue to study the subject of the em-

Pursuant to the UN "Uniting for Peace" resolution, a Collective Measures Committee was established to consider measures which might be taken to prevent or suppress some future, un-named aggressor. In July, a subcommittee concerned with economic sanctions reported that the cost of imposing economic sanctions would probably fall unevenly on cooperating nations, chiefly because of differences in geographical proximity to, or economic interdependence with, the offending country. As a means of attaining a more equitable sharing of the burden, it recommended that: "Countries that are relatively unaffected either by economic hardships or because of their inability to make military or other contributions, should be expected at least to provide alternative markets, raw materials and other assistance for those that are heavily affected. In certain cases, assistance may take the form of loans or grants."[3] The U.S. Government did not publish in 1951 a detailed statement as to its reaction to the portions of this report dealing with burden sharing.

C. *STOCKPILING*

For several years the U.S. Government, as a result of expensive and distressing experiences during World War II, has been accumulating a stockpile of strategic and critical materials.[4] The primary purpose of the program is to reduce wartime dependence (both for civilian and direct military needs) upon foreign sources of essential raw and semi-processed materials,[5] and it is designed

---

bargo and its effectiveness and other measures which might be taken through the UN.

[3] Report of the Collective Measures Committee, General Assembly, *Official Records*, 6th Session, Supplement No. 13 (A/1891) New York, 1951, p. 8. See *United Nations Bulletin*, August 15, 1951, pp. 152-153 and October 15, 1951, pp. 340-341; Department of State *Bulletin*, November 12, 1951, p. 771-774; also, for comment, *The Statist*, November 10, 1951, p. 606. This report also considers various types of sanctions and assesses their burdens on cooperating countries.

[4] See *Survey—1949*, pp. 162-168, and *Survey—1950*, pp. 212-221, for a brief account of the issues, activities, and shifting policies through 1950; see also "Stockpiling of Strategic and Critical Materials," *Hearings*, House of Rep., Special Subcommittee of the Committee on Armed Services, 81st Cong., 2d Sess., May-September, 1950. Fissionable materials are stockpiled by the Atomic Energy Commission; data on these operations are secret and not included in the following account.

[5] Through 1950 approximately 80 percent, by value, of the purchases had been from abroad; data for 1951 are not available, but the percentage may well have been lower as increasing attention was placed on developing domestic sources.

to make up the deficit between probable supplies and estimated total needs during a full-scale war.[6]

Program

The stockpile objectives are under more or less constant review and are frequently changed, both as to components and amounts, since they are based on strategic assumptions as to the nature and probable duration of a threatened war, the probable supplies available from accessible wartime sources, the probable requirements,

TABLE 14

Total United States Stockpile Objectives, 1946-1951

(billions of dollars)

Date	*Value*	
	At June 30, 1951 Prices	*At Dec. 31, 1951 Prices*
December 31, 1946	4.5	n.a.
December 31, 1947	4.5	n.a.
December 31, 1948	4.7	n.a.
December 31, 1949	4.9	n.a.
December 31, 1950	8.6	n.a.
June 30, 1951	8.3	9.1
December 31, 1951	n.a.	9.3

Source: Munitions Board, *Stockpile Report to Congress,* Washington, D.C., July 23, 1951, p. 11 and January 23, 1952, p. 1.

etc., which are themselves subject to constant reassessment. Many of the program details are secret, but data have been published on the total dollar value of the objectives and show that it was relatively stable in terms of constant dollars from 1946 up to 1950. In that year, following an extensive review, the total objectives were drastically increased, as Table 14 shows. It was only by coincidence

[6] For detailed information on the 1951 stockpiling activities, see Munitions Board, *Stockpile Report to Congress,* Washington, D.C., July 23, 1951 and January 23, 1952; "The Supplemental Appropriation Bill for 1952," *Hearings, Part 2,* House of Rep., Subcommittee of the Committee on Appropriations, 82d Cong., 1st Sess., May-June 1951, pp. 440-487; "Third Supplemental Appropriation Bill for 1951," *Hearings (on Emergency Agencies),* House of Rep., Subcommittee of the Committee on Appropriations, 82d Cong., 1st Sess., March 1951; the various 1951 commodity reports under the general title "Investigation of the Preparedness Program," Report of the Preparedness Subcommittee of the Committee on Armed Services, U.S. Senate, 82d Cong., 1st Sess.; the *Congressional Record,* March 22, 1951, pp. 2974 f., June 27, 1951, pp. A4093 f.; and the strategic and critical materials section of the 1951 quarterly Economic Cooperation Administration, *Report to Congress.*

that this increase occurred shortly after the outbreak of the war in Korea since it was based on studies virtually completed before that event. There was a small reduction in the objectives during 1951 as a result of a decision that excessive quantities of a few items had been programmed.

As in the preceding year, but in contrast to the period 1946-1949,[7] the stockpile program was regarded by both the Administration and Congress almost entirely in terms of its national security aspects and not as a method of bridging the "dollar gap" of foreign countries or as a threat to domestic producers of stockpile items. Following the $2.9 billion of new purchasing authority provided in 1950 for fiscal year 1951 (which brought the total available funds to $4.2 billion), the Administration requested only $800 million of new obligational authority for fiscal year 1952. This request, less a $10 million cut in the portion for administrative expenses, was granted by Congress without objection and without reduction. The Administration stated that more funds were not requested because the above amount was sufficient to purchase all the items available.

Procurement and Supply Development

During 1951, there was an extensive reshuffling of the complex structure of responsibility for determining the stockpile procurement activities.[8] An account of these organizational and administrative shifts is outside the scope of this document, but it should be noted that the primary purpose of the changes was to centralize responsibility in the face of increasing demands of United States industry for many of the materials in the stockpile list and increasing competition for the materials between private groups and the Government and among each. These administrative changes, in general, took the form of giving the civilian agencies charged with directing the mobilization of the domestic economy (the Defense Production Administration in particular, rather than the Munitions Board of the Defense Department) greater responsibility for determining how much should go into and out of the Government's stockpile.

Actual procurement for the official stockpile during 1951 was of

[7] See *Survey—1950*, pp. 212-217.

[8] See *Congressional Record*, July 13, 1951, p. 8344, for a listing of the agencies directly concerned with the stockpile program.

approximately the same dimensions as during the previous two years, and there remained a large gap between the objectives, the provision of funds, and the commodities on hand, as a comparison between Table 14 and Table 15 shows. Indeed, the General Services Administration stated in mid-1951 that it would take three and a half more years to purchase and take possession of all the items ordered and to be ordered with the funds ($5 billion) already made available by Congress.

TABLE 15

Value of United States Stockpile on Hand, 1946-1951

(billions of dollars)

Date	Value: At June 30, 1951 Prices	Value: At Dec. 31, 1951 Prices
December 31, 1946	0.3	n.a.
December 31, 1947	0.7	n.a.
December 31, 1948	1.1	n.a.
December 31, 1949	1.8	n.a.
December 31, 1950	2.5	2.6
June 30, 1951	3.0	3.1
December 31, 1951	n.a.	3.4

Source: Munitions Board, *Stockpile Report to Congress*, Washington, D.C., July 23, 1951, p. 11 and January 23, 1952, pp. 1 and 9.

a. PROCUREMENT[9]

The major problems with respect to actual procurement of current output during 1951 revolved around questions of prices, allocation of available supplies as among the allied countries,[1] and allocation among competing internal demands. The last problem is outside the purview of this survey; yet it should be recorded

[9] Throughout the first part of the year, responsibility for actual procurement and for expanding sources of supply was distributed among several Government agencies, but in August the President created a new independent agency—the Defense Materials Procurement Agency—which assumed all the procurement and development functions of the General Services Administration, the Economic Cooperation Administration, the Department of Interior, the Munitions Board, and the Defense Production Administration. (See *New York Times*, August 2 and 29, 1951.) It appears, however, that whereas this new agency did provide centralized direction, control, and coordination, several of the previous agencies continued to operate actively—either through, under, or as agents of the new organization.

[1] The United States export controls discussed above, by restricting and channelling exports of critical materials, served to protect domestic supplies and so was closely related to the United States stockpile program.

that diversions from the stockpile—primarily of commodities under contract but a few commodities on hand were also affected—to industrial consumers were of increasing importance as the rearmament programs got under way and were partly responsible for the failure of the official stockpile to increase at a faster rate. The problem of international allocations for several items in especially short supply are discussed in Section D below. Here it need only be noted that, as during the previous year, the United States was criticized, during the early months of 1951, by many foreign countries for "hogging" scarce materials and for "inept and uneconomic" stockpile procurement policies which, it was said, resulted in higher prices for all purchasers and in an "inequitable" distribution of available supplies. (Those making such charges almost always blamed the official stockpiling operations, but at least one observer wrote that the lenient credit and monetary policies were equally to blame by making possible the "runaway competition" of private industries among themselves and with the Government.)[2] During the last half of the year, the U.S. Government, heeding these complaints and in keeping with its avowed policy that available supplies should be equitably distributed among all her allies, adopted a general policy of reducing the current imports for the official stockpile, except in cases where supply was in excess of demands.[3] Thus, acquisitions during the last six months of the year were, in terms of constant prices, some 40 percent below those during the first six months. And as the year ended, foreign countries were again beginning to urge that the United States step up its procurement as a means of helping to cover their growing "dollar shortage."

The rapid rise in prices for most of the imported (as well as domestic) stockpile commodities after the outbreak of the Korean War in mid-1950 not only greatly increased the dollar cost of meeting the stockpile goals but also resulted in several other serious procurement problems. Price ceilings imposed on internal transactions during the first part of the year were lower than the world

[2] See Hobson, O. R., "The New Commodity Inflation," *Lloyds Bank Review*, April 1951, especially p. 38. In order to increase the supply of certain strategic and critical materials, the Bureau of Customs was ordered by the Secretary of Commerce to lift the prohibition on re-entry of United States nonagricultural surplus property held abroad if such items were to be used for defense purposes.

[3] See *The Economist*, August 25, 1951, p. 439, and *New York Times*, November 26, 1951.

market prices for some items on the stockpile list and so effectively curtailed foreign procurement. To remove this obstacle the Office of Price Stabilization first adopted a policy—when appeals were made to it—of sanctioning sales by private importers of unprocessed commodities to the official stockpile (but not to domestic consumers) at current world prices, and in July it issued a general regulation exempting sales to the Government of such commodities from price control.

Other problems arose in connection with certain commodities for which the U.S. Government was designated the sole buyer.[4] The General Services Administration had been named the sole importer of natural rubber at the end of 1950;[5] in order to lower the world price, it set a buying rate which was below the market. The Government also let it be known that it was increasing the production of synthetic rubber, and a senior official testified that foreign rubber interests were pricing themselves out of business. By July, the Government was able to purchase rubber at 45 cents per pound, as compared with a price of 85 cents earlier in the year. The American procurement practices were protested by the rubber-producing areas, and some of the British press was critical on the grounds that the United States action of sweeping into and then out of the rubber market on such a big scale was "making difficult conditions even more unmanageable." In early 1952 rubber imports were again returned to private channels.

More serious international tensions developed over the price of tin. In early 1951 the Reconstruction Finance Corporation had again been designated the sole importer of tin metal and tin concentrates. Shortly thereafter, in an effort to force a "reasonable price," it declared a buyers' strike—thus carrying out a recommendation of the Senate Armed Forces Committee that the United States stop buying tin at "gouging" prices (250 percent of the pre-Korean prices) which, it stated, were the results of the operations of a well-organized tin cartel. The world price dropped precipi-

[4] The possibility of a greater centralization of imports of strategic materials in the hands of the Government was increased by the 1951 amendment to the Defense Production Act which gave the Government wide authority to purchase abroad "metals, minerals and other materials" for its own use and for internal resale.

[5] For a review of "World Rubber Developments in 1950-1951," see W. N. Small's article in Department of Commerce, *Foreign Commerce Weekly*, March 3, 1952, pp. 3 f.

tously, from $1.82 to $1.34 per pound in a five-day period.[6] By mid-June the price was down to $1.06 as the RFC successively reduced its offer price. In late July, the RFC announced that the price "gouge" was ended. An interim agreement was then reached with Bolivia whereby shipments during the next few weeks would be paid for at the rate of $1.12 per pound, on the understanding that this price would be retroactively adjusted should a different price be agreed upon during pending negotiations. Bolivia continued to demand a price of $1.50, and no agreement had been reached at year's end.

Various of the foreign tin producers bitterly denounced the contention of certain members of Congress that an international cartel was operating. The press reported that Bolivia was protesting the RFC purchase policies to the State Department and to the President directly and that the State Department at least believed that the RFC offer should be raised to prevent a deterioration of friendly relations with foreign countries.[7] The head of the RFC resigned early in 1952, and the press interpreted this to be at least in part the result of disagreement within the Administration over the price to be paid for imported tin. In any case, the desires of the tin producers and those of the United States were not reconciled during the year.[8]

The GSA and the RFC were the major procurement agencies, but small additions to the stockpile were also made by ECA and the Commodity Credit Corporation (CCC). The former, out of its 5 percent counterpart funds plus a small amount of dollars from the GSA, entered into purchase *commitments* to the equivalent of $14.5 million, raising the total since the inception of ECA to $102.9 million, of which the equivalent of $81.3 million was out of 5 percent counterpart funds. The CCC was authorized in 1949 to barter surplus agricultural commodities held by it for strategic materials

[6] The press reported that British officials were pleased at this particular RFC action and the following price drop, arguing that it demonstrated that past United States buying policy, and not concerted sellers' action, was responsible for the high prices.

[7] See *New York Times*, December 22, 1951; *The Economist*, January 5, 1952, p. 47; and *The Statist*, January 19, 1952, p. 87.

[8] There was much disagreement between the United States and foreign officials as to the facts regarding the cost of production and the marketing arrangements for tin. In October the RFC sent a mission to Malaya to study the cost of production there. It was thought by some that a solution to the United States purchase price problem would await the report of this mission.

from foreign sources. These transactions have been small; during the year it obtained approximately $23 million of commodities, raising the total to $33 million, which were in turn purchased by the GSA.

b. SUPPLY DEVELOPMENT

The U.S. Government placed increasing emphasis during 1951 on developing new sources of supply and expanding the output of existing sources—both at home and abroad. Efforts to expand production *abroad* took many forms, in addition to paying high prices for current output.[9] Attention has already been given in this survey to the loans for such purposes which were made by the Export-Import Bank[10] and the International Bank, to the emphasis given such activities under the Point Four Program, and to the export license priorities on goods needed to expand such production and to meet certain other essential needs of the producing countries. In addition to these measures, the Government signed during 1951 a larger number than in previous years of long-term contracts at fixed or minimum prices, on the justification that foreign producers would be induced to expand output if assured of a certain market for a reasonably long period of time. Such contracts were, however, not a sufficient inducement in many instances; some foreign producers—of tin in particular—were reported as unwilling to expand output without guarantees of relief from possible overproduction in the future, including agreement for restriction of exports and/or production and the use of buffer stocks as well as price guarantees. For well-known reasons,[1] the United States opposed such international restrictive agreements.

Latin America was an important source, both actual and potential, of many of the stockpile commodities,[2] and discussions between these countries and the United States in 1951 focussed attention on, but did not solve, many of the problems faced by the

[9] For details on the program for expanding *domestic* sources of stockpile commodities, see *Stockpile Report to Congress*, January 23, 1952, *op.cit.*, pp. 21 ff.

[10] Total loans by the EIB for strategic materials, made with the advice of the Munitions Board, were $38 million during 1951, and at year's end EIB was studying applications for credits of $13.5 million to facilitate production of a variety of minerals.

[1] See *Survey—1950*, pp. 225-227.

[2] See "United States Relations with International Organizations," *H. Rpt. No. 671*, July 2, 1951, Appendix IV, and "Latin-American Business Highlights," Chase National Bank, *Quarterly Digest*, New York, February 1951.

United States in its efforts to get the so-called underdeveloped countries to step up their production of strategic raw materials.[3] At the Fourth Meeting of Consultation of Foreign Ministers of the American Republics held during the spring in Washington many resolutions were adopted which dealt with these problems.[4] While most of them were well-polished generalizations, they did seem to involve some responsibilities by the United States other than simply keeping the interests of its southern neighbors in mind. One stated that ". . . the American Republics agree to cooperate fully . . . to increase the availability of products in short supply to the countries of the free world." But the Latin American Republics were reluctant to make even this general commitment to step up the production of such goods without exacting conditions from the United States, not only because the latter's current demand was urgent but also because the future demand was uncertain and since part of the requested production was considered inconsistent with their own development programs. Thus, resolutions were also approved—clearly directed toward the United States—stating that the members agreed to facilitate, by priorities and export licenses, the obtaining of necessary machinery and materials; to provide "special and adequate technical and financial assistance when necessary and appropriate;" "to be prepared to enter into long-term or medium-term purchase and sale contracts for these basic and strategic materials;" "to establish common and mutually agreed-upon policies for liquidating government-accumulated stocks so as to avoid disturbance in the world markets for the particular products from a possible overhang on future markets;" and to protect the economic development programs and standards of the Latin American states by allocating scarce goods to meet the "essential needs of the civilian economy."

Nor was this all. The Latin American countries expressed much concern over the future purchasing power of the monetary reserves which might be accumulated through their exports. They pressed for a "guarantee of the purchasing power" of future dollar accumulations. The United States was not prepared to accede to this de-

[3] For a review of the "Effects of the United States Defense Programme on Trade with Latin America," see UN Doc. E/CN.12/234, May 5, 1951.

[4] For the text of the thirty-odd resolutions, see Department of State *Bulletin*, April 16, 1951, pp. 606-613.

mand,[5] but it did consent to consultation on the problem in the Inter-American Economic and Social Council. An extraordinary session of this body was held in August and United States representatives reported later that the session was characterized by "great preoccupation over the problem of maintaining purchasing power of monetary reserves." Again, the United States refused to assume any specific or contractual responsibility on this score. The published record does not show that an attempt was made to demonstrate that there was anything "wrong" with some kind of an escalator clause on reserves (after all, they had been recognized as "sound" for domestic wage contracts in the United States), but rather that the United States officials took the position that to date at least the problem was "more theoretical than real," that it was "only one aspect of the much greater problem . . . of the economic and financial disequilibrium" forced on the world by rearmament, and that examination of this problem should include a consideration of recent sacrifices during World War II and after by the United States in pursuit of mutual security for the free world.[6] *The Latin American States were not completely satisfied* with the general nature of the resolutions passed in the spring nor the American attitude on the purchasing power of accumulated dollar balances.

Although only a minor part of its activities, ECA gave increasing attention during 1951 to its strategic materials development program. This included providing dollars to purchase certain equipment and services in dollar areas and using some of its five-percent counterpart fund deposits to provide a part of the local currency needed to expand output. (The Mutual Security Act of 1951 removed the restriction that counterpart funds could be spent only in the country making the deposit or in its overseas territories.) All projects financed in this way involved an agreement by the recipient to repay the ECA advances (plus interest) in the materials produced by the expanded facilities, and in several instances the United States also received an option to purchase additional quantities. During 1951, ECA committed a total of $6.5 million in

[5] The resolution as finally approved stated that all members should adopt adequate internal measures to control prices and mitigate inflation.

[6] See Miller, E. G., Jr., "ECOSOC Meeting Seeks Solution of Hemisphere Economic Problems," Department of State *Bulletin*, September 17, 1951, pp. 475-476.

dollars and the equivalent of $61.7 million in counterpart funds for this purpose (raising the total from the beginning of ECA to $25.3 million and $83.9 million, respectively). Repayments were, as was to be expected, very small during the year. In addition to its own program, ECA in many cases actively encouraged the ERP recipient nations to use a part of their 95-percent counterpart fund deposit for expanding the production of scarce materials, particularly in the dependent overseas territories; it also allocated a part of its technical assistance funds for similar purposes. The United States received no special priorities with respect to the output from such projects.

During the year the Reconstruction Finance Corporation continued to finance improvements and expansion in certain abaca (hemp) plantations in four Central American states; and the Department of Agriculture continued to carry out research and experimentation in several foreign countries designed to increase the output of certain strategic agricultural-type commodities.

D. *INTERNATIONAL COMMODITY ARRANGEMENTS*

For several years the U.S. Government has actively participated in six intergovernmental commodity groups (or committees) concerned with wheat, sugar, rubber, tin, cotton, and wool. Except for wheat, however, these groups had only research and advisory functions, and during the latter part of 1950 the United States and some of its allies became convinced that additional international commodity arrangements were needed to insure that certain strategic raw materials were distributed in a manner best calculated to achieve the maximum common defense against Communist aggression.[7]

International Materials Conference[8]

The events and motives leading up to the establishment in March, 1951 of a Central Group of the International Materials Con-

[7] The UN Economic and Social Council at its Thirteenth Session in late 1951 had recommended [ECOSOC Resolution 373 (XIII)] that UN members continue to accept the principles of Chapter VI of the ITO Charter as a guide to international action or consultation on commodity problems. Further consideration of actual procedures was postponed until 1952. See also UN Doc.E/2039, June 27, 1951.

[8] Most of the data in this section have been taken from the various press releases of the International Materials Conference. These press releases were only

ference (IMC) and the organization of its seven "commodity committees" (paper-paper pulp, sulfur, cotton-cotton linters, wool, copper-zinc-lead, manganese-nickel-cobalt, and tungsten-molybdenum) were summarized in our *Survey—1950.*[9] It need be repeated here only that the chief function of the Central Group was to "formulate and coordinate international policy relating to the production, allocation, conservation, distribution, and utilization of certain strategic raw materials."[1] The individual commodity committees were, however, to have complete autonomy in conducting their work. These commodity committees were charged with making studies and specific recommendations to member governments as to means of expanding production and conserving supplies on specific commodities and, where deemed necessary, with making suggestions as to international allocations of the specific commodities under their purview. They were informal in the sense that they had no executive power or authority to impose sanctions. That is, the general approach of the International Materials Conference was to be one of voluntary cooperation which meant that "the solutions which are devised must be so reasonable and equitable as to command acceptance."[2]

The first meetings of the seven commodity committees took place during February, March, and April at the permanent office of the International Materials Conference in Washington.[3] Twenty-eight countries were included in the membership of the various commodity committees at year's end,[4] and in most cases the members

---

sporadically reported in the American press and various U.S. Government periodicals. For the convenience of those having access only to secondary sources, citations to such documents are frequently given.

[9] See pages 232-235. For a later and official statement on some of these preliminary issues, see Armstrong, W. C., "The International Materials Conference," Department of State *Bulletin,* July 2, 1951, pp. 23-30.

[1] Department of State *Bulletin,* April 16, 1951, p. 634.

[2] Thorp, W. L., "Security and Shortages," Department of State *Bulletin,* November 5, 1951, p. 730.

[3] The Central Group (composed of the United States, United Kingdom, France, Canada, Italy, India, Australia, Brazil, and representatives of OAS and OEEC) met at intervals to service the committees and to invite new members to participate in the committees when such participation was deemed desirable. The Organization of American States (OAS) and the Organization for European Economic Cooperation (OEEC) were represented in order to prevent regional solutions to allocation problems outside the IMC and to coordinate the actions of the members of these organizations who were not members of IMC.

[4] Only the United States, United Kingdom, France, West Germany, and Canada were on all seven committees.

accounted for between 80 and 90 percent of the production and consumption in the free world. Any nation with an avowed interest in the work of any committee was given permission to be heard so as to expand the coverage and to facilitate equitable distribution.

Early in its work, each commodity group sent out questionnaires asking the various countries for determinations of specific needs, production volumes, usual imports and exports, etc., with a view to making estimates of the degree and duration of specific commodity shortages, which estimates in turn would serve as a basis for allocation and conservation recommendations. These data were confidential, and deliberations of the committees were usually held in closed sessions.[5] While it was reported that one of the main tasks of the committees would be to consider means of conservation and of increasing production,[6] during 1951 most of their time was devoted to the problem of allocating available supplies. When allocations were agreed upon by a commodity group, they covered both member and nonmember countries. It appears that the *general* rule for making allocations was that defense requirements of each nation should be met first (including small amounts of some of the commodities for stockpiling) and any remaining supplies should be made available for civilian needs—using previous consumption levels as a guide.[7] Although no government was required to accept the recommendations of any commodity group, if it did it thereby undertook to carry out the allocation to the fullest extent possible.

[5] Such information if made public would of course affect the commodity markets. Thus, the press releases and information bulletins of the IMC frequently reported "No new developments" week after week. There was therefore seldom any official indication of whether the deliberations were marked by inability to agree on policy recommendations or whether general unanimity prevailed and the purely technical aspects of the work consumed weeks of effort.

[6] Including, it was officially stated, the consideration of new investment, of changes in pricing policies, of possible purchase agreements, of export controls, of restrictions on domestic consumption, and of other technical measures to increase conservation. For the first report on consumption and conservation of commodities under the IMC, see its "Utilization of Manganese, Nickel, Cobalt, Tungsten, Molybdenum: First Report of the Joint Subcommittee," Washington, D.C., December 1951.

[7] It was officially stated that each allocation system was predicated on assumptions of common principles in national stockpiling, uniform definitions of defense requirements, and agreement on relative priority of civilian needs among member countries. (See International Materials Conference; *Press Release No. 25,* May 24, 1951, and *Information Bulletin No. 38,* January 11, 1952. For an official statement of United States priority policy, see Armstrong, W. C., *op.cit.*, pp. 29-30.)

The paper-paper pulp committee did not make any general allocations of newsprint during the year, but it did recommend several "emergency" allocations to various countries (not including the United States) on the grounds that they were necessary to keep the free newspapers in these countries active and effective in propaganda warfare.[8] Since no supplies were available for distribution outside those already under contract, these allocations were diverted from Canadian and United States consumers. This commodity committee decided that the other goods under its responsibility (kraft and dissolving pulp) did not require allocation during the year.

Most of the free world's sulfur exports are produced in the United States. To give tangible evidence of United States support of the IMC concept,[9] to strengthen its request that other countries participate with respect to commodities of which the United States was a net importer, and to avoid frictions which might result from a unilateral distribution, the U.S. Government favored an allocation of sulfur via the new international machinery. The sulfur committee's recommendation for the third quarter of 1951 gave about two-thirds of the supply to the United States and Canada.[1] A similar allocation was made for the fourth quarter, along with certain recommendations for increasing the production in other countries, but apparently only after the United States withdrew some of its demands.[2] These allocations served to run down the United States reserves.

[8] Canadian producers in late 1951 stated that the aggregate supply of newsprint would be within 3 percent of world demand in 1952. But it should also be recorded that in May 1951 the Judiciary Committee of the House of Representatives "found" that companies in the United States and Canada had illegally contrived to reduce output and raise prices for newsprint in the United States and recommended strong antitrust action to induce greater production. This recommendation was not carried out, and a price increase by Canada in June resulted in some friction between the United States and Canadian Governments. (See *New York Times*, May 22, 1951, and June 13, 1951.)

[9] Some of the reasons for United States support of the IMC were discussed in *The Statist* (November 3, 1951, pp. 566-567) report on speeches made by Assistant Secretary of State Thorp and Mr. Stacy May. A more recent statement was that made by Charles E. Wilson before the Senate Committee on Banking and Currency on March 21, 1952. For a summary of this, see *New York Times*, March 22, 1952.

[1] See Department of State *Bulletin*, July 30, 1951, p. 194.

[2] For a statement on the sulfur shortage and means of increasing production, see *World Today*, September 1951, pp. 377-383, *The Statist*, November 17, 1951, p. 638, and the Department of State *Bulletin*, November 5, 1951, p. 730.

The cotton-cotton linters committee concluded in August, on the basis of an estimate of a United States cotton crop 70 percent greater than the previous year, an estimate which was later reduced somewhat, that no allocation was needed. Strong pressure by the U.S. Government in the wool committee to set up an allocation and price control scheme for wool ran into opposition from the growers of the United States and, especially, Australia and New Zealand. The wool committee terminated its meeting in August without making any allocation recommendations.[3] The official report was to the effect that recommendations were impossible because of differences of opinion as to the outlook for production and consumption.[4]

The committee considering copper-zinc-lead required seven months to reach conclusions as to allocations. No recommendations were found necessary for lead. Allocations finally were recommended for zinc and copper for the fourth quarter of 1951 and the first quarter of 1952, with the United States receiving half the supply of each commodity.[5] Chile, one of the world's largest producers of copper, reserved 20 percent of its supply to be sold without reference to the allocation scheme but stated that it would take the general allocations into account on this reserve 20 percent.[6]

The committee concerned with supplies of manganese-nickel-cobalt determined that manganese need not be allocated if available conservation techniques were put into force. The shortages of cobalt and nickel were found to be more acute.[7] The shortage of cobalt was found to be so great that the committee recommended that nickel be used where possible as a substitute, with

[3] See International Materials Conference, *Press Release No. 41,* August 25, 1951, and *New York Times,* August 23, and September 3, 1951. For an official account of recent developments in wool markets and international discussions thereon, see Grindle, N. L., "Recent International Discussions on Wool," Department of State *Bulletin,* July 16, 1951, pp. 116-119.

[4] During the year a British Commonwealth wool price-support scheme continued in operation. This scheme was virtually the same as that administered by the postwar Commonwealth Joint Organization and was essentially a producers' group and thus dissimilar from the IMC commodity groups. For a statement on this Commonwealth wool group, see *The Economist,* August 7, 1951, p. 367.

[5] Department of State *Bulletin,* January 7, 1952, pp. 15-16.

[6] Unofficial reports were that Chile opposed allocation of copper for fear of losing its bargaining position with Argentina.

[7] For a survey of the world nickel situation, see *The Statist,* September 27, 1951, pp. 538-540.

the resulting increased shortage of nickel being made up by other (unspecified) means. The United States was given nearly two-thirds the nickel and slightly over half the cobalt in the first allocations which were made—for the fourth quarter. In December a provisional allocation of cobalt for the first quarter of 1952 was accepted.[8]

The remaining committee was responsible for tungsten-molybdenum. This group recommended an allocation for the third quarter, with the United States scheduled to receive three-fourths of the molybdenum and almost half of the tungsten supplies.[9] Only ores and concentrates were allocated at that time; the committee considered that if it could solve the difficult problem of their distribution, primary products could be left to normal trade channels. This committee, unlike the others, also made recommendations as to prices; spot prices of tungsten were set, by agreement of all but one participating government, at between $55 and $65 per short ton, and the prevailing world prices (United States export price) of molybdenum were to be used. The allocation for the fourth quarter—considerably delayed by the disagreement of Brazil with the price ceiling on tungsten and the resultant resentment among other members—included primary products and set out specific quantities that producers should export; the price arrangements for the third quarter were not continued into the fourth quarter. A first quarter 1952 allocation was announced in December.[1]

The tungsten-molybdenum committee was the only one of the seven which produced a long-term (four-year) plan—for tungsten—designed to induce producers to expand production facilities. It reportedly stipulated a maximum price of $60 per unit—at which producers would guarantee to sell predetermined volumes—and a minimum price of $35 per unit—at which consumers would agree to buy predetermined volumes. The proposal contemplated that, so long as demand at the maximum price was greater than supply,

[8] Department of State *Bulletin*, January 14, 1952, p. 70.

[9] The large portion of each material allocated which went to the United States could perhaps *prima facie* be justified by the facts that United States gross national product was approximately three times that of all the other NATO countries combined and American total rearmament expenditures (excluding foreign aid) have been calculated at five times that of all the other NATO countries combined as of mid-1951.

[1] Department of State *Bulletin*, January 14, 1952, pp. 69-70.

allocations by the IMC would be made. The producers were apparently at best lukewarm toward the scheme, and the interested governments had not taken action on it at year's end.[2]

In reporting on its activities,[3] the IMC noted that, while its first allocation plans were not completed until the third quarter and then covered only three commodities, four others were also placed under allocation during the fourth quarter and that several others were under continuous review as the year ended, with the possibility that recommendations for allocations would be made for some of them in 1952. It noted that delays in receiving replies to questionnaires were hindering the work of the committees and that efforts were being made to suggest allocations for periods longer than one quarter. By and large, the allocations through 1951 were *ad hoc* measures and did not lend themselves to generalized description. The IMC stated in a year-end report that one of the immediate tasks was, indeed, to revise the basis and methods of allocation, but no details of the particular problems were given; earlier, it had reported that improved procedures for screening stated requirements, both for defense and civilian uses, were needed.

With respect to the implementation of its allocation recommendations, the IMC reported that there had been "general willingness of the member and nonmember governments to comply . . ." and that "it would appear that . . . implementation will even more closely follow the IMC recommendations" during future periods.[4] Nonetheless, future implementations were foreseen as beset with many problems. The IMC specifically mentioned, but did not detail, those revolving around the relationship of existing trade agreements to allocation plans, the maintenance of "normal" trade

[2] Official details of the scheme were not released, but it was reported that it left intact existing bilateral contracts. See *The Economist*, December 8, 1951, p. 1426; and December 29, 1951, pp. 1584-1585; *The Statist*, December 8, 1951, p. 736; and Heymann, H., "Raw Materials at the Crossroads," *Swiss Review of World Affairs*, August 1951, pp. 4-6, and "Commodity Markets in New Phase?" *ibid.*, December 1951, pp. 18-20, for a discussion of some of the issues involved. For a more general discussion of some of the problems of allocating raw materials, see Wolff, S., "Will Cooperation Solve Western Europe's Raw Material Problems?" *ibid.*, September 1951, pp. 13-15; and *World Today*, November 1951, pp. 474-480.

[3] See especially International Materials Conference, *Information Bulletin No. 22*, September 21, 1951, *No. 29*, November 9, 1951, and *No. 38*, January 11, 1952.

[4] International Materials Conference, *Information Bulletin No. 38*, *op.cit.*

patterns, the adequacy of controls over exports and imports, price discrepancies between different sources of supply, and the reporting methods of participating countries.[5] Although not mentioned by the IMC, attention should be drawn to the basic problem of the difference in interest with respect to prices as between producer and consumer nations and the importance to producer countries of using scarce material exports as levers in obtaining desired imports.[6]

While allocation problems had taken up the greater part of the committees' time during 1951, the IMC reported that, if its task were to be successfully discharged, it would be necessary in the immediate future to give more attention to the problems of increasing production and, even more urgently, to problems of conservation, including the substitution of alternative materials. Indeed, the conservation practices followed by the United States and Britain in particular had been of major importance in the 1951 successes of the IMC allocation proposals.[7] Observers seemed to be generally agreed that, considering the problems faced and the voluntary nature of the organization, the IMC was remarkably successful.[8] Certainly most of the panic buying which was so prevalent as the year began had stopped and prices of many of the commodities had fallen from their earlier peaks. Much of the IMC success may have been due to the willingness of its members to reduce hoarding once machinery was set up to insure them of continuing supplies.

[5] See *New York Times*, October 28, 1951, Department of State *Bulletin*, November 26, 1951, p. 869, and Canadian Department of Trade and Commerce, *Foreign Trade*, Ottawa, February 9, 1952, pp. 152-154, for other accounts of problems facing the IMC.

[6] See Section C above for an account of some of these problems as faced by the United States in its stockpiling operations during the year.

[7] For details on United States conservation activities, see Munitions Board, *Stockpile Report to Congress*, July 23, 1951, p. 31, and Thorp, W. L., "Security and Shortages," Department of State *Bulletin*, November 5, 1951, pp. 728-731.

[8] See, for example, the evaluation by Heymann, H., "International Materials Conference Six Months Old," *Swiss Review of World Affairs*, October 1951, pp. 10 and 11, and *The Economist*, September 15, 1951, pp. 610-611, and December 29, 1951, pp. 1584-1585.

Commodity Study Groups and Agreements[9]

a. INTERNATIONAL COTTON ADVISORY COMMITTEE

The International Cotton Advisory Committee held its tenth plenary session at Lahore, Pakistan, in early February. The major concern at the previous meeting, in 1950, had been the threat of a world surplus of cotton, but by early 1951 there appeared to be a prospect of a world deficit. The Committee therefore requested the secretariat to call to the attention of various international agencies concerned with financial and technical aid the benefits that would result from promoting increased cotton production in underdeveloped countries. The secretariat was also directed to continue its research into the question of the possibility of an intergovernmental agreement—the United States has consistently opposed such an agreement. Much time was also spent during the 1951 meeting discussing the problem of export taxes on cotton, with many of the importing countries arguing that such taxes, by increasing the price of cotton, were impairing the regular international flow of cotton, while some of the exporters asserted that the export taxes were not responsible for the recent price increases and had been imposed to suppress inflation in the exporting countries. No important substantive action was taken by the committee at this meeting, but the secretariat was instructed to prepare certain studies on various aspects of cotton and to cooperate with the cotton-cotton linters committee of the International Materials Conference.[1]

b. WOOL STUDY GROUP

The Wool Study Group did not meet during 1951, but, as noted above, a wool committee had been established under the International Materials Conference.

[9] See *Survey—1950*, pp. 223-231, for a summary of these pre-Korean organizations and United States participation in them through 1950. For an official report on these groups and their activities during 1951, see UN Interim Coordinating Committee for International Commodity Arrangements, *Review of International Commodity Problems, 1951*, New York, February 1952.

[1] For further details, see Edmond, L. E., "Recent International Discussions on Cotton," Department of State *Bulletin*, October 8, 1951, pp. 586-588.

c. RUBBER STUDY GROUP

The members of the Rubber Study Group held two unproductive meetings during the year—in February and in April. These sessions were chiefly concerned with possible action to secure agreement on a plan for the international allocation of both natural and synthetic rubber. The conclusion was reached that, barring all-out war, the world's rubber supply was more than adequate to meet the existing world demand. No allocations were recommended for this and the additional reason that the Rubber Study Group could not agree on quotas because of "serious practical difficulties." The producers of natural rubber wanted purchase guarantees of a minimum quantity at a set price as protection against overproduction after the emergency. Further, they wanted guarantees that they would be able to use foreign currencies earned to buy desired manufactured items. The United States representatives stated that their country could not meet either request.[2]

Meanwhile the importation of natural rubber in the United States had been centralized in the Government, synthetic production was being stepped up, and the world price had fallen from its previous high levels (see Section C above). At the end of the year the conditions of production and distribution out of Malaya at least had become so disrupted that it was being unofficially suggested that it might be necessary to place rubber under the IMC.[3]

d. TIN STUDY GROUP

The International Tin Study Group met in late September. The sharp disagreements between the United States as a consumer and the various producing countries which had prevented this group from reaching any agreements on intergovernmental control of tin during 1949 and 1950 were still unresolved,[4] and the meeting adjourned without making any recommendations as to allocations

[2] See *New York Times*, April 6, 21, and 22 and May 14, and 23, 1951. See also the account of the Rubber Study Group's activities in *International Organization*, November 1951, pp. 855-856. This journal is a convenient source of information on activities of a large number of the international organizations.

[3] See, in particular, *The Economist*, December 8, 1951, p. 1426.

[4] See *Survey—1950*, pp. 225-227.

or pricing.[5] In the meantime, as noted in Section C above, the United States had centralized the importation of tin in the RFC; by withdrawing from the market it had been successful in lowering the world price; but it was still involved in bitter disputes with foreign producers.

e. INTERNATIONAL SUGAR AGREEMENT

The International Sugar Agreement, which had been only nominally in effect for several years, appears to have lapsed so far as United States participation was concerned. During 1951, President Truman did request the advice and consent of the Senate for an extension of the Agreement, but that body took no action.[6] As in previous years, and as noted in the previous chapter, the United States continued to operate its own preferential trading system for sugar.

f. INTERNATIONAL WHEAT AGREEMENT

The International Wheat Agreement continued in full operation during 1951 and two major new developments took place.[7] First, Japan was admitted as an importing country. Her unrestricted membership had been supported by the United States in 1950, but Britain had opposed it on the ground that Japan would compete for the limited supplies of wheat purchaseable in sterling. Britain's counter proposal that Japan be admitted on condition that she agree to restrict her purchases of sterling wheat was unacceptable to the United States, which stated that such a qualification would alter the nondiscriminatory, multilateral aspects of the Agreement. In early 1951, Britain felt under less pressure to conserve dollars and agreed to Japanese membership, provided the latter's quota was reduced from the requested 1.2 million tons per year to 0.5 million tons. On this basis Japan joined.

The second major development concerned prices. As the free-

[5] See *New York Times*, September 29, 1951, and *The Statist*, October 6, 1951, p. 444, for accounts of this meeting. For "A Review of the World Tin Industry," see International Tin Study Group, *Tin, 1950-1951*, The Hague, 1951.

[6] See *Congressional Record*, June 7, 1951, p. 6395.

[7] In the fight against Communism, the U.S. Administration claimed that the International Wheat Agreement had, by assuring wheat supplies to importing nations, lessened the dependence on "Communist grain" and thus the hold of Russia on various countries in Europe. (See Department of Agriculture, "How is the Wheat Agreement Working?" *Agricultural Information Bulletin No. 74*, Washington, D.C., January 1952, p. 10.)

market price of wheat rose far beyond the maximum price specified in the Agreement, many producer nations became less interested in the insurance aspects of the undertaking and more interested in the prices currently obtained. Some of the exporting countries (but not the United States) were reported to have concluded that the maximum price under the Agreement hurt domestic producers and, not wanting to subsidize them, asked for an increase in the maximum price permitted in the Agreement. This was not granted, but the fixed maximum price was breached when Canada added a 6-cent per bushel carrying charge for wheat sold under the Agreement. The United States and Australia followed the Canadian lead. The consumer nations disputed this action, and at year's end the International Wheat Committee was studying its legality. Such fees are authorized in the Agreement, but it is specified that both the consumer and producer nation must agree on them, and the former insisted that they had not agreed and could see no justification for doing so since the charges had not been previously imposed and since carrying conditions and costs had not been changed.[8]

For the United States, the difference between the maximum price under the Agreement and the domestic price was about 75 cents per bushel during most of the year, the difference being provided as a subsidy to private American exporters by the CCC out of appropriated funds.[9] An average of $130 million in such payments were reported for each of the two years of operation, but two-thirds of the subsidized wheat went to ERP and other aid recipients, thus reducing the direct cost of such aid.[1]

E. *DOMESTIC PRICE CONTROLS AND INTERNATIONAL ECONOMIC POLICIES*

Export Price Control and Material Allocations

At a time when the Government was attempting to stabilize domestic price levels, it deemed it necessary to supplement other

[8] See *The Economist*, June 30, 1951, p. 1589; July 21, 1951, p. 179; and August 4, 1951, p. 306.

[9] Secretary of Agriculture Brannan emphasized that, without the Agreement, the United States would not have exported so much of its surpluses. (See "How is the Wheat Agreement Working?" *op.cit.*, p. 12.)

[1] *Ibid.*, p. 13.

measures with the imposition of price controls over exports. The Government also tried to use the existence of price controls on exports to persuade foreign countries to impose similar controls on their exports to the United States, and some American officials saw export price restrictions as a means of easing the drain on the dollar reserves of friendly nations and so of pressure for larger United States aid.

In most instances, exporters were placed under the general price ceiling regulations when these ceilings were initially imposed, but in April 1951, under pressure from exporter-producers facing rising supply prices, the Office of Price Stabilization announced that very soon a special price order would be issued allowing a mark-up based on the practices followed in a representative base period.[2] Three and a half months later the order was issued,[3] and, with subsequent amendments, allowed the exporter-producers to use as their ceiling price for exports either the domestic ceiling price or a price composed of the current domestic price plus the same mark-up for exports as was used just prior to Korea. Merchant-exporters operated under a similar percentage mark-up procedure, except that in their case the mark-up was based on their purchase price.

Some exporters also took strong exception to the notion that price restrictions on exports were justified as a method of getting other nations to control the price of their exports to the United States and as a means of easing the drain of foreign dollar reserves. They argued that other means should be found to achieve these broader international objectives,[4] but foreign countries stressed that the high prices they were paying for imports were a justification for their own high exports prices.

American producers of exports also claimed that they were being granted "unreasonably low" priorities in the allocation of scarce materials. In general, the Administration made no distinction in allocating scarce materials as between domestic or export uses, but individual firms could be and were given priorities if they were

[2] See *New York Times*, April 18, 1951.

[3] Special orders had been issued during March and May designed to allow exporters to fulfill existing contracts without serious financial losses.

[4] For a discussion of these points, see "Defense Production Act Amendments of 1951," *Hearings on H.R. 3871, Part III*, House of Rep., Committee on Banking and Currency, 82d Cong., 1st Sess., June 1951, *passim.*

exporting goods which fell within the categories of priority exports mentioned in Section A above.[5]

Import Price Controls[6]

The maintenance of effective, orderly, and equitable internal price controls requires the imposition of restrictions over the prices of imported goods. The problem is especially difficult since the producers are outside the jurisdiction of the importing country's government. During 1951 the United States began to tackle the problem on several fronts: international agreements to restrict price fluctuations and/or to allocate supplies so as to prevent "suicidal" competitive upbidding of prices of scarce items (discussed in Section D above); exercise of the quasi-monopsonistic position of the U.S. Government with respect to certain goods (discussed in Section C above); imposition of restrictions on resale prices in the United States and/or on the mark-up permitted on landed cost of imports; and reduction or suspension of the tariffs on certain imports. During the hearings on the amendments to the Defense Production Act, the question was raised of also granting import subsidies on certain products. Secretary of Agriculture Brannan replied that, so far as agricultural products were concerned at least, the Administration had given no consideration to this procedure except in the case of coffee, on which there had been some discussion but no significant support.[7]

[5] For some views of exporters on these questions, see the *New York Times*, February 23, March 27, May 3, and August 12, 19, and 22, 1951.

[6] With increasing numbers of domestically produced goods being brought under national allocation schemes, several members of Congress became concerned lest imports to meet the unrequited internal demand for such goods serve in the long run to deprive domestic producers of important parts of the home market. An amendment was proposed, on the House floor, to the Defense Production Act to require the President to prohibit the import of any items made of materials like or directly competitive with those under allocation in the United States unless the import were deemed necessary for national defense. The Administration strongly opposed the amendment, arguing that it would: (a) divert the embargoed products to Communist markets, (b) reduce the dollar earnings of friendly countries already receiving aid from the United States, (c) violate many trade agreements, (d) shut out useful and needed imports, and (e) contradict the United States efforts to gain cooperation abroad in the end-use control of essential commodities. The amendment was defeated but, in the face of United States programs to aid foreign countries and to reduce inflation at home, by the surprisingly close vote of 96 to 77. (For further details, see *Congressional Record*, July 9, 1951, pp. 8003 ff.)

[7] "Defense Production Act Amendments of 1951," *Hearings on S. 1397, Part 1*, U.S. Senate, Committee on Banking and Currency, 82d Cong., 1st Sess., May-June 1951, pp. 644-648.

Early in the year, imports other than those purchased directly by the Government were in most cases placed under the Temporary General Ceiling Price regulations applicable to domestic goods. That is, the regulations for imported commodities were identical with those for similar domestic commodities. Importers objected in principle to the base period selected for calculating the ceiling prices and to their inability to raise retail prices as the landed costs increased. Some foreign suppliers also objected to these regulations, and the President of Brazil charged that the United States had violated the Chapultepec resolution by imposing ceilings without consulting interested suppliers; the United States denied this charge, stating that it had held meetings with representatives of the coffee-producing countries.

On May 4 a special order for imports was announced. The new order allowed, subject to certain exceptions and adjustments, wholesaler-importers to add a dollar and cents mark-up on landed costs (no ceiling was placed on landed costs) calculated to be equal in amount to the percentage mark-up used in the twelve months prior to the Korean war. Retailer-importers were permitted to use a percentage mark-up on landed costs. The principle of a restricted mark-up was generally accepted by the trade as equitable. Manufacturing-importers had no specific import price ceiling imposed on them, but they were subject to the appropriate domestic price ceiling on their product.

For certain items whose prices were going up precipitously, "tailored" regulations were imposed, setting absolute ceilings on landed costs and/or domestic sales prices. Included were some goods regarded by the authorities as of special importance in household budgets and some strategic and critical materials; price ceilings were removed from imports of strategic and critical materials sold to the Government for the official stockpile.

Suspension of Import Taxes

Import duties and taxes tend to raise the price of imported commodities and may make more difficult efforts to lower or maintain a given internal price level. Duties not only tend to be pyramided if the imported good goes through processing in the United States, but in cases where the landed cost of imports is less than the domestic ceiling price imposed on them by an amount less than the duty, the existence of the duty clearly obstructs imports, thus causing a drop in import volumes at a time when larger supplies would serve to reduce inflation and to meet urgent rearmament demands. And if, under these conditions, to maintain the volume of imports while retaining the duty, an internal price ceiling is permitted on imports which exceeds the price ceiling for similar commodities produced domestically, the result is a two-price system. Such considerations, rather than the general policy of expanding trade by lowering barriers, led in 1951 to new efforts to suspend the duties on certain imports.

a. COPPER

Congress had in 1947 suspended the excise tax on imported copper and in 1949 had extended the suspension to June 30, 1950. The suspension was allowed to lapse on that date despite repeated Administration requests for its extension.[8] In April 1951, Congress again considered a proposal to reinstitute the suspension. The Administration based its support for the measure largely on the acute unsatisfied internal demand for copper and on the grounds that it would help narrow the gap between the domestic and the import prices,[9] and that it would not adversely affect the domestic industry since local production was less than 60 percent of current needs. Opposition came, as before, from those in Congress who believed that it would injure domestic producers, retard new explorations in the United States, constitute "primarily a sop to fabricators" rather than relief to consumers, and would set a precedent for removing duties on any commodity which the Administration believed was not being produced in adequate supply domestically. Nonetheless, the measure was approved without extensive debate. In its final form the law suspended the tax until June 30, 1953 or until the President proclaimed the end of the "national emergency," whichever is earlier. In order to protect domestic producers, how-

[8] See *Survey—1950*, pp. 197-198.

[9] In May the State Department announced that it had completed an agreement with Chile whereby the latter would increase production in return for a 3-cent per pound increase in price. This raised the foreign-supply price above most domestic price ceilings by 3 cents per pound even after the suspension of the import tax. The Government has not released the text of the agreement.

ever, it also provided that if the price of domestic copper fell below 24 cents per pound (the current price during the debate was 24½ cents) the President is required to reinstate the tax.[1]

b. METAL SCRAP

In 1950, Congress had reinstituted until June 30, 1951 the suspension of tariff duties on ferrous and non-ferrous metal scrap.[2] Without debate, following the unanimous approval by the relevant committees,[3] and in view of the acute shortage of scrap for the steel mills, Congress in 1951 approved an extension of this suspension until June 30, 1952.

C. LEAD, ZINC, TUNGSTEN, AND ALUMINUM

In April, a measure was introduced in the House to suspend the import tax on lead, on the grounds that domestic production was insufficient to meet internal demands and that foreign supplies were being directed away from the United States market because of the internal price ceilings.[4] In August, the House approved a bill almost identical with that suspending the copper tax,[5] and the Senate finally approved the measure in January 1952. In October the House also approved a bill to suspend the import duties on zinc for a two-year period, the duty to be reinstated if the domestic price fell below 18 cents per pound.[6] The Senate gave its approval in January 1952. Late in the year, the Defense Production Administration sent draft legislation to Congress providing for a two-year suspension of the duty on tungsten, citing the short supply of this metal and the absence of objections to the proposal by domestic producers. After adding a provision that the suspension would be revoked if the price fell below $63 per ton (the price, double the pre-Korean level, which the Government had

[1] The law makes no provision for reinstating the suspension should the price subsequently rise above 24 cents per pound.

[2] See *Survey—1950*, p. 198, fn. 4.

[3] See S. *Rpt. No. 497*, 82d. Cong., 1st Sess., June 29, 1951.

[4] The Emergency Lead Committee had earlier suggested that an escalator provision be imposed on critical materials under which, in general, no tariff would be in effect when domestic supplies were seriously deficient and foreign products urgently needed. (*New York Times*, March 11, 1951.)

[5] See *H. Rpt. No. 802*, 82d Cong., 1st Sess., August 7, 1951 and S. *Rpt. No. 1053*, 82d Cong., 1st Sess., October 19, 1951.

[6] See *H. Rpt.* No. *1214*, 82d Cong., 1st Sess., October 18, 1951 and S. *Rpt.* No. *1057*, 82d Cong., 1st Sess., October 20, 1951.

guaranteed domestic producers for a five-year period in order to encourage expansion of domestic production),[7] the House passed the measure on October 15, and with but little debate. The Senate took no action on this proposal in 1951. Finally, a bill to provide temporary duty-free importation of aluminum was introduced in the House on October 15, but that body adjourned without taking action.

[7] See *H. Rpt. No. 1152*, 82d Cong., 1st Sess., October 12, 1951.

VII · EUROPEAN ECONOMIC INTEGRATION[1]

A MAJOR aspect of United States foreign economic policy since 1948 has been to encourage the economic "integration" (or "unification" as it was usually called in 1951) of Western Europe; on this policy the Administration and Congress have been in agreement.[2] Few of those supporting or discussing the policy have taken time to define carefully the objective sought, but most appear to accept the definition given by Mr. Paul Hoffman, ECA Administrator, in late 1949 when he spoke of the creation within Europe of "a single large market within which quantitative restrictions on the movement of goods, monetary barriers to the flow of payments and, eventually, all tariffs are permanently swept away."[3]

The policy, which in 1950 had taken its most concrete forms in United States support of the European Payments Union (and the related relaxation of quantitative restrictions on trade within Europe) and the Schuman Plan, has been justified on several economic grounds,[4] the most important being that creating such a "single market" (a) would reintroduce into Europe the invigorating force of competition, thus making for a dynamic and expand-

[1] The present chapter is concerned only with those aspects of European economic integration in which the U.S. Government played an active role. For a comprehensive description and excellent analysis of *all* the trade and payments aspects of European economic integration from 1947 through mid-1951, see Diebold, W., Jr., *Trade and Payments in Western Europe*, Council on Foreign Relations, New York, 1952. This book has been drawn on heavily in the preparation of this chapter.

[2] During the hearings on the Mutual Security Program, the Administration was queried by Congress as to whether plans were being made for establishing regional economic cooperation organizations in the Near East and the Far East along the lines of those already operating in Europe. The ECA Administrator replied only that he believed that such plans and arrangements must come from the areas themselves and that they could not be successfully imposed from the outside by the United States.

[3] *New York Times*, November 1, 1949.

[4] Many have also justified the program on the political and military grounds that it provides the means whereby Germany could be brought fully into the Western European family of nations and could contribute to the North Atlantic defense arrangements.

ing economy, and (b) would permit European producers to take advantage of large-scale—always identified with low-cost—production. Those supporting the policy maintained, though the literature is characterized by the absence of detailed studies of individual industries and firms, that the results of such competition and larger markets would be to so increase total production and productivity in Europe as to allow European producers to compete more effectively in extra-European markets and thus not only mark progress toward nondiscriminatory trade on a world-wide basis but also permit Europe to maintain socially and politically acceptable levels of consumption and investment independent of United States aid. Following the outbreak of war in Korea and the resulting rearmament programs in Europe, official United States spokesmen rarely talked of Europe's being able, economically integrated or not, to dispense in the near future with American assistance. But integration was regarded as more, rather than less, important inasmuch as the defense crisis resulted in an even greater need for a more efficient use of resources for greater total production. At the end of 1950, most observers agreed that some progress had been made in these integration efforts but that Europe was still far short of Mr. Hoffman's one "mass market"; and many of the European countries were threatening to meet the various strains of rearmament by greater rather than less restrictions on their intra-European trade and payments.

A. *CONTINUED SUPPORT OF POLICY*

In the public hearings and debate on the Mutual Security Program in 1951 there was, as compared to the previous years, relatively little discussion of European economic integration.[5] In part, apparently, this was because no funds were being asked by the Administration specifically for supporting such integration efforts, but, more importantly, it was a reflection of the fact that Congress and the Administration were in accord as to the desirability of the economic integration policy and Congress was, by and large, satisfied with the Administration's statement that, among other things, it planned to "encourage" the Europeans to strengthen and continue the EPU, to extend the intra-European trade liberalization

[5] It may well be that the integration policy was discussed at length in the many executive sessions which characterized the 1951 hearings.

measures, to reduce disparities in European tariffs, to ratify the Schuman Plan, and to apply the principles of the Schuman Plan to the establishment of an European Army.[6] (A brief account of United States support for the establishment of an European Army was given in Chapter I above.)

In 1950 the House had written into the law amending the Economic Cooperation Act a statement that it was the policy of the people of the United States to encourage both the economic "unification" and the political "federation" of Europe. The reference to political federation was deleted in the finally approved measure after the Administration had stated that, while it would look with favor on such a development, it did not believe the United States should try to force it and that, in any case, it believed a political unification of a high order was not a prerequisite to economic "integration." During the 1951 public hearings on the Mutual Security Act the question of political federation was not discussed and no reference was made to it in the Administration's proposals. There are suggestions in the public record, however, that the question was discussed at length in executive session, and Congress incorporated in the final law a statement that one of the purposes of that aid program was to encourage "the economic unification and political federation of Europe," thus reflecting the conviction of the majority of Congress that the economic "unification" objectives could be achieved only if individual traders and investors throughout the area were subjected to the same laws, the same currency, and the same (or mutually harmonious and consistent) governmental economic policies.[7] During 1951, the State Department apparently came to believe that the U.S. Government should more actively "encourage" the political unification of Europe.[8]

[6] See "The Mutual Security Program," *Hearings (on H.R. 5020 and H.R. 5113)*, House of Rep., Committee on Foreign Affairs, 82d Cong., 1st Sess., June-July 1951, pp. 432-433.

[7] For a statement of Congressional sentiment in 1950 that political unification of Europe was both desirable and necessary if the economic integration objectives were to be realized, see *Conference Report No. 2117*, 81st Cong., 2d Sess., May 19, 1950. For a detailed nonofficial report arguing in some detail that Western Europe could not be made defensible with United States aid unless Europe were both integrated economically and federated politically, see Geiger, T., and Cleveland, H. van B., *Making Western Europe Defensible*, National Planning Association, Planning Pamphlet No. 74, Washington, D.C., 1951.

[8] For a general statement indicating such support for political federation of some kind in Europe, see Department of State, *Our Foreign Policy 1952*, General Foreign Policy Series 56, Washington, D.C., March 1952, pp. 23-30.

An important new consideration to the Administration in this policy shift was the fact that General Eisenhower was finding that his task of trying to create "balanced collective forces" among the European members of the North Atlantic Treaty Organization was being made especially difficult because there was no single strong political authority in Europe.[9]

There were relatively few public statements by senior United States officials during the first part of the year urging that the Europeans make greater efforts to integrate their economies—the attention of most American officials responsible for European policy was focussed on the more immediate problems of expanding rearmament in that area—and some of the European press reported that it appeared that United States enthusiasm for the policy was waning.[1] But in the hearings during the summer on the Mutual Security Program, Administration spokesmen assured Congress that they believed that economic integration was more important than ever and that they would like to see it "go faster."[2]

[9] An account of the discussion in the United States on the question of political unification of Europe is outside the scope of this document. Attention is drawn, however, to a resolution (S. Res. 269) introduced in the U.S. Senate on January 31, 1952, declaring that, since it was "well recognized" that many past wars had as one of their underlying causes political disunity in Europe, the U.S. Government was interested in the early creation of a united states of Europe, that it would welcome the calling of a European constitutional convention to lay the groundwork for European political federation, and that the U.S. Government would "cooperate" with any new European federal government. President Truman formally approved this resolution, and it was consistent with the various views which General Eisenhower had expressed in a January 22, 1952 statement. One of the sponsors of the resolution stated that unless there were political and economic unification of Europe "we shall not be able to relieve ourselves of the burden we are now carrying." The resolution was referred to the Senate Committee on Foreign Relations, but that body had taken no action by the time the present document went to press. (For the text of the resolution and the statements of President Truman and its sponsors, see Department of State *Bulletin*, February 18, 1952, pp. 275-276.)

[1] See, for example, *The Economist*, September 15, 1951, p. 625.

[2] In the spring, the Council of Europe had formally invited the U.S. Congress to send a group of its members to Europe to discuss with a group of representatives of the Consultative Assembly of the Council of Europe the general problem of European unification and other problems of mutual interest between the United States and Europe. By concurrent resolutions (S. Con. Res. 36 and H. Con. Res. 136, 82d Cong., 1st Sess.) Congress authorized seven members of each chamber to attend such a meeting in November; their expenses were met by Congress, but they went in their individual capacities without instructions and with no authority to represent the U.S. Government. These delegates informed their European hosts in no uncertain terms that they believed that the European countries could and should make much faster movements in the direction of eliminating the barriers among themselves to trade and payments and in breaking up trusts and cartels.

And, as noted above, the law not only repeated the earlier statements about economic "unification" but added "political federation."[3] More important, in July, General Eisenhower made a widely publicized speech putting all the weight of his authority behind "unification."[4] He stated that, while he had received ready cooperation from all the separate governments of Europe and progress was being recorded in building Atlantic defense forces, "we cannot reach maximum security without a united [economically and politically] Europe." Once Europe were "truly a unit" (the General did not define his terms, but in the context he apparently meant some sort of political federation and a removal of all trade and payments barriers within Europe) he stated, she could build adequate military security and at the same time improve the standard of living of her peoples. Further, "it would mean early independence of aid from America and other Atlantic countries." He then warned that, "The coffers, mines, and factories of that continent are not inexhaustible." Six months later (at a time when there was much speculation that he might become the next President of the United States) General Eisenhower said: "As time goes on, it seems obvious that [Europe] cannot gain strength and stability if it is

They also were critical of tax evasion in Europe and charged that there was a general lack of enterprise and competitive business competence in Europe. The American delegates stated at the time that they were not greatly impressed by the listing of the obstacles to European unity—language barriers, differences in social, political, and commercial conditions and institutions, the need to protect "legitimate" national interests, etc.—but later wrote that they "came away . . . more fully aware of the tremendous problems to be faced if European federation is to make any real progress." Even the friendly European press characterized the group as "naïve" and "overassured" as to the correctness of their integration prescription; less friendly journalists referred to them as "a band of evangelists and demagogues." In any event, the meeting served to give the Europeans firsthand evidence that this cross-section of the U.S. Congress (the fourteen representatives were chosen as representing a cross-section of the American public) was deeply convinced that Europe could and should "unify," both economically and politically, and that the United States "had been too gentle in the past in urging its point of view upon Western Europe." For the text of the group's report to Congress, see S. *Doc. No. 90*, 82d Cong., 2d Sess., January 21, 1952. For a British press account, see *The Economist*, December 1, 1951, pp. 1337-1338.

[3] The so-called Benton amendment, designed to encourage free private enterprise in Europe (for text see Chapter I, Section A,c,1, above), was regarded as supporting the economic unification policy.

[4] For the text of his speech, see *New York Times*, July 4, 1951. General Eisenhower was speaking in his capacity as Supreme Commander, Allied Powers, Europe, but it was commonly believed that his views had the full support of the U.S. Government.

to remain split up in a number of independent economies." . . . "In the light of cold, hard fact, I simply can't see any acceptable alternative to a union, an economic union, between the states of Western Europe. I can't see how economic union can be successful unless there is political union."[5]

Thus, although the United States presented no new specific proposals during 1951, it seemed clear at year's end that the U.S. Government planned to increase the pressure on the European nations to "unite"—both economically and politically.

B. *EUROPEAN PAYMENTS UNION*

In their program for encouraging European economic "integration," ECA and the OEEC had laid particular stress on the need for creating a multilateral system of payments which would provide for the transferability *within* Europe of European currencies and for some credit margins. The first major regional attack on this problem took the form of an Intra-European Payments Scheme.[6] This was followed by the European Payments Union (EPU), which began operating during the last half of 1950. The major objectives, provisions, and issues that were thrashed out in the creation of EPU, along with a summary of its operations during 1950, were described in the previous volume of this *Survey*. While the agreement is technical and complex, the fundamental principles of the Union are simple. Once a month the central bank of each EPU member (including its associated monetary area, if any) reports to the Bank for International Settlements (the agent for the EPU) the net surplus or deficit of its current transactions with each of the other members. The BIS then offsets each country's total net surplus and total net deficits and arrives at a single net figure (surplus or deficit) for each member vis-à-vis all the other members as a group. (Thus, the members' currencies are

[5] For the text of his January 22, 1952 remarks to the press, see *New York Times*, January 23, 1952. The press at the time referred to "political cooperation," but the State Department subsequently (*Our Foreign Policy 1952, op.cit.*, p. 26) quoted Eisenhower as saying "political union."

[6] For a critical account of European regional payments arrangements before the Marshall Plan, as well as a discussion of the Intra-European Payments Scheme and the European Payments Union through mid-1951, see Diebold, W., Jr., *Trade and Payments in Western Europe*, Chapters 3-6. See also our *Survey—1949*, pp. 136-139, and *Survey—1950*, pp. 240-255, for a summary account of the policies and activities during those years.

transferable among themselves at the central bank level.)[7] The net balance for each member, expressed in units of account equal to one United States dollar, is cumulated month by month. This net cumulative credit or debit balance is then set off—month by month—first against the "initial position,"[8] if any, and then against the "quota"[9] assigned each country. A cumulative balance up to one-fifth of the quota is carried forward simply as a credit to the EPU from that country or vice versa. Beyond one-fifth of the quota, cumulative credit balances are settled one-half in dollar (or gold) payments from the Union to the creditor and one-half in credit from the creditor to the EPU; a cumulative debit balance must be settled by the debtor paying an increasing proportion of it in dollars, rising progressively from 20 percent to 80 percent, with the balance being settled in the form of a debt on the Union's books.[1] The agreement provided that if a debtor country exhausted its quota it was to pay subsequent deficits 100 percent in gold or dollars, but the action to be required of creditors who exceeded their quotas was left to future determination.

Operations during 1951

Extreme debit and credit positions create serious obstacles to any multilateral payments scheme, and throughout 1951 the EPU was subjected to a series of crises resulting from the emergence of several extreme debtors and creditors. In meeting these prob-

[7] Individual importers and exporters make payments as before and are still subject to the exchange control systems of their separate countries.

[8] Belgium-Luxembourg, Sweden, and the United Kingdom were thought likely to be structural creditors and were saddled at the outset with a specific *debit* balance for the first year of the Union; in return they received an equivalent amount of "conditional aid" from ECA. Austria, Greece, Iceland, Netherlands, Norway, and Turkey were thought likely to be structural debtors and so started off with a specific *credit* balance on the books of the EPU. These "initial positions" were granted only for the period July 1, 1950 through June 30, 1951. Following mid-1951, the U.S. Government provided Austria, Greece, Italy, and Turkey with dollars ("special resources") to cover in whole or in part their EPU deficits.

[9] In general, the quotas were fixed at approximately 15 percent of each member's intra-European payments and receipts in 1949. The major exception to this rule was Belgium-Luxembourg, whose quota plus her initial debit balance was equal to approximately 15 percent of her payments and receipts in 1949. Greece, Austria, and Iceland were regarded as having such weak currencies that any credit extended to them by the Union was likely to turn out to be uncollectible and so they were denied the right to the use of their quotas.

[1] The percentages are so calculated that once a given country's quota is exhausted, a creditor (debtor) has received (paid) 40 percent of the quota in dollars and extended (received) 60 percent in credit.

lems the EPU Managing Board, which includes a United States official as a nonvoting member, made many investigations and tendered much advice as to the specific actions to be undertaken by individual countries. The Managing Board and the parent OEEC Council frequently urged, with varying degrees of success, that extreme EPU debtors pursue more stringent internal fiscal and credit policies, and creditors more lenient monetary policies, but resort was frequently had by the individual countries to more direct controls, especially to quantitative restrictions on imports and exports.[2] Thus, in the face of an "alarming" EPU deficit during late 1950 and early 1951, Germany was not only given a special credit by the EPU but one of the conditions attached was that she impose more stringent internal fiscal and credit measures. When these measures failed to stop quickly the increase in her deficit, she was urged not only to pursue these restrictive internal financial policies more energetically but was also authorized to cancel outstanding import licenses and reimpose many of the quantitative restrictions on imports which she had previously removed. Further, the EPU creditors were urged by the OEEC to discriminate in favor of imports from Germany. Shortly thereafter, her position quickly improved. She had paid off her special credit by May, and at the end of the year had become a small net creditor; early in 1952 she again relaxed her import restrictions.[3]

[2] Official and detailed accounts of the operations of the EPU may be found in the Organization for European Economic Cooperation: *European Payments Union, First Annual Report of the Managing Board,* Paris, August 1951; *Report of the Managing Board of the European Payments Union on the Operation of the Union After 30th June 1952* (OEEC *Press Release A* (*52*) *14,* 1952); *European Economic Cooperation, A Survey prepared by the Organization for European Economic Cooperation,* Paris, May 1951, and *European Economic Cooperation, A Second Survey,* Paris, November 1951; and the OEEC's Third Annual Report, *Economic Progress and Problems of Western Europe,* Paris, June 1951. These official documents have been heavily drawn upon in the preparation of this section and the following section on trade liberalization measures. For a detailed account of the mechanics and procedures of the EPU, see Bank for International Settlements, *Twenty-first Annual Report,* Basle, June 1951, pp. 222-238.

[3] In June 1951, the German EPU quota was increased from 320 to 500 million units of account. For details on the German crisis, see Diebold, W., Jr., *Trade and Payments in Western Europe, op.cit.,* Chapter 6, and Organization for European Economic Cooperation, *European Economic Cooperation. . . ,* May 1951, *op.cit.,* pp. 24-26. For an analysis crediting monetary policy as the major factor in the German improvement, see *The Banker* (London), September 1951, pp. 171-177. For an analysis giving large credit also to the reversal of price trends as between Germany's imports and exports, decline in inventory accumulations, and the reimposition of direct controls on imports, see Board of Governors of the Federal Reserve System, *Federal Reserve Bulletin,* Washington, D.C., March 1952, pp. 237-243.

Certain other countries, especially Greece, Austria, and Iceland, were extreme debtors throughout the period and by early 1951 had run up deficits beyond the limits of their "initial credit positions." Thereupon, not only did the OEEC authorize them to reimpose many of their previously removed import quotas but also ECA provided all, or a large part, of the dollars needed by these countries to settle their deficits in excess of their "initial positions."[4] The Netherlands, Norway, and Turkey also quickly exceeded their "initial credit positions" and were relieved by the OEEC of many of their commitments to liberalize intra-European trade. The Netherlands and Norway were subsequently able to keep their deficits within the quotas assigned them[5] and received no special assistance from the ECA; by the end of the year, Turkey had exceeded her quota but had covered this deficit from her own reserves. Although Denmark's deficit did not seriously threaten to exceed her quota, the deficit was increasing during the first part of 1951, with the result that she was being threatened with the requirement for making what she regarded as unacceptably large gold payments to the Union; the OEEC thereupon relieved her of some of the obligations she had undertaken to remove additional import quotas. Late in the year, Denmark was able to reduce the size of her deficit and recover part of her previous gold payments.

The United Kingdom and France, which had been assigned the biggest quotas, had registered large surpluses during 1950 and the first few months of 1951. These surpluses caused some anxiety to the EPU Managing Board on the grounds that their counterpart—deficits by countries with relatively small quotas—might result in large gold payments which the debtor countries might find "difficult" to make. Both the United Kingdom and France agreed to pursue more liberal import policies vis-à-vis other EPU members. But, beginning in May and April, respectively, Britain and France began to record large deficits, as the price of raw mate-

[4] For the second year of EPU operations the U.S. Government allotted Greece, Turkey, Austria, and Iceland "special resources" to cover anticipated deficits with the EPU. As these "special resources" are used, the MSA pays the dollar equivalent in dollars to the Union. Such payments by the United States to the Union through 1951 totalled $130 million.

[5] The Netherlands quota was increased in June from 330 to 355 million units of account.

rials sold by countries in their monetary areas to Europe fell, as they (especially Britain) increasingly directed internal resources to rearmament and away from exports to other European countries, and as their imports from Europe and certain overseas territories of other members expanded. By the end of 1951, the large cumulative surpluses of these two countries had changed into large and growing deficits. In October, Britain, reportedly without prior consultations with the OEEC, reimposed many quantitative restrictions, and France followed suit in early February 1952. Britain was subjected to especially large gold payments to the EPU in the last three months of the year, and, in late December, ECA transferred $40 million to her in accordance with the 1950 agreement to reimburse the United Kingdom for any net payment of dollars made by her to EPU because other EPU debtors had used pre-EPU accumulated sterling balances to cover their deficits with the Union.

Three extreme creditors, Portugal, Belgium-Luxembourg, and Italy, also created crises in EPU and, as a temporary solution, agreed in effect to an increase in their quotas. The EPU Agreement made no specific provision for the action to be taken when creditors exhausted their quotas, saying only that such surpluses would be settled according to decisions to be taken by OEEC at such time. Portugal's surplus approached the limit of her quota early in 1951. The OEEC thereupon urged the Portuguese to pursue less stringent internal credit policies and to lower import barriers against European imports. It was then agreed between Portugal and the OEEC Council that, up to a specified limit, any surplus above the quota would be settled half by gold payments from the Union to Portugal and half by Portuguese credits to the Union. In January 1952, Portugal, with its EPU surplus still increasing, announced that as an experiment it was increasing to 100 percent the liberalization of imports from OEEC countries and that imports from the United States would be further restricted in order to divert purchases to European sources.

The Belgian credit surplus began to exceed its quota in August and that of Italy in November. These two countries reluctantly agreed, for a limited period of time and up to specified amounts, to receive gold for approximately half of any surplus beyond their quotas and to finance the remainder by extending credit to the

EPU. Belgium was extremely loath so to finance her surplus. To help redress her position she resorted, with many misgivings, to a series of direct control devices—notably stricter export licensing, freezing of a certain percentage of export proceeds, and imposition of export taxes. She also reduced her quantitative restrictions on European imports and increased such restrictions on dollar imports.[6] Late in the year and early in 1952, Italy eliminated all quantitative restrictions on imports from European sources and reduced some customs duties on such imports, but did not increase (or decrease) barriers against dollar imports. Sweden[7] and Switzerland were also creditors of EPU through 1951 but neither was in imminent danger of exceeding its quota.

Thus, as Table 16 shows, while six of the fifteen member coun-

TABLE 16

Position of Member Countries with the European Payments Union, 1950-1951

(millions of dollar equivalents and percentages)

Member Country[a]	*Cumulative Net Position: Surplus (+) or Deficit (−) as of December 31*		*Percentage of Quota Used,*[b] *as Creditor (+) or Debtor (−) as of December 31*	
	1950	*1951*	*1950*	*1951*
Austria	−37.4	−130.6	(c)	(c)
Belgium-Luxembourg	+21.8	+601.5	0	+164[d]
Denmark	−38.4	−32.3	−20	−20
France	+212.4	−199.7	+41	−35
Germany	−356.7	+36.0	−112[e]	+9
Greece	−70.8	−186.7	(c)	(c)
Iceland	−3.3	−8.5	(c)	(c)
Italy	−30.9	+194.7	−15	+116[d]
Netherlands	−107.9	−50.0	−24	−7
Norway	−51.1	−69.6	0	−5
Portugal	+36.8	+96.5	+53	+139[d]
Sweden	0	+177.5	0	+66
Switzerland	−12.6	+141.2	−5	+57
Turkey	+5.3	−98.2	+11	−108[f]
United Kingdom	+433.0	−471.8	+27	−67

(*Notes to table on next page*)

[6] As noted in Chapter V above, this discrimination against imports from the dollar area resulted, during the Sixth Session of the GATT, in charges by the United States delegates, along with certain others of the Contracting Parties, that this was in violation of Belgium's obligations under the GATT. For details on the Belgium-EPU issue and particularly the various direct control devices so reluctantly resorted to by Belgium in an effort to restrain her EPU surplus, see *The Economist*, September 8, pp. 586-588; October 13, pp. 881-882; October 20, p. 938; November 10, p. 1131; December 8, pp. 1422-1424; December 22, 1951, p. 1543; and January 5, 1952, p. 40.

[7] Sweden had earlier agreed to handle any surplus she might have over her quota on a 50-50 credit-gold basis.

tries shifted during the year from creditor to debtor positions or vice versa, by the end of 1951 three members were such extreme debtors that they had not even been permitted to use their quotas, one country was a debtor to the extent that it had exceeded its quota, and three countries had reached such extreme creditor positions that they had exceeded their quotas and had been kept as active members in the Union only by temporary and provisional arrangements.

---

a) Ireland (together with the nonparticipating sterling area and the dependent overseas territories) is included with the United Kingdom. Trieste is included in the monetary area of Italy.

b) The "net accounting position" of each member vis-à-vis the Union (the figure used to calculate the percentage of quotas utilized) differs from the "cumulative net position" of each member as cited in the above table. In arriving at the former, account must be taken of the use of "initial positions," "existing resources" (bilateral debts—mostly sterling—outstanding on June 30, 1950 for which no specific amortization plans had been agreed bilaterally and which go through the Union mechanism) and "special resources" (dollars provided by the U.S. Government to cover in whole or in part the deficits of Austria, Greece, Iceland, and Turkey). Further, interest paid or received on loans granted to or received from the Union by members is included in the "net accounting position" but not in the above figures on "cumulative net position." The quotas for all members were the same at the end of 1951 as at the end of 1950, except for Germany, which was increased in June 1951 from $320 to $500 million, and for the Netherlands, which was increased in June 1951 from $330 to $355 million. The most convenient sources for details on these transactions for each country are the monthly International Monetary Fund, *International Financial Statistics*, Washington, D.C., and the *New York Herald Tribune*, European Edition, "Monthly Economic Review," Paris.

c) The OEEC decided that when these countries were in a deficit position they would not be permitted to use their quotas since their currencies were regarded as so weak that any credit extended to them by the Union would be considered by the other members as uncollectible. As noted in the text, each of these countries paid some dollars into the EPU to cover deficits in excess of their "initial credit balances" and their net use of "existing resources." All of these dollars were supplied by the U.S. Government, except for $17.6 million which Austria supplied from its own resources.

d) As noted in the text, special arrangements were made for creditors who exceeded their quotas. In general, these took the form of the creditors agreeing, within limits and for specified periods of time, to financing any such excess one-half by further extensions of credit to the Union and one-half in the form of gold payments to them from the Union. The total amount so settled outside the quotas as of December 31, 1951 were: Belgium-Luxembourg, $260.1 million; Italy, $32.7 million; and Portugal, $27.4 million.

e) By a special decision of the OEEC Council, the German deficit in excess of the quota in late 1950 and early 1951 was settled under terms of a special credit from the Union plus some dollar payments by Germany out of its own resources. As of the end of 1951, $36.7 million dollars had been so settled outside the quota. All of the special credit to Germany had been repaid by mid-1951.

f) Turkey's deficit in excess of the quota as of December 31, 1951 had been settled by the payment to the Union of $3.8 million by Turkey from its own resources.

Accomplishments and Problems

In recording the accomplishments and problems of the EPU, it must be kept in mind that the Union was conceived, and its details were more or less settled, before the Korean war began but that from the beginning it has been operating in a rearming world. The mobilization programs not only resulted in uneven increases in internal inflationary pressures (and so resulted in new and more intense balance of payments difficulties for certain members) but they also forced unforeseen changes in international prices, the composition of trade, and the direction of its movement. Especially important was the uneven effect on members' terms of trade resulting from the violent fluctuations in raw material prices. Further, the rearmament efforts of the several countries varied greatly, and those pursuing relatively more energetic programs were forced to increase imports by a larger amount and to divert more domestic resources from exports to rearmament than was done by those carrying out relatively smaller defense efforts. These "temporary" factors were important in the violent swings of members' balances of payments during the year and in the emergence of so many extreme debtors and creditors. Further, the changes in members' balance of payments positions were often rapid, thus "forcing" each member to take unilateral action via direct controls rather than "cooperative" action with reliance on the more slowly operating indirect monetary and credit controls.

On an operational level, it appeared during the fall of 1951 that EPU might soon face a cash crisis. The organization began operations with liquid resources of $350 million, representing dollars set aside by ECA out of its fiscal year 1951-1952 appropriation.[8] During the first year of its operation the Union had been able to increase its liquid reserves by a small amount since the creditors tended to be countries with large quotas while the debtors tended to be nations with relatively small quotas; thus, larger dollar payments were made into than out of the Union. In view of this increase in the Union's dollar resources, ECA did not make a direct dollar grant to EPU for its second year. As noted above, during

[8] This was subsequently increased to $361 million when Sweden relinquished $11 million of ECA "conditional aid" and ECA transferred this to the capital of the EPU.

the last half of 1951, however, several countries reached the upper ranges of their creditor position and thus were entitled to receive increasing proportions of any surplus in gold, while some of the previous creditors, especially Britain and France, had cumulative positions in the tranches of their quotas where only small amounts of gold had to be paid to the Union. As a result, at the end of October the liquid reserves of the Union had fallen to $179 million. But a rise to $217 million was recorded at the end of the year as the deficits of Britain and France began to put them into a tranche calling for larger percentages of gold payments and this particular cash crisis was averted.[9]

Nonetheless, in its early 1952 report on the future operations of the Union, the Managing Board stressed that if the Union were to operate effectively it needed additional "convertible assets" (that is, dollars), not only to provide funds to meet current operations so as to avoid the sort of crisis which threatened it in November, but also (a) to serve as security to its creditors for the day when the Union was liquidated (otherwise creditors would be less willing to extend credit to the Union); (b) to give confidence to members that the Union would remain a solvent and continuing organization and so encourage them to undertake further trade liberalization measures; and (c) to enable the Union better to meet the "needs" of members reaching extreme positions. The U.S. Administration, however, was of the view in early 1952 that while an increase in the dollar assets of the Union was desirable on its own merits, there were more urgent and critical needs for any dollars that Congress might provide for aiding Europe in the immediate future.

The EPU, along with the associated trade liberalization measures discussed in the next section, had three major objectives: to facilitate (a) the expansion of trade on a nondiscriminatory basis among the members, (b) the ending of dependence of members upon extraordinary assistance from the United States, and (c) the return by members to the practice of worldwide currency convertibility and nondiscriminatory trade.

The available data indicate that moderate success was achieved

[9] By the end of 1951, $238.1 million had actually been transferred to the Union by the U.S. Government and the remainder of the $361 million was still held by the U.S. Government.

with respect to the first listed objective. Bilateral trade and payments agreements and discrimination on currency grounds as to source of imports within Europe, which had characterized much of the trade before EPU began, were virtually ended.[1] That is, the Union did contribute to the development of intra-European trade on a nondiscriminatory basis. Presumably the result was to widen the area of competition but enough time had not elapsed to be able to determine whether this resulted in the hoped-for increase in productivity and total production which in turn was supposed to increase the ability of Europe to compete in third markets. The EPU multilateral clearing and settlement worked well.[2] Of the total bilateral surpluses or deficits incurred during each month of the period July 1950 to December 1951 (equivalent to $5.6 billion), just over three-quarters were cleared by the process of multilateral compensation and the operation of the cumulative principle, thus economizing on the use of the members' reserves. Dollar payments from the Union settled 9 percent of the total surpluses of members and dollar payments to the Union[3] settled 6 percent of the deficits; the balance was settled via the use of credits to or from the EPU, initial balances, and "existing resources."[4]

Not the least of the accomplishments of the EPU was its facilitating the repayment of accumulated intra-European indebtedness, both via amortization and the use of "existing resources." From July 1, 1950 through 1951 more than one-half of the $861 million of such reported unfunded indebtedness outstanding on June 30, 1950 had been repaid through the Union—the largest repayments were those made by the United Kingdom.[5] In some cases the old debts were replaced by new ones, but the EPU Managing Board stated that even here "the process itself has been sane and

[1] However, in December Switzerland imposed restrictions on certain exports to the sterling area in an effort to reduce its EPU surplus.

[2] For details on these operations for the period through 1951, see *New York Herald Tribune*, European Edition, "Monthly Economic Review," Paris, February 4, 1952.

[3] Including the use of $130 million of "special resources"—that is, dollars provided the Union by the U.S. Government to cover, in whole or in part, the deficits of Austria, Greece, Iceland, and Turkey.

[4] "Existing resources" refer to bilateral debts—mostly sterling—outstanding as of June 30, 1950 for which no specific amortization arrangements had been agreed upon bilaterally. The equivalent of $100 million of such resources were used from July 1, 1950 to December 31, 1951.

[5] For details through June 30, 1951, see Organization for European Economic Cooperation, *European Payments Union, op.cit.*, pp. 18-20.

healthy in that it has introduced order into a hitherto confused field and has thus contributed to the restoration of confidence in intra-European financial arrangements."[6]

Still, while the total value, and volume, of intra-European trade increased substantially during 1951, this was in the context of expanding trade throughout the world, and as Table 17 shows, the value of the members' intra-European merchandise trade as a *percentage* of their total commodity trade not only did not increase but declined slightly during the year as compared with 1950.[7] It may, of course, be true that in the absence of the EPU and the trade liberalization measures Europe, under the stresses of the rearmament programs, would have reverted to the previous bilateral arrangements with a sharp curtailment of intra-European trade.

TABLE 17

Value of Intra-European Merchandise Trade as Percentage of Members' Total Trade, 1938, 1948-1951[a]

(monthly averages)

Year		*Exports*	*Imports*
1938		50	39
1948		45	32
1949		46	35
1950	first half	50	40
	third quarter	50	41
	fourth quarter	49	42
1951	first quarter	50	40
	second quarter	48	37
	third quarter	47	38
	fourth quarter[b]	47	40

a) These data refer to trade among the metropolitan countries only; the trade liberalization measures did not apply completely to trade with members' overseas territories. Imports are on a c.i.f. and exports on an f.o.b. basis.
b) Monthly average for October and November only.
Source: Calculated from data given in Organization for European Economic Cooperation, *General Statistics*, Paris, March 1952, pp. 82-83. These data for 1938, 1948-1950 differ slightly from those given in our *Survey—1950*, p. 269, which data were taken from Economic Cooperation Administration sources.

Little, if any, progress was recorded during the year toward the second and third objectives of the EPU which were cited above.

[6] *Ibid.*, p. 35.

[7] The decline in the percentage of intra-European imports can perhaps be explained by the roughly estimated 10 percent deterioration in European commodity terms of trade during 1951 as compared with 1950; this consideration, however, probably does not explain the decline in the export percentage.

Indeed, on balance, at the end of 1951 Europe seemed further from these goals than when the EPU was inaugurated, but again there were so many new factors operating as a result of the rearmament programs that it is impossible from publicly available data to assess the influence of the EPU. Nonetheless, some fundamental problems and some limitations on the ability of the EPU to promote progress toward these broader goals became evident during the year.

As the EPU Managing Board has pointed out,[8] achievement of independence from extraordinary outside financial assistance and of world-wide currency convertibility and nondiscrimination requires that each of the countries reach and maintain both internal and external equilibrium. This in turn depends, to a major extent, on the actions that each member takes as to the extent and type of its rearmament program, internal credit and fiscal policy, investments, wage policy, etc. Although the EPU Managing Board is authorized to study and review developments and to counsel the members as to methods of avoiding such disequilibria, it has no executive authority in these matters.[9] The EPU Agreement does contain one set of automatic checks and incentives designed to force debtors and creditors to achieve international equilibrium: the partial dollar settlements of intra-European deficits and surpluses. But the experience of 1951 showed that these were not adequate, that many countries quickly approached the limits of their quotas, and that when debtors did so their first reaction was to reimpose quantitative restrictions on their imports. Still, it may be that this was only a reflection of the unusually large swings in various members' balance of payments positions arising out of the rearmament program and out of the fact that sufficient time had not elapsed for other measures to have their full effect. Certainly, as noted above, not enough time had passed to determine whether

[8] *European Payments Union, op.cit.,* p. 35. See Chapter III of this report and Part II of the *Report of the Managing Board of the European Payments Union on the Operations of the Union after 30th June 1952, op.cit.,* for a critical account of the EPU by its own Managing Board. These are the sources of much of the information given here.

[9] The record shows that the EPU Managing Board, together with other OEEC bodies, did provide an important "focal point" for intra-European "consultations," "exchange of views," and "cooperation" on a wide variety of financial and economic questions. The advice of the EPU Managing Board was followed by at least Germany with what most observers regarded as conspicuous success.

the EPU and the trade liberalization measures were resulting in a more efficient use of European resources—that is, in increasing both production and productivity—which would constitute a major attack on the basic causes of the dollar shortage and of European discrimination against imports of many non-European goods and services.

On the basis of the record through 1951, the query must be raised of whether the EPU was actually operating to create a balanced trading system *within* Europe. Both ECA and OEEC officials have insisted that this was never the intention, but the official report of the EPU Managing Board[1] shows that considerable pressure was applied by it to the member countries during the year to achieve a greater degree of balance within Europe. In particular, the record shows that intra-European creditors who approached the limit of their quotas were encouraged by the OEEC and the EPU Managing Board to be especially generous in importing from and loaning to EPU debtors—the debtors were also encouraged to take "whatever steps are open" to them to increase exports to their EPU creditors—and to look increasingly to non-European markets for their exports. To the extent these things were done the EPU *was operating to defeat its third major objective.*

The EPU Managing Board itself also raised the question of whether there was not a fundamental defect and an "inherent contradiction" in the EPU which served at least to postpone the time when those members with the stronger currencies could achieve general convertibility. A basic and integral aspect of the EPU is that it operates on the basis that all members' currencies are equally valuable; that is, that there is "equality" in terms of purchasing power among the currencies of all members at the established exchange rates. This, however, has not been true, and serious problems have resulted from the full transferability of currencies provided under the EPU. In particular, the Managing Board reported that an increasing amount of capital was moving from the weaker to the stronger currencies. (It would also seem likely, although no concrete instances are known, that, since the countries with stronger currencies usually pursue more liberal commercial policies with the non-EPU area, weaker currency countries may have imported commodities from the dollar area via the strong currency

[1] *European Payments Union, op.cit.,* especially p. 37.

EPU countries.) If these capital movements also move out of the stronger European currencies into dollars, for example (or if dollar imports by strong currency countries are reexported to weaker currency countries) the strong currency countries to that extent are retarded in their advance toward general convertibility since they receive only a portion (0-50 percent) of their EPU surplus in dollars. The EPU Managing Board concluded that, "It seems clear that the Union must always be in difficulty from this cause unless Member countries follow internal and external policies which will result in a reasonable parity between the 'nominal' and the 'real' values of their currencies."[2]

This problem became acute when, in the latter part of 1951, certain countries—Belgium-Luxembourg, Portugal, and Italy—accumulated surpluses in excess of their quotas. These creditor countries desired to receive full settlement of any such excess in dollars. Failure to do so might (as it did in the case of Belgium and Portugal) result in the creditor restricting dollar imports in favor of European exports, that is, in moving away from general convertibility. Internally, financing these unrequited exports to EPU partners would seem to involve for the creditor either adding to domestic inflationary pressures (also serving to retard progress toward convertibility) or postponing investment or rearmament projects. On the other hand, to permit a full settlement of such surpluses in gold or dollars would have meant that the debtors were paying dollars for imports which they were committed to importing relatively freely from Europe under the OEEC-ECA-sponsored intra-European trade liberalization program, even though many of these debtors maintained severe restrictions on such imports from the dollar area. Further, full settlement in gold was frowned on by EPU officials since it would remove the incentive for creditors to help the debtors via more liberal import policies. That is to say, under these conditions there developed a conflict between regional liberalization and convertibility and global convertibility and nondiscriminatory trade. In practice, this conflict appears, on balance, to have been resolved in favor of the former.

It had been the hope of those who established the EPU that before some members exceeded their quotas, the weaker currency

[2] *Report of the Managing Board of the European Payments Union on the Operation of the Union after 30th June, 1952, op.cit.*, p. 13.

countries would—with the assistance of ECA and the Union's financial resources, the complementary trade liberalization program, and the advice and cooperation of the OEEC and all of its members—have taken such internal and external action as would have permitted them to pay increasing percentages of dollars for any intra-European deficit with the result that the EPU would "open out to cover world-wide payments."[3] These hopes were not realized for many reasons: the defects of the EPU noted above; the extension by EPU and ECA of financial resources to debtors which relieved the pressure on them to reach equilibrium positions; the intractability of the problems of the structural debtors, the solution of which seemed to require a large and steady inflow of foreign long-term capital over many years; the uneven impact of rearmament on internal prices; and the uneven diversion of internal resources from exports and civilian consumption and investment to defense.

The EPU was in difficulties at the end of 1951 and little if any progress had been made in achieving two of its major goals. It appeared that if the EPU were to continue—as the U.S. Government and the EPU member governments wished—the existing pattern of intra-European surpluses and deficits must be drastically altered, and/or the United States would have to make another dollar contribution to the EPU, and/or some means would have to be found of financing intra-European defense trade,[4] and/or the EPU mechanism itself would have to be revised. The most common suggestions with respect to the last possibility[5] were that the powers and responsibilities of the Managing Board be increased so as to permit it to "harmonize" the policies of the various mem-

[3] *European Payments Union, op.cit.*, p. 39. In the light of the downward trend of the gold and dollar reserves of many of the countries, the ratio of gold to credit in the settling of members' balances with EPU was not increased at the June 1951 annual review of the Union; such an increase was regarded by many as a necessary step in the transition toward general convertibility.

[4] See Diebold, W., Jr., *Trade and Payments in Western Europe, op.cit.*, Chapter 23, for a discussion of some of the problems of separating such trade for special financing.

[5] See especially *Report of the Managing Board of the European Payments Union on the Operation of the Union after 30th June, 1952, op.cit.*, and Carli, G., (Chairman of the EPU Managing Board), "EPU Problems," *Banca Nazionale del Lavoro Quarterly Review*, Rome, October-December, 1951, pp. 179-187.

bers, that members' quotas be revised, and that changes be made in the percentages governing gold and credit settlements.[6] Most of those who publicly expressed views on the Union agreed with its Managing Board's statement that, while modifications in the EPU agreement would be needed in 1952 if it were to continue, the situation in 1951 was "more satisfactory than the position which would have emerged in the absence of E.P.U.,"[7] since the actual alternative was probably a network of bilateral agreements providing for almost constant balance.

C. *TRADE LIBERALIZATION MEASURES*

The ECA-encouraged efforts by the OEEC countries to "integrate" their economies by removing certain monetary barriers were preceded, accompanied, or closely followed, by measures designed to remove or relax other barriers to trade within the area. The most important of these other barriers were seen as quantitative restrictions and tariffs, but cartels and such practices as "dual pricing" were also regarded as significant. ECA and the OEEC decided to concentrate their efforts on reducing quantitative restrictions, and especially import quotas. This decision was taken because quotas were regarded as exceptionally restrictive and rigid and as much the most important of the postwar increases in barriers but ones which had not yet served to encourage much investment and production dependent on them. Negotiations for tariff reductions were regarded as too complicated, time-consuming, and onerous a task for the OEEC; further, most of the OEEC countries were Contracting Parties to the GATT, which organization was concentrating on the lowering of tariffs.[8] Nonetheless, by the end of 1950 the low-

[6] The EPU was "reviewed" at the end of its first year of operations—June 1951—but no important changes, other than increasing the quotas of Germany and the Netherlands, were made. At that time the problems of the extreme creditors were still in the future, the cash position of the Union was still strong, and there was considerable uncertainty as to the impact of rearmament on the members' balances of payments. There are no public indications that serious thought was given to reallocating quotas so as to favor those countries making the greater defense contributions. (Such a possibility had been suggested by Hirschman, A. O., "The European Payments Union: Negotiations and the Issues," *The Review of Economics and Statistics,* February 1951, pp. 49-55.) The EPU agreement stipulates that the OEEC shall undertake a general review of EPU operations by June 30, 1952.

[7] *European Payments Union, op.cit.,* p. 40.

[8] See Chapter V above. The GATT also concerns itself with quantitative restrictions but the emphasis in the negotiations on reducing trade barriers has been on lowering tariffs.

tariff countries in Western Europe, especially the Benelux and some of the Scandinavian countries, were protesting against demands for further removal of quantitative restrictions so long as certain other countries—especially France—maintained such high tariffs that the removing of import quotas was having little effect on their imports. Following the round of tariff negotiations held at Torquay, England in late 1950 and early 1951,[9] which resulted in no significant reductions in the disparities in European tariffs, the Contracting Parties set up an intersessional Working Party (in which the United States was represented) to study proposals and make recommendations for reducing such disparities. The group met during the summer and the problem was discussed at the Sixth Session of GATT during the autumn of 1951, but by the end of the year no recommendations or "statements of progress" had been published.[1]

The general formula agreed upon by ECA and the OEEC in 1949 for reducing quantitative restrictions on trade was that each country would remove quotas on private account imports from other OEEC members *as a group*, to an agreed-upon percentage of its imports from them in the base year 1948.[2] The percentage was to apply separately to each of the three major categories of imports: foodstuffs, raw materials, and manufactured goods. Many "safeguards," especially in the form of escape provisions for those countries suffering adverse balances of payments, were included, but any country taking advantage of these was required to be prepared to justify its action to the OEEC.[3] The percentage was first fixed (in late 1949) at 50 percent. Shortly after the EPU began operations in September 1950 it was raised to 60 percent, and,

[9] See Chapter V above.

[1] *The Economist*, October 27, 1951, p. 991, reported that the Working Party had agreed that the disparities would not be removed by the low-tariff countries increasing their rates on liberalized goods but had as yet made no progress toward reducing existing tariffs by the high-tariff countries.

[2] Imports on government account, a significant proportion of the total for several of the countries, were exempt, it merely being stated that such imports should be transacted on commercial principles as specified in the ITO Charter. In most instances, imports from the outer sterling area and from the overseas territories of member countries were included, but in several cases these overseas areas themselves did not reduce their restrictions *pari passu* with the mother country. For Germany the base year for calculating the percentages was 1949.

[3] A brief summary of these escape clauses may be found in our *Survey—1950*, pp. 257-259. All of the decisions on liberalization by the OEEC have been codified and the most recent version, published in 1951, is Organization for European Economic Cooperation, *Code of Liberalisation*, Paris, July 1951.

since EPU provided for transferability of European currencies, it was agreed that there should be no discrimination on liberalized imports as among European sources after January 1, 1951.[4] These goals were reported as having been met or exceeded by most if not all of the participating countries, but when the member countries agreed "in principle" in late 1950 to proceed to a 75 percent level as of February 1951 many obstacles were encountered,[5] and, during 1951, the defects of this percentage approach became more apparent. First, each country had begun with the "easy" commodities—that is, those which were not subject to quotas, or which were not pressing on previous quotas, or which were noncompetitive internally, or which were effectively kept out by tariffs. Second, those goods whose importation had been severely restricted in the base period and which, by that fact, it might be most desirable, from the point of view of expanding trade and obtaining the most economical use of resources within Europe, to free of restrictions were usually not selected for liberalization since, among other reasons, including them would add little to the percentage of liberalization achieved. Third, so long as each member was free to select the individual commodities in its list there were few if any cases where a single good was permitted to compete on equal terms (except for tariffs and transportation costs) with domestic products in the whole European market—the objective so frequently stressed by ECA officials.

In an effort to remove some of these defects, the OEEC secretariat prepared a list of commodities—the so-called "common list"—which all member countries able to reach the 75 percent goal would be asked to include in their list of commodities not subject to import quotas.[6] The list was composed of commodities which the

[4] The OEEC Council also "agreed" that there should be no discrimination as regards nonliberalized imports, but through 1951 this decision had not been put into force since some of the countries were unwilling to apply it. See Diebold, W., Jr., *Trade and Payments in Western Europe, op.cit.*, Table 7, for the percentages each country had reached by the end of 1950. Chapter 11 of Diebold's book presents an excellent description and analysis of these trade liberalization measures and the obstacles which they encountered.

[5] See *Survey—1950*, pp. 258-259 for some of the obstacles encountered immediately, including the unwillingness of several of the countries to apply the 75 percent to each of the three categories (especially agricultural products) with the resultant agreement that the additional 15 percent would apply to the *total* imports on private account but not necessarily to each of the three categories.

[6] The list may be found as Section 3 of Annex A of the *Code of Liberalisation, op.cit.*

OEEC believed could be imported without quotas by all members without serious damage to domestic producers but which were of importance to the exporting countries. Several of the items were goods which the member countries were anxious to buy in any case, but it also included textiles and textile machinery and fresh vegetables, of which the supplies were relatively abundant and competition among the European producers keen.[7] The list was adopted by the OEEC Council in April 1951[8] and went into effect during the summer. But several countries did not reach the 75 percent goal or apply the common list.

As noted above, Germany took advantage of the escape clause and reimposed early in the year the quantitative restrictions which she had previously withdrawn; at the beginning of 1952, she again removed certain of the reimposed import quotas, but even so reached a percentage figure of only 62 percent, raised to 70 percent a few weeks later. By mid-1951, Austria, Denmark, Greece, Iceland, and Norway, stressing the adverse effects on their balances of payments of their rearmament programs, the impact on their economies of the German restrictions on imports, and the deterioration of their terms of trade[9] had applied for relief under the escape clause and had been temporarily exempted by the OEEC from their general commitments to reach the 75 percent—or even the 60 percent—liberalization goals and from applying the "common list." Austria and Greece suspended all of their previous liberalization measures and as of the end of the year the percentage of liberalization achieved by Denmark, Iceland, and Norway was 63, 41, and 68, respectively. Turkey had also failed to reach the 75 percent goal by the end of the year, but Sweden, Switzerland, the

[7] During the latter part of the year the OEEC secretariat was preparing a second "list," but this had not been approved by the OEEC Council, as planned, by the end of the year.

[8] At the same time the members "agreed" to "consolidate" the previous 60 percent liberalization, which meant that except under the safeguard or escape clauses of the liberalization code no consolidated item could be withdrawn even though the minimum percentage was still honored. By the end of the year all but four countries had specifically committed themselves to such a "consolidation."

[9] The rearmament-induced shortages of many goods were also reported as tempting some countries to return to bilateral bargain procedures (including export quotas) as a device for obtaining larger quantities of urgently needed commodities in exchange for their products which were in great demand. To forestall such action, the OEEC urged all members to agree on certain end-use prohibitions of scarce materials, and the International Materials Conference (see Chapter VI above) was making international allocations of several commodities.

Netherlands, Ireland, and Belgium had achieved it. And, as noted above, Italy and Portugal had, by early 1952, removed all quantitative restrictions on private imports from European sources.

Especially severe setbacks to the liberalization program were recorded late in the year and early in 1952. Faced with what was regarded as a rearmament-induced rapid inflation, depletion in gold and dollar reserves, and a mounting EPU deficit, the United Kingdom in early November revoked many of the existing open general licenses for private imports from Europe (as well as other nonsterling area countries) and reestablished quotas, the effect of which was to reduce the percentage of liberalized European imports from more than 90 percent to some 45 percent. In an attempt "to keep the essence of liberalisation alive,"[1] the new quotas applied to EPU members as a group and so were not discriminatory within that region and, with a few exceptions, quotas were not reimposed on the items on the "common list." Shortly thereafter, the French Government, also faced with a growing EPU deficit and fast declining foreign exchange reserves, reimposed quantitative restrictions on all those imports from which they had earlier been withdrawn. It should be noted here that while many of the countries reimposed restrictions on imports during the year, none of these led to retaliatory action of the sort which had been common before the EPU and the trade liberalization program were adopted.

At the beginning of 1951, the OEEC had planned that all member countries would reach the 75 percent goal by February, but by early 1952 nine of the sixteen member countries—Austria, Denmark, France, Germany, Britain, Greece, Iceland, Norway, and Turkey—had not reached, or had retreated from, that objective. From available data, it seems likely that on balance the trade liberalization program retrogressed during the year,[2] and that more intra-European trade was being subjected to quantitative restric-

[1] See *The Economist*, November 19, 1951, p. 1129, and November 17, 1951, pp. 1169-1170, for a detailed account of this British action. As noted in Chapter V, above, the British action was referred to a committee of the Contracting Parties of the GATT concerned with quantitative restrictions, but it deferred examination of the action during 1951.

[2] The record shows that members were quick to reimpose restrictions on imports when their balance of payments positions deteriorated but were slow to remove them when their positions improved.

tions at the end than at the beginning of 1951.[3] The general conclusion reached by the Bank for International Settlements in early 1951 was still valid at the beginning of 1952. "In no case has as much as one-half of a country's total imports been subject to O.E.E.C. liberalisation—and for some countries (especially those which practise the method of purchase by official agencies) not even a quarter of their total imports has been involved. It is also a fact that in 1950, when the original liberalisation was first extended, a number of countries raised protectionist duties in their tariffs, and in that way attenuated the practical influence of the liberalisation."[4]

D. *EUROPEAN COAL AND STEEL COMMUNITY*

As summarized in the previous volume of this series,[5] the United States—both the public and private sectors—gave enthusiastic and almost unqualified support to the May 1950 proposal of then French Foreign Minister Schuman[6] that the coal and steel industries of France and Germany (together with those of any other European country wishing to join) be merged into a single market and placed under the control of a supra-national authority.[7] The U.S. Government actively intervened at various times, especially with the German authorities, to obtain agreement on the proposal because it believed that it would make war between Germany and France "impossible"; that it was a necessary prerequisite if German forces and productive capacity were to be incorporated

[3] It should be noted that a comprehensive set of rules on liberalization of invisible transactions within Europe was finally agreed upon in July and published as part of the revised *Code of Liberalisation*. However, available evidence indicates that these called for few changes in previous practices, and during late 1951 the United Kingdom, at least, greatly restricted the amount which British tourists were permitted to spend abroad. W. J. Diebold in his *Trade and Payments in Western Europe*, cited above, reports that, "Robert Marjolin, the Secretary General of the OEEC, said that in his opinion the decision liberalizing invisible transactions 'equals in importance' the decision to remove quotas on 50 percent of intra-European trade."

[4] Bank for International Settlements, *Twenty-first Annual Report*, Basle, June 11, 1951, p. 122.

[5] *Survey—1950*, pp. 260-264.

[6] Jean Monnet was commonly given credit for conceiving the scheme as well as for working out many of its details.

[7] It was never intended to, and in its present form, as approved by some of the governments by the end of 1951, it does not, prejudice the ownership of the coal and steel industries in the various countries.

into the North Atlantic mutual defense efforts; and that it would result in more competition and so more efficient production and lower prices within Europe, thus going far toward achieving the broad objectives of the European Recovery Program. A draft of the plan was signed by delegates of France, Germany, the Netherlands, Belgium, Luxembourg, and Italy in March 1951, and the next month a fifty-year treaty constituting the "European Coal and Steel Community" was signed by the Foreign Ministers of these six countries.[8] The Netherlands ratified the treaty in late 1951, and in December the French National Assembly ratified it. Early in 1952 it was ratified by the German Parliament, following agreement by the occupying powers that the International Authority for the Ruhr would be liquidated and current limitations on German coal and steel production would be removed once the proposed High Authority was actually operating.[9]

A detailed description of the treaty—long, one hundred articles and several annexes, and complex—is outside the scope of this document, but in view of the support it has received from the United States a brief survey of its most important provisions is appropriate.[1] At the outset, it should be recorded that there are exceptions to most of the general principles, and it is therefore impossible to know how it will work out when the treaty is translated from paper into concrete action.

The major tasks of the Community are seen as creating conditions for a more competitive market with the aim of (a) improving the efficiency of coal and steel production in the member countries and so lowering prices while insuring that the single market, and third areas, are regularly supplied with coal and steel, and (b) assuring each nation access on equal terms to the various coal and steel products and raw materials, and so removing what many believed was one of the major causes of political antagonisms be-

[8] The U.S. Congress and the American press had been critical of the refusal of the United Kingdom to participate in the negotiations. Late in 1951 the British Government announced its intention to send a permanent delegation to the High Authority, but no information was made public as to the specific functions or instructions which the delegation would have.

[9] The occupying powers retained the right to supervise the dissolution of the Ruhr trusts, and at year's end final agreement had not been reached on all the details for the dissolution of the Central German Coal Sales Agency.

[1] For an official United States "Analysis of the Schuman Plan," see Department of State *Bulletin*, Washington, D.C., April 2, 1951, pp. 523-528.

tween Germany and France. The treaty[2] provides that a "common market" for iron and steel products[3] shall be established as among the signatories in the sense that, in general, the following shall be abolished and prohibited: import and export duties and quantitative restrictions on the movements of steel and coal;[4] discriminatory practices among buyers, producers, or consumers with respect to prices and delivery terms; all forms of state subsidies, assistance, or charges; and "restrictive practices tending toward the division of markets or the exploitation of consumers." In addition, there are to be no restrictions, based on nationality, on the movements among the six nations of coal and steel workers of "proven qualifications." During a five-year transitional period a series of special protective measures are authorized to mitigate the effects on existing producers of increased competition; the two most important of these are (a) restrictions on shipments within the region, and (b) subsidies, to be paid out of equalization funds raised by levies on low-cost producers and paid, in tapering amounts, to high-cost producers.

The Community is to be administered by an elaborate structure of four new institutions, the High Authority, the Council of Ministers, the Common Assembly, and the Court of Justice. The High Authority is the executive body and has day-by-day responsibility for carrying out the provisions of the treaty. Its nine members,[5] taking decisions by majority vote, are designated by the govern-

[2] The quotations in this description of the treaty have been taken from the "Treaty Constituting the European Coal and Steel Community," as distributed by the Press and Information Division of the French Embassy in New York. It varies in some details from the text of an earlier draft published by the State Department as Publication 4173, European and British Commonwealth Series 22, Washington, D.C., April 1951.

[3] The terms "coal" and "steel" are defined in the treaty. As regards steel it includes raw materials for the production of pig iron and steel, pig iron and ferro-alloys, and a list of specified raw and semi-finished products of steel such as rails, wire rods, etc., as well as certain finished products of steel, such as tin plate, etc.

[4] Since each of the members is also a member of the GATT and bound by the most-favored-nation clause of that agreement, it will be necessary to obtain release from that clause before the internal tariffs can be reduced or removed. This is a question of discrimination, and at the Sixth Session of the Contracting Parties to the GATT in the fall of 1951 a Working Party was set up to "undertake the necessary examination of the treaty."

[5] It was agreed during the negotiations that one of these members would be chosen from a list prepared by the International Confederation of Free Trade Unions. For an analysis of the significance of the Plan for labor, see Roux, R., "The Position of Labour Under the Schuman Plan," *International Labour Review*, Geneva, March 1952, pp. 289-320.

ments of the member states but are to exercise their functions in "complete independence" and are neither to solicit nor accept instructions from any government or organization.[6] The major link between the High Authority and the member governments is the Council, which is composed of one minister from each member government. The system of checks and balances between the High Authority and the Council is complex and many of the Authority's decisions or recommendations require the concurrence of the Council—usually by a simple majority vote when the Council is supporting the action of the High Authority but by a unanimous vote when it is over-ruling or acting in place of the High Authority. In general, the High Authority has great powers with respect to gathering and publishing information, preventing the growth of cartels, and of stopping or breaking up mergers which violate the nondiscriminatory aspects of the treaty, while to the Council is reserved much authority on many investment and production matters. The Common Assembly, seventy-eight members selected by the Parliaments of the member states or by direct voting, has general supervisory powers over the Community. In its annual meeting it is to receive and discuss a "general report" submitted by the High Authority and by a two-thirds vote can force the resignation of the High Authority. Finally, the seven-man Court, appointed by agreement among the member governments, is to sit in continuous session and has responsibility for enforcing the treaty, including the right to nullify the decisions of the other three institutions. Appeals to the Court can be made by the High Authority, the Council, governments of member states, and individual concerns.

The High Authority is entitled to raise funds (in addition to imposing fines) by receiving grants, by borrowing, and by placing certain levies on the production of coal and steel, and, with the unanimous approval of the Council, may grant loans, or give its guarantee to loans which enterprises raise elsewhere, to assist in the carrying out of approved investment programs. (ECA Administrator Foster testified before Congress that, after much thought, ECA had decided that the U.S. Government probably

[6] The High Authority is to be assisted by a consultative committee of between 30 and 51 members representing, in equal numbers, producers, workers, consumers, and dealers.

should not extend a grant to the Community. As to a loan, another ECA official stated only that a loan would be preferable to a grant.) To "encourage a coordinated development of investments" the High Authority may require enterprises to submit their individual programs in advance and must publicly issue its opinion of such programs, but if the proposed investment, or the operation of the resulting installations, requires subsidies, protection, or discrimination the High Authority, without referring the question to the Council, can forbid—and impose fines for violations—the enterprise from using funds other than from its own reserves. If new equipment or techniques in the coal and steel industries result in serious unemployment, the Authority, with the consent of the Council, may help finance (by loans) other "new and economically sound activities" capable of reemploying such workers and may also provide aid (in the form of grants) to such unemployed workers by means of separation pay and by helping to meet retraining and resettlement expenses.

As regards the commercial policies on coal and steel of the member states vis-à-vis third countries, the treaty provides, subject to international agreements to which the members are parties, that by unanimous decision the Council may establish both minimum and maximum customs duties—within which limits each government may set its tariffs "according to its national procedure." The High Authority is also empowered to "supervise the administration and control" of such import and export licensing as the member states impose and to make recommendations for the establishment of quantitative restrictions. (This last power is regarded by the State Department as analogous to the so-called escape clause rights under the GATT.) The press reported that it was the intention that, in time, each member country would adopt a uniform tariff on coal and steel vis-à-vis third countries and that the final level, it was hoped, would be close to that of the current rates of the Benelux countries.

With respect to cartels—seen by many in the United States as the most important problem of the Plan—the treaty forbids, and provides heavy fines for violations, all private agreements and "concerted practices" which would tend to "fix or influence prices; restrict or control investment, production, or technical development, or allocate markets or sources of supply." Further, mergers of any kind require the approval of the High Authority, which approval may not be granted if such a merger violates the principles cited in the previous sentence. On the other hand, in case of a decline in demand which the High Authority deems to face the Community with a period of "manifest crisis" it can, with the concurrence of the Council (if it fails to act the Council can force it to), establish a system of production quotas, including levies on tonnages exceeding the quotas, which sums will be earmarked for those whose production drops below "the level envisaged," and the High Authority may also impose import quotas on imports from third areas. And if a serious shortage develops, there are elaborate provisions whereby the Council and/or High Authority can allocate available supplies of coal and steel among member states, among different types of consumers, and for export.[7]

The generally approved price scheme is something of a multiple basing point system and producers are prohibited from charging "discriminatory" prices, especially according to the nationality of the buyer within the Community, or to engage in "unfair competitive practices," especially temporary or local price cuts designed to acquire a monopoly position. Restrictions are also imposed in the treaty on wage cuts as a "weapon of competition." The High Authority is granted extensive regulatory power over prices and can itself fix minimum prices within the common market, "if it deems that a manifest crisis exists or is imminent," and under certain conditions can also fix maximum prices. The treaty has very little to say regarding the treatment to be accorded by the Community to outside countries which import coal and steel from the Community.

To repeat, the treaty as of the end of 1951 was still only on paper, and it is not possible to be confident as to how it will work out in practice. *The Economist* reported[8] that in Europe there were many who believed it would "turn out to be the old cartel writ large" since the High Authority and the Council seemed to have greater powers than the old private cartels ever possessed. With so much of

[7] The authority with respect to exports is intended to be a substitute for the existing jurisdiction of the Ruhr Authority which decides how much coal Germany shall export.

[8] May 26, 1951, pp. 1216-1218. See also McKesson, J. A., "The Schuman Plan," *Political Science Quarterly*, March 1952, pp. 18-35, for a general description of the Plan and some of the criticisms which have been levied against it.

the final authority in political organs (the Council and the Assembly), many thought it likely that the powers would be used mostly for restrictive and short-term purposes. Others—some thought the majority of people who had examined it carefully—anticipated that there were so many checks and balances that the Community would accomplish very little and that the coal and steel enterprises would go on pretty much as if the treaty had never been signed. Nevertheless, one gathers from the press that the feeling was widespread in Europe that the Plan was clearly preferable to what was regarded as the most likely alternative—a rapidly recovering Ruhr under the unfettered control of the German Government and the reemergence of private cartels with government support.

The public statements of United States officials showed few worries as to the success of the Plan. Most who spoke in public on it agreed with Secretary Acheson's statement at the end of 1951 that the Plan was "a major step in the direction of building up a strong and unified Western Europe,"[9] with his earlier statement that it carried forward the fundamental concept of the European Recovery Program—"a joint effort among the nations of Europe toward greater freedom of trade, leading to higher standards of living for their people"[1]—with the U.S. High Commissioner for Germany's conclusion that it would free markets and develop new economic opportunities, and with ECA's repeated assertion that it should increase productivity in Europe. United States officials also expressed the belief and hope that it would set the pattern "for other similar kinds of economic pools" in Europe.[2]

E. *OTHER ECONOMIC INTEGRATION PROPOSALS*

The United States had looked with favor in 1950 on the so-called Stikker Plan, the Pella Plan, and the Petsche Plan (named after the European officials who presented them) which were designed to further, in various ways, the economic integration of Europe.[3] There is no evidence, however, that ECA actually intervened in

[9] Department of State *Bulletin*, December 24, 1951, p. 1013.

[1] Department of State *Bulletin*, April 9, 1951, p. 590.

[2] See statement by ECA Administrator Foster in *Hearings on H.R. 5020, op.cit.*, p. 212.

[3] See *Survey—1950* for a brief characterization of each of these schemes. See Diebold, W., Jr., *Trade and Payments in Western Europe, op.cit.*, Chapter 11, for a detailed description and analysis of these plans, especially the one credited to Mr. Stikker.

their behalf, and the only official report on them during the year was that they were being "studied." In mid-1950 the representatives of several European countries put forward tentative and general proposals for creating a single market in Europe for selected agricultural products. In general, these proposals for establishing a so-called "green pool" were along the general lines proposed by French Foreign Minister Schuman for coal and steel.[4] In March 1952, a conference was called by France of the agricultural ministers of eighteen countries to "sound out" the sentiment for establishing such a pool. The Director of the European Office of the Mutual Security Agency blessed the calling of the meeting and stated that "The establishment of a common agricultural market would be another step in uniting and strengthening the free peoples of Western Europe" and would be in accord with United States policy.[5]

In the early days of its integration drive, ECA had encouraged customs unions within Europe and had been especially hopeful that the proposed Benelux Economic Union would provide an impressive example of the benefits to be derived from integration. The date for that economic union was again postponed on January 1, 1951—this time for an indefinite period—and during the year not only were the previous difficulties unresolved but the sharply discrepant positions of Belgium-Luxembourg and Holland in the EPU, noted above, resulted in those nations agreeing to reduce (by unpublicized methods) the volume of Belgian exports to the Netherlands for at least a temporary period. Instead of providing a shining example of the potentialities of economic unification, the Benelux experiment through 1951 had provided excellent examples of some of the difficulties.

In addition to the specific plans and schemes noted above, the United States also took an active part during 1951 in certain other of the "economic cooperation" activities of the OEEC,[6] in which organization the United States and Canada became in 1950 informal but active members. Most important here were efforts, es-

[4] See Diebold, W., Jr., *Trade and Payments in Western Europe, op.cit.*, Chapter 13, for a description and analysis of some of these proposals. See also Strange, S., "A European Agricultural Authority," *World Affairs*, October 1951, pp. 454-466.

[5] For a press report of this statement, see *New York Times*, March 24, 1952.

[6] For details of these activities, see Organization for European Economic Cooperation, *European Economic Cooperation, op.cit.*

sentially advisory, to (a) "harmonize" the monetary policies of the various members so as to make possible the progressive reduction of trade and payments restrictions, (b) prevent the post-Korean export restrictions by member countries from denying other members certain essential goods, (c) reduce the practice of "dual pricing," and (d) obtain agreement by all members for prohibiting certain end-uses for selected strategic and critical materials.

F. EUROPEAN VERSUS NORTH ATLANTIC INTEGRATION

There was much discussion during the year as to whether the economic "unification" efforts should be broadened, as so many Europeans desired, to include all members of the North Atlantic Treaty Organization—the so-called Atlantic Community. While there was an increasing amount of "acting in concert" among this broader group, especially in military matters[7] and on political questions so far as they involved East versus West disputes, the U.S. Government was exceedingly chary of any economic "integration" of this area in the sense that they were pressing it for Europe.[8]

Thus, the import restrictions which the United States reduced during the year (see Chapter V) were on a global rather than a regional basis; there was no public consideration given in official United States circles to joining a regional payments union such as the EPU, or special economic "pools" such as the Schuman Plan; and in such new cooperative enterprises as the International Materials Conference (see Chapter VI) the membership was not restricted to any one geographic region.

Nonetheless, United States officials did talk in glowing, but very general, terms of the desirability of developing an "Atlantic Community," the legal basis for the economic aspects of which is pro-

[7] At noted in Chapter I, the United States did subject its rearmament proposals to the scrutiny of various NATO groups; and, though no data are publicly available, it may be that certain adjustments were made in them in an effort to "coordinate" them with the military production programs of the other North Atlantic Pact countries.

[8] No action was taken by Congress during the year on the Atlantic Union proposal which had been submitted to it in 1950. (See *Survey—1950*, p. 237n.) The Congressional group which visited as a delegation to the Council of Europe in November stated that responsible Americans had not "thought through" the implications of the Atlantic Union proposal nor had the Government established a "clear" policy with respect to Atlantic integration. (See S. *Doc. No. 90, op.cit.*, pp. 11-14.)

vided in Article 2 of the North Atlantic Treaty, which states that members will ". . . encourage economic collaboration between any or all of them."[9] In September, United States officials supported the creation within the North Atlantic Treaty Organization of an Atlantic Community Committee—of which it was not a member—to recommend action which might be taken to implement this Article. At the Lisbon meeting of NATO in February this particular committee was disbanded, but the United States representatives there supported the decision that the North Atlantic Council should concern itself with a wide variety of economic problems affecting all the members.

There was, however, other evidence that the U.S. Government was not yet prepared energetically to pursue a policy of Atlantic integration. For example, the United States had through 1951 placed very few orders in other North Atlantic nations for military equipment for its own use, although the press reported that the capacity for such production did exist in several of the other countries. On the other hand, the United States was placing an increasing volume of orders for military supplies in certain European countries for delivery to other European countries, thus forcing some coordinated military production within Europe.[1] More significant as an indication of United States policy of encouraging European but not Atlantic economic integration was the United States insistence in March 1952 that the Organization for European Economic Cooperation continue to function pretty much as it had in the past. The British Government, which had long favored a North Atlantic rather than a European economic grouping, proposed that the OEEC functions be drastically curtailed on the grounds that these duties could and should be carried out by the North Atlantic Treaty Organization. The press reported[2] that United States officials emphatically opposed the British suggestion, chiefly on the

[9] In early 1952 a communique issued by President Truman and Prime Minister Churchill stated that "We are resolved to build an Atlantic Community, not only for immediate defense, but for enduring progress." (For text of the whole communique, see Department of State *Bulletin*, January 21, 1952, pp. 83-84.)

[1] Available evidence—most of the facts are secret—suggest that the European countries themselves were doing little in the way of placing orders among themselves for military supplies. See, e.g., *New York Times*, May 23, 1951, and "Mutual Security Act of 1951," *Hearings on S. 1762*, U.S. Senate, Committee on Foreign Relations and Committee on Armed Services, 82d Cong., 1st Sess., July-August 1951, p. 180.

[2] See especially *New York Times*, March 25, March 29, and March 30, 1952.

grounds that the OEEC had been the major organization for fostering economic integration *within* Europe and that such integration was and continued to be the declared policy of the United States.[3] In this connection it is to be remembered that one of the major objectives of the United States policy of encouraging European economic integration has been to reduce, rather than to increase, formal governmental economic ties between the United States and Europe.

[3] The press reported (*New York Times*, March 30, 1951) that the United States did agree that in the future the Organization for European Economic Cooperation Council's annual review of the economic and financial situation of the member countries, made with the aim of harmonizing their financial and economic policies, should include a similar "review" of the United States and Canadian economies.

VIII · UNITED STATES BALANCE OF INTERNATIONAL PAYMENTS 1951

THE balance of international payments of the United States in 1951 not only reflected a continuing disequilibrium in the nation's international economic affairs but also showed the effects of some new types of disturbances and disequilibria which distinguished it from the World War II years as well as the immediate postwar period.[1]

The value of imports of goods and services was at an all-time high and the value of exports also exceeded those of any year, except 1944, in the nation's history. The current account surplus, at approximately $5 billion, was smaller than it had been for any year during the period 1942 through 1949, but it was more than double that of 1950. With net unilateral transfers of the U.S. Government only slightly higher than in 1950 and a one-third decline in the net outflow of private capital and remittances, the rest of the world, in their transactions with the United States, were able to increase their gold and dollar reserves by only about $400 million, as compared with $3.6 billion in 1950. These yearly figures hide the fact that the disequilibrium was greater in the latter part of the year than it was in the first part. Thus, during the last quarter the current account export surplus was at a rate of nearly $7.5 billion, and the rest of the world was liquidating its gold and dollar reserves in its trade with the United States at an annual rate of nearly $1.6 billion.

[1] In view of the excellent quality and general availability of the Department of Commerce publications on the United States balance of payments, this chapter merely outlines the major developments during the year. The reader desiring details is referred especially to the following documents, which are the source of most of the information presented here: Department of Commerce, *Survey of Current Business*, June 1951, pp. 15-23; September 1951, pp. 9-12; October 1951, pp. 7-14; February 1952, pp. 23-26; and March 1952, pp. 15-21. See also Board of Governors of the Federal Reserve System, *Federal Reserve Bulletin*, March 1952, pp. 227-236.

Statistical details of the 1951 developments by quarters, and the revised data for the years 1948, 1949, and 1950, are given in Table 18.[2]

A. CURRENT ACCOUNT

Merchandise Trade

a. EXPORTS

The value of United States merchandise exports, which had been falling more or less steadily since 1947, began to rise in September 1950 and continued sharply upward to mid-1951 when it leveled off at an average annual rate of around $16 billion—an amount equivalent in value, but not in volume, to that of 1947 when the wartime backlog of foreign demand for American goods to meet pent-up consumer demands, to rebuild inventories, and for physical reconstruction were at their peak. For the year 1951, the value of United States commodity exports at $15.4 billion was some one-half greater than in 1950 and the volume was approximately one-third larger.

This increase in exports was attributed to many factors. The rising defense expenditures and growing inflation in many parts of the world resulted in an increased demand for many American goods, which, for most items, continued to be in plentiful supply. Foreign nations were able to increase their purchases, as compared with 1950, because their dollar receipts were well above the 1950 levels, because over the year they practically stopped building up their gold and dollar reserves, and because of a small increase in the volume of official United States aid. In addition to these general factors, several more or less special but unrelated developments accounted for the rise in exports. The stoppage of petroleum production in Iran, the poor grain harvests in many countries, especially in India, Argentina, and Canada, and the curtailment of exports of many commodities from Western Europe all served to create large demands for United States exports. In addition, once again European coal production fell substantially below the growing domestic requirements and shipments of this commodity

[2] For a detailed review of some "Recent Developments in the U.S. Balance of Payments" for these years, see the article so titled by H. K. Zassenhaus and F. C. Dirks in International Monetary Fund, *Staff Papers*, April 1952, pp. 213-262.

TABLE 18

International Transactions of the United States, 1948-1951

(millions of dollars)

Type of Transaction	*1948*[r]	*1949*[r]	*1950*[r]	*1951*[p] *and by Quarters* *Total*	*I*	*II*	*III*	*IV*
Exports of Goods and Services								
Merchandise, adjusted[a]	13346	12337	10658	15424	3414	4091	3842	4077
Income on investments	1375	1405	1743	1905	396	471	458	580
Transportation	1299	1176	926	1495	284	389	399	423
Travel	308	363	377	444	83	115	151	95
Miscellaneous services	639	693	721	872	198	217	219	238
Total Exports	16967	15974	14425	20140	4375	5283	5069	5413
Imports of Goods and Services								
Merchandise, adjusted[a]	7822	7066	9315	11663	3217	3133	2680	2633
Income on investments	284	353	437	400	86	99	93	122
Transportation	630	676	798	917	221	251	233	212
Travel	600	678	727	733	120	167	308	138
Miscellaneous services	931	830	851	1398	271	288	394	445
Total Imports	10268	9603	12128	15111	3915	3938	3708	3550
Surplus of Exports of Goods and Services								
Merchandise	5524	5271	1343	3761	197	958	1162	1444
Income on investments	1091	1052	1306	1505	310	372	365	458
Transportation	669	500	128	578	63	138	166	211
Travel	−292	−315	−350	−289	−37	−52	−157	−43
Miscellaneous	−292	−137	−130	−526	−73	−71	−175	−207
Total Export Surplus	6699	6371	2297	5029	460	1345	1361	1863

Net Means of Financing Surplus								
Liquidation of gold and dollar assets[b]	780	−60	−3645	−362	−855	−159	257	395
Dollar disbursements by:								
International Monetary Fund	203	99	−20	−24	−10	−11	*	−3
International Bank	176	38	37	81	16	10	23	32
U.S. Government sources:								
Grants and unilateral transfers	4157	5321	4120	4534	1035	1279	1131	1089
Long and short-term loans	886	647	164	159	59	83	27	−10
U.S. private sources:								
Remittances	678	552	481	405	112	96	90	107
Long and short-term capital[c]	857	589	1316	747	249	284	−16	230
Total Net Financing	7736	7156	2453	5540	606	1582	1512	1840
Errors and Omissions	−1037	−785	−156	−511	−146	−237	−151	+23

r. Revised

p. Preliminary

* Less than $500,000

a) Includes goods sold or bought from other countries that have not been shipped from or into United States customs areas (e.g., with respect to imports, purchases abroad by U.S. Government agencies for transfer to third countries under various foreign aid programs and purchases abroad for the use of American military establishments overseas; with respect to exports, commodities furnished by the U.S. Government from overseas stocks—such as surplus property—and goods sold from overseas purchases, particularly under the various foreign aid programs). The United States customs area includes continental United States, Alaska, Hawaii, Puerto Rico, the Virgin Islands, the Panama Canal Zone, American Samoa, and certain minor American islands in the Pacific.

b) Excludes the increase in short-term balances and gold holdings of the International Bank and Monetary Fund resulting from payment of United States subscriptions, sales of debentures and notes in the United States, and the reduction of such balances and gold holdings resulting from dollar disbursements to foreign countries.

c) Excludes net purchases of debentures sold or guaranteed by the International Bank (1948, $7 million; 1949, $20 million; 1950, $1 million; and 1951, $147 million).

Sources: Department of Commerce, *Survey of Current Business*, June 1951, pp. 18-22 and March 1952, pp. 16 and 20.

again bulked large in American exports. During 1950 the United States had imposed restrictions on the export of cotton in the face of a small crop, but these were removed after the good 1951 harvest, with the result that exports of this commodity were unusually large in the latter part of the year as foreign countries replenished their inventories.

For reasons of national security, relatively large amounts of exports during the year are excluded from the detailed statistics and it is therefore not possible to make precise statements as to the area, distribution, and commodity composition of the nation's exports. Such data as are available, however, indicate that, as compared with 1950, all major areas increased their imports from the United States, with over half (52 percent) of the increase going to Europe and with relative declines in the proportion of the total destined for Canada and Latin America.

The increase during the year in the value (and volume) of exports was shared by all major commodity groups, with crude foodstuffs showing the greatest percentage value increase, in part a reflection of the enlarged relief wheat shipments. Crude materials shared least in the increase, and a slightly smaller proportion of the enlarged total, as compared with 1950, was also taken by manufactured foodstuffs. There was only a slight increase in the proportion of the nation's total exports represented by semi-manufactures and finished manufactures, but together they still accounted for over two-thirds of the total.

b. IMPORTS

At nearly $11.7 billion, the value of United States merchandise imports was at an all-time high but, as contrasted with exports, the entire increase of $2.4 billion over 1950 was accounted for by price increases; in fact, the *volume* of imports showed a fractional decline from the 1950 record level. The United States commodity terms of trade, as measured by the ratios of the index of unit values compiled by the Department of Commerce, stood at 75 in June 1950 (1936-1938 = 100) and had fallen to 70 by the end of that year. There was some further decline during the first half of 1951 and the monthly average for the year was 68 but had risen to 70 by December. Stated otherwise, the 1951 average unit value for exports was roughly 14 percent higher than in 1950, while that for imports exceeded 1950 by 26 percent.

The value of commodity imports, which had begun to expand during the last quarter of 1949, increased rapidly after the outbreak of war in Korea (only about one-fourth of the increased value of imports in 1950 over 1949 was represented by higher prices) and reached an annual rate of nearly $13 billion during the first quarter of 1951. A small reduction in the total was recorded in the second quarter and a substantial cut in the third quarter when imports leveled off at an annual rate of about $10.5 billion. The decline after the first quarter has been officially attributed to the fact that for many industries inventories of imported products were unusually high relative to sales. This decline in purchases brought about a drop, after June, in the prices of some of the major import commodities, especially wool, copra, tin, and burlap, and strengthened the "wait-and-see" policy of importers and their customers who had already been made cautious by the softening of the domestic consumers' goods market and the feeling that the political conditions abroad had become more or less "stabilized." The Department of Commerce concluded, however, that the reduced level of imports at the end of the year was probably temporary since there are limits to the ability to consume stocks and that if, as expected, national output and income of the United States continued to expand, the volume of imports would also rise.

As compared with 1950, the value of imports for consumption[3] of all the five major categories increased during the year under review, with the largest increase recorded for crude materials (the *volume* of such imports actually declined 7 percent). The percentage of the total for finished manufactures also increased, but by a smaller amount, while those of crude foodstuffs, manufactured foodstuffs, and semi-manufactured goods all declined. All the major areas of the world shared in the increased value of American imports for consumption, but Canada, Latin America, and Africa took a smaller proportion of the total than they had in 1950,

[3] Imports for consumption comprise goods entering consumption channels immediately upon arrival in the United States customs area plus *withdrawals* from bonded warehouses. Not included are goods purchased abroad by United States agencies for transfer to third countries under the various foreign aid programs and procurement abroad for the use of American overseas military establishments.

while Europe, Asia, and Oceania increased their proportions. Just over half of total United States imports were supplied by countries in the Western Hemisphere.

Invisibles

a. INCOME ON INVESTMENTS[4]

United States income on foreign investments[5] has risen steadily since World War II, starting at $0.8 billion in 1946, reaching $1.7 billion in 1950, with 1951 receipts estimated provisionally at $1.9 billion.[6] The exceptionally high returns in 1950 and 1951 arose out of higher prices and increased production, plus, in a few important cases, dividends paid out of past earnings. These balance of payments inflows were offset by payments from the United States ranging from just over $200 million in 1946 to about $440 million in 1950 and an estimated $400 million in 1951.

The growth in investment income receipts since 1946 resulted not only from the expansion of total foreign investment but also from the fact that, as compared with prewar, new private investments were predominantly in high-yielding direct investments rather than in low-yielding portfolio investments and that in direct investments there was a shift in composition away from public utilities into the production of raw materials (particularly petroleum, mining, and smelting) and in manufacturing. The *rates* of return on direct investment rose from about 6 percent of book

[4] For a detailed account of income and earnings on United States investments abroad and foreign investments in the United States during the period 1946-1950, see Pizer, S., "Income on International Investments of the United States," *Survey of Current Business,* October 1951, pp. 7-14, from which most of the following information was taken.

[5] Income is defined in the official statistics as the sum of interest and dividends from portfolio investments and dividends, interest, and branch profits from direct investments. Income from direct-investment companies excludes undistributed profits of subsidiaries which are, however, included in "earnings," and all income as officially reported for balance of payments purposes is taken after the payment of any foreign taxes thereon.

[6] Undistributed earnings of direct-investment subsidiaries, not included in the above figures on "income," reached a peak of $581 million in 1948, having risen from $303 million in 1946. The total dropped to some $443 million in 1950; data on 1951 are not available. Undistributed earnings on direct-investment subsidiaries of foreigners in the United States increased from $37 million in 1946 to about $172 million in 1950.

In the period 1946-1950 approximately half of the direct-investment earnings of United States investments abroad were retained abroad and reinvested, accounting for $3.8 billion of the total additions to United States direct investments abroad.

value in 1929 to an average of about 15 percent in 1950; the rate was probably about the same in 1951.[7] The rate of return on portfolio investments, on the other hand, dropped to 3 percent in 1950, compared with 6 percent in 1929, reflecting defaults, retirements, and refunding operations which scaled down interest rates on outstanding obligations. Thus, private direct investments were the source of 84 percent of 1950 income receipts while portfolio investments accounted for less than 9 percent.[8] Most of the balance represented payments to the U.S. Government on official loans.[9] Interest receipts on government lending have increased steadily since 1946 as a result of the large amounts of postwar official lending. Thus, gross receipts of $21 million in 1946 had risen to approximately $100 million during each of the three years 1948 through 1950 and increased to $192 million in 1951, as interest became due on the 1946 loan to Britain. It was officially anticipated that the yearly average ($170 million) of such receipts during the 1950 decade would be about $40 million more than the annual average received during the 1920's on World War I loans.

Areas returning the most income on United States investments abroad coincided broadly with the distribution of outstanding investments, with nearly 40 percent of the income received during 1946-1950 originating in Latin America, and 26 percent coming from Canada. In both areas the income was primarily from direct investments.

Income payments on foreign investments in the United States grew at approximately the same rate as income receipts, but the absolute size of the gap increased; the Department of Commerce concluded that it would probably continue to grow since it was anticipated that United States investments abroad would continue in much larger amounts than foreign investments in the United States. In contrast to increases in investment receipts, payments by the United States to foreigners have been concentrated on portfolio investments. Thus, out of total payments of approximately

[7] While such comparisons are subject to many qualifications, it appears that for many comparable industries the rates of return on United States domestic investments were as high or higher than the rates of return on foreign investments.

[8] This contrasts sharply with the situation in 1929 when income from private portfolio investments accounted for 50 percent of total receipts from income on foreign investments.

[9] Less than 1 percent of the total payments represented income from private short-term investments abroad.

$1.5 billion over the period 1946 through 1950, more than half were on publicly held securities (almost all stocks of American corporations) and some 40 percent was derived from direct investments in the United States. The balance represented payments on long- and short-term obligations of the U.S. Government held abroad, largely the result of foreign governments and central banks investing a portion of their dollar reserves in such interest-bearing securities. ERP Europe received over 70 percent of the total payments from the United States during the period and Canada received 18 percent.

Since 1947, investment receipts have been second only to merchandise exports as a source of inpayments in the nation's balance of payments, and in the six-year period since the end of the war (1946-1951) have accounted for over 8 percent of the total proceeds from United States exports of goods and services. Further, the trend increased steadily from just over 5 percent in 1946 to nearly 12 percent in 1950. Despite the increase in total income receipts on investment during 1951, such income fell to 9.5 percent of total receipts as the result of the huge expansion in proceeds from merchandise exports. Receipts from foreign investments have in recent years followed the general trend of American imports; roughly parallel movements in these two series are in part the result of the fact that a large portion (perhaps as much as one-third during recent years) of the production of American direct investments abroad are sold in the United States. The Department of Commerce has estimated that in the five years ending in 1950 approximately one-quarter of the nation's merchandise imports came from United States-controlled companies abroad.[1]

b. TRANSPORTATION

Receipts on transportation account rose sharply during the year to almost $1.5 billion due in large part to the increased volume of exports, especially to the larger shipments of coal and grain, and

[1] See Pizer, S., "Income on International Investments of the United States," *op.cit.*, for a detailed discussion of this question. Mr. Pizer also tentatively concludes that in 1950, at least, the dollar proceeds of sales of such United States-controlled companies abroad plus dollar capital outflow from the United States were greater than the amount of dollars required by these companies to finance their purchases in the United States and to transfer earnings into dollars. That is, these investments represented a net dollar gain for the foreign countries.

somewhat less importantly, to the rise in outbound rates of some 10 to 15 percent. Save for 1947, United States receipts from this source were the largest since the war. *Payments* for transportation reached a postwar peak as a result primarily of the increased rates charged by foreign vessels. Net receipts on transportation account were well above those recorded during the previous year but substantially below those registered in the first three postwar years. This was to be expected since the net shipping balance tends to vary directly with the net merchandise export balance inasmuch as the United States receives payments on international account by carrying its own exports (and goods between foreign countries) but pays on international account only for foreign vessels carrying United States imports.[2]

C. TRAVEL AND MISCELLANEOUS SERVICES

At nearly three-quarters of a billion dollars, foreign travel expenditures by Americans were slightly higher than in 1950, and the drop, which some had anticipated after the Holy Year in 1950 and in view of the increasing international tensions, did not materialize. Expenditures in Europe by United States travelers declined by about 10 percent,[3] but those with Latin American countries increased. The effect of the post-Korean international tensions on tourist expenditures was still not clear but may have been responsible for the decline in trips to Europe.[4] Receipts from tourism rose, however, by over 17 percent during the year as compared with 1950, due in large part to increased travel in the United States by Canadians, with the result that the tourism account between these two countries was almost balanced.

Expenditures for miscellaneous services rose sharply during 1951 to about $1.4 billion, primarily as a result of increased payments by the U.S. Government for the construction and maintenance of military facilities and installations abroad and the spend-

[2] It should be recognized that United States balance of payments statistics on shipping receipts are not the same as earnings by American ships in foreign trade since carriage payments for imports transported in United States bottoms are not included in the former.

[3] For comments on tourism as a European asset, see *The Statist*, July 28, 1951, pp. 118-119, and Organization for European Economic Cooperation, *Tourism in European Recovery*, Paris, 1951.

[4] See Department of Commerce, *Foreign Commerce Weekly*, September 3, 1951, pp. 3 f.

ing by military personnel stationed in foreign countries. The large increase in the last two quarters reflected, however, only a better statistical coverage and prior data were scheduled for revision. Receipts from miscellaneous services also rose—due in large part to larger earnings by American contractors for construction overseas—but the net deficit of almost $0.5 billion on the miscellaneous services account was the largest since the end of the war.

Export Surplus

As a result of the above developments, the current account export surplus of the United States rose from $2.3 billion in 1950 to $5.0 billion in 1951. In the last quarter it was at an annual rate of over $7.5 billion—well in excess of the rate during each of the previous three years but still only about two-thirds of that recorded

TABLE 19

United States Current Account Surplus, by Area, 1950-1951

(millions of dollars)

		1951p				
	1950r	Total	First Quarter	Second Quarter	Third Quarter	Fourth Quarter
Canada	293	672	178	280	87	127
Latin America	357	1017	−82	235	474	390
ERP Countries	1734	3041	526	880	708	927
ERP Dependencies	−312	−518	−196	−133	−106	−83
Other Europe	−44	105	7	30	34	34
All Other Countries	219	703	26	43	175	459
International Institutions	50	9	1	10	−11	9
Total	2297	5029	460	1345	1361	1863

r) Revised
p) Preliminary
Source: Department of Commerce, *Survey of Current Business,* June 1951, p. 18 and March 1952, pp. 16-17.

in 1947. Practically all of the 1951 increase was accounted for by the sharp rise in merchandise exports. There was also an increase during the year in the export surplus in the transportation and income-on-investments accounts, but these were in large measure offset by the increase in net payments on other invisibles—especially miscellaneous services.

As Table 19 shows, the increase in the surplus extended to all major areas except the ERP dependencies, which were the source of many of the strategic and critical materials whose prices had risen so much during late 1950 and early 1951. The amount of the deficit with the various ERP dependencies was, however, declining throughout the year as inventories in the United States reached higher levels and as prices for many of the commodities receded from their previous levels. The 1950 deficit with the non-ERP countries in Europe was changed into a surplus during 1951 as shipments under various official aid programs to Yugoslavia and Spain were increased.

The surplus account with the ERP countries increased by $1.3 billion. This increase was due in large part to the greater volume of United States exports (plus transportation services) of foods, fuel, cotton, and chemicals (as well as military equipment) to replace supplies previously obtained by Europe from other sources, to build up inventories, and to meet the expanded industrial requirements growing out of the rearmament programs. The value of Europe's exports to the United States also increased during the year but not sufficiently to offset this expansion in its imports from America. Further, while the terms of trade between Western Europe and the United States did not alter much, prices of both imports and exports were higher than in 1950 and thus served to increase the amount of the United States export surplus. While both imports and exports with Canada rose during the year, the latter increased by more than the former, due in part to inventory buying and to expanded Canadian purchases of military supplies and equipment in the United States which were not matched by United States purchases of such equipment in Canada. A small import surplus was recorded with Latin America during the first quarter of the year when seasonal coffee purchases by the United States were large but was thereafter replaced with a large export surplus, reflecting in part an extensive wave of inventory buying which in turn reflected concern in that area over the future purchasing power of their dollar reserves.

B. *CAPITAL ACCOUNT*

Foreign Gold and Dollar Assets

During the first half of 1951, the rest of the world in its transactions with the United States was able to build up its gold and dollar assets (both long- and short-term) as the result of continued high volumes of grants and loans from the United States and rising purchases by it of foreign goods and services. During this period the accumulations totalled over $1 billion, bringing the aggregate increase since the September 1949 devaluations to $5.1 billion, thus recouping two-thirds of the reserves lost to the United States during the previous four years. During the last half of 1951, however, the decline in United States imports and continued high exports, together with a decrease in the outflow of private capital and no significant change in the volume of official aid, resulted in a drain of some $650 million in these assets. Thus, for the year, the rest of the world accumulated an estimated $362 million in its transactions with the United States, one-tenth that of the previous year.

Detailed data as to the area distribution of the accumulation of gold and dollar assets in the transactions of the rest of the world with the United States are not available and intra-transfers among the other countries of the world of such assets were large. If newly-mined gold is taken into account, as well as their transactions with the United States (but *excluding* changes of long-term dollar holdings), the combined gold reserves and dollar holdings of the rest of the world increased by $939 million in the first half of the year and declined by $900 million during the last half, leaving total holdings at an estimated $19.2 billion, only slightly greater than at the beginning of the year.[5] As Table 20 shows, the United Kingdom (which holds the central monetary reserves of the entire sterling area) accounted for the largest part of the movements in

[5] This increase of only $39 million in the total reserves is $323 million less than the recorded accumulations of the rest of the world in their transactions with the United States, despite the fact that newly mined gold is taken into account in the former figure. The statistics for transactions with the United States and for the total changes in the rest of the world's gold and dollar holdings are taken from different sources, the first being taken from Department of Commerce publications and the latter from the public reports of the Board of Governors of the Federal Reserve System. From the available data it is not possible to reconcile this discrepancy. It should be noted, however, that including newly mined gold makes relatively little difference in 1951 since $600 million of the estimated total foreign production (excluding the USSR and the United States) of $750 million went into private industrial uses or private hoards or was otherwise unaccounted for. The inclusion of Federal Reserve data of changes in long-term dollar assets (mostly United States Government securities whose original maturity was longer than twenty months) also accounts for some of the differences in the figures and the balance is thought to be due to differences in estimates of privately held bank balances as between the two sources.

TABLE 20

Estimated Changes in Foreign Gold and Dollar Reserves, 1951[a]

(millions of dollars)

Area or Country	*First Half*	*Second Half*[p]	*Total*[p]	*Holdings as of Dec. 31, 1951*[p]
Sterling Area[b]	+596	−1285	−688	3733
Continental ERP Countries[c]	+39	+243	+281	6913
Other Continental Europe[d]	−23	−4	−27	545
Canada	−6	+172	+166	2154
Latin America	+200	−312	−113	3342
Asia	+65	+228	+293	2162
Other	+68	+58	+127	328
Total	+939	−900	+39	19176

p) Preliminary. Totals may not add due to rounding.
a) Dollar holdings represent official and private balances reported by banks in the United States and include holdings of United States securities with original maturities up to twenty months.
b) Excludes Eire and Iceland, which are included in "Continental ERP Countries."
c) Includes Bank for International Settlements, European Payments Union, Belgian Congo, French and Portuguese dependencies, and the Netherlands West Indies and Surinam. Also included are estimates of certain unpublished gold reserves of ERP countries and the gold to be distributed by the Tripartite Commission for Restitution of Monetary Gold. With respect to France, includes only the gold reserves of the Bank of France and French dependencies; and with respect to Italy, includes only reserves of Bank of Italy plus certain earmarked gold.
d) Excludes gold reserves of, but includes dollar balances held by, the USSR.
Source: Board of Governors of the Federal Reserve System, *Federal Reserve Bulletin*, March 1952, p. 232. See this table for further details. The accompanying article, "International Flow of Gold and Dollars, 1951," is the source of most of the information given here.

gold and dollar holdings during the year. The sharp drain in the reserves of the sterling area during the last half of the year was in part due to the development of an adverse trade balance of that area with Canada, Latin America, and continental Western Europe, and in part was the result of capital movements. The reversal in the United Kingdom's trade balance with the United States was also significant, especially since it coincided with the reduction in the disbursements to the United Kingdom by the Economic Cooperation Administration. Continental Western Europe increased its reserves by some $281 million, with Belgium, Germany, and Italy, registering the largest increases. These countries had a deficit with the United States, but it was more than offset by financial assistance from the U.S. Government together with dollar receipts from the United Kingdom via the European Payments Union. The reserves of the Latin American countries rose during the first few months of 1951, in part because of the seasonal high sales of wool and coffee to the United States, but this trend was reversed during the second quarter as United States imports declined and anticipatory buying by these countries increased. As noted in Table 19, Canada had a large import surplus with the United States, but this deficit was more than offset during the year by the proceeds of dollars from Canada's export surplus with other countries combined with her domestic gold production and the sizable capital inflow from the United States. Asia recorded the largest increase in reserves during the year, with Japan accounting for nearly half the total increase, and Indonesia representing nearly a third of the total. Japan's position improved primarily as a result of the procurement by the United Nations forces in Korea of goods and services in Japan, together with an expansion in Japan's commercial exports. The increases registered for Indonesia were in large part the result of the expanded exports of strategic raw materials to the United States.

During the last part of 1950 many countries rushed to convert an abnormally large portion of their dollar accumulations into gold, and this policy continued during the first quarter of 1951 when the gold outflow from the United States reached an annual rate of over $3.5 billion. This practice ceased in March along with the announcement of more restrictive monetary and debt-management policies by the U.S. Government and with the cessation abroad of speculation that the United States might change the official price of gold. During the last two quarters of the year the United States again made large gold purchases, and the ratio of gold to total gold and dollars held by foreigners was the same as it had been at the beginning of the year.

There was some evidence during the year that certain countries faced with heavy drains in their international reserves were beginning to rely more on traditional fiscal and monetary measures to restore equilibrium in their balance of payments, but in the world as a whole international payments deficits were controlled chiefly through imposing new exchange and quantitative trade restrictions. The large drain experienced by certain countries and the failure of others to increase their reserves appreciably, despite direct trade and payments restrictions and, in some cases, more restrictive monetary and credit policies, increased the concern felt for several years as to the adequacy of the monetary reserves of most foreign countries. The U.S. Government (The National Advisory Council on International Monetary and Financial Problems), however, stated late in the year its conclusion that grant assistance should not be extended for the purpose of increasing the reserves of foreign countries, and there was no public discussion of loans for this purpose.

Other Items

The other means of financing the surplus of United States exports of goods and services—dollars furnished by the International Monetary Fund and the International Bank, official Government gifts and loans, and private gifts and loans—have been discussed in Chapters I through IV and need not be reviewed here.

C. *ERRORS AND OMISSIONS*

The errors and omissions figure in the United States balance of payments was reported tentatively at zero during 1950, but revised data place it at $156 million, compared with $785 million in 1949; in 1951 it was preliminarily estimated at $511 million. This item has been largest during times of financial stress and international tension, and thus has been attributed largely to unrecorded capital movements, but at times the undervaluation of exports in the official statistics and overvaluation of payments for imports have also been important. The Department of Commerce has estimated that during 1951 there was an increase in speculative capital movements to the United States in anticipation of renewed sterling devaluations as well as a flight of capital from certain politically disturbed areas and that such movements account for most of the errors and omissions during the year under review.

SUMMARY

1951 WAS a year of widespread adaptation and reorientation of United States foreign economic policies toward the primary objective of strengthening the military defenses of the non-Communist world. Defense considerations had been brought sharply to the fore by the outbreak of war in Korea in mid-1950, and during the later part of that year the military assistance program was expanded, stockpiling of critical and strategic imported materials was accelerated, arrangements were inaugurated to create intergovernmental machinery for the international allocation of many scarce commodities, more rigid and extensive export controls were imposed, efforts were intensified to restrict strategic trade between East and West Europe, and greater attention was being given to non-European areas. During 1951, the previous shifts in emphasis toward national security and away from economic recovery and development and the longer-run policy goal of multilateral, nondiscriminatory trade were accentuated.

Although the actual fighting was in the Far East, there was no serious questioning during 1951 of the earlier conclusion that the bulk of American financial aid should go to Europe. It was generally accepted (by Congress, the Administration, and the public) that, as compared to other areas, Europe was in a position to make effective use of larger amounts of aid, that if a general war with the Soviet bloc were to start it was likely to be centered in Western Europe, and that the subjugation by Russia of that area would be disastrous to American security.[1] Still, it was decided to increase the amount of aid to other areas.

In 1951 all but a few of the official foreign aid activities of the

[1] There was disagreement within the Government as to the policy of extending aid to Spain. The majority of Congress believed that Spain's record of anti-Communism and its strategic location warranted the extension of financial support. The State Department at least was at best reluctant to assist a country with which it had had so many differences in the past and which was so mistrusted by the other members of the North Atlantic Treaty, but Congress specified in the mutual security legislation that Spain would receive $100 million of aid out of the 1952 appropriations. This was in addition to a $62.5 million loan authorized in the 1950 law appropriating funds for the third year of the Marshall Plan.

U.S. Government were subsumed under a single Mutual Security Program,[2] but it was still true throughout the year that assistance was being extended to foreign nations via a series of more or less distinct programs with different, though frequently overlapping, objectives—rearmament, economic development, economic recovery, relief—administered by separate organizations, principally the Economic Cooperation Administration (later the Mutual Security Agency), the Department of Defense, and the State Department. Congress attempted to solve some of the problems of conflicting authority and inconsistent action among the responsible agencies by providing greater centralization (via the newly created Office of Director for Mutual Security) in the administration of the aid programs than there had been in the previous years.[3] It had not been demonstrated by year's end whether this was providing a greater degree of coherence and consistency in the foreign aid policies of the United States.[4] The Mutual Security Act of 1951 made, in one piece of legislation, provision for aiding friendly countries all over the world, but the approach was regional, with the law specifying that the aid was to be distributed in certain amounts as among four major areas: Europe, the Near East and Africa, Asia and the Pacific, and Latin America. The law also divided, both as to purpose and to form, the aid for each area between "military" and "economic."

Military end-items were to account for some three-quarters of

[2] Outside the Mutual Security Program, special emergency food programs were also authorized and carried out for Yugoslavia and India and emergency refugee aid was continued in small amounts for the International Refugee Organization. Some contributions were also made to the International Children's Emergency Fund during the year. Except for the Ryukyus, aid under the Occupied Areas Program was terminated during the year. The Export-Import Bank remained a separate and distinct institution.

[3] Congress also specified that the Director for Mutual Security was to be responsible for administering United States policy in East-West trade.

[4] In view of the conflicts and inconsistencies within and among the various international economic policies and activities of the United States, many of which have been noted in the foregoing chapters, there was increasing questioning during the year of whether the U.S. Government was appropriately organized to formulate and carry out a consistent and coherent foreign economic policy. At the request of the Bureau of the Budget, the Brookings Institution made a study of *The Administration of Foreign Affairs and Overseas Operations* (Washington, D.C., June 1951). This study was restricted to the organization of the Executive Branch. W. J. Parks, in his book, *United States Administration of its International Affairs* (Johns Hopkins University Press, 1951), gives some consideration to the organization of Congress and the relations between the Executive and Legislative Branches.

United States aid to Europe under the first year of the Mutual Security Program on the ground that United States security depended on increased military strength abroad. Actual shipments of such items, under this program and its predecessor, the Mutual Defense Assistance Program, during calendar year 1951 were less than $1 billion. This relatively small amount of aid extended was the result in large part of the long time required to produce many of the items and of the competing demands for United States production by American forces stationed in the United States and the United Nations forces in Korea. But the slowness in implementing the program of building "balanced collective forces" in the North Atlantic area, begun late in 1949, was the result only in part of the relatively small amounts of military supplies furnished by the United States to the other signers of the North Atlantic Pact. Details on the mobilization programs of individual countries are not public, but the U.S. Administration stated during the year that, although great efforts were being made by the European members, their level of rearmament was not up to that hoped for. It appears that during 1950 and most of 1951 the force plans of the military officials of each member country and of the North Atlantic Treaty Organization were made more or less independently of the estimates of capabilities being made by the various financial and economic officials, with the result that a large gap developed between the two. At its September meeting, the NATO Council publicly recognized that the plans of the military authorities must be reconciled with the political-economic capabilities of each member country, as assessed by the financial and economic authorities, and therefore a special committee of senior officials, including Mr. Harriman (the Director of the Mutual Security Program), was constituted to bring about such a "confrontation" and to make the necessary reconciliation. This group of "Three Wise Men" made its report in late February 1952. Its "plan of action" was accepted by the various ministers of finance, economy, foreign affairs, and defense of the member countries. The details of these decisions were not made public, and some of them require parliamentary approval to become effective. Nonetheless, they did represent an important step forward in implementing the program of mutual security in the North Atlantic area for they constituted, for the first time, agreement at the executive level and in concrete and specific terms on many previously disputed problems. The agreement was not only among the various members of the North Atlantic Treaty Organization but also as between the "civilian" and "military" sectors of the governments of each country. In general, it was decided that the previous force plans, even after many reductions had been made in the estimated costs of creating and maintaining such forces, were beyond the economic capabilities of most members but that the latter were somewhat greater than those most of the ministers of finance had previously stated; that emphasis in 1952 should be on raising and equipping the maximum number of forces by the end of that year, rather than concentrating on the larger goals previously set for 1953 and 1954; that the United States should accelerate the rate of flow to Europe of military equipment already authorized by Congress; that more attention should be given to correlating United States shipments with the domestic production of recipient nations; that although the maintenance of civilian standards of consumption could not have priority over rearmament as had been planned in 1950, it was necessary that each member's economy be kept in a "sound" condition; and that through various devices—including purchases of military end-items for Europe in Europe and the transfer, up to the limit specified by Congress, of funds from "military" to "economic" aid—the United States should supply the European countries with more "free" dollars and more commodities other than military end-items than had been planned.

Some persons, especially in England, hoped that the program for developing collective and balanced military defenses in the North Atlantic area would be expanded into a high order of "economic cooperation" or "integration" of the economies of that area. United States officials gave lip service to the concept of developing a North Atlantic Community for other than defense purposes but carefully refrained from making any commitments which could be regarded as creating for this area a regional economic bloc of the sort which it was urging Western Europe to create. Congress stated in the Mutual Security Act its, and the Administration's, conviction that Western Europe should "unite"; in the 1951 law this statement included political "federation" as well as economic "unification" and reflected the growing conviction in official circles that the latter was feasible only if accompanied by the former.[5]

Except for general statements urging that "action be taken,"[6] the United States apparently offered no concrete or specific proposals for the political federation of Europe, but it did actively support the creation of the European Defense Community, and officials expressed great satisfaction with the preliminary agreement on many, but not all, aspects of the so-called European Army which was reached in early 1952 among representatives of Germany, France, Italy, Belgium, Luxembourg, and the Netherlands. Continued support was given to the efforts among the same six countries to create a European Coal and Steel Community (the Schuman Plan), and by early 1952 the Parliaments of Netherlands, France, and Germany had ratified the treaty. While American officials believed that the effect of the Coal and Steel Community would be to increase competition and result in increased efficiency and lower prices for coal and steel products, the major reason for supporting both the defense and the steel and coal projects was the belief that they would reduce the threat to the other Western European countries of German military aggression and so would make it possible to incorporate German forces and production into the joint defense of the North Atlantic area.

The United States continued to support and partially finance the European Payments Union, through which the equivalent of some $4 billion of transactions were cleared or settled during the year. But the Union was being subjected to a series of crises resulting from the emergence of several extreme debtors and extreme creditors, and Europe as a whole, and on the average, probably retreated on the front of intra-European trade liberalization. Most of the difficulties faced were the result not of the operations of the Union but of the uneven effects upon members' balances of payments of the rearmament programs. Still, during the year some inherent defects of the Union became increasingly apparent and by year's end it had made little if any progress toward one of its major objectives

[5] Congress also inserted in the Mutual Security Act the so-called Benton Amendment, designed to encourage competition in Europe. This was seen as supporting the various other European economic integration proposals of the United States.

[6] General Eisenhower, as Supreme Commander of Allied Powers in Europe, was very outspoken in his conviction that Europe must unite—both economically and politically—but he did not publicly provide any blueprints.

which had often been stressed by United States officials—facilitating a movement by the members toward general convertibility and world-wide nondiscriminatory trade practices. Indeed, there was some evidence that the Union was operating, as some had feared when it was being created, in the direction of encouraging a closed and balanced trading system *within* Europe. Nonetheless, most observers agreed that members pursued more liberal trade and payments policies among themselves, and so facilitated their rearmament efforts, than would have been possible in the absence of the Union and the associated trade liberalization measures since the alternative, most believed, was the return to a network of strictly balanced bilateral accounts.

One of the major issues within the U.S. Government on the question of aiding European mobilization was the extent to which American aid should take forms other than military end-items. The majority in Congress, impressed by the reports of the Administration in earlier years as to the accomplishments of the Marshall Plan, believed that the European Recovery Program had already adequately restored the ability of those economies to shoulder (with the help of military end-items from the United States) the necessary rearmament burdens while maintaining socially and politically acceptable internal standards of consumption and investment. The Administration argued that some $1.6 billion of nonmilitary end-items should be provided during the first year of the Mutual Security Program not for "recovery" purposes *per se* but to permit the European nations to expand their own production of military matériel, to finish certain "recovery" projects already well on the way toward completion, and to cushion the rearmament-induced decline in internal consumption and investment levels so as to strengthen the moral and the psychological support of the people of Europe for the rearmament effort. Congress agreed that aid which would directly result in the multiple expansion of the production in Europe of military equipment and supplies was desirable and concluded that approximately $1 billion for fiscal year 1952–1953 were justified for these purposes. Congress made it clear that it regarded the European Recovery Program, as originally conceived, as completed and that the U.S. Government could no longer provide grants to expand the production of civilian-type goods in Europe. As a result, the European

Recovery Program was formally declared by the Administration to have ended on December 31, 1951—six months earlier than originally planned—after the extension of some $12 billion of aid (including goods in the pipeline) and after only moderate success had been recorded in attaining the stated objectives of the program.

As a part of its policy of strengthening the defense of the West against possible aggression of the Soviet bloc, the U.S. Government held that in addition to accelerating their rearmament, all non-Soviet bloc countries should greatly restrict their exports to Russia and her satellites. For several years the United States had been imposing increasingly stringent controls on its own exports to such countries and by 1951 had reduced the shipments to a trickle of nonstrategic goods. The Administration had also been urging other members, especially those in Western Europe, to apply controls parallel to those of the United States and believed that, by and large, these efforts had met with success. The majority of Congress did not share this belief, and in the spring it passed a law the intent of which was to deny United States financial aid to any country which did not apply a virtual embargo on exports to the Soviet bloc. The European countries objected strongly to this law and the Administration argued, among other things, that an embargo on trade would weaken the West more than the East, that exports by the West should be prohibited only when they strengthened the military potential of the Soviet bloc more than the resulting imports strengthened the West, and that, therefore, considerable discretion was needed by the Administration in implementing the accepted general policy of restricting East-West trade. Late in the year, the previous law was repealed and a new one was approved which again required that United States aid be suspended to countries shipping items of strategic value to the Soviet bloc, but it also gave the Administration some authority to waive the law if it deemed it in the interest of national security to do so. No aid was denied to a foreign country on the basis of these laws during 1951.

Apart from questions of shipments to Russia, the supply of several strategic items was found in late 1950 and during 1951 to be inadequate to meet the current demands of the West, swollen because of the rearmament programs and the accelerated stockpiling activities, especially in the United States. To facilitate the equitable distribution of some fourteen commodities important in international trade and the rearmament programs, and to keep their prices down, most of the Western nations, with strong encouragement from the United States, joined in an International Materials Conference composed of "commodity groups" which in turn were to recommend allocations of the current production of these commodities among the non-Communist nations. The committees succeeded in setting up acceptable allocations schemes for seven commodities during the latter part of 1951, and one commodity was placed under a general price ceiling and floor. Many of the problems of allocation, price regulation, and conservation were not resolved during the year, but an auspicious beginning was made toward agreement in what was generally regarded as an exceedingly difficult field of international economic relations.

During the year the United States continued its efforts, which had been expanded after the start of the Korean war, to add to the official stockpile of strategic and critical materials. Official stockpile goals were slightly reduced during the year following a reassessment which led to the conclusion that more than adequate amounts of certain goods had previously been scheduled. Actual procurement was at approximately the same rate as the previous year and would have been larger had not some of the materials previously ordered been directed to current industrial production. As compared with the previous year, the "mad scramble" for such goods had virtually ended and relatively few complaints were registered that the United States was "hogging" such supplies.[7]

It was the United States position that primary reliance in solving the problem of shortages of critical raw materials should be placed on greater production, both at home and abroad. To encourage such production abroad, the United States not only stood ready to purchase large amounts of the output for the official stockpile, but, through the Export-Import Bank and the Economic Cooperation Administration, made several loans to finance at least part of the cost of new or enlarged production projects; in addition, the Export-Import Bank's lending authority was raised by $1 billion dur-

[7] Indeed, by the end of the year some of the European countries whose overseas territories were important suppliers were urging that the United States increase its purchases of certain items as a means of providing dollars to such countries to help cover their reemerging "dollar shortages."

ing the year, it being planned that a large part of this would be available for helping to finance raw material projects.

Many of the supplying nations were reluctant to expand their capacity to produce such goods, fearing that the increased demand was but a temporary phenomenon and that they would not be permitted currently to use the proceeds from larger sales to purchase goods in the United States. Further, many of the countries complained of the low prices being set for their commodities by the United States, both directly when the U.S. Government was the purchaser, as in rubber and tin, and indirectly via the price ceilings set for sales inside the United States by the Office of Price Stabilization. Representatives of these countries frequently stated that entirely apart from the above considerations, the resulting production pattern would not be in keeping with their own plans for economic development.

The United States recognized these arguments in various ways—though not by any means to the full satisfaction of the so-called underdeveloped countries. Administration officials flatly refused even to consider seriously a request by certain of the Latin American countries that the United States guarantee the purchasing power of the dollars the latter received from sales of raw materials, but they did stress that the United States was controlling the prices of most exports and that various duties and taxes on imports of some of these commodities had been temporarily suspended by Congress during the year, thus permitting the supplier to receive higher prices. And in administering its export controls the Administration attempted—subject always to the overriding priority of the rearmament programs of the Western world and of the requirements for civilian production in the United States—to insure that the suppliers of strategic and critical raw materials received export licenses, not only for the equipment and supplies needed to expand the production of such goods but also for relatively large supplies of essential consumer goods and capital goods needed to carry out diversified economic development programs.

The problem of the economic development of the so-called underdeveloped areas (usually defined to include Africa, the Near East, most of non-Communist Asia, and Latin America) and the role they could play in the defense of the West, other than as sources of raw materials desperately needed by the North Atlantic countries, was discussed at length during the year. Europe continued to occupy the central position in the international economic policies of the United States, but the trend of the previous year of giving increasing aid and attention to other areas was intensified. It was recognized that these countries could contribute little in the way of armed forces for the defense of the West, but a considerable expansion in the amount of military equipment was sent some of them during the year—not all countries in the area received military assistance and some did not request it—in an effort to bolster their ability to prevent internal subversion and to deter possible outside aggression. Still, as contrasted with Europe, the United States planned to devote a larger portion of its assistance to these areas in the form of goods and technical aid to meet their pressing economic needs, it being argued by the Administration, and accepted by Congress, that this was an effective way of keeping these people sympathetic to the cause of the West.

The total value of the financial assistance on a grant basis extended by the U.S. Government to the areas of Asia and the Pacific, the Near East and Africa,[8] and Latin America during the year was about $1 billion. If to this are added the disbursements on a credit basis from Export-Import Bank loans, the special food loan to India, and the dollar disbursements by the International Bank and the International Monetary Fund, total gross dollar assistance from public sources amounted to approximately $1.5 billion. Such a sum was regarded as grossly inadequate by the spokesmen for most of the underdeveloped countries.

Many differences developed during 1951 between the United States, usually supported by the other historically capital-exporting countries, and the so-called underdeveloped countries on the general question of financing economic development. Most of these discussions took place in various United Nations meetings, but very much at issue was the United States Point Four Program "for the improvement and growth of underdeveloped areas." United States spokesmen laid great stress on the contribution which technical assistance could make, but most of the delegates from the underdeveloped countries, while recognizing the importance of technical assistance, insisted that it was of little use unless it was accompanied by large amounts of capital assistance—preferably

[8] Excluding Greece and Turkey.

on a grant basis. In their emphasis on large-scale capital aid—both on a grant and a loan basis—the underdeveloped countries had been encouraged by the November 1950 *Report to the President on Foreign Economic Policies* (the Gray *Report*) and the October 1951 report of the President's International Development Advisory Board (the Rockefeller report, *Partners in Progress*).

In the United Nations, the United States delegates maintained that the bulk of the capital needed should come from within the country concerned and urged the countries to take measures for increasing and mobilizing domestic savings, but they received the reply that, although something might be done along this line, the level of incomes was so low that internal savings were completely inadequate. The United States recognized that some foreign investment was required but believed that the bulk of it should be on a loan basis[9] and pointed out that both the International Bank and the Export-Import Bank stood ready to loan on "worthwhile" projects, but they repeated that major reliance must be placed on private sources. There was in the debates an apparent general hostility on the part of the underdeveloped countries toward attempts to encourage private capital flows; during the year the United States achieved only modest success in signing investment treaties with foreign countries, in negotiating new tax conventions, or in encouraging private American investments via issuing investment guarantees. The outflow of private long-term capital declined by some $400 million from the previous year to a total of about $800 million, of which the bulk, as in each year since World War II, was in petroleum, mining, and smelting.

As to loans from public sources, the spokesmen for the underdeveloped countries expressed a decided preference for receiving them from international institutions rather than such national institutions as the Export-Import Bank. In particular, they urged that the International Bank should, as a matter of policy, guarantee to lend at least $1 billion a year for economic development purposes, and that study should be given to establishing an International Finance Corporation, to make equity investments, and a new International Development Authority, to extend both grants

[9] In the debates and hearings on the Mutual Security Program, Congress had made it clear that it believed most of the aid the U.S. Government extended for economic development purposes should be on a loan basis.

and loans to the underdeveloped countries for basic non-self-liquidating projects. Both the Bank and United States officials opposed the first as not feasible but agreed to study the second. The United States strongly, but unsuccessfully, opposed the United Nations taking any resolution favoring a formal study of the third proposal, arguing that the present was an inappropriate time since the funds for such an institution would have to come from the United States, Canada, and the Western European nations and that none of these countries could provide such aid during the current rearmament effort.

In sum, 1951 witnessed a decided cleavage between the United States and the underdeveloped countries on almost every aspect of the broad problem of economic development of underdeveloped areas. Further, there were indications that within the U.S. Government there was disagreement as to precisely what constituted economic development and what the United States could or should do to facilitate it.[1] Nonetheless, the President stated in early 1952 that the Point Four Program constituted one of the most important elements of the nation's foreign policy.

As noted above, the commercial policy of the United States was dominated during the year by the strategic problems of stockpiling, restricting East-West trade, export controls, and the international allocation of scarce materials, but considerable attention was also given to the Reciprocal Trade Agreements Program. This program, which has constituted the core of American international commercial policy since 1934, suffered severe setbacks during 1951. The third round of tariff negotiations under the General Agreement on Tariffs and Trade was completed in April, and significant reductions in duties were made by the United States on its imports and by other countries on their imports from the United States. But the United States failed (except with respect to Canada) to obtain any reduction in the British imperial preferences—long a goal of American policy.

More important, despite the facts that the United States surplus on current account during the year was more than double that of the previous year, that the amount of official grants and loans

[1] For a recent statement of some of the basic conceptual problems, see Frankel, S. H., "Some Conceptual Aspects of the Economic Development of Underdeveloped Territories," *Essays in International Finance No. 15*, May 1952, International Finance Section, Princeton University.

provided foreigners was larger than in 1950, that internal inflationary pressures were strong, and that alternative employment possibilities for those suffering import competition were good, the Administration, by and large, adopted before Congress a defensive attitude toward the reduction of United States import restrictions and, in the main, asked Congress only to give its approval to legislation which would permit a consolidation of past actions. But Congress was not prepared to do even this and insisted on increasing the protection afforded American producers from foreign competition. In the process the foundations of the Reciprocal Trade Agreements Program were weakened.

In particular, in extending the Reciprocal Trade Agreements Act for another three years, Congress, over the objection of the Administration, inserted several restrictive clauses. The "peril points" clause was again written into the law; an escape clause was inserted and the conditions under which it could be invoked were broader than those previously honored by the Administration; and the Administration was ordered to withdraw concessions from Soviet bloc countries. Congress also stated during the year that it intended to reassume some of the authority previously granted the President for determining specific tariff rates, and while the House finally approved a diluted version of the Administration's customs simplification bill, the Senate took no action on the measure. Although the State Department again repeated that it did not plan to resubmit the ITO Charter to Congress, the latter body in 1951 registered reservations to full future American participation in the General Agreement on Tariffs and Trade.

A more publicized action by Congress was the extension of the earlier authority to impose quantitative restrictions on imports of fats and oils and the broadening of the provision specifically to include dairy products and, in particular, cheese. As a consequence, stringent quotas were applied on cheese imports. This gave rise to bitter objections by officials of several of the European countries who not only threatened retaliation but found the United States guilty of violating the General Agreement. This action, together with the United States insistence that its trade agreement with Czechoslovakia be cancelled and the increase in the number of applications by importers for relief under the new escape clause, resulted in the United States being severely criticized during the

Sixth Session of the Contracting Parties to the General Agreement, and many observers believed that the United States was in danger of losing its leadership role in that organization and in the program for expanding trade and lowering barriers to it.

The Administration "recognized" in 1951 that little progress could be hoped for in the immediate future toward its long-established policy of a world-wide reduction of quantitative restrictions on imports and exchange controls, especially those involving discrimination as to source, and did not press energetically other nations to remove such barriers. At year's end there was some evidence that the United States was reconsidering its previous policy which had effectively denied access to the resources of the International Monetary Fund by any country which maintained exchange restrictions on current account transactions or made use of quantitative import controls.

In sum, the record for 1951 shows that the United States effectively abandoned the immediate pursuit of most of its previously established long-term economic objectives and that almost all of its international economic and financial policies and activities were dominated by short-term strategic considerations. Though not explicitly stated by responsible officials, there seemed to be developing within the U.S. Government a conviction that the state planning, discrimination, and interference with the free market which were inevitable during an extended period of intensive rearmament (to say nothing of the intensification of state planning and controls in many countries even prior to the present mobilization period) had removed many of the basic assumptions on which the previous international commercial and financial policies of the United States had been based.

Nonetheless, the Administration did not agree with those members of the Fund and the General Agreement on Tariffs and Trade who favored making fundamental changes in the policies and terms of reference of these two institutions. It argued that, although many exceptions to the "rules of conduct" of these institutions were called for under the existing conditions, their approach and long-term objectives were the proper ones for the post-crisis period and that if they were abandoned now there was no foreseeable likelihood of getting international agreement on principles to replace them.

APPENDIX TABLES

APPENDIX TABLE I

Aid Provided by ECA to ERP Participants,
April 3, 1948 through December 31, 1951
(millions of dollars)

Country	1951		1948-1951			Approximate Net Aid Received After Operation of IEPS and EPU 1948-1951[c]
	Grants[a]	Credits[b]	Grants[a]	Credits[b]	Total	
France	460.2	16.0	2074	194	2268	2570
United Kingdom	224.5	11.2	2407	353	2760	2290
Germany (Federal Republic)	378.1	3.6	1289	4	1293	1190
Netherlands-Indonesia	153.3	—	798	151	949	1140
Italy	298.8	0.8	1069	75	1144	1060
Greece	203.8	1.3	507	1	508	830
Austria	160.8	—	574	0	574	800
Norway	49.3	—	186	35	221	400
Denmark	62.0	—	229	31	260	290
Turkey	39.1	19.5	56	74	129	210
Ireland	15.1	9.5	18	128	146	150
Belgium-Luxembourg	52.6	2.7	498	54	552	90
Portugal	1.4	18.9	10	29	39	50
Sweden	27.0	—	90	20	111	30
Iceland	7.4	1.8	18	4	22	20
Trieste	7.8	—	32	0	32	15
EPU	195.4	—	238	0	238	
Unclassified Areas[d]	63.1	—	143	0	143	
Total	2436.3	85.3	10237	1153	11391	

a) Includes expenditures out of MDAP transfers to ECA.
b) Includes, under the metropolitan country, loans to dependent overseas territories for development of deficiency materials projects.
c) These data are the result of *adding* to the total aid extended to each country by ECA the "drawing rights" received by each under the Intra-European Payments Scheme and the amount of "initial credit balances" utilized under the European Payments Union and *subtracting* the "drawing rights" extended and "initial debit balances" utilized. The detailed statistics of the operations under these two payments plans are given in *Survey—1950*, p. 241 and in Chapter VII *supra*. The totals of the net aid received as estimated in this column exceed the total

(*Notes continued on next page*)

ECA aid provided the individual countries as given in the total column in the above table because of rounding and, more importantly, because a proportion of the aid provided by ECA to the EPU was in turn used by the latter to make dollar payments to EPU creditors. Thus, the net aid received by the various countries as distributed in this column includes a part, but not all, of the aid provided by ECA to the EPU.

d) Includes both dollars and counterpart funds used for certain ECA administrative expenses, certain technical assistance supplied by ECA, and postal and subsidy payments on relief parcels.

Source: Department of Commerce, "Foreign Aid," *Foreign Transactions of the U.S. Government,* Washington, D.C., April 1952, Table A and Appendix Tables 6 and 9.

APPENDIX TABLE II

ECA Paid Shipments, by Commodity Group and by Area of Origin, April 3, 1948-December 31, 1951

(millions of dollars)

	Area of Origin					
Commodity Group	*Total*	*United States*	*Canada*	*Latin America*	*OEEC Countries*	*Other*
Food, Feed, & Fertilizer	3209.5	2140.6	603.0	375.4	48.9	41.6
Fuel	1552.4	534.0	0.1	151.6	388.8	477.8
Raw Materials and Semi-Finished Products	3280.9[b]	2308.5[b]	557.7	283.9	58.8	72.0
Machinery and Vehicles	1428.1	1386.1	36.8	—	5.2	0.1
Tobacco	444.5	439.2	—	4.7	0.6	—
Miscellaneous Products	101.0	76.8	17.8	4.1	1.5	0.8
Commodity Total[c]	10004.3[a]	6885.2	1215.4	819.8	503.7	592.3

a) $12 million of unallocable commodity returns are deducted from the total only.

b) Cotton composed $1398 million of the total and of the United States shipments in this group.

c) The grand total of paid shipments of $11348.2 million is composed of the above plus $36.8 of technical services, $8.8 of ship disbursements, $515.3 to EPU, and $783.0 for ocean freight—all unallocable by source.

Source: Mutual Security Agency, *Monthly Report for the Public Advisory Board,* Washington, D.C., December 31, 1951, pp. 42-43.

APPENDIX TABLE III

ECA-Financed Shipments, by Major Commodity Groups, 1948-1951

Commodities	*1948*	*1949*	*1950*	*1951*	*Total*
			(percentages)		
Food, Feed, & Fertilizer[a]	51.8	37.9	29.1	28.9	36.4
Fuel	21.7	13.4	12.3	17.9	15.5
Raw Materials and Semi-Finished Products	22.6	34.3	37.3	33.5	32.8
Machinery and Vehicles	3.7	13.6	19.8	18.4	14.3
Miscellaneous	0.2	0.8	1.5	1.3	1.0
	100.0	100.0	100.0	100.0	100.0
			(millions of dollars)		
Total Commodities	1870	3641	2643	1862	10016[d]
Ocean Freight[b]	184	279	170	196	829
EPU—Capital Fund	—	—	43	307	350
Assistance via EPU	—	—	—	165	165
Grand Total	2054	3920	2856[c]	2530[c]	11360[d]

a) Including tobacco.
b) Includes some $46 million of technical services and ship disbursements.
c) Includes shipments for Overseas Territory Development beginning in the fourth quarter of 1950.
d) $12 million of commodities returned, which are unallocable by type, are *not* deducted; $1 million occurred in 1950 and $11 million in 1951.
Sources: Economic Cooperation Administration, "Paid Shipments," Washington, D.C., December 31, 1949, December 31, 1950, and Mutual Security Agency, "Paid Shipments," Washington, D.C., December 31, 1951.

APPENDIX TABLE IV

ECA-Financed Shipments, by Commodity Group and Area of Origin, 1948-1951

(percentages)

	Agricultural Commodities					*Industrial Commodities*				
Area of Origin	*1948*	*1949*	*1950*	*1951*	*Total*	*1948*	*1949*	*1950*	*1951*	*Total*
United States	60.7	78.0	84.6	92.7	78.5	43.4	61.3	61.4	61.6	58.6
Canada	28.3	9.8	8.6	0	11.7	19.1	13.3	11.2	8.1	12.5
Latin America	6.7	10.1	5.8	6.5	7.7	8.9	7.5	8.6	10.6	8.6
Participating Countries	3.1	0.7	0	0.4	1.0	16.7	8.5	8.5	5.7	9.3
Other	1.2	1.4	1.0	0.4	1.1	11.9	9.4	10.3	14.0	11.0
Total	100.0	100.0	100.0	100.0	100.0	100.0	100.0	100.0	100.0	100.0
Total by Value (millions of dollars)	1086	1914	1248	899	5147	784	1727	1395	963	4869

Sources: Economic Cooperation Administration, "Paid Shipments," Washington, D.C., December 31, 1949 and December 31, 1950; Mutual Security Agency, "Paid Shipments," Washington, D.C., December 31, 1951.

APPENDIX TABLE V

ECA Technical Assistance Program, 1949-1951[a]

(millions of dollars)

	Authorizations		Expenditures	
Field of Activity	*1951*	*1949-1951*	*1951*	*1949-1951*
Industrial Productivity	9.7	17.9	3.9	7.4
Agricultural Productivity	2.2	5.2	1.7	3.1
Manpower Utilization	.2	2.5	.6	1.2
Public Administration	.5	2.7	.6	1.8
Transportation and Communications	.6	2.4	.7	1.6
Marketing	.3	.7	.1	.3
Development of Overseas Territories	.6	.9	.1	.2
Tourism	*	.2	*	.1
Program Management[b]	.5	1.7	1.6	2.2
Total	14.7	34.1	9.4	17.9

* Less than $50,000.

a) The technical assistance program of ECA was not begun until 1949. Includes assistance under the MDAP.

b) This item represents the costs to ECA of managing the entire program.

Sources: Mutual Security Agency, "The Mutual Security Program," *First Report to Congress*, Washington, D.C., December 31, 1951, Tables C-6 and C-7; and Economic Cooperation Administration, *Thirty-First Report for the Public Advisory Board*, Washington, D.C., January 31, 1951, pp. 46-47.

APPENDIX TABLE VI

ECA Industrial Projects, by Type and by Country, 1948-1951
(millions of dollars)

	1951		*1948-1951*		
	Total Cost[b]	*ECA Cost*	*Total Cost*[b]	*ECA Cost*	*Paid Shipments*
Type of Project[a]					
Manufacturing:	37	8	1365	346	209
Iron and steel	3	3	842	216	144
Petroleum refining	16	1	250	36	16
Automotive products	0	0	106	38	28
Other	18	4	167	56	21
Power facilities	44	2	394	136	65
Raw materials extraction	3	1	261	40	25
Transportation and Communications	8	6	172	40	23
Irrigation and reclamation	0	0	78	4	1
Engineering and technical services	0	1	12	3	1
Total	91	18	2281	568	325
Country[c]					
France	31	4	782	150	93
Italy	20	4	435	171	101
United Kingdom	0	0	421	51	40
Turkey	4	5	205	53	32
Austria	4	2	82	37	23
Greece	0	1	113	32	5
Netherlands	0	0	67	27	12
Belgium	0	0	51	15	9
Iceland	0	0	16	8	3
Portugal	3	2	29	9	2
Denmark	0	0	10	5	3
Norway	1	*	30	5	2
Germany (Federal Republic)	0	0	11	2	1
International	28	1	29	1	—
Total[d]	91	18	2281	568	325

* Less than $500,000.

a) Industrial projects exclude technical assistance projects, strategic materials development projects, and counterpart fund projects.

b) Total cost includes ECA dollars, other dollars, and dollar equivalents of local currencies.

c) Overseas territories are reported with recipient mother country.

d) Refers only to European programs. There were small project approvals in Korea and other areas.

Sources: Economic Cooperation Administration, *Thirty-First Report for the Public Advisory Board,* Washington, D.C., January 31, 1951, pp. 44-45; and Mutual Security Agency, *Monthly Report for the Public Advisory Board,* Washington, D.C., December 31, 1951, pp. 60-61.

APPENDIX TABLE VII

ECA Counterpart Funds, 1948-1951

(millions of dollar equivalents)

	1951	*1948-1951*
Total deposits	*2061*	*9100*
95 percent deposits:	1956	8662
Withdrawals for:		
Debt retirement	178	2180
Promotion of utilities	136	879
Promotion of manufacturing	350	731
Promotion of transportation and communications	137	704
Promotion of agriculture	124	642
Promotion of extractive industries	53	452
Promotion of stockpile materials	1	39
Promotion of other production	52	220
Construction of public buildings and housing	291	625
Military production, construction, and matériel	116	116
Special relief projects	15	160
Other	50	311
Total	1502	7058
5 percent deposits:	105	438
Obligations for:		
ECA administration and operating expenses	(a)	43
Deficiency materials	(a)	178
Information and special purposes	(a)	54
Transfers to U.S. Treasury	20	50
Other transfers	3	4

a) During August 1951, ECA changed its basis of reporting on use of 5 percent counterpart from "expenditures" to "obligations." It is, therefore, impossible to determine the magnitude of either for 1951. As of July 31, 1951, "expenditures" were $156 million plus $72 million committed for deficiency materials projects, and as of August 30, 1951, "obligations" were $245 million including deficiency materials commitments. Expenditures for all items, other than deficiency materials, were nearly equal to obligations, but expenditures for deficiency materials were lagging about 50 percent behind commitments.

Source: Economic Cooperation Administration, "Local Currency Counterpart Funds," Washington, D.C., December 31, 1950 and Mutual Security Agency, "Local Currency Counterpart Funds," Washington, D.C., December 31, 1951.

APPENDIX TABLE VIII

ECA-Southeast Asia Program,
Paid Shipments, by Commodity and Country of Destination,
Cumulative, June 5, 1950-December 31, 1951

(millions of dollars)

Item	*Total*	*Burma*	*China*	*Indo-china*	*Indo-nesia*	*Philip-pines*	*Thai-land*	*Unallo-cated*[a]
Food, feed and fertilizer	43.1	*	39.2	1.7	0.1	2.0	*	—
Fuel	5.6	—	4.8	0.8	—	*	*	—
Raw materials and semi-finished products	32.8	3.9	18.5	6.1	1.0	2.0	1.2	—
Machinery and vehicles	9.1	0.4	1.8	3.2	0.8	0.3	2.6	*
Miscellaneous	3.8	0.9	1.0	1.0	0.3	0.2	0.5	—
Total commodities	94.5	5.3	65.4	12.7	2.3	4.5	4.3	*
Plus:								
Technical assistance services	2.6	0.4	0.7[b]	0.2	0.4	0.2	0.4	0.3
Ocean freight	6.2	*	4.8	1.1	0.1	—	0.2	—
Grand total	103.4	5.8	70.9	14.0	2.8	4.7	4.8	0.3

* Less than $50,000.

a) Includes "Far East general account" and "Far East inventory" which were unassigned to any country.

b) Includes Joint Commission of Rural Reconstruction expenses.

Source: Mutual Security Agency, "Mutual Security Program," *First Report to Congress,* Washington, D.C., December 31, 1951, Table D-4.

APPENDIX TABLE IX

Calendar of Tax Conventions, as of December 31, 1951

Country	*Signed*	*Effective Date*[a]
Conventions relating to taxes on income:		
Sweden	Mar. 23, 1939	Jan. 1, 1940
France (2d treaty)	July 25, 1939	Jan. 1, 1945
Supplemental	Oct. 18, 1946	Jan. 1, 1950
Canada	Mar. 4, 1942	Jan. 1, 1941
Supplemental	June 12, 1950	Jan. 1, 1951
United Kingdom	Apr. 16, 1945	Jan. 1, 1945
Netherlands	Apr. 29, 1948	Jan. 1, 1947
Denmark	May 6, 1948	Jan. 1, 1948
Union of South Africa	Dec. 13, 1946	(b)
Supplemental	July 14, 1950	(b)
New Zealand	Mar. 16, 1948	Jan. 1, 1951
Belgium	Oct. 28, 1948	(c)
Norway	June 13, 1949	Jan. 1, 1951
Ireland	Sept. 13, 1949	Jan. 1, 1951
Greece	Feb. 20, 1950	(b)
Switzerland	May 24, 1951	Jan. 1, 1951
Conventions relating to taxes on estates and inheritances:		
Canada	June 8, 1944	June 14, 1941
Supplemental	June 12, 1950	Nov. 21, 1951
United Kingdom	Apr. 16, 1945	July 25, 1946
France	Oct. 18, 1946	Oct. 17, 1942
Union of South Africa	Apr. 10, 1947	(b)
Supplemental	July 14, 1950	(b)
Norway	June 13, 1949	Dec. 11, 1951
Ireland	Sept. 13, 1949	Dec. 20, 1951
Greece	Feb. 20, 1950	(b)
Switzerland	July 9, 1951	(c)

a) Most of the income tax conventions provided that they go into effect on the first day of the calendar year in which the ratifications were exchanged. The estates and inheritances tax conventions usually provided that they go into effect on the day that the ratifications were exchanged, but some (e.g., those with Canada and France) were made to go into force retroactively.

b) Ratified by the U.S. Senate on September 17, 1951 but ratifications not yet exchanged.

c) Not yet ratified by the United States.

Sources: U.S. Treasury Department and miscellaneous sources cited in Chapter II.

APPENDIX TABLE X

Calendar of Treaties of Friendship, Commerce and Navigation, as of December 31, 1951

Country	*Signed*	*Effective Date*
Argentina	July 27, 1853	Dec. 20, 1854
Austria	June 19, 1928	May 27, 1931
Belgium	Mar. 8, 1875	June 11, 1875
Bolivia	May 13, 1858	Nov. 9, 1862
Borneo	June 23, 1850	July 11, 1853
China	Nov. 4, 1946	Nov. 30, 1948
Colombia[a]	Dec. 16, 1846	June 10, 1848
Costa Rica	July 10, 1851	May 26, 1852
Denmark[b]	Apr. 26, 1826	Aug. 10, 1826
El Salvador	Feb. 22, 1926	Sept. 5, 1930
Estonia	Dec. 23, 1925	May 22, 1926
Ethiopia	Sept. 7, 1951	(f)
Finland	Feb. 13, 1934	Aug. 9, 1934
Germany[c]	Dec. 8, 1923	Oct. 14, 1925
Greece	Aug. 3, 1951	(f)
Honduras	Dec. 7, 1927	July 19, 1928
Hungary[d]	June 24, 1925	Oct. 4, 1926
Ireland	Jan. 21, 1950	Sept. 14, 1950
Israel	Aug. 23, 1951	(f)
Italy	Feb. 2, 1948	July 26, 1949
Latvia	Apr. 20, 1928	July 25, 1928
Liberia	Aug. 8, 1938	Nov. 21, 1939
Morocco	Sept. 16, 1836	Jan. 28, 1837
Muscat (& Zanzibar)	Sept. 21, 1833	Sept. 30, 1835
Norway	June 5, 1928	Sept. 13, 1932
Paraguay	Feb. 4, 1859	Mar. 7, 1860
Poland[e]	June 15, 1931	July 9, 1933
Spain	July 3, 1902	Apr. 14, 1903
Switzerland	Nov. 25, 1850	Nov. 8, 1855
Thailand	Nov. 13, 1937	Oct. 1, 1938
United Kingdom	July 3, 1815	July 3, 1815
Uruguay	Nov. 23, 1949	(g)
Yugoslavia	Oct. 14, 1881	Nov. 15, 1882

a) To be replaced by a treaty signed on April 26, 1951 but which was not ratified by the United States during 1951.

b) To be replaced by a treaty signed on October 1, 1951 but which was not ratified by the United States during 1951.

c) With respect to the effect of war on the operation of the provisions of this treaty and of treaties in general, see the decision of the U.S. Supreme Court in *Clark v. Allen*, 331 U.S. 503, and the cases cited therein.

d) Notification of termination of this treaty as of July 1952 was given by the United States in July 1951.

e) Notification of termination of this treaty as of January 5, 1952 was given by the United States in July 1951.

f) Not yet ratified by the United States; the treaties with Ethiopia and Greece will replace less comprehensive ones signed in 1914 and 1936 respectively. There was also in force less comprehensive treaties relating to commerce and general economic relations with France (1822), Iraq (1938), Netherlands (1852), and Turkey (1929, 1931).

g) Ratified by the U.S. Senate on August 9, 1950 but as of January 1952 not ratified by the Uruguayan General Assembly.

Source: Department of State, Office of Public Affairs, "Commercial Treaty Program of the United States," Commercial Policy Series 141 Washington, D.C., April 1952, p. 6.

APPENDIX TABLE XI

Calendar of United States Reciprocal Trade Agreements, as of December 31, 1951

Country	*Date Concluded*	*Date Effective*
Argentina	Oct. 14, 1941	Nov. 15, 1941
Australia (G)	Oct. 30, 1947	Jan. 1, 1948
Austria (T)	Apr. 21, 1951	Oct. 19, 1951
Belgium (G)*	Oct. 30, 1947	Jan. 1, 1948
Brazil (G)*	Oct. 30, 1947	July 31, 1948
Burma (G)	Oct. 30, 1947	July 30, 1948
Canada (G)*	Oct. 30, 1947	Jan. 1, 1948
Ceylon (G)	Oct. 30, 1947	July 30, 1948
Chile (G)	Oct. 30, 1947	Mar. 16, 1949
Cuba (G)*	Oct. 30, 1947	Jan. 1, 1948
Denmark (A)	Oct. 10, 1949	May 28, 1950
Dominican Republic (A)	Oct. 10, 1949	May 19, 1950
Ecuador	Aug. 6, 1938	Oct. 23, 1938
El Salvador	Feb. 19, 1937	May 31, 1937
Finland (A)*	Oct. 10, 1949	May 25, 1950
France (G)*	Oct. 30, 1947	Jan. 1, 1948
Germany (T)	Apr. 21, 1951	Oct. 1, 1951
Greece (A)	Oct. 10, 1949	Mar. 9, 1950
Guatemala	Apr. 24, 1936	June 15, 1936
Haiti (A)*	Oct. 10, 1949	Jan. 1, 1950
Honduras	Dec. 18, 1935	Mar. 2, 1936
Iceland	Aug. 27, 1943	Nov. 19, 1943
India (G)	Oct. 30, 1947	July 9, 1948
Indonesia (G)[1]	Oct. 30, 1947	Jan. 1, 1948
Iran	Apr. 8, 1943	June 28, 1944
Italy (A)	Oct. 10, 1949	May 30, 1950
Liberia (A)	Oct. 10, 1949	May 20, 1950
Luxembourg (G)*	Oct. 30, 1947	Jan. 1, 1948
Netherlands (G)*	Oct. 30, 1947	Jan. 1, 1948
New Zealand (G)	Oct. 30, 1947	July 31, 1948
Nicaragua (A)*	Oct. 10, 1949	May 28, 1950
Norway (G)	Oct. 30, 1947	July 11, 1948
Pakistan (G)	Oct. 30, 1947	July 31, 1948
Paraguay	Sept. 12, 1946	Apr. 9, 1947
Peru (T)*	Apr. 21, 1951	Oct. 7, 1951
Southern Rhodesia (G)	Oct. 30, 1947	July 12, 1948
Sweden (A)*	Oct. 10, 1949	Apr. 30, 1950
Switzerland	Jan. 9, 1936	Feb. 15, 1936
Turkey (T)*	Apr. 21, 1951	Oct. 17, 1951
Union of South Africa (G)	Oct. 30, 1947	June 14, 1948
United Kingdom (G)*	Oct. 30, 1947	Jan. 1, 1948
Uruguay	July 21, 1942	Jan. 1, 1943
Venezuela[2]	Nov. 6, 1939	Dec. 16, 1939

Note: Countries designated with (G) are those which became contracting parties to the General Agreement at Geneva in 1947, those with an (A) joined at Annecy in 1949, and those with a (T) acceded at Torquay in 1951. The asterisk indicates that the country previously had a bilateral agreement with the United

(*Notes continued on next page*)

States which was superseded, terminated, or made inoperative by accession to GATT. Those without symbols are countries not parties to the GATT and with which the United States concluded agreements prior to GATT; since 1947, the United States had not concluded any trade agreements outside the GATT.

1) The Netherlands signed the GATT at Geneva in 1947 in behalf of the Netherlands Indies. As the Republic of Indonesia, the latter became a party to the agreement as an independent country on February 24, 1950.

2) The United States and Venezuela were renegotiating their treaty during 1951 and 1952.

Sources: Department of Commerce, *Foreign Commerce Weekly*, Washington, D.C. (various issues) and sources cited in Chapter V; see also any issue of the *American Import and Export Bulletin*.

INDEX